Time Out

Amsterdam

timeout.com/amsterdam

Time Out Guides Ltd
Universal House
251 Tottenham Court Road
London W1T 7AB
United Kingdom
Tel: +44 (0)20 7813 3000
Fax: +44 (0)20 7813 6001
Email: guides@timeout.com
www.timeout.com

Published by Time Out Guides Ltd, a wholly owned subsidiary
of Time Out Group Ltd. Time Out and the Time Out logo are
trademarks of Time Out Group Ltd.

© **Time Out Group Ltd 2014**
Previous editions 1991, 1993, 1995, 1996, 1998, 2000, 2002, 2004, 2005,
2007, 2011.

10 9 8 7 6 5 4 3 2 1

This edition first published in Great Britain in 2014 by Ebury Publishing.
A Random House Group Company
20 Vauxhall Bridge Road, London SW1V 2SA

Random House Australia Pty Ltd 20 Alfred Street, Milsons Point, Sydney,
New South Wales 2061, Australia

Random House New Zealand Ltd 18 Poland Road, Glenfield, Auckland 10,
New Zealand

Random House South Africa (Pty) Ltd Isle of Houghton, Corner Boundary
Road & Carse O'Gowrie, Houghton 2198, South Africa

Random House UK Limited Reg. No. 954009

Distributed in the US and Latin America by Publishers Group West
(1-510-809-3700)

For further distribution details, see www.timeout.com.

ISBN: 978-1-84670-329-4

A CIP catalogue record for this book is available from the British Library.

Printed and bound in China by Leo Paper Products Ltd.

The Random House Group Limited supports The Forest Stewardship Council®
(FSC®), the leading international forest-certification organisation. Our books
carrying the FSC label are printed on FSC®-certified paper. FSC is the only
forest-certification scheme supported by the leading environmental
organisations, including Greenpeace. Our paper procurement policy can be
found at www.randomhouse.co.uk/environment.

MIX
Paper from
responsible sources
FSC® C020056
www.fsc.org

Contents

78

69

122

281

Time Out Amsterdam

Out

Editorial
Editor Steve Korver
Researcher Floris Dogterom
Copy Editors Cath Phillips, Dominic Earle
Proofreader John Shandy Watson
Indexer Tom Smith

Editorial Director Sarah Guy
Management Accountant Margaret Wright

Design
Senior Designer Kei Ishimaru
Designer Thomas Havell
Group Commercial Senior Designer Jason Tansley

Picture Desk
Picture Editor Jael Marschner
Deputy Picture Editor Ben Rowe
Freelance Picture Researchers Lizzy Owen

Advertising
Managing Director of Advertising St John Betteridge
Advertising (Amsterdam) Jinga Media Ltd
(www.jingamedia.com)

Marketing
Senior Publishing Brand Manager Luthfa Begum
Head of Circulation Dan Collins

Production
Production Controller Katie Mulhern-Bhudia

Time Out Group
Chairman & Founder Tony Elliott
Chief Executive Officer Tim Arthur
Publisher Alex Batho
Group IT Director Simon Chappell
Group Marketing Director Carolyn Sims

Contributors
Top 20 Steve Korver **Amsterdam Today** Steve Korver **Itineraries** Steve Korver **Diary** Willem de Blauw, Sarah Gehrke, Steve Korver, Anna Whitehouse **Amsterdam's Best** Steve Korver **Explore** Erin Farber, Sarah Gehrke, Charley Harrison, Karina Hof, Leisha Jones, Steve Korver, Lake Montgomery, Christine O'Hara, Tim Peterson, Kim Renfrew, Nina Siegal, Tim Skelton, Catherine Somzé, Lena Vazifdar, Mark Wedin, Anna Whitehouse **Children** Georgina Bean, Julia Gorodecky, Jane Hannon **Film** Luuk Van Huët, Marjanne de Haan, Steve Korver, Mark Smith **Music & Nightlife** Niels Carels, Joost Baaij, Steve Korver, Steven McCarron, Lake Montgomery, Nina Siegal, Arun Sood, Mark Wedin, Christiaan de Wit **Performing Arts** Shyama Daryanani, Monique Gruter, Steve Korver, Steven McCarron, Malcolm Rock **Escapes & Excursions** Steve Korver, Marinus De Ruiter, Steve McCarron, Kim Renfrew, Tim Peterson, Megan Roberts **In Focus** Steve Korver **Essentials** Floris Dogterom, Steve Korver, Kim Renfrew.

The editor would like to thank Karen Willey, Floris Dogterom, Nel & Klaas, Will Fulford-Jones, Ruth Jarvis and all contributors to previous additions of Time Out Amsterdam, whose work forms the basis of parts of this book.

Maps JS Graphics Ltd (john@jsgraphics.co.uk). New mapping on the Amsterdam pull out map is based on data supplied by © OpenStreetMap contributors (www.openstreetmap.org)

Cover photograph Sandra Raccanello/SIME/4Corners

Back cover photography Clockwise from top left: Alexander Demyanenko/Shutterstock.com; John Lewis Marshall; Eric Gevaert/Shutterstock.com; Judith Fereday; Dennis van de Water/Shutterstock.com

Photography Pages 2/3, 26, 32 Holland Media Bank/Guus Schoonewille; 10 Radu Razvan/Shutterstock.com; 10/11, 108 villorejo/Shutterstock.com; 11 JeniFoto/Shutterstock.com; 12 (top and middle), 16 (middle), 29 (bottom), 44/45 (top), 82, 92, 128, 148, 160, 173, 175, 176, 190, 203, 229, 248, 255 Michelle Grant; 12 (bottom) Jaroslav Moravcik/Shutterstock.com; 13 (top) Kevin Dooley; 15 (top), 17 (top right), 57 (bottom), 69, 116, 132 (top), 156, 158, 171, 201 Marie-Charlotte Pezé; 16 (top), 30, 60, 131, 216 Dennis van de Water/Shutterstock.com; 16 (bottom) Ronald van Weeren; 17 (top left) M R/Shutterstock.com; 19 Holland Media Bank/Jose Alberto Mateo; 20 Frantisek Gela / Shutterstock.com; 21, 256 (bottom) Anne Binckebank; 24 (bottom) Holland Media Bank/Martin Waalboer; 27, 102 Ivica Drusany/Shutterstock.com; 28 (top), 34/35, 36 (bottom), 48/49 dev/Shutterstock.com; 28 (middle) Wladyslaw/Wikimedia Commons; 28 (bottom), 150 Jvhertum/Wikimedia Commons; 31 (top) Deningrad/Wikimedia Commons; 31 (bottom) Trey Guinn; 32/33 Ridgers/Shutterstock.com; 33 (middle) Cris Toala Olivares; 33 (bottom), 44/45 (bottom), 47 Holland Media Bank; 36 (top) Roel Bakker; 36/37 Jasper Faber/Rollende Keukens; 38 (bottom), 187 Worldpics/Shutterstock.com; 38/39 (top) Peter Kooijman; 39 Mauvries/Shutterstock.com; 40 (top) Arthur de Smidt; 40 (middle) Ronald Knapp; 40 (bottom) Maeve Stam; 40/41, 65 (bottom) Jan Kranendonk/Shutterstock.com; 42 Rob van Esch/Shutterstock.com; 43 (top) Aico Lind; 43 (bottom) SCS/Soenar Chamid; 46/47, 71, 84, 100, 101, 111, 120 (bottom) Maria Cavali; 54/55 Giancarlo Liguori/Shutterstock.com; 56 VanderWolf Images/Shutterstock.com; 57(top) Rostislav Glinsky/Shutterstock.com; 61 Estea/Shutterstock.com; 62 Cassander EeftinckSchattenkerk; 63 J.M.P.M. Seijger/Shutterstock.com; 64 (top) Ramunas Bruzas/Shutterstock.com; 64 (bottom), 119, 121 Kei Ishimaru; 65 (top) Matthew Dixon/Shutterstock.com; 72 Thijs Wolzak; 73 Abel Minnee; 74 pisaphotography/Shutterstock.com; 75 Victor Torres/Shutterstock.com; 76 Carolien Sikkenk; 15 (bottom), 77, 112, 126, 140, 170, 192 Olivia Rutherford; 78 emei/Shutterstock.com; 79 (top), 230/231, 258 Hans Engbers/Shutterstock.com; 79 (bottom) hipproductions/Shutterstock.com; 81 (left) Paul Winch-Furness; 86, 151 Karl O'Brien; 86/87 Alexander Demyanenko/Shutterstock.com; 89, 103, 112/113, 140/141 Artur Bogacki/Shutterstock.com; 94 Mikhail Markovskiy/Shutterstock.com; 97 Paule Kijne; 31 (middle), 104 104, 213 (bottom) Wilmar Dik; 106 (top and bottom left) Doriann Kransberg; 106 (bottom right) Bas Uterwijk; 109, 253, 267, 304/305 TonyV3112/Shutterstock.com; 120 (top) Taiga/Shutterstock.com; 123, 146, 166, 188 Christina Theisen; 124 Gert Jan van Rooij, courtesy Galerie Fons Welters Amsterdam; 126/127 Alchena/Shutterstock.com; 132 (bottom), 256 (top) John Lewis Marshall; 135 saaton/Shutterstock.com; 137 (top) Jessica Spengler; 137 (bottom) Ed Gilbert; 138 Henni van Beek; 139 A.Storm Photography/Shutterstock.com; 142 (top) Luuk Kramer; 142 (bottom) Roos Aldershoff Fotografie; 143 (top) Marijke Volkers; 143 (bottom) Ruud van Zwet; 149 (bottom) Goia de Bruijn; 152/153 Eddo Hartmann; 160/161 Ingolf Pompe/Getty Images; 172, 174 Nick_Nick/Shutterstock.com; 179 Iwan Baan; 189 Erik Verheggen; 191 Maarten Tromp; 200 Aija Lehtonen/Shutterstock.com; 204 nexus 7/Shutterstock.com; 207 (bottom) Hanne Nijhuis; 208 Henze Boekhout; 209 Alwin Poiana; 210 Coco Duivenoorde; 213 (top) Jan Versweyveld; 214/215 Neirfy/Shutterstock.com; 217 Evgeny Prokofyev/Shutterstock.com; 218 (top) iPics/Shutterstock.com; 218 (bottom) Paulina Grunwald/Shutterstock.com; 221 (top) Mediagram/Shutterstock.com; 221 (bottom) elvisvaughn/Shutterstock.com; 222 Eric Gevaert/Shutterstock.com; 223 Patricia Hofmeester/Shutterstock.com; 224 Boris Stroujko/Shutterstock.com; 226 Brasilnut1/Shutterstock.com; 227 Regien Paassen/Shutterstock.com; 232/233 Universal History Archive/Universal Images Group/REX; 235 Getty Images/The Bridgeman Art Library; 238 Dirk Verwoerd; 241 Keystone/Getty Images; 243 Planet News Archive/SSPL/Getty Images; 244 Alex Bowie/Getty Images; 246/247 Ppl/Shutterstock.com; 250 Oleg Senkov/Shutterstock.com; 251 Janericloebe/Wikimedia Commons; 254 Mark Wolters/Shutterstock.com; 257 Yamandu Roos; 262 Amsterdam Museum, Ioan Rijksmuseum Amsterdam; 265 Dom Brady/Wikimedia Commons; 266 Copyright Studio Roosegaarde, Amsterdam; 268 Isantilli/Shutterstock.com; 281 Amy Murrell; 282 Kasia Gatkowska; 287 Gourmantine; 289 Rob 't Hart Photography.

The following images were supplied by the featured establishments: pages 13 (middle), 24 (top), 29 (top), 50, 51, 52, 54, 68, 70, 81 (right), 83, 88, 95, 98, 107, 117, 122, 136, 147, 149 (top), 152, 168/169, 180, 182, 185, 193, 194, 196, 197, 198, 202, 207 (top), 211, 212, 259, 260, 261, 263, 264, 272, 274/275, 276, 277, 278, 279, 283, 285, 286

About the Guide

GETTING AROUND

Each sightseeing chapter contains a street map of the area marked with the locations of sights and museums (❶), restaurants (❶), cafés and bars (❶), shops (❶) and coffeeshops (❶). There are also street maps of Amsterdam at the back of the book, along with an overview map of the city and transport map. In addition, there is now a detachable fold-out street map inside the back cover.

THE ESSENTIALS

For practical information, including visas, disabled access, emergency numbers, lost property, useful websites and local transport, see *pp290-297*.

THE LISTINGS

Addresses, phone numbers, websites, transport information, hours and prices are all included in our listings, as are selected other facilities. All were checked and correct at press time. However, business owners can alter their arrangements at any time, and fluctuating economic conditions can cause prices to change rapidly.

The very best venues in Amsterdam, the must-sees and must-dos in each category of this book, have been indicated with a red star (★). In the Sightseeing chapters, we've also marked those venues with free admission with a FREE symbol.

PHONE NUMBERS

The area code for Amsterdam is 020. All of the phone numbers given in this guide, when dialled from outside the city, take this code unless otherwise stated. Dialling from abroad you'll need to preface them with the country code for the Netherlands, 31, and then the 020 city code (but first dropping the initial zero). We have stipulated where phone numbers are charged at non-standard rates – such as 0800 numbers (free) and 0900 (premium rate). For more information on telephone codes and charges, *see p297*.

FEEDBACK

We welcome feedback on this guide, both on the venues we've included and on any other locations that you'd like to see featured in future editions. Please email us at guides@timeout.com.

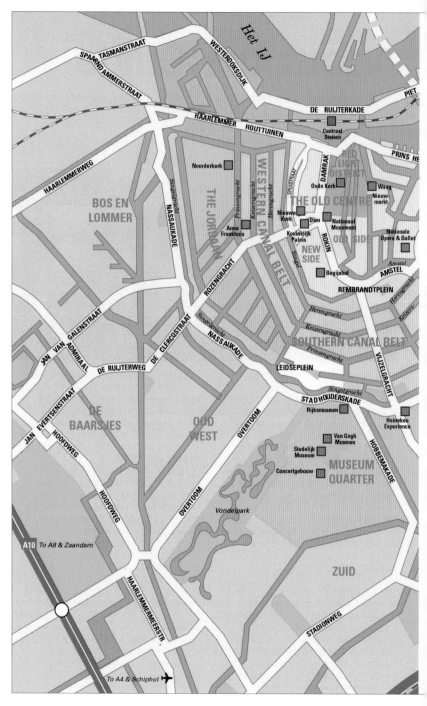

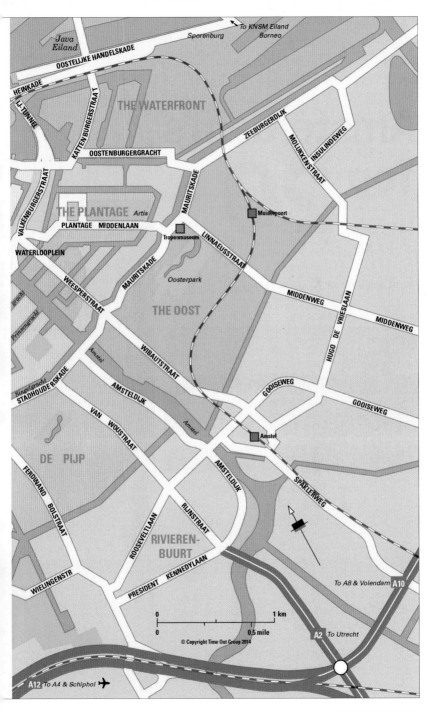

Java Eiland

To KNSM Eiland Borneo

Sporenburg

OOSTELIJKE HANDELSKADE

HEINKADE

IJ-TUNNEL

KATTENBURGERSTRAAT

THE WATERFRONT

ZEEBURGERDIJK

MOLUKKENSTRAAT

INSULINDEWEG

OOSTENBURGERGRACHT

VALKENBURGERSTRAAT

MAURITSKADE

THE PLANTAGE Artis

PLANTAGE MIDDENLAAN

Tropenmuseum

Muiderpoort

LINNAEUSSTRAAT

WATERLOOPLEIN

MAURITSKADE

Oosterpark

WEESPERSTRAAT

THE OOST

MIDDENWEG

MIDDENWEG

HUGO DE VRIESLAAN

gracht

Prinsengracht

WIBAUTSTRAAT

Amstel

Singelgracht

STADHOUDERSKADE

AMSTELDIJK

GOOISEWEG

GOOISEWEG

VAN WOUSTRAAT

Amstel

Amstel

DE PIJP

Amstel

SPAKLERWEG

FERDINAND BOLSTRAAT

AMSTELDIJK

ROOSEVELTLAAN

RIJNSTRAAT

RIVIEREN-
BUURT

To A8 & Volendam A10

WIELINGENSTR

PRESIDENT KENNEDYLAAN

0   1 km

0   0,5 mile

© Copyright Time Out Group 2014

A2 To Utrecht

A12 To A4 & Schiphol ✈

Amsterdam's
Top **20**

*From Rembrandt to
the Red Light District, we
count down the city's finest.*

❶

1 Van Gogh Museum
(page 133)

While there's a whole town in China
pumping out Van Gogh copies for the
hotel walls of the world, there's still
nothing quite like admiring the real
thing – just ask the almost 1.5 million
people who visit this museum every
year. The permanent exhibition features
some 200 paintings and 500 drawings
by Van Gogh, and temporary shows
explore his contemporaries and his
influence on other artists. To avoid
the queues, be sure to book tickets
online, or try visiting around noon
or late afternoon.

❷

2 Rijksmuseum
(page 130)

The nation's 'treasure house' makes one proud to be human – which is always refreshing. It's also reassuring to discover that Rembrandt's *The Night Watch* and Vermeer's *The Milkmaid* are not at all overrated. The Rijksmuseum's refurbished palatial interior – all gold leaf and intricate art nouveau woodwork and patterns – is worthy of a day's admiration in itself. As for the artworks, you'll need a week. And don't forget to practise some Mongolian throat-singing under the vaulted ceiling of the bike path that runs through the building.

3 Canal cruising
(page 88)

Sure, you can enjoy the bird's-eye view of Amsterdam from the new public library OBA (*see p156*), the rooftop lounge of DoubleTree by Hilton (*see p289*), the Twenty Third Bar (*see p166*) and the iconic Westerkerk tower (*see p93*). But it's the eel's-eye view best enjoyed from a watery cruise that gives you the most insightful and scenic views of the city. And if you can arrange to navigate your own smaller boat, so much the better.

4 Anne Frank Huis
(page 92)

One of the 20th century's most famous and best-selling authors was dead at 15. Her book, *The Diary of Anne Frank*, documented the two years her Jewish family spent hiding from the Nazis in a small 'back house'. After being betrayed, the family members were sent to concentration camps – only her father survived. The family's preserved hiding place and the accompanying exhibitions resonate with a simple message – 'Never again' – which remains as relevant as ever.

5 Begijnhof
(page 75)

This hidden courtyard near the chaos that is high-street shopping strip Kalverstraat is the perfect place to regain a sense of peace. Just avoid treading on the slab of pink granite by the walkway: it's the grave of a nun and former resident. Begijnhof and its two churches are also handily adjacent to the bookish square Spui (with its Friday book market and numerous bookshops and cafés) and the freely accessible Civic Guard's Gallery of the Amsterdam Museum.

6 Red Light District
(page 56)

Yes, this is a red-light district where women get paid for sex. But Amsterdam's sleaze zone also remains one of the city's oldest neighbourhoods, and as such contains many ancient houses, squares and churches, along with nurseries, schools and locals casually – and socially – going about their business. Chief annoyance: roving packs of drunken British stag partygoers – oh, the shame.

7 Jordaan
(page 112)

The laid-back Jordaan is a compelling neighbourhood and the perfect place for a spot of aimless wandering. Higgledy-piggledy streets offer a surprise around almost every corner: it may be a seemingly forgotten café, a hip art gallery or a window into a living room filled with plain weird stuff. In fact, a semi-random approach can also be applied to the rest of Amsterdam with its eternally looping streets. But keep an eye out for the bikes.

8 Amsterdam Museum
(page 76)

A couple of hours in this rather high-tech historical museum will certainly enhance your future wanderings around the city. Marvel at how Amsterdam evolved out of bog. Respect how local business people gave the middle finger to royalty while creating their own Golden Age. Dig the wacky antics employed by local hippy activists during the halcyon 1960s. Raise your eyebrows at how much ecstasy was consumed in the clubbing heyday of the '80s and '90s.

The 2nd most popular spot in Amsterdam welcomes you.

Artis Royal Zoo of Amsterdam

natura
ARTIS
magistra

9 NDSM
(page 158)

This former shipyard is now home to a heady, post-industrial mix of commerce and art. MTV's European headquarters contrasts nicely with shipping containers used by noisy bands for rehearsal spaces. Restaurant ships compete with former petrol stations revamped as organic snack bars. An indoor city of studios for hundreds of professional creatives is surrounded by work by the who's who of the local graffiti scene. And as a bonus – you can access it all via a free 20-minute ferry ride from Centraal Station.

10 Stedelijk Museum
(page 130)

After reopening following almost a decade of expansion and renovation, the Netherlands' premier modern-art museum was keen to be taken seriously as one of the globe's finest institutions of its kind. General acclaim greeted exhibitions of Mike Kelley, Kazimir Malevich and homegrown design wonderboy Marcel Wanders. The locals, while visiting in droves, seemed to take it a bit less seriously – by nicknaming the new plastic extension the 'bathtub'.

11 Paradiso
(page 192)

The Paradiso was never technically a church, but rather a congregational meeting hall. But with all the stained glass, it's churchy enough. And since the 1960s, it's been the 'pop temple' for every relevant genre that followed – from punk to hip hop and dance. The world's biggest musical legends regularly forego a stadium gig to play here. And in its smaller upstairs hall, Paradiso books the legends of tomorrow. The nearby Melkweg (*see p192*) is also a legendary music venue.

12 Westergasfabriek
(page 116)

The city's vast former gasworks on the western edge of the city has been transformed into an award-winning cultural park with clubs, music venues, restaurants, the Het Ketelhuis art-house cinema (*see p176*) and plenty of green space, which also plays host to stellar concerts and festivals. Designed by American landscape architect Kathryn Gustafson, Westergasfabriek is a wonderful example of urban reuse.

13 Concertgebouw
(page 203)

Could this late 19th-century building topped with a shiny golden lyre have the best acoustics on the planet? You can decide while sunk into one of the comfy seats as you absorb the planet's best orchestras, conductors, ensembles and soloists. If you're already a classical music fan, you undoubtedly have some tracks played by the house band, the Royal Concertgebouw Orchestra.

14 Vondelpark
(page 128)

OK, you might still hear some bongo playing on occasion, but it's not nearly so rampant as it was in the 1970s, when KLM airways lured American longhairs to visit Amsterdam with the slogan: 'Come sleep in Hippie Park.' Today, Vondelpark is merely a people's park and the city's green lung. On sunny days and Sundays, it becomes the most densely populated spot in the city.

15 Noordermarkt Monday Flea Market
(page 122)

When the sun glimmers through the antiques-laden stalls, this church square achieves an old-fashioned vibe that's hard to match. Browse away. And if you want to be tradition-bound, have coffee and apple pie in one of the surrounding cafés. The same square also hosts a lovely Saturday organic farmer's market.

TOWN PLAN

Amsterdam is awash with all manner of city tours, by bus, boat, bike and more. If you fancy a helping hand round the *hofjes*, turn to p50 Tour Amsterdam.

16 Nine Streets
(page 97)

Obviously, the UNESCO-crowned Canal Ring is essential viewing on any visit to Amsterdam. However, make sure you don't miss the intersecting streets, where most of the city's living, eating and drinking takes place. The Nine Streets is where people go to indulge in quirky shopping – from wonderful cheeses to Karl Lagerfeld's flagship store to toothbrushes to 19th-century spectacles to 21st-century denim.

17 EYE
(page 159)

This new film institute building resembles a shiny white bird about to take flight – which contrasts nicely with the sinking-ship appearance of another Waterfront modern architectural icon, Renzo Piano's NEMO Science Center (*see p154*). EYE has been very effective in luring people over to Amsterdam Noord – an area long ignored – and it will only become hipper with the 2014 opening of arts centre Tolhuistuin.

18 Foam
(page 104)

The Photography Museum Amsterdam, located in a renovated canal house, displays a comprehensive array of camera-clicking talent. It not only focuses on global icons – recent retrospectives have covered William Klein and Diane Arbus – but also zooms in on the domestic scene by exhibiting work by local photographers, and hosting courses, events and pop-ups. There's an excellent café on site too.

19 Artis Royal Zoo
(page 147)

One of Europe's oldest zoos has been a fine day out for the whole family since the mid 19th century. And it's continuing to expand its ambitions in 2014, with the opening of Micropia (the world's first 'microlife experience'), a new public square and a restaurant with a view of the famously flaming pink flamingos. If green is more your thing, Hortus Botanicus (*see p148*) is just a few palm fronds away.

20 Haarlem and beyond
(page 216)

The Netherlands is a dinky country and you should take advantage of that with a day trip or two. Haarlem is 20 minutes away by train, Utrecht 30 minutes, Rotterdam less than an hour and Belgium just two. So make the most of the opportunity to compare and contrast. But don't forget to come back to the canals of Amsterdam…

Amsterdam Today

Getting in touch with the Dutch.

TEXT: STEVE KORVER

'The most relaxed city in Europe'. 'It has everything, from the best art and new design to the old sex, drugs and rock'n'roll'. 'The people are so friendly'. 'It's compact and beautiful, you can bike and walk everywhere and everybody speaks English'. These are just a few of the reasons why tourists continue to flock en masse to the Dutch capital – though a lot has changed in recent years. Compared to London or Paris, Amsterdam used to be like a kid brother who didn't want to grow up; it was a playground where all involved had a jolly good time, bar a few superficial bumps. During recent years, though, the city has had to grow up fast.

CHRISTMAS CONTROVERSY

The tradition of Zwarte Piet divides the nation.

Each year in the Netherlands during the Christmas season, the tone around the debate on whether Zwarte Piet ('Black Peter') is a form of racism gets darker. On one side are protestors with their 'Black Peter is racism' T-shirts. On the other are the two million who signed a Facebook 'Pietition' and treat such talk as a threat against their culture.

For the outsider, it remains a curious tradition: countless Dutch adults putting on black faces, smearing on red, red lipstick, popping on a wig of kinky hair and adorning their ears with large golden hoops – and doing all this without any sense of malice. Then they hit the streets like a pack of highly caffeinated Al Jolsons to help St Nick distribute sweets to children.

Local Dutch cultural history only goes so far in giving a reasonable explanation behind the Black Peter tradition. Once upon a pagan time, this was slaughter season when meat was both stored for the long winter and sacrificed to Odin – the Germanic God of War, Sea and Hunt. It became a celebration of life and was accompanied, one assumes, with lots of blood and bonking. So when the Church came to town to tone down the whole process, they decided the party should be rebranded around Saint Nicholas, patron saint of children, whose birthday conveniently fell on 6 December.

The Dutch were forced to repress their natural urges for communal butchery by aggressively baking huge mounds of animal-shaped cookies and chewing on marrow-textured marzipan. Later, Sinterklaas mutated further by heading to America with the settlers, eventually getting drawled out to become Santa Claus. Meanwhile Black Peter's blackened face is explained away as resulting from his assigned job of delivering the sweets to the awaiting shoes via that dirtiest of orifices, the chimney. (But, of course, this doesn't explain Black Peter's exaggerated lips, kinky hair, golden-hooped earrings and, often enough, Surinamese accent.)

Another rationalisation has the tradition going back to when darkness represented evil; that Black Peter is actually the conquered devil, and that his colour and joy of mischief are the only leftovers of an evil beaten out of him by St Nick. Either way – may it be through soot or sin – blackness tends to cling. As does St Nick during the rest of the year as the official patron saint of not only Amsterdam itself, but also other favourites of Odin such as merchants, prostitutes, thieves and sailors (who, interestingly, paid tribute to their patron saint for centuries by using the term 'doing the St Nicholas' as slang for intercourse).

Odin not only shares the same followers as St Nick, but also rides the same kind of white horse and, in some stories, has some dark sidekicks chained to him – with such similarities it's easy to assume that St Nick is simply Odin cross-dressed as a bishop. And, in turn, Odin is the devil – or so said the Church when they came to town. But as long as Satan continues to bring joy to the hearts of millions of kiddies each year, what's the problem? As for Zwarte Piet, controversy will no doubt continue to reign for many Christmases to come.

Red Light District.

POLITICAL LIFE

'Tolerance' is a word that gets bandied about a lot in Amsterdam, but the word doesn't necessarily mean acceptance of all kinds of behaviour. It's more likely to translate as: 'Do your thing, as long as it doesn't interfere with my thing – and especially my business thing.' But whatever the nature of the city's famed tolerance, it has made it a safe haven for displaced people for centuries. Its atmosphere of intellectual and artistic freedom has also made it a refuge for thinkers and creative types ever since René Descartes rocked up.

However, it could be argued that the same tolerance that allowed Amsterdam to become known as a Jewish capital of Europe before World War II (engendering the nickname Mokum or 'home') was counteracted by the Dutch 'tolerance' of the deportation and extermination of the same Jewish community under Nazi occupation. There may have been a resistance movement here, but in the end 90 per cent of the Netherlands' Jews were killed during the war – the highest proportion of any western European country, and the second highest in Europe after Poland.

The city's perceived tolerance was also shaken to its very core by a more recent event: the murder of film director, writer and big mouth Theo van Gogh, shot and knifed in broad daylight in November 2004 by a young Dutch-Moroccan man incensed by Van Gogh's constant moaning about Islam – notably in his much-hyped movie *Submission*. Racial tension was in the air. The mayor at the time, Job Cohen, gave a speech immediately following the brutal event that included the now-famous line, '*We moeten de boel bij elkaar houden*' (We have to keep our stuff together). And that's exactly what he did.

Many Amsterdammers praised Cohen's swift, balanced response, focusing more on dialogue than action to keep the peace in the multicultural city that Amsterdam had become over the years. Others, however, felt that he wasn't tough enough and spent too much time drinking mint tea in mosques with Muslim delegates instead of setting an example by taking firm measures.

The current mayor, Eberhard van der Laan, is also taking an inclusive approach by 'keeping the stuff together', but perhaps with a slightly firmer hand. He's also building on Cohen's pet project of cleaning up the Red Light District (*see p57* **Red Light Blues**). Both these men make a solid case for the effectiveness of appointing mayors instead of electing them – for politicians they are shockingly reasonable (and tolerant).

There's a sharp distinction between Amsterdam's politics and that of the country as a whole, with its recent pull towards populism and the right-wing. Relatively few Amsterdammers would be caught dead voting for populist politician Geert Wilders,

who blames everything on Islam and the EU. While Amsterdam may have been a birthplace of capitalism, it remains a staunchly left-wing town with the Labour Party (PvDA) holding power for over a century.

While the national government toughens up its immigration policies, Amsterdam responds by actively finding housing for illegal refugees. While the national government comes up with ideas to limit the trade on soft drugs, the city points out the crazy nature of such ideas.

Change may be afoot, though, and local elections in March 2014 could lead to the Labour Party finally losing its all-pervasive powers. While few expect any radical swing to the right, some disturbing trends are emerging: compared to five years ago, a third of all Amsterdammers feel the city has become less tolerant, and a majority of gays and Muslims feel 'less free', according to a recent survey.

Physically, much of the city's charm lies in how little has changed – Amsterdam was spared the devastation of many nearby cities during World War II. Several modern schemes are keeping the city in flux – especially the Noord-Zuidlijn metro line and developments around Centraal Station, and directly across the IJ in Amsterdam Noord (see p74 **Old Station, New Hub**) – but most of the more appealing sights have been around for many decades or, more usually, for centuries.

Like any big city, Amsterdam has its fair share of crime and violence. That said, crime rates have been steadily decreasing during the last few years. Numbers for robbery, shoplifting, pickpocketing and theft of cars and bikes are all spiralling downwards, and even the number of road accidents in the city is on the decline. You're also unlikely to get shot unless you're a high-flying criminal (there are regular gangland assassinations), so relax and enjoy.

BUSINESS LIFE

The global financial crisis was slow to affect the Netherlands. Of course, there were plenty of banks that needed bailing out, but the general populace seemed to continue to spend. Fashion icon Karl Lagerfeld recently saw fit to open his second flagship shop in Amsterdam, and ultimate lifestyle car

'While Amsterdam may have been a birthplace of capitalism, it remains a staunchly left-wing town.'

brand Tesla chose the city for its latest showroom. At the other end of the scale, the adorable Uke Boutique (www.uke boutique.nl), dedicated to that cutest of instruments, the ukelele, is managing to survive in the current climate. Others are even flourishing: Hutspot (see p167), a department store for pop-ups, plans to open a third location in 2014.

The buoyancy of the retail sector could be explained by the fact that the Netherlands is a wealthy country (it came fifth in the EU's rich list). Indeed, the Port of Amsterdam was founded on the principles of exchange. Yet the population is perhaps less obsessed with shopping than residents of other countries. The influence of Calvinism, that most pared-down of lifestyle choices, is still etched deep into the national psyche, and most people are happy to pack a cheese sandwich for lunch rather than eat out at a stylish café. Contradictions abound, but whatever your outlook, you shouldn't feel guilty for spending a little here.

Besides being home to the European headquarters of some of the world's largest corporations, Amsterdam is also home to a whole slew of advertising firms such as They, Sid Lee, Wieden+Kennedy and DDB Tribal. Other creative agencies such as VandeJong, Kesselskramer and Submarine combine working for big brand clients with more quirky and non-commercial projects. And there's another major industry that's doing very well from the crossover between art and commerce: the local gaming development industry is showing no signs of downturn. With so many global firms in town, 'Western foreigners' now make up 15 per cent of the population, and they seem universlly determined to embrace a lifestyle that involves ferrying kids to school by cargo bike.

Centraal Station.

For its part, the city actively campaigns to make the city more appealing for foreign businesses and their employees, creating a special bureau for all aspects of being an expat in the city, and organising special training for civil servants and those working in the hotel and catering industry to become more polite and flexible. Of course, Amsterdam's economic resilience is also greatly thanks to the more than 16 million tourists who pour in every year.

CULTURAL LIFE

Amsterdam's museum scene has officially awakened from a long slumber with four major reopenings. After a full decade of renovation, the Rijksmuseum (*see p130*) is back to delirious acclaim – predictable since it houses some of the world's greatest art treasures; the Stedelijk Museum of Modern Art (*see p130*) has also reopened in the hope of getting delirious acclaim in the future – but it's tricky if your budget keeps getting cut; the Scheepvaartmuseum (Maritime Museum; *see p154*) is once again glorifying Dutch sea savvy; and the EYE Film Institute (*see p159*) has now settled into an eye-catching riverside building across from Centraal Station. Feeling overwhelmed yet?

There has always been plenty to keep visitors amused in Amsterdam, whether they're inclined towards experimenting with vices or more cerebral, nobler pursuits. But sadly, the squat scene – always an

Scheepvaartmuseum.

incubator of interesting and edgy art, ideas and initiatives – was allowed to disintegrate during the last decade. Recently, though, the powers-that-be realised that Amsterdam needs creative souls if it wants to compete with the likes of Berlin, and they began setting up 'breeding grounds' for the arts (*see p263* **Giving a Squat**). As a result, the current chaos of economic crisis and subsidy cuts has been greeted by local creatives as a challenge rather than a death knoll.

Football remains the city's main game, with fans still pining for the glory days of Johan Cruijff and Marco van Basten. While plenty of Dutch stars, such as Arjen Robben and Robin van Persie, have made their names and riches internationally, the magic spark is still missing from the national side.

The same goes for local team Ajax, which has never really hit its stride on the global scene since occupying the Amsterdam ArenA 20 years ago. Fans complain that while the squad is a great training ground, the best players get sold to the major clubs abroad when they reach their peak. Klaas-Jan Huntelaar (Schalke), Rafael van der Vaart (Hamburg) and Wesley Sneijder (Galatasaray), are three prime examples. All is not lost, though. With Dutch footballing legends Frank de Boer and Dennis Bergkamp installed as manager and assistant manager respectively, Ajax hopes to translate its recent national successes to the international stage once again.

Beyond football, Dutch stars manage to bag medals on a regular basis in ice skating, field hockey, swimming, darts and cycling. There have even been murmurings about Amsterdam hosting the 2028 Olympics, but no one should book a hotel room quite yet.

SOCIAL LIFE

Where are all the above issues discussed most feverishly? *Horeca*, of course. The hotel-restaurant-café business is a crazy rollercoaster, with an almost endless stream of new and often daring ventures popping up (and closing down). Clubbing, in particular, seems to be enjoying a renaissance thanks in part to 24-hour licensing (*see p193* **24-hour Party Town**), reviving memories of the late 1980s when clubs such as RoXY and iT ruled the DJ roost and achieved global fame. But in among all this flux, café culture remains the centre of Dutch social life. Indeed, like most places, it's all about food, drink and *geouwehoer* (as gabbing endlessly is called locally).

It used to be that the term 'Dutch cuisine' inspired only mirth in serious foodies; these days that's been reduced to the occasional chuckle. Well-travelled native chefs have returned home to apply their skills to fresh, local and often organic ingredients. The land is most suited to growing spuds, cabbage, kale and carrots, but the nation is now using its greenhouses to grow a startling array of ingredients, year-round. In short, things have improved immensely.

In medieval days it was fish, gruel and beer that formed the holy diet. During the Golden Age, the rich indulged in hogs and

DUTCH DISNEYLAND
Ain't Amsterdam cute?

It's certainly hard not to be charmed by Amsterdam's cutesy doll's house proportions, and it only makes sense that the radical hippy party that arose from the ashes of Provo (*see p241*), and ended up winning five seats in city government in 1970, called themselves the Kabouters, after the word for happy-go-lucky forest-dwelling dwarves common in local folk tales. It's also no great surprise that the Dutch have a reputation for quality theme parks: the Efteling (*see p174*) is a favourite among connoisseurs who like a dash of surreal with their rollercoaster experiences, and Madurodam proudly claims the title of 'world's largest miniature village' (*see p174*).

In many ways, Amsterdam can be seen as one giant theme park – or at least well on the way to becoming one. Take the Red Light District, which seems to contradict the rampant idea of sex being something dirty and dangerous. In fact, it's probably the closest a sex district can get to being 'fun for the whole family'. Long gone are the days when you'd walk through the neighbourhood and see – as you still could back in the 1960s – condoms hanging out to dry until their next go.

Certainly, there are plenty of locals who warn of the 'Disneyfication' of Amsterdam, with residents being pushed out of the centre in favour of hotels and restaurants for well-heeled tourists. And this scenario seems backed up by the fact that all visitors, from stoners to business folk, rarely bother to look both ways when crossing a road, tramline or bike path.

The intimate dimensions of Amsterdam seem to lull people into a false sense of security – as if they were in a theme park. Regardless, you shouldn't make the same mistake. For now, at least, Amsterdam remains a very real city where one can still be rendered into road pizza in the blink of an eye. You've been warned.

pheasants. Then, with Napoleonic rule at the dawn of the 19th century, the middle classes were seduced by the Mediterranean flavours of herbs and spices. Only in the last century has Amsterdam taken to global cuisine, with waves of immigrants helping to create today's vortex of culinary diversity (*see p104* **Seriously Hot Stuff**).

Of course, there's still nothing quite like a hotchpotch of mashed potato, crispy bacon and crunchy greens, holding a well of gravy and loads of smoked sausage, to prove that traditional Dutch food can still hit the spot. But the most feverish buzz is around places that combine straight, honest cooking with eccentric ingredients and often out-of-the-way locations. There's also much talk of a new 'nouveau rough' school that combines rough interiors, an obsession for fresh and well-sourced ingredients, and reasonable prices. This move towards unpretentious, straightforward cooking can also be seen in the rise of street food.

Another relatively new development is the emergence of several 'culinary boulevards': Haarlemmerstraat/Haarlemmerdijk, the stretch of connected streets in the Jordaan centred on the Spanish La Oliva (*see p117*), Amstelveenseweg south of Vondelpark, and most recently Van Woustraat in De Pijp.

As the local barfly-cum-columnist Simon Carmiggelt once observed: 'Going for one drink is like jumping off a roof with the plan

of falling only one floor.' So knowing some basic rules when out drinking in Amsterdam is a plus. Perhaps the most fundamental rule for Brits is not to whine about the 'two fingers' of head that come with a glass of draft pils ('lager'). You're not being ripped off. It's the 'crown' and the reasoning behind it is sound: by letting a head form during tapping, the beer's hoppy aroma – and hence full flavour – is released, and the drinker's gas intake is minimised (leaving more room for more beer of course).

Another handy tip is to avoid getting completely legless by acquiring a sound knowledge of *borrel hapjes* (booze bites). These tasty bar snacks are formulated to line the stomach during drinking sessions. Inevitably, such menus begin with the strongest of stereotypes: *kaas* (cheese), which can be ingested either via *tostis* (grilled cheese sandwiches) or pure with dipping mustard. But the most universal and tastiest of *hapjes* are definitely *bitterballen* ('bitter balls'), which are essentially cocktail versions of the *kroket*.

A barfly can also score some major points by giving the Dutch rightful credit for inventing gin. In around 1650, a doctor in Leiden came up with the process that allowed juniper berries to be infused into distilled spirits and gin was born – or rather *jenever*, as the original Dutch version is called. A few decades later, the Dutch were exporting ten million gallons of the stuff, as a supposedly innocuous cure for stomach and kidney ailments. They graded the *jenever* by age – *jong*, *oud* and *zeer oud* (young, old and very old) – but also by adding various herbs, spices and flavours. Such liquid elixirs can still be found at *proeflokalen* (tasting houses) such as Wynand Fockink (*see p70*). But there are also new boutique distillers on the block, such as Distilleerderij 't Nieuwe Diep (www.nwediep.nl), along with an emerging craft beer scene (*see p150* **What's Brewing?**).

Although it may seem that Amsterdam has lost some of its underground feel, the city is still a magnet for inspiring people who'll always find a way to make sure the city's sheer individuality will remain and – by doing so – keep it one of the most wonderful places on the planet to work, live and spend time in.

I THINK, THEREFORE I AMSTERDAM
Living with a logo.

It was all so much simpler in the 1970s. To entice people to visit Amsterdam, all KLM had to do was put out some posters cajoling its long-haired American target audience to come 'Sleep in Hippie Park'. Word of mouth did the rest. And before that there was the tourist board's 'Get in Touch with the Dutch' campaign in the 1960s – surely a slogan from a more innocent period. Compared to that halcyon era, the boom years of the 1990s were the most boring of times, with tedious slogans such as 'Capital of Inspiration' and 'Business Gateway to Europe'.

Now, in the 21st century, every city needs its own marketing campaign to establish its advantages over the rest of the planet, spurred on by the stratospheric success of the original 'I heart NY' logo.

Amsterdam's slogan can perhaps be seen as a twist on local boy René Descartes' insight: 'I think, therefore I am.' Like those other inspired plays on the city's name, 'Amsterdamned' and the even better 'Amsterdamaged', 'I amsterdam' works through its utter simplicity.

The only really annoying thing about the campaign is that it tries to peddle the idea that the logo will not only attract outside business, but also work to unify regular Amsterdammers. This is solidly contradicted whenever an actual Dutchie tries to say 'I amsterdam' out loud. Their accent makes them stutter out something that sounds more like 'I hamster', as if they were arrogant rodents rather than proud Amsterdammers.

Okay, it's easy to mock. We admit that marketing a city can't be easy, and there must be more to it than producing a catchy T-shirt slogan. And what other choices were there? 'Handy airport, lotsa coffeeshops', while appealing to both the business and leisure markets, lacks something in the way of elegance.

It could be argued that 'Amsterdamned' and 'Amsterdamaged' are much better ambassadors for the city. After all, today's visiting dopeheads may hold the city's economic future in their rather shaky hands. It's happened before: sentimental (and rich) ex-hippies, looking for somewhere to recover their lost youth and salve their conscience, were the ones who invested in the place during the booming 1990s. They figured that it would be a good excuse to come and visit a few times a year, in the hope of re-creating those relaxed coffeeshop moments from decades long past.

Thinking of which, isn't being relaxed one of the things Amsterdam has always been famous for? This logo stamped all over the city does little to contribute to this most obvious of brand benefits.

Itineraries

Sure you can spend your day in a stoned stupor – we're not judging. But you can also try to stay a bit focussed.

10AM

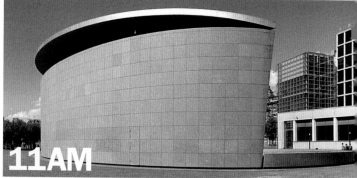

11AM

1:30PM

Day 1

10AM You can easily walk around town, but why not rent a bike from, for example, StarBikes (p292), just east of Centraal Station. They're friendly folks who also serve great coffee. Otherwise just cruise up to Nieuwmarkt (p77) square to settle on the one of the terraces around De Waag.

11AM Naturally, you've pre-booked a ticket online for the Van Gogh Museum (p133) or Rijksmuseum (p130) so you can skip the queues. Get there via art and antique gallery streets Nieuwe Spiegelstraat and Spiegelgracht.

1:30PM Neutralise your eyes from the onslaught of colours from all that art, by absorbing the green of Vondelpark (p128) while lunching at Blauwe Theehuis ('Blue Tea House', p134).

3:30PM Do some window shopping of the quirky offerings of the 'Nine Streets' (p97), a series of side streets connecting the

Left from top: **Nieuwmarkt, Van Gogh Museum, Blauwe Theehuis.** Right: **Nam Kee, FEBO.**

three main canals of the iconic grachtengordel.

4:30PM Again: you've really been on the ball and pre-booked a ticket online for the Anne Frankhuis (p92). Good work!

6:30PM Go back over 350 years at Wynand Fockink (p70) for a shot or two of jenever, the original gin. Opt for a kopstoot ('head butt') which pairs such a shot with a beer. If you have to return that bicycle, stop on the way at the city's Central OBA Libraray (p171) to check out the view.

9PM Head into the Old Side for a late meal: at the Chinese Nam Kee (p68), the Korean Yokiyo (p68) or the cheese fondu-ists Café Bern (p67).

11PM Nightcap in the more civilised zones of the Red Light District, such as straight-friendly gay/lesbian bar Getto (p187), updated pinball arcade the TonTon Club (p70) or in former gambling hall Mata Hari (p69). If you have one too many, gel your belly back together by pulling a greasy kroket out of the wall of a FEBO (p137).

11AM

Day 2

10AM You loved that kroket from last night so much you want it for breakfast. Van Dobben (p107) has perhaps the best in the city. But they also have gentler Dutch sandwich fare…

11AM Admire the crazy architecture of the city's most over-the-top cinema Tuschinski (p176) before walking the very filmic Staalstraat and dropping in on Dutch modern design mecca Hotel Droog (p72). Then enter the past at Oudemanhuis Book Market (p73) to browse, as Van Gogh did before you, through the old prints and books.

1:30PM Cross over to the New Side towards Spui square. You might want to chug back a herring at the fish stall on the left. It will give you strength to absorb the city's living history at Amsterdam Museum (p76) and the hidden courtyard Begijnhof (p75).

Left: **Staalstraat**.
Right from top:
Oudemanhuispoort,
Blauw, **Paradiso**.

11AM

3:30PM Your sense of focus has been admirable. So take a break. The sculptured glass bongs of the Original Dampkring Gallery (p99) will set your imagination free – if not, there's always the conveniently nearby coffeeshops.

4:30PM Energised by the scope of the human spirit, take a semi-ambitious bike ride to Oost to enjoy some locally brewed beer in the shadow of a windmill on the packed terrace of Brouwerij 't IJ (p151). They also serve excellent sausage and cheese.

6:30PM

6:30PM Perhaps it's time for a power nap? Otherwise go out for some Indonesian food (p104).

9PM But be on time for that excellent gig likely happening at Paradiso (p197) or Melkweg (p197).

11PM If you decide not to stay for the post-gig clubnight, take the roundabout route back to your hotel. Who knows what you will find?

9PM

Itineraries

Free Stuff

GARDENS & FLOWERS
The Rijksmuseum (p130) has free sculpture gardens – highlights including the organic curves of Henry Moore.
Open-air concerts and the great outdoors of Vondelpark (see p129).
The Bloemenmarkt (p110) has every manner of blooms and bulbs.

CULTURE
The Concertgebouw (p203) hosts free lunchtime concerts on Wednesdays – as does the Nationale Opera & Ballet (p204) on Tuesdays.
The Civic Guard Gallery at the Amsterdam Museum (see p76), plus the neighbouring atmospheric inner courtyard Begijnhof (p75).
Watching horseriding in the epic Holland's Manege (Vondelstraat 140, 618 0942).
Lounging at one of the city beaches (p191).
Reading through the international papers and glossies at the public library Openbare Bibliotheek Amsterdam (p171). And then proceeding to the top floor café to take in the view.
Visiting the City Archives (see p105 Stadsarchief Amsterdam).
Interactive Dutch films at EYE Film Institute (p159).
Free jazz jams at the Bimhuis (p201) every Tuesday at 10pm from September to June.

Sculpture gardens by the Rijksmuseum.

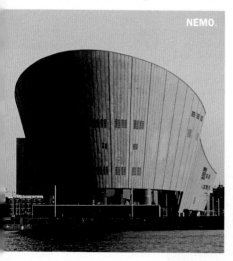
NEMO.

ONE-OFFS
The free ferries from behind Centraal Station can motor you over to Noord and further Oost. So just get on board.
The view from NEMO (see p154).
Checking the biggest barometer in the Netherlands; the neon light on the Hotel Okura Amsterdam (see p289) tells you what tomorrow's weather will be like: blue for good; green for bad; white for changeable.
Noord/Zuidlijn viewpoint: across from Rokin 96 in the middle of the street, descend the stairs to see the current state of Amsterdam's new subway.
Free diamond factory tour at Gassan Diamonds (see p147).
The Monday morning flea market (p122) and the Saturday organic market, Boerenmarkt (p121), both on Noordermarkt square, is a one-way ticket to old world charms. They combine nicely with exploring the Jordaan's hofjes (hidden courtyards, p123).

FOOD & DRINK
Complimentary coffee at various branches of Albert Heijn (see p81).
Tasting free samples of organic foodstuffs at the Saturday farmers' market on Noordermarkt (see above).

City Archives.

Noordermarkt flea market.

TWILIGHT TOUR
Night-time is the right time.

If night has fallen, there's nothing like a scenic stroll in the Canal Ring while enjoying the wiggly reflections of those iconic canal houses in the waters below. Albert Camus in *The Fall* described how the city's radiating canals resembled the circles of hell. And appropriately enough, the Red Light District forms the inner pit. You may have already found yourself as you randomly wandered the city, endlessly looping in towards the red lights of the city's geographical centre. No one is sure if the city was designed like this on purpose, but this phenomenon has acted as a form of social control: it has traditionally kept visiting sailors (and later packs of stag-celebrating Brits) centralised, while leaving the rest of the city for residents to live their daily lives.

So if you want to break free from this eerie gravitational pull, head to the Jordaan to take in some casual, local nightlife at a traditional 'brown cafe'. If you are in search of a more youthful frenzy, then check out the strip of bars running west from Leidseplein on Marnixstraat, or along 1e Van de Helststraat in De Pijp.

You can also pay tribute at Amstelstraat 24, just off Rembrandtplein, where Manfred Langer opened one of the city's most legendary nightclubs, iT, in 1989. It was intended to be the ultimate gay disco, and indeed became a magnet for two-metre tall transvestites wearing acres of leather. Soon straights and international names were clamouring to get in, but the club started to fade when Langer died in 1994 (he was taken to his final resting place in a pink Chevrolet convertible). Langer's dream does linger on in the building's current occupant, Air (p191).

However, today's club scene is more defined by a more low-tech aesthetic and approach exhibited by relative new locations such as the urban beach Roest (p156). Then there are such cosy, funky clubs such as De Nieuwe Anita (p179) and the newly revamped Canvas (p194).

Diary

*Plan ahead with our year-round
guide to the best festivals and events.*

Koningsdag

One may sometimes think that the Dutch are a fairly reserved bunch. But when they shed their inhibitions and dive into a fun-seeking frenzy, they dive deep. On the likes of Oudejaarsavond (New Year's Eve) and Koningsdag (King's Day, the day formerly known as Queen's Day) – and whenever Ajax win a big game – the city falls into a joyous, orange-tinted psychosis of song, drink and dance. Happily, orange doesn't play a huge role during FashionWeek (but – who knows? – perhaps next year orange will become the new black). Dance, meanwhile, plays a huge role in the city's two major annual clubbing events: 5 Days Off and the Amsterdam Dance Event. Other cultural gems abound, running from Open Monument Days and the ever-popular Museum Night to the world's largest documentary film festival. Or there's a dedicated cello biennale, a curate-it-yourself festival and – don't laugh – a National Windmill Day.

Spring

5 Days Off

Various venues (www.5daysoff.nl).
Date early Mar.
Taking Amsterdam by storm every March, 5 Days Off is – yep, you guessed it – a five-day festival, which features a host of international artists and the latest talent in the fields of electronic music, art and media art. It started in 2001 as a shorter version of the 10 Days Off festival in Ghent, Belgium. Venues include the Paradiso (*see p197*), Melkweg (*see p192*) and De Balie (*see p211*). Check the website for ticket prices and more information.

★ Amsterdam Restaurant Week

Various venues (www.restaurantweek.nl).
Date Mar, Aug.
A three-course gourmet dinner in a top restaurant for only €27.50? Possibly only during Amsterdam Restaurant Week (in fact, it lasts two weeks). Just as in New York, where the idea originated, restaurant owners think this is a great way to promote their businesses. The food isn't fast, but your reservation really needs to be, especially for the high-end restaurants: bookings start as early as a month before.

Stille Omgang

The Old Centre (www.stille-omgang.nl).
Date mid Mar.
The candlelit night-time Silent Procession, a key event for Catholics, commemorates the 14th-century Miracle of Amsterdam. It follows a circular route from the Spui, north on Nieuwendijk and back on Warmoesstraat and Nes, between midnight on Saturday and 4am on Sunday. It's a sight that becomes particularly surreal as the procession snakes through the Red Light District.

National Museum Weekend

Around the Netherlands (www.museum weekend.nl). **Date** early-mid Apr.
Around a million visitors flock to the country's 500 or so state-funded museums, which offer free or discounted admission and special activities for this one weekend.

★ World Press Photo

Nieuwe Kerk, Dam, The Old Centre: Old Side (www.worldpressphoto.org). Tram 1, 2, 4, 5, 9, 16, 24. **Date** mid Apr.
Launched in 1955, this is the world's largest photography competition, with exhibits from thousands of photojournalists. The show is held in the Nieuwe Kerk (*see p56*); after kicking off in Amsterdam, it then tours to another 100 locations around the world.

★ Koningsdag (King's Day)

Throughout the city. **Date** 27 Apr.
The day-formerly-known-as-Queen's-Day, the most popular event in the city actually kicks off the night

Diary

PUBLIC HOLIDAYS

Nieuwjaarsdag (New Year's Day)
1 Jan

Goede Vrijdag (Good Friday)
3 Apr 2015, 25 Mar 2016

Eerste Paasdag (Easter Sunday)
5 Apr 2015, 27 Mar 2016

Tweede Paasdag (Easter Monday)
6 Apr 2015, 28 Mar 2016

King's Day
27 Apr

Bevrijdingsdag (Liberation Day)
5 May

Hemelvaartsdag (Ascension Day)
14 May 2015, 5 May 2016

Pinksteren (Whit/Pentecost Sunday)
24 May 2015, 15 May 2016

**Pinkstermaandag
(Whit/Pentecost Monday)**
25 May 2015, 16 May 2016

Eerste Kerstdag (Christmas)
25 Dec

Tweede Kerstdag (Boxing Day)
26 Dec

Christmas.

Top:
**National
Windmill Day.**
Bottom:
**Rollende
Keukens**.

before, with street parties and late-night drinking sessions in cafés. It's all quite insane. *See p39* **The Queen, Um, King of All Parties**.

Herdenkingsdag & Bevrijdingsdag (Remembrance Day & Liberation Day)
Remembrance Day *Various locations.* **Date** 4 May, 7.30pm. **Liberation Day** *Various locations.* **Date** 5 May.
In the presence of the King and many dignitaries, those who lost their lives during World War II are remembered at the Nationaal Monument on Dam Square (*see p56*). Gays and lesbians have their own ceremony with a remembrance service at the Homomonument (*see p180*), and there are also other events in various quarters of the city. The two-minute silence is usually respected in the city's bars and restaurants – so keep your cakehole shut.

Liberation Day (to mark the end of Nazi occupation in World War II) is celebrated the following day, with music and speeches. The best places for visitors are Museumplein, Leidseplein and Westermarkt (the focal point of the gay commemorations).

London Calling
Paradiso, Weteringschans 6-8, Southern Canal Belt (www.londoncalling.nl). Tram 1, 2, 5, 7, 10. **Date** May, Nov.
Taking place twice a year, this two-day indie music festival at the Paradiso (*see p197*) is a showcase for new bands, with special focus on the UK and USA. The festival started in 1992, and since then has welcomed the likes of Bloc Party, White Lies,

Florence and the Machine, the XX, Hudson Mohawke and Franz Ferdinand.

Kunstvlaai
Various venues (www.kunstvlaai.nl). **Date** May 2016.
This biennial art market is the very much hipper twin to KunstRAI (*see below*), focusing on new and more original artists, groups and galleries.

KunstRAI
RAI Convention Centre, Europaplein, Zuid (626 4020, www.kunstrai.nl). Tram 4 or RAI rail station. **Date** mid May-early June.
A hundred or so galleries, both national and international, present their artists' work at this huge commercial five-day exhibition. (For a few years, it was known as Art Amsterdam, in an attempt to piggyback on the much more successful and inspired Art Rotterdam that takes place in February.)

National Windmill Day
Around the Netherlands (623 8703, www.nationalemolendag.nl). **Date** mid May.
Got a windmill on your mind? On the second Saturday in May, about 600 state-subsidised windmills open their doors and spin their sails. Most have demonstrations and activities, and you can buy flour and bread made the traditional way.

★ Rollende Keukens
Westergasfabriek, Westerpark, West (www.rollendekeukens.nl). Tram 3, 10 or bus 18, 21, 22. **Date** late May-early June.
Street food festival 'Rolling Kitchens', with its massive serving of food trucks, is a much-loved event at Westergasfabriek (*see p213*). Bands and DJs expand the gastronomic weirdness.

Open Ateliers (Open Studios): Kunstroute de Westelijke Eilanden
Prinseneiland, Bickerseiland & Realeneiland, West (www.oawe.nl). Tram 3 or bus 18, 21, 22. **Date** late May-early June.
Most neighbourhoods with a significant number of artists' studios hold an annual open weekend, when artists open their doors to the general public. The Westelijke Eilanden event, covering the picturesque and peaceful islands around Prinseneiland, is the most popular.
▶ *The Jordaan also hosts an Open Ateliers in late spring; details on www.openateliersjordaan.nl.*

ArtZuid
Various venues (www.artzuid.com). **Date** late May-late Sept 2015.
An installation of modern sculptures that snakes through Amsterdam South every other year. In the past, ArtZuid has included work by such heavy hitters as Ai Weiwei, Richard Serra and Atelier Van Lieshout.

Summer

Amsterdam Tattoo Convention
*RAI Convention Centre, Europaplein, Zuid
(www.tattooexpo.eu). Tram 4 or RAI rail.*
Date early June.
All the big names from the global tattoo scene swoop
down to Amsterdam for a weekend to ink up all the
needy bikers and housewives.

★ Vondelpark Openluchttheater
*Vondelpark, Zuid (www.openluchttheater.nl). Tram
1, 2, 3, 5, 12.* **Date** early June-mid Aug.
The big open-air stage in this popular park is used
to the max with a free programme that ranges from
classical music to stand-up to pop. There are dance
nights, and kids' afternoons too. Few places capture
the laid-back vibe of Amsterdam in the summer with
quite such conviction.

Holland Festival
*Various venues (523 7787, www.holland
festival.nl).* **Date** June.
This hugely popular month-long event (established
in 1947) is the Netherlands' leading performing-arts
festival. It takes a refreshing approach to dance, literature, visual arts, theatre and film, but there's no
doubting that music is its central theme, particularly
in the realms of contemporary classical, experimental and electronic music. It attracts international
stars and composers each year, and you're guaranteed a series of groundbreaking premieres and
reworkings that'll move on to make waves in other
cultural capitals around the world. Tickets go on sale
months beforehand; check the website for the programme and to book.

Oerol
Terschelling (www.oerol.nl). **Date** mid June.
Amsterdammers leave in droves for this ten-day theatre festival on the Frisian island of Terschelling,
120km (75 miles) north of the city. Rent a bike and
enjoy the dunes and the 200 shows – some of which
are in the dunes. *See p220* **Wadden Islands**.

Canal Gardens in Bloom
Various locations (www.opentuinendagen.nl).
Date late June.
On the third weekend in June, the owners of the
beautiful, hidden gardens behind the city's posh
canal houses open their doors, giving the public a
chance to have a peek at these stunning secret gems.
Sadly, dogs and prams are not allowed, and wheelchair access is almost impossible.

Amsterdam Roots Festival
Various venues (www.amsterdamroots.nl).
Date early July.
World music acts from around the globe flock to
Amsterdam for this four-day shindig. It culminates
in a free open-air extravaganza in Oosterpark, which

Top:
**Canal
Gardens in
Bloom**.
Bottom:
**Amsterdam
Gay Pride**.

IN THE KNOW FILM FESTIVALS

Whether you want to submerge yourself
fully in the film experience or simply dip
your toe in the celluloid pool, Amsterdam's
numerous film festivals have much to
offer. *See p178* **Festival Fever**.

THE QUEEN, UM, KING OF ALL PARTIES

Just how much orange do you think you can take?

starts at noon and goes on until late. Cubia All Stars from Peru were the highlight of the 2013 line-up.

Over het IJ
NDSM, Noord (www.overhetij.nl). Ferry from CS to NDSM. **Date** early-mid July
This is a ten-day international festival of large-scale, avant-garde theatrical projects, which takes over the former NDSM shipyard (*see p158* **Northern Lights**).

Julidans
Various venues (www.julidans.nl). **Date** July.
This international contemporary dance festival provides a taster of what's going on – and what's to come – in the field of dance theatre. It features internationally renowned dance artists as well as newcomers that now rank among the greatest in their fields, such as Akram Khan, Dave St-Pierre and Sidi Larbi Cherkaoui.

★ Kwaku
Bijlmerpark, Zuidoost (www.kwakufestival.nl). Bijlmer ArenA rail. **Date** mid July-mid Aug.
'Kwaku' is the word that symbolises the emancipation of the people of Suriname, and also the name of this family-oriented festival, which takes place every weekend throughout the summer in the multicultural 'hood around ArenA stadium. Come for excellent ass-shaking music, plus theatre, film, literature, sport and Caribbean food.

★ Amsterdam Gay Pride
Prinsengracht, Canal Belt (www.amsterdam gaypride.nl). Tram 10. **Date** early Aug.
Although Gay Pride is always surrounded by drama and controversy, whether around money, politics or big egos, the atmosphere during the spectacular boat parade on the first Saturday in August is simply

If first-time visitors to Amsterdam arrived on a certain day at the end of April, they would often get confused and exclaim, 'I heard Amsterdam was a happening town, but this is crazy!' And it's lucky for everyone that this chaotic day only occurs once a year. Party-lovers, rubbish collectors and students of the surreal should, however, make sure that their visit coincides with this date, when up to a million extra people pour into the city.

Queen's Day (Koninginnedag), which was always held on 30 April, was rebranded as **King's Day** (**Koningsdag**) when Willem-Alexander took over the throne from his mother Beatrix in 2013. And the official date was moved to 27 April, to coincide with his birthday.

Confused? It doesn't matter. The royal family is soon forgotten amid all the revelry. You're as likely to happen upon a leather-boy disco party on one side street, or an old-school crooner on the other, as you are to witness a boat bellowing out heavy metal, only to have its amps short-circuited at the next bridge by a gang of boys – dressed head-to-toe in orange – urinating on them. To add to the chaos, everyone is permitted to sell their household junk out on the street. If you have offspring in tow, head to Vondelpark (*see p128*), which is dedicated to children. Meanwhile, Dam Square becomes a fairground, while the gay and lesbian festivities spread out like ripples from the Homomonument (*see p180*) and Reguliersdwaarsstraat.

What with all the performances, the markets, the crowds and, of course, the readily flowing alcohol, the streets of Amsterdam offer all anyone could dream of – at least for a day.

MAGNETIC FIELD

Curate your own festival!

Encompassing music, theatre, experimental arts and all means of creative expression, **Magneet Festival** (www.magneetfestival.nl) brings a little bit of Burning Man to a man-made stretch of sand on Zeeburgereiland in Amsterdam Oost.

The man behind the concept, Jesse Limmen, started a decade or so ago in the hippy village of Ruigoord with €200 worth of beer, a ramshackle bar and a microphone. Later, the alternative Lowlands festival invited him to create a do-it-yourself bar. People would enter their names at a check-in desk, describe their act – whether it be comedy, hip hop, spoken word or whatever – then grab a beer and a silly costume while waiting for their turn to climb on stage. As long as the crowd liked it, they could continue; if not, an MC would intervene. The approach proved insanely popular. Highlights included Dutch rocker Anouk casually coming in for a seven-song set and the Eagles of Death Metal destroying the drum kit.

Since then, the idea has evolved into a festival covering four consecutive weekends in late August/early September, involving experimental constructions, tents and podiums that ring with music, theatre, children's activities and more. While the offerings are diverse, the philosophy remains the same: 'No spectators, only participators'. In a truly collaborative effort, people can pitch their ideas via the festival website.

A more idyllic and relaxed version of the festival continues all year round at café-restaurant **Magnetico** (IJdijk 8, 06 4364 0522 mobile, www.magnetico-s114.nl). In an expanse of sand near highway S114 and the bridge going over to IJburg, a corrugated shed surrounded by lots of picnic tables and general arty weirdness is now Jesse's full-time home base.

Top:
Sail Amsterdam.
Middle:
Grachtenfestival.
Bottom:
Appelsap.

water music has expanded to offer almost 100 classical music concerts, each set somewhere near or on the water.

Sail Amsterdam
Waterfront (www.sail.nl). **Date** 19-23 Aug 2015.
Every five years, dozens of tall ships and hundreds of modern boats sail into Amsterdam, and huge crowds gather along the harbour to admire them.

Netherlands Theater Festival
Various venues (624 2311, www.tf.nl).
Date end Aug-early Sept.
This ten-day festival showcases an edited selection of the best Dutch and Belgian theatre of the previous year. As at the Edinburgh Festival, the accompanying Amsterdam Fringe event is uncurated, and brings a heady mix of more experimental productions. *See also p205*.

Uitmarkt
Various locations (www.uitmarkt.nl).
Date end Aug.
Ove the last weekend in August, the chaotic Uitmarkt whets appetites for the coming cultural season with previews of theatre, opera, dance and music events. Everything is free, and as a result it all gets very crowded.

Magneet Festival
Oostpunt, IJdijk 10, Oost (www.magneetfestival.nl).
Tram 26 or bus 37. **Date** late Aug-mid Sept.
See p40 **Magnetic Field**.

fabulous. Around 350,000 spectators line the Prinsengracht to watch the boats, each with garish decorations, loud sound system and a crew of bare-chested sailors. *See p187* **A Straight Guide to Gay Pride**.

★ De Parade
Martin Luther Kingpark, Zuid (033 465 4555, www.deparade.nl). *Tram 12*. **Date** Aug.
When this touring show lands in Amsterdam (Rotterdam, The Hague and Utrecht are also on the route), locals flock to eat, drink and be merry. And to catch an act – cabaret, music, comedy, drama – outside or in one of the many kitschly decorated tents that give the vibe of an old-fashioned carnival. Afternoons are child-friendly.

Appelsap
Oosterpark, Oost (www.appelsap.net). *Tram 3, 9, 14*. **Date** mid Aug.
The atmosphere at this outdoor hip hop festival is always hot. Attracting around 5,000 visitors, the programme takes hip hop back to its roots and includes up-and-coming artists as well as some local favourites. The location may change in 2015.

Grachtenfestival
Various venues (421 4542, www.grachtenfestival.nl).
Date mid Aug.
What started out in 1997 as a single free concert from an orchestra floating on a pontoon in front of the Hotel Pulitzer has grown into the 'Canal Festival'. Handel would be delighted to hear that this modern

Autumn

Open Monument Days
Various venues (552 4888, www.open monumentendag.nl). **Date** mid Sept.
On the second weekend in September, you get the chance to visit buildings that are normally closed to the public. Some are breathtaking historic buildings from the Golden Age; others are schools, farms or ex-industrial buildings. Look out for the Open Monumentendag flag, check the website or pick up a booklet. It's all part of European Heritage Days, involving around 4,000 sites across the Netherlands.
▶ *Architecture fans, take note: the must-see Museum Het Schip also runs boat tours exploring the architecture around the waterfront; see p251.*

Unseen
Westergasfabriek, Westerpark, West (www.unseen amsterdam.com). *Tram 3, 10 or bus 18, 21, 22*.
Date late Sept.
This new four-day 'photo fair with a festival flair', based in the Westergasfabriek (*see p213*), not only includes exhibitions but also books, talks, city-wide projects and a lot of parties.

Dam tot Damloop

Across Amsterdam (www.damloop.nl).
Date late Sept.
Taking place on the third Sunday in September, the Dam to Dam Run stretches 16.1km (ten miles) from Amsterdam to the town of Zaandam. Up to 200,000 people gather to watch the 30,000 participants trying to finish within the two-hour limit. Bands line the route and a circus in Zaandam keeps the little ones amused. There's also a 6.5km (four-mile) course.

Affordable Art Fair

Kromhouthal, Gedempt Hamerkanaal 231, Noord (622 7728, www.affordableartfair.com). Bus 32, 33, 38 or ferry from Centraal Station to IJplein.
Date Oct.
For one weekend in October, it's all about affordable art. Launched in Amsterdam in 2006, this art phenomenon presents work from local and international galleries. The wide range of art on sale – from figurative to abstract, traditional to avant-garde – ranges in price from around €100 to €5,000.
▶ *Follow our Jordaan gallery route – see p124 Art Throb.*

Amsterdam Dance Event

Various venues (www.amsterdam-dance-event.nl).
Date mid Oct.
The organisers claim this five-day event is the world's biggest festival of clubbing, involving some 2,000 artists. It combines business with pleasure: during the day, there are conferences and workshops, while at night, roughly 400 international acts and DJs make sure your feet keep moving.

Amsterdamse Cello Biennale

Muziekgebouw, Piet Heinkade 1, Waterfront (519 1808, www.cellobiennale.nl). Tram 25, 26.
Date mid Oct 2014, 2016.
Muziekgebouw plays host to this nine-day festival of daytime and evening concerts, masterclasses and presentations. Spanning generations and genres, it shows off the cello as an artistic, a virtuosic and a versatile element in its own right. Musicians and ensembles come from around the world.

PINT Bokbierfestival

Beurs van Berlage, Damrak 243, The Old Centre: Old Side (www.pint.nl). Tram 4, 9, 14, 16, 24.
Date end Oct.

The Beurs van Berlage plays host to this three-day beer festival, the largest in the Netherlands. Enjoy tastings of the 50 or so different varieties of the full-bodied, slightly sweet and usually dark German bock beer. Boozehounds should check the website of PINT (a similar organisation to the UK's CAMRA) for details of other beer festivals.

Amsterdam Spook Halloween Festival

Various venues (www.halloweenamsterdam.com).
Date end Oct.
During the last decade, Amsterdam has embraced Halloween as a new celebration. While there are many imitators, Amsterdam Spook has spent years bringing buckets of blood to the masses. An over-the-top party in a scary location is the main attraction, but the festival also includes make-up workshops, boat cruises and plenty of other ghoul-infested activities.

★ N8 (Museum Night)

Various venues (527 0785, www.n8.nl).
Date Nov.
The success of Museum Night shows that Amsterdammers like to mix art with entertainment. Almost every museum and gallery in town opens late and organises something special to complement the regular exhibits. You might see a take on Rembrandt's *The Night Watch* made out of Chupa Chups lollies, or dance the night away in the Anne Frank Huis. Tickets sell fast.

Amsterdam Light Festival

Various venues (www.amsterdamlightfestival.com).
Date mid Nov-mid Jan.
Some 30 light sculptures and projections by the world's best light artists will brighten up town in this new annual festival. Follow the special route from Amstel to the Maritime Museum to see Amsterdam in a whole new shiny way.

Clockwise from left: **Amsterdam Light Festival**; **Amsterdam Dance Event**; **Dam tot Damloop**.

are the wickedest, dude. The event is scattered all over town (as, frankly, are the minds of the participants), but it's invariably focused on the Melkweg (*see p192*) at night.

Winter

Oudejaarsavond (New Year's Eve)
Various venues. **Date** 31 Dec.
No, you haven't got off the wrong train or plane, and you're not in a war zone: New Year's Eve – and seeing out the *oud* and welcoming in the new – is a riot of champagne, *oliebollen* (greasy deep-fried blobs of dough, apple and raisins), and tons and tons of scary fireworks that officially only go on sale the day before. Come midnight, people take to the streets (and bars, many of which only open at midnight) to celebrate. The best areas to head for are Nieuwmarkt and Dam Square; the latter often stages a big council-sponsored concert, with Dutch acts and DJs to help keep things moving. Not for the faint-hearted.

FashionWeek Amsterdam
Various venues (www.fashionweek.nl).
Date mid Jan.
Even with such home-grown talent as Viktor&Rolf, Amsterdam has never been a cutting-edge fashion centre. But FashionWeek is out to change this with catwalk shows taking place in unique locations, plus exhibitions and readings.

Chinese New Year
Nieuwmarkt, Old Centre: Old Side (www.zeedijk.nl). Tram 4, 9, 16, 24 or Metro Nieuwmarkt. **Date** late Jan/early Feb.
The Nieuwmarkt is a focal point for Amsterdam's Chinatown, and Chinese New Year is welcomed during the daytime with lion dances, firecrackers and Chinese drums and gongs.

Sinterklaas
By boat: Amstel, Nieuwe Herengracht. Then city route: Prins Hendrikkade, Damrak, Dam, Raadhuisstraat, Rozengracht, Marnixstraat, Leidseplein. **Date** mid Nov-5 Dec.
Sinterklaas (St Nicholas) marks the start of three weeks of Christmassy festivities by sailing into town on his steamboat in mid November. With a white beard, red robe and mitre, he parades around the centre of town on his horse, while his staff – dozens of blacked-up *Zwarte Pieten* (Black Peters) – hand out sweets. The celebrations continue, with little gifts being left in children's shoes at night, until Pakjesavond on 5 December, when families celebrate by exchanging presents and poems.

High Times Cannabis Cup
Various venues (www.cannabiscup.com).
Date end Nov.
All things wastedness are celebrated over five days of banquets, bands, cultivation seminars and a competition where hundreds of judges (including you, if you wish) ascertain which of the hundreds of weeds

Amsterdam's Best

Check off all the city essentials with our list of handpicked highlights.

OBA.

Sightseeing

VIEWS

Westerkerk p93
Climb the tower for a higgledy-piggledy view of the Jordaan.

OBA p171
Gaze out across the Old Centre and beyond from the new central library.

NEMO p154
Climb the sloped roof of the science museum to take in the watery vistas.

DoubleTree by Hilton p289
The poshest choice: this hotel's rooftop affords views of both the Old Centre and Noord.

ART

Rijksmuseum p130
Rembrandt, Vermeer, Frans Hals. Get lost for days...

Van Gogh Museum p133
The largest cache of expressionism's wonderboy.

Stedelijk Museum p130
World-class modern art in an eye-catching building.

Jordaan p112
Take an arty wander in this gallery-rich neighbourhood.

NDSM p158
Creative hotspot – worth it for the graffiti alone.

Mediamatic p154
Can urban farming be art?

HISTORY

Amsterdam Museum p76
City museum of history – both past and living.

Anne Frank Huis p92
Never again.

Stadsarchief p105
City archives has a small, dazzling collection in a large, dazzling building.

Vondelpark.

Oudekerk p64
The city's oldest church surrounded by the world's oldest trade.

OUTDOORS
Vondelpark p129
The city's green lung and people's park.
Amsterdamse Bos p139
After nearly a century of growth, an artificial forest can become convincing.
Begijnhof p75
Peaceful inner courtyard remains tucked away for your hidden pleasure.
Urban beaches
Roest (p156), Hannekes Boom (p156) and Blijburg (p157) offer some great urban outdoors.

CHEERFUL DUTCH CLICHES
Bloemenmarkt p110
Flower market has it blooming all.
Brouwerij 't IJ p151
Why not have a beer in the shadow of a windmill?
Erotic Museum p63
If you really can't leave it at a quick gawp of the Red Light District.

CHILDREN
TunFun p173
Head underground for this huge play park. Parents can nurse a beer.
Canal cruise p88
No guarantees, but the waters have the power to hypnotise…
Madurodam p174
You'll have to head to the Hague for the world's largest miniature village.

WILDLIFE
ARTIS Zoo p147
The city zoo is even wilder than the Red Light District.

Hortus Botanicus p148
It's all about plants, but one greenhouse is filled with butterflies.

Eating & drinking

BLOWOUTS
La Rive p106
The city's poshest of posh eateries is still going strong.
Bridges p67
Young chef making big statements at the grand Grand Hotel.
&samhoud places p156
Molecular, witty and expensive.
5&33 p80
Breakfast, lunch, dinner or drinking at this new hotspot in the Art'otel.

GLOBAL
Nam Kee p68
Chinatown classic serving iconic oysters with black bean sauce.
Yokiyo p68
Disciples of David Chang bring Korean to the Red Light masses.
Blauw p104
Indonesian rice tables worth going out of your way for.
Société Wunderbar p80
From Asia to America with all stops in between.

LOCAL
Comestibles Kinders p117
Are these the finest sandwiches in town, or is it Small World (p119), Hartenkaas (p94), 't Kuyltje (p94) or good ol' Van Dobben (p107)?
De Vegetarische Slager p125
This vegetarian butcher/deli knows how to make converts with its meaty secrets.

Hap Hmm p133
Home cooking at
bargain prices.
Rijssel p151
Locally sourced food,
cooked wildly.
Vleminckx p81
OK, they sell Belgian
chips, but it's close enough.

BARS & CAFES

Belgique p80
It's tiny but the selection
of Belgian beers is large.
Hiding in Plain Sight p146
Embrace liquid danger with
a Walking Dead cocktail in
cosy surrounds.
Café de Doktor p80
It doesn't come much
more old school than this.
Café Welling p134
Brown café with a classical
touch thanks to neighbour
Concertgebouw.
Kingfisher p166
Friendly neighbourhood
bar in De Pijp.
Wynand Fockink p70
Taste the old school of the
original gin, *jenever*.
't Arendsnest p94
Dutch beers of distinction
with snacks to match.
Barco (p156)
All aboard the boat.
Getto p187
Straight-friendly gay/lesbian
bar serves up the finest
cocktails and burgers.
Gollem's Proeflokaal p135
A gathering place for
the beers and people
of the world.
Mata Hari p69
Stylish Red Light drinking
and eating.
TonTon Club p70
Updated arcade with
local beer.
Papeneiland p121
Bill Clinton sent them
a thank-you note for the
apple pie.

OUTDOOR DRINKING

't Blauwe Theehuis p134
In the heart of Vondelpark,
flying saucer-shaped venue
with expansive patio.
Brouwerij 't IJ p151
You might have to adjust
your seating to get out of
the shade of a windmill.
**Distillerij 't Nieuwe
Diep** p149
This old mill in a park in
deepest Oost serves
homebrewed elixirs.
't Smalle p121
So gorgeously charming,
the Japanese recreated it
for a theme park.

Shopping

GIFTS & SOUVENIRS

Otherist p99
Quirky gifts made for
quirky minds.
**Antiek Centrum
Amsterdam** p125
Antiques, treasures and
weirdness – all for sale.

BOOKS & MUSIC

**Athenaeum
Nieuwscentrum** p82
Mags and papers from
around the world, with
books on all things
Amsterdam.
Friday Book Market p76
The already bookish Spui
square has a weekly
antiquarian book bonanza.
Concerto p110
One of the last CD shops
standing – and with
good reason.

FASHION

SPRMRKT p125
Keeping it glam, keeping
it local.
2 p135
Something for all the
fancy boys.

Otherist.

Margriet Nannings p99
Local designer with a bevy
of boutiques.

DESIGN MINDED

Hay p82
Retro Scandinavian design
for modern times.
Hotel Droog p72
Design for home, garden
and beyond.
Frozen Fountain p98
Witty and ageless
Dutch design.
Moooi p122
Marcel Wanders and friends
ask for the big bucks.

MARKETS

Albert Cuypmarkt p167
The nation's longest
street market.
Noordermarkt p122
A Monday morning flea
market not to be missed.

Albert Cuypmarkt.

Boerenmarkt p121
Organic farmer's market
with a lot of taste, held
in the Noordermarkt.

Nightlife

CLUBS
Trouw Amsterdam p194
Catch it while you can:
the city's most happening
club, with a 24-hour
party licence.
Canvas p194
Reopened in 2014 and
the party view is better
than ever.
De Nieuwe Anita p179
Keeping clubbing close
and cosy in this buzzing
hive of hipster activity.
Club Church p185
A gay cruising club with
a difference.

MUSIC
Paradiso p192
'Pop temple' for bands
and club nights.
Melkweg p192
Bands and club nights in
former milk factory.
Concertgebouw p203
Grand setting and
glorious acoustics.
Tolhuistuinen p198
New cultural hotspot
in Noord.
Bimhuis p201
Jazz venue between
water and rail.
Westergasfabriek p213
Former gasworks has a
location for everything:
jazz, urban, rock'n'roll
and dance music

Arts

FESTIVALS
Gay Pride p39
Countless events
overshadowed by one
big event: the Canal
Pride parade.
King's Day p35
It's no longer called
Queen's Day, but it's
still a right royal party.

Parade p41
A festival with lots of theatre
and the atmosphere of an
old-fashioned carnival.

THEATRE
Stadsschouwburg p207
Home to the brilliant
Toneelgroep Amsterdam.
Boom Chicago
American improv comedians
grounded deep in the 'Dam.
Over 't IJ Festival p205
Absurdist theatre has a home.
**Amsterdam Fringe
Festival** p205
Welcome to the deep,
deep underground.

FILM
EYE p159
Stunning film institute at the
heart of new Noord.
Pathé Tuschinski p176
The most over-the-top
cinema on earth?
Movies p175
Old world atmosphere for
films old and new.

OPERA & BALLET
**Nationale Opera
& Ballet** p204
Ground zero for homegrown
singers and leapers.

Explore

Tour Amsterdam

Tourists who know Amsterdam primarily through its reputation as the capital of sex, drugs and rock 'n' roll are often stunned by the physical beauty of the city, which is apparent even in its seedier districts. Your main intention may be simply to get hammered for the weekend, but it's worth escaping the well-trodden tourist centre to have a nose about. You can wander around aimlessly and enjoy all kinds of scenic experiences in this compact city, but the U-shaped canals and winding byways can make it tricky for novices to find their way without getting lost. To orient yourself and make sure you don't miss the city's highlights, we recommend a tour. There are plenty on offer, employing various modes of transport – by bicycle, by bus, on foot and, naturally in a city filled with water, by boat.

BY BICYCLE

Joy Ride Tours
Departs from behind the Rijksmuseum, Museumstraat 1, Museum Quarter (06 4361 1798 mobile, www.joyridetours.nl). Tram 2, 5, 7, 10, 12. **Tours** *Apr-Nov* 4pm Mon, Thur-Sun. **Tickets** €24-€27. **Map** p314 K13.
Hop into the saddle of a *fiets* (bike) and cruise around the major sights and lesser-known landmarks of Amsterdam for two or three hours, with resident experts guiding you all the way.

MacBike
620 0985, www.macbike.nl.
This outfit offers a wide array of guided tours, lasting between two and four hours: windmills, Jewish

Amsterdam, Waterland and the general city tour, which starts at noon daily from Centraal Station (€18.50 with bike rental, no reservations needed). You can also opt for MacBike's printed routes (€1-€2 each), including an 'Art on the Edge' guide that takes you past many of the city's outdoor sculptures and art monuments.

Yellow Bike
Nieuwezijds Kolk 29, Old Centre: New Side (620 6940, www.yellowbike.nl). Tram 1, 2, 5, 13, 17. **Open** *Mar-Oct* 9am-5.30pm daily. *Nov-Feb* 9.30am-5pm daily. **Tickets** from €21. **No credit cards. Map** p312 J8.
Yellow Bike offers two- and three-hour city tours, and a four-hour Waterland tour including a visit to a pancake house.

BY BOAT

Unless specified, all the boat companies listed here offer a wide range of cruises, each varying in price, length and departure time – check individual websites for more details. Alternatively, you can visit the different jetties in front of Centraal Station and up Damrak and simply chance upon a cruise that's about to depart.

IN THE KNOW
LANGUAGE MATTERS

All the tours listed here are available in English. However, not every company offers them all the time, or they may have to be requested specially, so it's best to check in advance.

Amsterdam Canal Cruises

626 5636, www.amsterdamcanalcruises.nl.
Canal, lunch, dinner and candlelight cruises, and charter boats for all occasions. The city canal cruises depart every half hour from opposite the Heineken Brewery, while charter boats will pick you up from an agreed location.

Blue Boat Company

679 1370, www.blueboat.nl.
Take the city cruise from Stadhouderskade 30 (opposite the Hard Rock Café) or rent a boat by the hour, with the possibility of booking lunch or dinner, drink arrangements and entertainment.

Boat Trip to Museum Het Schip

418 2885, www.hetschip.nl. **Tickets** €42.50.
No credit cards.
Organised by Museum Het Schip, these tours focus on the architecture around Java and KNSM islands, former wharfs, and renovated warehouses and silos. The boat tour ends at Spaarndammerbuurt's Houthaven (timber docks), but a guided walk follows along the 'Workers' Palaces' that are found on Spaarndammerplantsoen, and concludes with a visit to the Museum Het Schip.
▶ *For more about Museum Het Schip, the Amsterdam School's architectural gem, see p114.*

Canal Bus

Departs from Artis, Centraal Station, Keizersgracht, Leidseplein, Rijksmuseum, Scheepvaartmuseum, Tropenmuseum, Westerkerk, NEMO, Rembrandthuis (623 9886, www.canal.nl/canal-bus). **Tickets** €20/24hrs; €33/48hrs; half-price for 4-12s.
These fun hop-on, hop-off canal boats take three different routes through the city: green, red and orange. You can also get combination tickets that

Blue Boat Company.

include admission to the Rijksmuseum, Van Gogh Museum and Heineken Experience, thereby avoiding the queues at these popular destinations. Book online for a 10% discount.

Canal Rondvaart/Holland International

www.canal.nl/rondvaarten-amsterdam.
Holland International has a variety of boats for rent (including canal boats), with or without catering. Cruise options include the '100 Highlights Cruise', focusing on the city's Golden Age heritage, and other more obviously named ones, such as 'Candlelight and Dinner' and 'Cocktail'.

EXPLORE

Canal Bus.

Gondola Tours

686 9868, 06 4746 4545 mobile, www.
gondel.nl. **Open** May-Nov. **Rates** €140/hr.
No credit cards.
Amsterdam is often referred to as the Venice of the
North, so what better way to explore its waterways
than by gondola? Tirza Mol rents out her (own-built)
gondola seasonally to groups of up to six people. Mol
or her partner, Hans Lentz, the city's only two gon-
doliers, can take you anywhere: you choose where
and when you board, and they do the rest.

Lovers Company

530 5412, www.lovers.nl.
Not just for lovers (the owner's surname is Lover),
this company offers a wide variety of cruises, from
museum tours, dinner cruises and winter candlelight
cruises to boat-plus-bike trips out of town.

Water Taxi/VIP Water Taxi

Lovers Company jetty, Prins Hendrikkade 25,
Old Centre: New Side (535 6363, www.water-
taxi.nl). Tram 1, 2, 4, 5, 9, 13, 16, 17, 24, 26.
Open varies. **Rates** Central Amsterdam €7.50
pick-up, plus €1.75/min.
Hailed spontaneously or prearranged by phone,
Water Taxi's floating yellow cabs can carry up to
eight people. It's worth storing the number for next
time you and your buddies are caught up Jacob's
Creek without a paddle. The VIP version offers
bigger boats and various organised cruises.

Wetlands Safari

Departs from IJ-side bus terminal, Centraal Station
(686 3445, 06 5355 2669 mobile, www.wetlands
safari.nl). Tram 1, 2, 4, 5, 9, 13, 14, 16, 17, 24.
Tours *May-mid Sept* 9.30am Mon-Fri; 10am Sun.
Tickets €48; €29 7-16s. **Map** p312 J6.
These guided canoe trips (5.5hrs) take you through
17th-century waterside villages and the reedlands
north of Amsterdam. They include short walks in
the moorland meadows where possible and a picnic
using local produce. Custom-made tours with bikes
and canoes are available too.

Row Your Own

Canal Bike

623 9886, www.canal.nl/canal-bike. **Open**
Summer 10am-8pm daily. *Winter* 10am-5pm
daily. **Rates** from €8 per person/hr.

Wetlands Safari.

EXPLORE

The humble pedalo has been repackaged (complete with a snazzy little rain shield) and rebranded for a whole new generation. Choose to pedal aimlessly around the canals or opt instead for one of the self-guided tours, such as Rembrandt's Amsterdam, the Jordaan or the Mystery Tour. There are three rental piers to choose from: the Rijksmuseum, Leidseplein and Westerkerk.

Canal Motorboats
Zandhoek 10a, Westelijke Eilanden, Waterfront (422 7007, www.canalmotorboats.com). Tram 3 or bus 18, 21, 22. **Open** 10am-sunset daily. **Rates** €50 1st hr, then sliding scale. **Map** p311 F5.
This electric motorboat is an environmentalist's (ahem) wet dream: low on both emissions and noise pollution. Made of aluminium, with a maximum capacity of six and a top speed of 7km/h, it's also the biggest and fastest vessel you're allowed to charter without a licence.

ON FOOT

Amsterdamsel Tours
06 2516 1727 mobile, www.amsterdamsel. org. **Tours** by appt. **Tickets** from €20. **No credit cards.**
Take a stroll through town to the rhythm of Mozart, Chet Baker and, yup, Eddie van Halen and find out what traces they left behind in tours such as 'Sex, Drugs and Rock 'n' Roll.' You'll also learn about famous local artists and government-funded rock 'n' roll. Other tours cover culinary Amsterdam and the city's Jewish heritage.

Dutch Delicacy Tour
Departs from entrance of Victoria Hotel, Damrak 1-5, Old Centre: New Side (06 4169 1779 mobile, www.dutchdelicacytour.com). Tram 1, 2, 4, 5, 9, 13, 16, 17, 24, 25, 26. **Tours** by appt Tue-Sat afternoons. **Tickets** €59.50. **No credit cards.** **Map** p312 J7.
A mouth-watering walking tour highlighting the centuries-old trade in food, coffee and spices that once brought wealth to Amsterdam. Lasting almost five hours, the tour includes tasting sessions at various spots along the way. There's a maximum of 15 people per group.

History Walks: Amsterdam in World War II
337 9733, 06 4098 3208 mobile, www.history walks.eu. **Tickets** €25. **No credit cards.**
Guided by university history students specialising in the period, this informative, two- to three-hour walking tour teaches you about the Amsterdam of 1940-45, from the beginning of German occupation all the way through to liberation. Note that visits to such topic-relevant locations as the Hollandsche Schouwburg (*see p147*), Verzetsmuseum (Museum

of the Dutch Resistance; *see p148*) or Anne Frank Huis (*see p92*) are not part of the tour. They also organise World War II-related excursions further afield; for example, to Arnhem.

Mee in Mokum
Departs from Museumcafé Mokum, Amsterdam Museum, Kalverstraat 92, Old Centre: New Side (625 1390, www.gildeamsterdam.nl/ stadswandelingen/general-info). Tram 1, 2, 4, 5, 9, 14, 16, 24. **Tours** 11am, 2pm Tue-Sun. **Tickets** €7.50; €5 reductions. **No credit cards.** **Map** p312 J10.
Amsterdammers from all walks of life show you around their city, leading you to their favourite spots and relating stories along the way. Tour options include the Old Centre, the Jordaan, Amsterdam's seaports or further afield.

Urban Home & Garden Tours
Usually departs from Museum Willet-Holthuysen, Herengracht 605, Southern Canal Belt (06 2168 1918 mobile, www.uhgt.nl). Tram 4, 9, 14, 16, 24 or Metro Waterlooplein. **Tours** mid Apr-mid Oct 10.30am Fri; 11.30am Sat; 12.30pm Sun. **Tickets** €34. **No credit cards.** **Map** p315 L10.
Professional garden designers and art historians lead these delightful three-hour tours of various 17th-, 18th- and 19th-century canal houses. Advance booking is essential.

IN THE KNOW
APP AMSTERDAM

Organisations such as **Waag Society** (www.waag.org) and **Appsterdam** (www.appsterdam.rs) are helping to ensure that Amsterdam develops as a global hub for app developers, and as the home town of augmented-reality pioneers **Layar** (www.layar.com), the city has long had various apps that can augment the reality of your wandering experiences.

Most of the city's major museums have apps for touring their collections and also investigating the city; in particular, the **Joods Historisch Museum** (Jewish Historical Museum; *see p143*) has a great app for exploring the old Jewish quarter.

Another inspiring local initiative, **Soundtrackcity** (www.soundtrackcity.nl), collaborates with artists and writers to make (mostly Dutch) audio walks, which you can download from its website or via its app. 'Secrets of the Amsterdam Canals' is filled with obscure anecdotes about the canals, complete with watery sound effects and ambient music.

EXPLORE

The Old Centre

EXPLORE

Amsterdam's ground zero of vice, consumerism and entertainment is also – by contrast – its compelling historic core. Some key buildings in the city's Old Centre, among them the wooden-roofed Oude Kerk (Old Church), date back to the 14th century, while the castle-like De Waag (the old weighing house) is an impressive 17th-century construction with 15th-century origins.

Bounded by Centraal Station, Singel and Zwanenburgwal, the area is roughly bisected by Damrak, which turns into Rokin south of Dam Square. Within the Old Centre, the saucier area to the east is the Oude Zijde (Old Side), which includes the Red Light District. The gentler area to the west is the far-from-new Nieuwe Zijde (New Side). And between them lies Dam Square, the city's meeting point, and home of the monumental Koninklijk Paleis (Royal Palace).

Amsterdam Museum

Don't Miss

1 Oude Kerk Oldest church surrounded by the oldest trade (p64).

2 Nieuwmarkt People-watching terraces with medieval centrepiece (p77).

3 Spui and **Begijnhof** Peaceful courtyard and bookish pursuits (p75).

4 Amsterdam Museum One-way to Amsterdam's DNA (p76).

5 Wynand Fockink Sagging shelves of original gins (p70).

Nationaal Monument, Dam Square.

THE OLD SIDE

The Old Side is the edgiest part of Amsterdam and includes the city's most unusual asset, the Red Light District (*see right*), where the window girls practising the world's oldest profession are increasingly being surrounded by more high-end shops and cafés. However, the scent of marijuana still pours out of overcrowded coffeeshops in narrow byways, and it's not unusual to hear groups of drunken tourists singing at the top of their lungs at 4am. It's hard to imagine that this area used to be the most religious part of town. The Old Side is also home to a very small but nonetheless authentic Chinatown on the Zeedijk.

Around the Dam

Straight up from Centraal Station, just beyond the once watery but now paved and touristy strip named Damrak, lies **Dam Square**, the heart of the city since the first dam was built here back in 1270.

Once a hub of social and political activities and protests, today it's a convenient meeting point for throngs of tourists, the majority of whom convene under its mildly phallic centrepiece, the **Nationaal Monument**. The 22-metre (70-foot) white obelisk is dedicated to the Dutch servicemen who died in World War II. Designed by JJP Oud, with sculptures by John Raedecker, it features 12 urns: 11 are filled with earth collected from the (back then) 11 Dutch provinces, while the 12th contains soil taken from war cemeteries in long-time Dutch colony Indonesia.

The west side of Dam Square, on the New Side, is flanked by the **Koninklijk Paleis** (Royal Palace); next to it is the 600-year-old **Nieuwe Kerk** (New Church – so named as it was built a century after the Oude Kerk, or Old Church, in the Red Light District). In kitsch contrast, over on the south side is **Madame Tussaud's Scenerama** (*see p78*).

The Red Light District

The Red Light District, which is situated in a rough triangle formed by Centraal Station, Nieuwmarkt and the Dam, is at the very root of Amsterdam's international notoriety. While overheated imaginations might construct images of wild sexual abandon framed in red neon-lit windows, the reality depicted in the postcards on sale locally is a sort of small, cutesy version of Las Vegas. If truth be told, the cheesy joke shop has here been supplanted by the cheesy sex shop: instead of electric palm buzzers and comedy nose glasses, you get multi-orifice inflatables and huge dildos.

Most of the historical significance of the Red Light District – of which there is plenty, this being the oldest part of Amsterdam – has been veneered by another old and very greasy trade: marketing. Although sex is the hook upon which the whole area hangs its reputation, it's actually secondary to window-shopping. People do buy – it's estimated to be a €450m-per-year trade – but mostly they simply wander around, gawping at the live exhibits.

Most of the window girls are self-employed and, even though prostitution was defined as a legal and taxable profession only in 1988 and bordellos have been officially legitimate only since October 2000 (a tactic intended to make taxation easier), the women have had their own union since 1984.

The Oudezijds Achterburgwal is dominated by sleaze and stag parties. But it does offer some of the more 'tasteful' choices for the eroto-clubber. The **Casa Rosso** nightclub (Oudezijds Achterburgwal 106-108, 627 8954) is certainly worth a look, even though the famed and peculiar marble cock-and-rotary-ball water fountain at its entrance has been removed. A short walk away at no.37 is the **Bananenbar** (627 8954), where improbably dexterous female genitalia can be seen performing night after night – and, as the central part of their belief-buggering act, spitting out an average of 15kg (33lb) of fruit every evening.

A former owner of the Bananenbar once tried to stave off taxmen – and get round the fact that his drinking licence had lapsed – by picking Satan as a deity and registering the Bananenbar as a church. It was a scam that worked for years – until 1988, when the 'Church

RED LIGHT BLUES

Cleaning up the city's most notorious postcode.

Red Light District.

Are you a loud, obnoxious tourist prone to trawling through the Red Light District in a drunken pack? If so, your time is running out.

In 2008, a plan was launched to clean up the infamous district. When he presented Project 1012 (1012 is the area's postcode), then-deputy mayor Lodewijk Asscher cited his inspiration as the clean-up of New York City by mayor Rudy Giuliani (despite the vast difference in the size of the two cities). New legislation gave the city the power to withdraw property rights from those suspected of criminal activities and to buy their properties — which the city did, but at what turned out to be hugely inflated prices. Ultimately, the city wants to close 200 of the nearly 500 window brothels and 26 of the 76 coffeeshops. For PR value, some windows became temporary 'fashion booths' as part of the 2009 initiative Red Light Fashion, in which designers were offered former bordello rooms as affordable studios for a year.

More high-end restaurants such as **Anna** (Warmoesstraat 111, www.restaurant anna.nl) and bars such as **Mata Hari** (*see p69*) have already entered the picture. And there are also many smaller businesses being – perhaps grudgingly – accepted into the mix. These include art and design bookshop **San Serriffe** (Sint Annenstraat 30, www.san-serriffe.com) and the cookie,

cake and cupcake artistry of **Cake Amsterdam** (Sint Jansstraat 61, www.cake amsterdam.com, open by appointment only). **Red Light Radio** (Oudekerksplein 22, www.redlightradio.net) is one of the more inspired complexes to arise. As local DJs spin on air – everything from black metal to dubstep – in a former bordello window, music hounds come from afar to browse the two record shops or simply hang out.

Although most Amsterdammers support the idea of stamping out the criminal elements behind the sex and drug traffic, many say the plans will deter tourism. Others argue the area is already the closest thing to a happy safe-sex Disneyland. But the area is certainly changing – and drunken hordes may soon be a thing of the past.

Mata Hari.

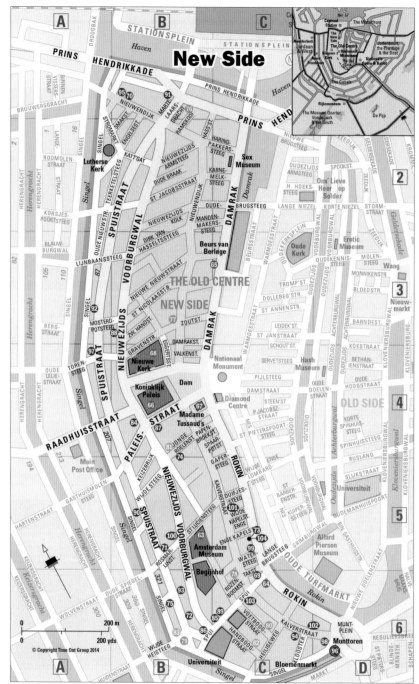

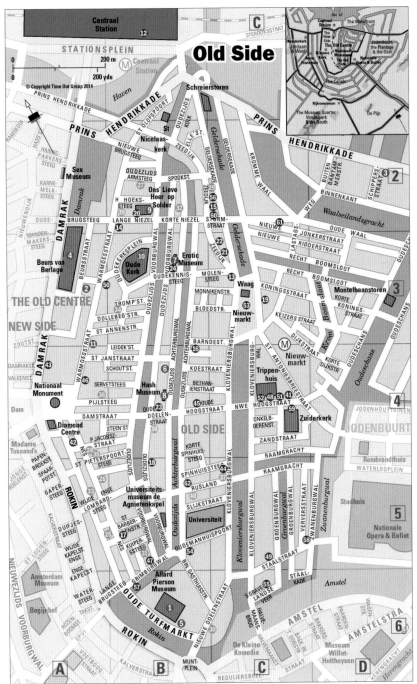

Old Side

Centraal Station

STATIONSPLEIN

© Copyright Time Out Group 2014

PRINS HENDRIKKADE

Schreierstoren

PRINS HENDRIKKADE

Haven

St Olofspoort

St Nicolaaskerk

Sex Museum

Oude Kerk

Beurs van Berlage

THE OLD CENTRE

NEW SIDE

DAMRAK

Ons' Lieve Heer op Solder

Erotic Museum

Waag

Nieuwmarkt

Montelbaanstoren

Hash Museum

OLD SIDE

Trippenhuis

Zuiderkerk

JODENHOUTTUINEN

JODENBUURT

Nationaal Monument

Dam

Madame Tussaud's

Diamond Centre

Universiteitsmuseum de Agnietenkapel

Universiteit

Rembrandthuis

WATERLOOPLEIN

Stadhuis

Nationale Opera & Ballet

Amsterdam Museum

Begijnhof

ROKIN

Allard Pierson Museum

OUDE TURFMARKT

ROKIN

Amstel

AMSTEL

Museum Willet-Holthuysen

De Kleine Komedie

MUNTPLEIN

EXPLORE

of Satan' claimed a membership of 40,000 overseen by a council of nine anonymous persons. The tax police were called in to bust the joint, but the bar was tipped off and the 'church' disbanded. Now under the same ownership as the Erotic Museum, the Bananenbar has kept its name and returned to its roots as a purveyor of sleaze.

If your urges are more academic, you can conduct some, ahem, research at the **Erotic Museum**, following it in semi-traditional fashion with a smoke at the **Hash Marihuana & Hemp Museum** (which doesn't actually sell dope, but you get the picture).

For more on the recent development of the area, *see p57* **Red Light Blues**. For more on the sex trade, *see pp267-271.*

Zeedijk

Before this dyke was built, some time around 1300, Amsterdam was a fishing village with barely enough bog to stand on. By the 15th and 16th centuries, with the East India Company raking in the imperialist spoils, Zeedijk was the street where sailors came to catch up on their boozing, brawling and bonking – or 'doing the St Nicolaas', as it was fondly termed in those days (a tribute to their patron saint, an extremely busy chap who watches over children, thieves, prostitutes and the city of Amsterdam).

Zeedijk.

Sailors who had lost all their money could trade in their pet monkey for a flea-infested bed at Zeedijk 1, which still retains its original name – **In't Aepjen**, meaning 'In the Monkeys' – and is today one of the oldest and most charming wooden houses in the city centre and still in business as a bar. Just off the street, down Oudezijds Kolk, is the **Schreierstoren**, aka the 'Weeping Tower'. Built in 1487, and successfully restored in 1966, it's the most interesting relic of Amsterdam's medieval city wall. It is said that wives would cry there (perhaps with relief) when their husbands set off on a voyage, then cry again if the ship returned with news that said spouse was lost at sea. If the latter happened, it was but a short walk to Zeedijk, where the bereaved lady would often continue life as a 'merry widow'. Prostitution was often the female equivalent of joining the navy: the last economic option.

During the 20th century, Zeedijk has been enlivened by the influx of different nationalities, in particular the Chinese. The first openly gay establishment appeared in the 1930s, closed, and recently reopened: at **Café 't Mandje** (no.63), there's a window shrine to flamboyant former owner Bet van Beeren (1902-67), who has gone down in local mythology as the original lesbian biker chick. In the '50s, jazz greats Chet Baker and Gerry Mulligan came to jam and hang out in the many after-hours clubs here, among them the 'still functioning as a shadow of what it was' **Casablanca** (no.26).

Unfortunately, this subculture marked Zeedijk as a place where heroin could be scored with comparative ease. By the 1970s the street had become crowded with dealers, junkies and indifferent cops, with most of the restaurants and cafés renting their tables to dealers. It was one big druggie convention. The junkies' magic number was 27: 25 guilders for the drugs and two guilders for the drink that owners insisted the junkies purchase to maintain the façade of legality.

Amsterdam's reputation became littered with needles and foil, never more so than when a wasted Chet Baker took his final curtain call in 1988 – on to a cement parking pole – from a window (second floor on the left) of the Prins Hendrik Hotel at the entrance of Zeedijk. A brass plaque commemorating the crooning trumpeter has been put up to the left of the hotel's entrance. Although there was a time when a German tour operator tried to run a 'criminal safari' along Zeedijk and street cleaners needed armed escorts, nowadays the street is very safe – mostly thanks to the efforts of local residents and shopkeepers.

You'll also find the city's very small Chinatown here – about half a block long; *see p65* **Tiny Chinatown**.

Schreierstoren.

Oudezijds main streets

The two canals known as 'De Wallen' –
Oudezijds Voorburgwal and Oudezijds
Achterburgwal – with their quaint
interconnecting streets, are where carnal sin
screams loudest. So it's ironic that, right in
the middle of Sin City, you'll stumble across
a pair of old churches. The **Oude Kerk**,
Amsterdam's oldest building, is literally in the
centre of the sleazy action, with hookers in
windows surrounding the mammoth church
like bullies taunting the class geek. Keep your
eyes peeled for the small brass bosom laid by a
mystery artist into the pavement by the front
entrance. The 17th-century attic church, **Ons'
Lieve Heer op Solder**, meanwhile, is tucked
away some distance from the red-lit action, but
still shouldn't be overlooked on your journey
around the area.

The **Agnietenkapel** (Oudezijds
Voorburgwal 231) is one of Amsterdam's
17 medieval convents. Built in the 1470s and
part of the University of Amsterdam since its
foundation in 1632, the chapel has an austere,
Calvinistic beauty highlighted by its stained-
glass windows, wooden beams and benches,
not to mention a collection of portraits of
humanist thinkers. The Grote Gehoorzaal
(Large Auditorium), the country's oldest lecture
hall, is where 17th-century scholars Vossius
and Barlaeus first taught; the wooden ceiling is
painted with soberly ornamental Renaissance
motifs including angels and flowers. Now, it's
used mostly for readings and congresses, and
the occasional exhibition.

The **Spinhuis**, a former convent tucked
away at the southern end of Oudezijds
Achterburgwal (on Spinhuissteeg), used to
set 'wayward women' to work spinning wool.
The male equivalent was over on the New
Side at Heiligeweg 9 – now an entrance to
the Kalvertoren shopping complex – where
audiences came to watch the prisoners being
branded and beaten with a bull's penis. In a
rather curious foreshadowing of Amsterdam's
contemporary S&M scene, the entrance gate
sports a statue that bears a striking
resemblance to a scolding dominatrix.

Warmoesstraat

It's now hard to believe that Warmoesstraat,
Amsterdam's oldest street, was once the most
beautiful of lanes, providing a sharp contrast
to its evil and rowdy twin, Zeedijk. The 17th-
century poet Joost van den Vondel ran a hosiery
business at Warmoesstraat 101; Mozart's dad
tried to flog tickets at the posh bars for his
young son's concerts; and Marx came here to
write in peace (or so he claimed – he was more
likely to have been in town to borrow money
from his cousin by marriage, the extremely
wealthy Gerard Philips, founder of the globe-
dominating Philips corporate machine).

But with the influx of sailors, the law of
supply and demand engineered a heavy fall
from grace for Warmoesstraat. Adam and Eve
in their salad days can still be seen etched in
stone at no.25, but for the most part, this street
has fallen to accommodating only the low-end
traveller. However, hipper hangouts such as
gay/mixed bar **Getto** (*see p187*), excellent
breakfast and lunch spot **De Bakkerswinkel**
and the **Winston Hotel** (*see p281*), plus shops
including the **Condomerie** and gallery **W139**,
have ensured that the strip has retained some
brighter and less corporate colours, while the
council's serial clean-up operation reached the
street lately and has at least had some of
the desired cosmetic effect.

EXPLORE

IN THE KNOW
AS SEEN ON SCREEN

The incredibly scenic Staalstraat is the
city's most popular film location, having
appeared in everything from *The Diary
of Anne Frank* to *Amsterdamned*.

De Appel

The Nes

Just as Warmoesstraat stretches north from the Nationaal Monument towards Centraal Station, so Nes leaves the same spot to the south, parallel and to the west of Oudezijds Achterburgwal. Dating from the Middle Ages, this street was once home to the city's tobacco trade and the Jewish philosopher Benedict Spinoza (1623-77), who saw body and mind as the two aspects of a single substance. Appropriate, then, that you can now witness the alignment of body and mind on the stages of the theatres that have long graced this street. You can also stop, recharge and realign your own essence at one of the many charming cafés hereabouts. At the end of Nes, either take a turn left to cross a bridge towards **Oudemanhuis Book Market** (where Van Gogh bought prints to decorate his room) on the University of Amsterdam campus; or turn right to cross over to the Spui in the New Side.

Sights & Museums

Allard Pierson Museum

Oude Turfmarkt 127 (525 2556, www.allard piersonmuseum.nl). Tram 4, 9, 14, 16, 24. **Open** 10am-5pm Tue-Fri; 1-5pm Sat, Sun. **Admission** €10; €5 reductions; free under-4s, IAmsterdam, MK. **No credit cards. Map** p59 B6 ❶
Established in 1934, the Allard Pierson is the University of Amsterdam's archaeological museum. It's home to one of the world's richest university

collections, and contains archaeological exhibits from Ancient Egypt, Greece, Rome and the Near East. Admission includes entrance to Bijzondere Collecties (*see p63*).

Amsterdam Exchange Experience

Beursplein 5 (550 5500, www.aex.nl). Tram 4, 9, 14, 16, 24. **Open** 3pm Mon-Fri (tours only, book ahead online). **Admission** €7.50. **Map** p59 A3 ❷
The Amsterdam Stock Exchange recently opened an 'experience' tour that covers the establishment of the world's first corporation (the Dutch East India Company) right through to the chaos of modern floor-trading. Note the bronze *Charging Bull* sculpture by artist Arturo Di Modica near the entrance.

De Appel

Prins Hendrikkade 142 (625 5651, www. deappel.nl). Bus 22, 48. **Open** noon-8pm Tue-Sat; noon-6pm Sun. **Admission** €7; €4.50 reductions; free under-12s, IAmsterdam, MK. **Map** p59 D2 ❸
This recently reopened arts centre prefers not to use labels like 'museum' or 'gallery'. Its glamorous new premises, a stone's throw from Central Station, showcase highly conceptual work by promising artists such as Allard van Hoorn, whose glowing 'Skies over Snaefell' installation is a treat in itself. Don't miss the café or the rear courtyard.

Beurs van Berlage

Damrak 243, entrance at Beursplein 1 (530 4141, www.beursvanberlage.nl). Tram 4, 9, 14,

16, 24. **Admission** varies. **No credit cards.**
Map p59 A3 ❹
Designed in 1896 by Hendrik Berlage as the city's
stock exchange, the palatial Beurs, while incorporating a broad range of traditional building styles, represents a break from the prevailing tastes of
19th-century architects and, as such, prepared the
way for the Amsterdam School. Although critics
thought it 'a big block with a cigar box on top,' it's
now considered the country's most important piece
of 20th-century architecture and a powerful socialist
statement: much of the artwork warns against capitalism, and each of the nine million bricks was
intended to represent the individual, with the building as a whole standing for society. Having long
driven out the money changers, the Beurs is now all
things to all other people: a conference centre, a café-
restaurant, and an exhibition space for shows that
range from Dutch design to beer festivals.
▶ *For more detail on the Amsterdam School's*
socialist vision and architectural works, see p251
School of Rock.

Bijzondere Collecties

Oude Turfmarkt 129 (525 7300, www.bijzondere
collecties.uva.nl). Tram 4, 9, 14, 16, 24. **Open**
9.30am-5pm Mon-Fri; 1-5pm Sat, Sun. Library
closed on weekends. **Admission** €7.50; €3.75-
€6.50 reductions; free IAmsterdam, MK.
Map p59 B6 ❺
They like their paper products at the University of
Amsterdam's 'Special Collections': documents,
prints, maps, photos and endless rows of books. The
invaluable pre-1850 collection is especially strong on
the history of printing, Hebrew and Judaica studies,
Protestantism, and medicine; the post-1850 collection focuses more on meritorious design, with exhibitions ranging from '1001 women' to the history of
atlases. The shop has an excellent selection of
design-related books. Admission includes entrance
to the Allard Pierson Museum (*see p62*).

FREE Cannabis College

Oudezijds Achterburgwal 124 (423 4420,
cannabiscollege.com). Tram 4, 9, 14, 16, 24
or Metro Nieuwmarkt. **Open** 11am-7pm daily.
Admission free. **Map** p59 B4 ❻
Founded by hemp activist Henk Poncin and a group
called Green Prisoners Release, Cannabis College is
a non-profit organisation, whose mission is to provide free, accurate and unbiased information concerning all aspects of the cannabis plant. The
volunteer staff ask for a small donation if you want
to wander around the indoor garden.

Erotic Museum

Oudezijds Achterburgwal 54 (624 7303, www.
erotisch-museum.nl). Tram 4, 9, 14, 16, 24
or Metro Nieuwmarkt. **Open** 11am-1am Mon-
Thur, Sun; 11am-2am Fri, Sat. **Admission** €7.
No credit cards. Map p59 B3 ❼

While the Sexmuseum (Damrak 18, www.sexmuse-
umamsterdam.nl) benefits from its Damrak site in
terms of passing trade, the Erotic Museum is in the
more appropriate location: slap bang in the Red
Light District. That's not to say, though, that it's any
more authentic or interesting. Its prize exhibits are
a bicycle-powered dildo and a few of John Lennon's
erotic drawings, while lovers of Bettie Page (and
there are many) will enjoy the original photos of the
S&M muse on display. It also puts on temporary
exhibits in the Sexy Art Gallery on the third floor.
In general, the museum's name is somewhat inaccurate: despite its best intentions and desperate desire
to shock, it's as unsexy as can be. You're probably
best off going to one of the many nearby sex shops
for your kicks.

Hash Marihuana & Hemp Museum

Oudezijds Achterburgwal 148 (624 8926,
www.hashmuseum.com). Tram 4, 9, 14, 16, 24
or Metro Nieuwmarkt. **Open** 10am-11pm daily.
Admission €9; free under-13s (must be
accompanied by an adult). **Map** p59 B4 ❽
Cannabis connoisseurs will lose themselves ogling
larger-than-life pictures of perfect plants and gleaming balls of hash in this museum in the Red Light
District. But this shrine to skunk is not only for
smokers. Strait-laced visitors will be entertained by

Erotic Museum.

Oude Kerk.

the detailed history of the plant. There's plenty of pro-cannabis propaganda too, including info about its medicinal uses, the environmental benefits of hemp and the cannabis culture of today. Don't miss the indoor 'grow-op' that showcases plants being lovingly cultivated for their seeds, guarded by a guru of ganja who offers advice on using a vaporiser.

★ Ons' Lieve Heer op Solder

Oudezijds Voorburgwal 40 (624 6604, www. opsolder.nl). Tram 4, 9, 14, 16, 24 or Metro Nieuwmarkt. **Open** 10am-5pm Mon-Sat; 1-5pm Sun. **Admission** €8; €4 reductions; free under-5s, IAmsterdam, MK. **No credit cards. Map** p59 B2 ❾

'Our Lord in the Attic' is one of Amsterdam's most unusual spots, and one of its best-kept secrets. The lower floors of the canal house have been wonderfully preserved since the late 17th century, and offer an insight into what life might have been like back then. But the main attraction is upstairs. Built in 1663, this attic church was used by Catholics when they were banned from public worship after the Alteration. It's been beautifully preserved too, the altarpiece featuring a painting by 18th-century artist Jacob de Wit, and was recently entirely renovated. The church is often used for services. Don't miss it.

★ Oude Kerk

Oudekerksplein 23 (625 8284, www.oudekerk.nl). Tram 4, 9, 14, 16, 24 or Metro Nieuwmarkt. **Open** 10am-6pm Mon-Sat; 1-5pm Sun. **Admission** €7.50; €5 reductions; free under-12s, IAmsterdam, MK. *Temporary exhibitions* varies. **No credit cards. Map** p59 B3 ❿

Built in 1306 as a wooden chapel, and constantly renovated and extended between 1330 and 1571, the Oude Kerk is the city's oldest and most interesting church. One can only imagine the Sunday Mass chaos during its heyday of the mid 1500s, when it contained 38 altars, each with its own guild-sponsored priest. The original furnishings were removed by iconoclasts during the Reformation, but the church has retained its wooden roof, which was painted in the 15th century with figurative images. Look out for the mixed Gothic and Renaissance façade above the northern portal, and the stained-glass windows, parts of which date from the 16th and 17th centuries. Rembrandt's wife, Saskia, who died in 1642, is buried here. The inscription over the bridal chamber, which translates as 'Marry in haste, mourn at leisure,' is in keeping with the church's location in the heart of the Red Light District, though this is more by accident than design. If you want to be semi-shocked, check out the carvings in the choir benches of men evacuating their bowels – apparently they tell a moralistic tale. Now with a charming café and terrace, Koffieschenkerij De Oude Kerk, the church is as much an exhibition centre as anything else, with shows focused on modern and mainly locally created art.

EXPLORE

TINY CHINATOWN

Small but perfectly formed. Take it away…

Fo Guang Shan He Hua.

EXPLORE

A string of no-frills restaurants on the Zeedijk, winding from Centraal Station towards Nieuwmarkt, makes up what is perhaps the world's smallest Chinatown. Here, you can eat authentic fare for under a tenner. Among the top local picks are award-winning Chinese eateries **Nam Kee** (*see p68*) and **New King** (Zeedijk 115-117, 625 2180), and Thai restaurant **Bird** (*see p67*), which has a very popular fast-food and takeaway outlet (the 'Snackbar') across the street from its more spacious and elegant restaurant. You'll also find Japanese, Malaysian, Vietnamese and pan-Asian restaurants up and down the street, as well as further east, on Koningsstraat past Nieuwmarkt.

If you want some Asian snacks or plan to cook an Asian meal at home, **Toko Dun Yong** (*see p74*) is the perfect shop. Its shelves, fridges and freezers heave with wonderful products, including frozen dumplings, preserved tofu, handmade noodles, saké and exotic fruit and vegetables, while the basement has kitsch and well-priced Asian crockery. On the southern edge of the square, **Oriental Commodities** (Nieuwmarkt 27, 626 2797, www.amazingoriental.com) sells handmade noodles, dumplings and all the Asian veg that you can't find at the Albert Heijn.

And don't miss the Chinese Buddhist temple **Fo Guang Shan He Hua** (Zeedijk 106-118, 420 2357, open noon-5pm Tue-Sat, 10am-5pm Sun), with its bluestone steps, roof tiles and ornaments imported directly from China. Monks and nuns still practise their faith here, but tours are available – you'll be asked to remove your shoes as you're guided through the surprisingly spacious complex.

Chinatown is where to experience street celebrations for **Chinese New Year** (*see p43*), including a traditional Lion Dance performed with live drumming.

wagamama

love noodles
love wagamama

wagamama amsterdam
amstelstraat 8 | rembrandtplein
max euweplein 10 | leidseplein
zuidplein 12 | wtc | station zuid

opening hours
12.00 - 22.00

wagamama.nl

FREE W139

Warmoesstraat 139 (622 9434, www.w139.nl).
Tram 4, 9, 14, 16, 24 or Metro Nieuwmarkt.
Open noon-6pm Mon-Wed, Fri-Sun; noon-10pm
Thur. **Admission** free. **No credit cards.**
Map p59 A3 ⑪
In its two decades of existence, this contemporary
art gallery has never lost its squat aesthetics or
sometimes overly conceptual edge, with legendary
openings that often spill out on to the street.

Restaurants

1e Klas

Centraal Station, Platform 2B (625 0131,
www. restaurant1eklas.nl). Tram 1, 2, 4, 5,
9, 13, 14, 16, 17, 24. **Open** 8.30am-11pm
daily. **Main courses** €19-€26. **Map** p59 B1
⑫ **Brasserie/pub**
This former brasserie for first-class commuters is
now open to anyone who wants to kill some time in
style – with a full meal, snack or drink – while waiting for a train. The art nouveau interior will whisk
you straight back to the 1890s. The adjoining pub is
also a treat and hosts regular jazz concerts. But if
you're running for the train, score something to go
from Shakies (423 4377, www.shakies.nl), in the west
tunnel by the stairs to platforms 10/11.

A Fusion

Zeedijk 130 (330 4068, www.a-fusion.nl).
Tram 4, 9, 16, 24 or Metro Nieuwmarkt.
Open noon-11pm daily. **Main courses**
€12-€20. **Map** p59 C3 ⑬ **Asian**
This loungey restaurant obviously took notes from
the hip side of Chinatown in New York City. The
interior is dark and inviting, and you can drink
bubble teas (lychee!) and eat some of the tastiest
confusion-free pan-Asian dishes in town. The dim
sum and satay dishes are particularly recommended.

De Bakkerswinkel

Warmoesstraat 69 (489 8000, www.
debakkerswinkel.nl). Tram 1, 2, 4, 5, 9,
13, 14, 16, 17, 24. **Open** 8am-5.30pm Tue-
Fri; 8am-6pm Sat, Sun. **Main courses** €3.50-
€11. **Map** p59 B2 ⑭ **Café**
A bakery-tearoom where you can indulge in lovingly
prepared and hearty sandwiches, soups and the
most divine slabs of quiche.
Other locations Roelof Hartstraat 68,
Museum Quarter (662 3594); Polonceaukade 1,
Westerpark (688 0632).

Bird

Zeedijk 72-74 & 77 (snack bar 420 6289,
restaurant 620 1442, www.thai-bird.nl). Tram 4,
9, 16, 24 or Metro Nieuwmarkt. **Open** *Restaurant*
5-11pm daily. *Snack bar* 1-10pm daily. **Main**
courses *Restaurant* €12.50-€25. **No credit**
cards (snack bar). **Map** p59 C2 ⑮ **Thai**

The most authentic Thai place in town. As a result,
it's also the most crowded, but the food is worth the
wait, whether you're dropping by to pick up a pot of
tom yam soup or want a full-blown meal. The snack
bar is at no.77; the restaurant – open only for dinner
– is across the street at nos.72-74 and is the best
choice if you plan to linger.

Blauw aan de Wal

Oudezijds Achterburgwal 99 (330 2257, www.
blauwaandewal.com). Tram 4, 9, 14, 16, 24 or
Metro Nieuwmarkt. **Open** 6-11.30pm Tue-Sat.
Main courses €30. **Set meal** €62.50 3 courses.
Map p59 B4 ⑯ **Mediterranean**
The hallmarks of this mainstay in the heart of the
Red Light District, complete with a peaceful court-
yard, are tempting Mediterranean dishes and a wine
list likely to inspire long bouts of grateful contem-
plation in visiting oenophiles.

Brasserie Harkema

Nes 67 (428 2222, www.brasserieharkema.nl).
Tram 4, 9, 14, 16, 24. **Open** noon-1am (kitchen
noon-4pm, 5.30-11pm) daily. **Main courses**
lunch €9-€20, dinner €15-€20. **Map** p59 B5
⑰ **French**
This former tobacco factory is a popular spot,
thanks to its stylish surroundings, excellent wines
and a kitchen that pumps out reasonably priced
French classics until late.

★ Bridges

Oudezijds Voorburgwal 197 (555 3560,
www.bridgesrestaurant.nl). Tram 4, 9, 14,
16, 24. **Open** 6.30-10.30am, noon-2.30pm, 6.30-
10.30pm Mon-Fri; 6.30-11am, 12.30-2.30pm, 6.30-
10.30pm Sat, Sun. **Main courses** €21-€55.
Map p59 B5 ⑱ **French/Dutch**
Young Dutch cooking talent Joris Bijendijk really
hit the headlines in 2013 when he became a surprise
finalist in France's version of *MasterChef*. Now,
he's executive chef at the Bridges restaurant in the
Grand Amsterdam hotel (*see p278*) and a commit-
ted proponent of slow food. The menu features
locally caught, seasonal seafood and five-star ingredients, such as oysters (from the raw bar) and
caviar. Be sure to admire the Karel Appel mural
upon entering.

Café Bern

Nieuwmarkt 9 (622 0034). Tram 4, 9, 14,
16, 24 or Metro Nieuwmarkt. **Open** 4pm-1am
(kitchen 6-11pm) daily. Closed mid July-mid Aug.
Main courses €12-€18. **No credit cards.**
Map p59 C3 ⑲ **Swiss**
Despite its Swiss origins, the Dutch adopted the
cheese fondue as a 'national dish' long ago. Sample
its culinary conviviality at this suitably cosy 'brown
café', which was established by a nuclear physicist
who knew his way around the fusion of cheese with
wine – and was also smart enough to know that a

EXPLORE

menu should be affordable and a bar should be stocked with a generous variety of grease-cutting agents. It's best to book ahead.

Centra
Lange Niezel 29 (622 3050, www.restaurant centra.nl). Tram 4, 9, 14, 16, 24. **Open** noon-11pm daily. **Main courses** €16.50-€22.50. **No credit cards. Map** p59 B2 ⑳ **Spanish**
Centra serves decent, wholesome, homely Spanish cooking in a suitably unpretentious atmosphere. The seafood paella is especially good.

Latei
Zeedijk 143 (625 7485, www.latei.net). Tram 4, 9, 14, 16, 24 or Metro Nieuwmarkt. **Open** 8am-6pm Mon-Wed; 8am-10pm Thur, Fri; 9am-10pm Sat; 11am-6pm Sun. **Main courses** €3-€8. **No credit cards. Map** p59 C3 ㉑ **Café**
Packed with kitsch and decorated with funky Finnish wallpaper – all of which, including the wallpaper, is for sale – this little café serves healthy juices and snacks all day long, plus Indonesian vegetarian dinners (from 6pm Thur-Sat).

★ Nam Kee
Zeedijk 111-113 (624 3470, www.namkee.net). Tram 4, 9, 14, 16, 24 or Metro Nieuwmarkt. **Open** noon-11pm daily. **Main courses** €8-€20. **No credit cards. Map** p59 C3 ㉒ **Chinese**
Cheap and terrific food has earned this Chinese joint a devoted following: the oysters in black bean sauce has achieved classic status. If it's too crowded, try one of the equally excellent nearby alternatives: New King (Zeedijk 115-117, 625 2180), Wing Kee (Zeedijk 76, 623 5683) or Si Chuan (Warmoesstraat 17, 420 7833).

Oriental City
Oudezijds Voorburgwal 177-179 (626 8352, www.oriental-city.nl). Tram 4, 9, 14, 16, 24 or Metro Nieuwmarkt. **Open** 11.30am-10.30pm daily. **Main courses** €8-€23. **Map** p59 B4 ㉓ **Chinese**
The location is simply marvellous: overlooking Damstraat, the Royal Palace and the canals. But that's not even the best bit: Oriental City serves some of Amsterdam's most authentic dim sum.

Yokiyo
Oudezijds Voorburgwal 67 (331 4562, www.yokiyo.nl). Tram 4, 9, 14, 16, 24 or Metro Nieuwmarkt. **Open** noon-5pm, 6-10pm Tue-Thur, Sun; noon-5pm, 6-11pm Fri, Sat. **Main courses** €13.50-€18. **Map** p59 B3 ㉔ **Korean**
Influential Korean-American chef David Chang has some worthy disciples at this new 'Korean Social Food Experience' with BBQ, kimchi and other bold-flavoured foodstuffs. Join the fun at the bar, on the long dining table or upstairs on one of the round tables with built-in barbecues.

Bars

Bierfabriek
Rokin 75 & Nes 92 (528 9910, www.bierfabriek. com). Tram 4, 9, 14, 16, 24. **Open** 4pm-1am Mon-Thur; 4pm-3am Fri; 2pm-3am Sat; 2pm-1am Sun. **Map** p59 A5 ㉕
With an industrial look and laid-back attitude, the Beer Factory pulls in a young crowd for its own-brewed beers and excellent roast chicken. *See p150* **What's Brewing?**

De Brakke Grond
Nes 45 (422 2666, www.brakkegrond.nl). Tram 4, 9, 14, 16, 24. **Open** noon-1am daily. **No credit cards. Map** p59 A5 ㉖
Belgian culture does stretch beyond beer, and cultural centre De Brakke Grond is here to prove it. Mind you, indulging in some good Belgian beer at the centre's café-restaurant will go down a treat after visiting the gallery or checking out a band.

Brouwerij de Prael
Oudezijds Armsteeg 26 & Oudezijds Voorburgwal 30 (408 4470, www.deprael.nl). Tram 1, 2, 4, 5, 9, 13, 14, 16, 17, 24. **Open** *Bar* noon-midnight Tue-Wed; noon-1am Thur-Sat; noon-11pm Sun. *Shop* noon-7pm daily. **Map** p59 B2 ㉗
An unusual venture: a microbrewery and shop set up to provide employment for people with psychiatric conditions. *See p150* **What's Brewing?**

Yokiyo

EXPLORE

Mata Hari.

Bubbles & Wines

Nes 37 (422 3318, www.bubblesandwines.com).
Tram 4, 9, 14, 16, 24. **Open** 3.30pm-1am
Mon-Sat; 2-9pm Sun. **Map** p59 A4 ㉘
This long, low-ceilinged room has the feel of a wine
cellar, albeit one with mood lighting and banquettes.
There are more than 50 wines available by the glass
and 180 by the bottle, and accompanying posh nosh
(Osetra caviar, truffle cheese, foie gras). Wine flights
are also served.

Café 't Mandje

Zeedijk 63 (622 5375, www.cafetmandje.nl).
Tram 4, 9, 16, 24 or Metro Nieuwmarkt.
Open 4pm-1am Mon-Wed; 3pm-1am Thur;
2pm-3am Fri, Sat; 2pm-1am Sun. **No credit
cards. Map** p59 C2 ㉙
Launched more than 80 years ago, this historic café
was the city's first (moderately) openly gay and lesbian bar. The original proprietor, Bet van Beeren
(who died over 40 years ago), was legendary for her
role as (probably) the world's first lesbian biker chick.
After years of closure, the café reopened recently, to
suggest that time can stand still. A replica of the café
can be seen at the Amsterdam Museum (*see p76*).

★ De Jaren

Nieuwe Doelenstraat 20-22 (625 5771,
www.cafedejaren.nl). Tram 4, 9, 16, 24. **Open**
9.30am-1am Mon-Thur, Sun; 9.30am-2am Fri,
Sat. **Map** p59 C6 ㉚
All of Amsterdam – students, tourists, lesbigays,
cinemagoers, the fashion pack – comes here for
lunch, coffee or something stronger all day long,
making it sometimes difficult to bag a seat. Upstairs
becomes a restaurant after 5.30pm. Be prepared to
fight for a spot on the Amstel-side terrace in summer,
as its sweeping views are beloved of tourists.

Kapitein Zeppos

Gebed Zonder End 5 (624 2057, www.zeppos.nl).
Tram 4, 9, 14, 16, 24. **Open** noon-1am Mon-
Thur, Sun; noon-3am Fri, Sat. **Map** p59 B5 ㉛
Tucked away down the poetically named 'Prayer
Without End' alley (a reference to the Santa Clara
convent that stood here in the 17th century), this
light-drenched, multifaceted café and restaurant has
an understated Belgian theme: it's named after a
1960s Flemish TV detective; there's Belgian beer on
tap; and the most frequently heard soundtrack is
chanson. Upstairs, the new Claires Ballroom features
live music and theatre.

Mata Hari

Oudezijds Achterburgwal 22 (205 0919,
www.matahari-amsterdam.nl). Tram 4, 9, 16,
24 or Metro Nieuwmarkt. **Open** noon-1am Mon-
Thur, Sun; noon-3am Fri, Sat. **Map** p59 B2 ㉜
Named after the exotic but tricksy Dutch courtesan,
it's appropriate that this new bar, restaurant and
lounge has brought a touch of comfort and class to
the Red Light District. Sympathetic lighting, retro
furniture and an open kitchen serving exquisite
dishes such as 'chocolate salami with forget-me-not
liqueur' make the seduction complete.

NRC Restaurant-Café

Rokin 65 (755 3553, www.nrcrestaurantcafe.nl).
Tram 4, 9, 14, 16, 24. **Open** 9am-midnight Mon-
Fri; 10am-midnight Sat, Sun. **Map** p59 A5 ㉝
The Netherlands' premier-quality newspaper
recently moved from Rotterdam to the big city of
Amsterdam and wanted to make a splash. So they
added a café-restaurant to their new offices, with
which to attract the local intelligentsia. You can
opt for a full-blown meal of inspired French country
cooking or just linger over a coffee and a flambée

EXPLORE

NRC Restaurant-Café. See p69.

(a German-French pizza-like dish). Don't miss the excellent, small bookshop.

TonTon Club

Sint Annendwarsstraat 6 (www.tontonclub.nl).
Tram 4, 9, 16, 24 or Metro Nieuwmarkt.
Open 5-11pm Tue-Thur; 11am-11pm Fri-Sun.
No credit cards. Map p59 B3 ㉞
This arcade bar in the heart of the Red Light District does feature old-school games such as pinball, but most have been hacked to do such things as print out chocolate – making TonTon more of a platform and meeting place for local game designers and artists. Besides offering coffee, beer and snacks, TonTon also regularly brings in local chefs to provide meals – from Korean tacos to Dutch Weed Burgers.

Van Kerkwijk

Nes 41 (620 3316, www.caferestaurant
vankerkwijk.nl). Tram 4, 9, 14, 16, 24. **Open**
11am-1am Mon-Thur, Sun; 11am-3am Fri, Sat.
Map p59 A4 ㉟
Far from the bustle of Dam Square, though really just a few strides away on one of Amsterdam's most charming streets, Van Kerkwijk is airy by day, romantic and candlelit by night – and equally good for group gatherings or intimate tête-à-têtes. You'll find sandwiches at lunch and more substantial food in the evening, though the emphasis is as much on genteel drinking. (Beware the near-vertical stairs leading down to the toilets.)

★ Wynand Fockink

Pijlsteeg 31 (639 2695, www.wynand-fockink.nl).
Tram 4, 9, 14, 16, 24. **Open** 3-9pm daily.
No credit cards. Map p59 A4 ㊱
It's standing room only at this historic tasting house. Hidden behind the Krasnapolsky hotel, and unchanged since 1679, this has been a meeting place for Freemasons since the beginning; past visitors include Churchill and Chagall. The menu of liqueurs

and *jenevers* (many available in take-out bottles) reads like a list of unwritten novels: Parrot Soup; The Longer the Better; Rose Without Thorns.

Coffeeshops

Basjoe

Kloveniersburgwal 62 (627 3858). Metro
Nieuwmarkt. **Open** 10am-1am daily. **No**
credit cards. Map p59 C5 ㊲
The canal view alone places Basjoe among our favourite coffeeshops in Amsterdam. Candlelit, with a plain decor of terracotta soft vinyl booths, cream walls and wooden tables, it's all about the weed here – but the coffee is also outstanding.

Greenhouse

Oudezijds Voorburgwal 191 (627 1739).
Tram 4, 9, 14, 16, 24. **Open** 9am-1am daily.
No credit cards. Map p59 B4 ㊳
This legendary coffeeshop offers highly potent weed with some fairly strong prices to match – it's won the High Times Cannabis Cup more than 30 times. The Grand Hotel is next door, so the occasional celebrity stops by to get hammered. The vibe inside has grown quite commercial, but it's still worth a peek, if only to see the beautifully handmade interior with its sunken floors, mosaic stones and blown-glass lamps.
Other locations Waterlooplein 345, Jodenbuurt; Tolstraat 91, De Pijp.

Greenhouse Effect

Warmoesstraat 53-55 (624 4974). Tram 4,
9, 16, 24. **Open** 9am-1am daily. **No credit**
cards. Map p59 B2 ㊴
This snug shop is shaped like a long, sleek train carriage, and features a polished interior and reliably high-quality ganja. It tends to fill up fast, but there's a sister operation across the street (Hill Street Blues, Warmoesstraat 52, open 9am-1am Mon-Thur, Sun,

EXPLORE

9am-3am Fri, Sat) where you'll discover a full bar and regular DJs. If the drink and dope combination renders you immobile, make a beeline for the hotel upstairs (*see p281*).

Rusland
Rusland 16 (627 9468, www.coffeeshop-rusland-amsterdam.com). Tram 4, 9, 14, 16, 24 or Metro Nieuwmarkt. **Open** 8am-12.30am daily. **No credit cards.** **Map** p59 B5 ㊵
Well known as the longest-running coffeeshop in the city, this 'Russian' den has hardwood floors and colourful cushions that complement an efficient multi-level design. The top-floor bar serves more than 40 different loose teas and healthy fruit shakes; below is a decent pipe display. It's off the well-trodden tourist path, which means cheaper prices and smaller crowds.

Shops & Services

A Boeken Stoffen & Fournituren
Nieuwe Hoogstraat 31 (626 7205, www. aboeken.nl). Tram 4, 9, 16, 24 or Metro Nieuwmarkt. **Open** noon-6pm Mon; 10am-6pm Tue, Wed, Fri; 10am-8pm Thur; 10am-5pm Sat. **Map** p59 C4 ㊶ **Homewares**
The Boeken family has been hawking fabrics since 1920. Just try to find anywhere else with the same range: latex, Lycra, fake fur and sequins abound.

Betsy Palmer
Rokin 9-15 (422 1040, www.betsypalmer.com). Tram 4, 9, 16, 24. **Open** noon-6pm Mon;

10am-6pm Tue-Sat; 1-6pm Sun. **Map** p59 A4 ㊷ **Accessories**
Tired of seeing the same shoes in every store, Dutch fashion buyer Gertie Gerards put her money where her mouth was and set up her own shop. Betsy Palmer is her in-house label, displayed alongside a huge variety of other brands, which change as soon as they sell out.
Other locations Van Woustraat 46, De Pijp (470 9795).

★ De Bijenkorf
Dam 1 (0800 0818, www.bijenkorf.nl). Tram 1, 2, 4, 5, 9, 13, 14, 16, 17, 24. **Open** 11am-8pm Mon, Sun; 10am-8pm Tue, Wed; 10am-9pm Thur, Fri; 9.30am-9pm Sat. **Map** p59 A4 ㊸ **Department store**
De Bijenkorf means 'the Beehive' – an apt moniker for this busy department store. Set in a grandiose building on Dam Square, this luxe temple to consumerism is arguably on a par with London's Harrods and Berlin's KaDeWe.

Book Exchange
Kloveniersburgwal 58 (626 6266, www. bookexchange.nl). Tram 4, 9, 14, 16, 24 or Metro Nieuwmarkt. **Open** 10am-6pm Mon-Sat; 11.30am-4pm Sun. **Map** p59 C5 ㊹ **Books & music**
The owner of this bibliophiles' treasure trove is a shrewd buyer who's willing to do trade deals. Choose from a plethora of second-hand English and American titles (mainly paperbacks), and the biggest science-fiction collection in the city.

EXPLORE

TonTon Club.

★ Capsicum

*Oude Hoogstraat 1 (623 1016, www.capsicum.nl).
Tram 4, 9, 14, 16, 24 or Metro Nieuwmarkt.*
Open 11am-6pm Mon; 10am-6pm Tue-Sat;
1-5pm Sun. **Map** p59 B4 **④⑤ Homewares**
All the fabrics on sale here are made from natural
fibres, such as cotton woven in India. Staff spin
the provenance of each fabric into the sale, and the
store has a covetable stash of cushions and shawls.
An absolute gem.

Condomerie

*Warmoesstraat 141 (627 4174, www.condomerie.
com). Tram 4, 9, 14, 16, 24 or Metro Nieuwmarkt.*
Open 11am-6pm Mon-Sat; 1-5pm Sun. **Map**
p59 A4 **④⑥ Sex shop**
A variety of rubbers of the non-erasing kind, to wrap
up trouser snakes of all shapes and sizes, in a store
that's equal parts amusing and inspiring.

Grimm Sieraden

*Grimburgwal 9 (622 0501, www.grimm
sieraden.nl). Tram 4, 9, 14, 16, 24.* **Open**
11am-6pm Wed-Fri; 11am-5pm Sat. **Map**
p59 B5 **④⑦ Accessories**
While this shop features the most avant-garde of
Dutch jewellery designers, it has the decency –
not to mention the sound commercial sense – to con-
centrate its stock on the most wearable pieces from
their various ranges.

Hotel Droog.

De Hoed van Tijn

*Nieuwe Hoogstraat 15 (623 2759, www.
dehoedvantijn.nl). Tram 4, 9, 16, 24 or Metro
Nieuwmarkt.* **Open** noon-6pm Mon; 11am-6pm
Tue-Fri; 11am-5.30pm Sat. (Oct-Dec only) noon-
5pm Sun. **Map** p59 C4 **④⑧ Accessories**
Mad hatters will delight in this vast range of bon-
nets, homburgs, bowlers, sombreros and caps,
including second-hand and handmade items.

★ Hotel Droog

*Staalstraat 7 (523 5059, www.hoteldroog.com/).
Tram 4, 9, 14, 16, 24.* **Open** 11am-6pm Tue-Sun.
Map p59 C5 **④⑨ Homewares**
Dutch design dynamo Droog has expanded its HQ
into a flagship 'hotel' – a city-centre design mall
where you can attend a lecture series or an exhibition, get beauty advice at Cosmania and, yes, even
spend the night in the single suite. The historic
building's rag trade origins continue at ice-cool
boutique Kabinet. The Droog shop still sells some
of the wittiest ranges around: Jurgen Bey, Richard
Hutten, Hella Jongerius and Marcel Wanders.
Also see p287.

★ Jemi

*Warmoesstraat 83A (625 6034, www.jemi.nl).
Tram 4, 9, 14, 16, 24 or Metro Nieuwmarkt.*
Open 9am-5pm Mon-Fri. **No credit cards**.
Map p59 A3 **⑤⓪ Gifts & souvenirs**
Amsterdam's first stone-built house is now occupied
by a delightfully colourful florist. Jemi arranges
splendid bouquets, provides tuition in the art of
flower arranging, and stocks tons of pots and plants.

Joe's Vliegerwinkel

*Nieuwe Hoogstraat 19 (625 0139, www.
joesvliegerwinkel.nl). Tram 4, 9, 16, 24 or
Metro Nieuwmarkt.* **Open** noon-6pm Tue-
Fri; noon-5pm Sat. **Map** p59 C4 **⑤① Gifts
& souvenirs**
Kites, kites and yet more kites – well, you've got to
do something with all the Dutch wind. A quirky
array of boomerangs, yo-yos and kaleidoscopes can
also be found at this wonderfully colourful shop.

't Klompenhuisje

*Nieuwe Hoogstraat 9A (622 8100, www.
klompenhuisje.nl). Tram 4, 9, 16, 24 or Metro
Nieuwmarkt.* **Open** 10am-6pm Mon-Sat.
Map p59 C4 **⑤② Children**
For delightfully crafted and reasonably priced shoes,
traditional clogs and handmade leather and woollen
slippers from baby sizes up to size 35, this is the
perfect place for turning kids into pint-sized
Dutchies for the day.

Nieuwmarkt Antique Market

*Nieuwmarkt (no phone). Tram 4, 9, 14, 16, 24
or Metro Nieuwmarkt.* **Open** *May-Oct* 9am-5pm
Sun. **Map** p59 C3 **⑤③ Market**

Patta.

A few streets away from the ladies in the windows, this antiques and bric-a-brac market attracts browsers looking for other kinds of pleasures: old books, furniture and objets d'art.

★ Oudemanhuis Book Market
Oudemanhuispoort (no phone). Tram 4, 9, 14, 16, 24. **Open** 9am-5pm Mon-Sat. **No credit cards. Map** p59 B5 ❸❹ **Market**
People have been buying and selling books, prints and sheet music from this indoor row of shops since the 18th century.

Palm Guitars
's Gravelandseveer 5 (422 0445, www.palm guitars.nl). Tram 4, 9, 14, 16, 24. **Open** noon-6pm Tue-Sat. **Map** p59 C6 ❺❺ **Books & music**
Palm Guitars stocks new, antique, used and rare musical instruments (and their parts) and, as such, is the gathering point for both the local and international roots and world music scenes.

Patta
Zeedijk 67 (331 8571, www.patta.nl). Tram 4, 9, 16, 24 or Metro Nieuwmarkt. **Open** noon-7pm Mon-Wed, Fri, Sat; noon-9pm Thur; 1-6pm Sun. **Map** p59 C2 ❺❻ **Accessories**
Named after the Surinamese slang for shoes, this store is where street-trainer fetishists come to commune: all the expected brands, from Adidas to New Balance, are here. Plus clothing by Stüssy and Rockwell.

Printed in Space
Grimburgwal 2 (624 7225, www.printed inspace.nl). Tram 4, 9, 14, 16, 24. **Open** 1-6pm Mon, Sun; noon-7pm Tue-Sat. **Map** p59 B6 ❺❼ **Gifts & souvenirs**
While DUS architects are busy 3D-printing a canal-house in Amsterdam North, this little shop is using the tech to fill your home. Got an idea for a vase? Then bring it in to be printed in bio-plastic, wood or nylon. Or just peruse their selection of already 3D-printed jewellery, lampshades, vases and, yes, miniature wooden shoes. And for just over €2,000, you can walk away with your own printer.

Puccini Bomboni
Staalstraat 17 (626 5474, www.puccini bomboni.com). Tram 9, 14 or Metro Waterlooplein. **Open** noon-6pm Mon, Sun; 9am-6pm Tue-Sat. **Map** p59 C5 ❺❽ **Food & drink**
Tamarind, thyme, lemongrass, pepper and gin are just some of the flavours of these delicious handmade chocolates, which are created without any artificial ingredients.
Other locations Singel 184, Western Canal Belt (427 8341).

Seventy Five
Nieuwe Hoogstraat 24 (626 4611, www. seventyfive.com). Tram 4, 9, 16, 24 or Metro Nieuwmarkt. **Open** noon-6pm Mon, Sun; 10am-6pm Tue-Sat. **Map** p59 C4 ❺❾ **Accessories**

Trainers for folk who have no intention of wearing them long enough to consider inserting a pair of Odor-Eaters: high fashion styles from Asics, Nike, Puma, Converse and Diesel.
Other locations Haarlemmerdijk 55C, The Jordaan (330 6328); Van Woustraat 14, De Pijp (379 5335).

Toko Dun Yong

Stormsteeg 9 (622 1763, www.dunyong.com). Tram 4, 9, 14, 16, 24 or Metro Nieuwmarkt. **Open** 9am-6pm Mon-Sat; noon-5pm Sun. **Map** p59 C2 ③ **Food & drink**
Visit Amsterdam's largest Chinese food emporium for the full spectrum of Asian foods and ingredients, ranging from shrimp- and scallop-flavoured egg noodles to fried tofu balls and fresh veg. You can also seek out a fine range of traditional Chinese cooking appliances and utensils, as well as indulge in Japanese ramen soups at Le Fou Fow (12.30-5pm Wed-Sun) on the second floor.

De Wijnerij

Binnen Bantammerstraat 8 (625 6433, www.dewijnerij.com). Tram 4, 9, 14, 16, 24 or Metro Nieuwmarkt. **Open** 11am-6.30pm Tue-Fri; 10am-6.30pm Sat. **Map** p59 C2 ③ **Food & drink**
This friendly and passionate shop specialises in French wine – usually from organic producers – and unique local distillates such as *jenever* (Dutch gin). With another wine and liquor shop, De Twee Engelen (no.19), and the relaxed café/terrace Cafe Captein en Co (no.27), this street is a delight for thirsty people.

WonderWood

Rusland 3 (625 3738, www.wonderwood.nl). *Tram 4, 9, 16, 24.* **Open** noon-6pm Wed-Sat. **Map** p59 B5 ③ **Homewares**
The name says it all: beautifully crafted wooden furniture (mainly chairs) in the form of shop-made originals, re-editions of global classics and original plywood designs from the 1940s and '50s.

OLD STATION, NEW HUB

A new Metro line is changing the face of Amsterdam.

Amsterdam is being ripped apart. The redevelopment activity is an attempt to right a wrong: the building of Centraal Station during 1882-89. Although it's impossible to imagine Amsterdam without its 'Old Holland'-style masterpiece (or its mirror-image, the Rijksmuseum), the building acted as a cultural divider, separating the city from its harbour and Amsterdam North across the IJ river – as well as from its history as the world's richest city port during its 17th-century Golden Age.

When the 9.5-kilometre (six-mile) Noord-Zuidlijn Metro link is completed, supposedly in 2017, the north will be connected to the outlying south via Centraal Station, which is also undergoing a total refurbishment that's due to be finished in 2015. The station will finally become truly central, with two front sides: one will face across the water towards a rapidly gentrifying north, while the other, the traditional front side, will look towards the Old Centre and the radiating horseshoe of canals with their gabled houses. It's hoped that the Metro line will give a boost to the rising business

centre Zuidas in the south, where many new office blocks lie largely empty.

Work on the Noord-Zuidlijn started in 2003 and was always a point of controversy. Most of the aldermen responsible for initiating the project have now moved on, leaving the city with a legacy that's at best merely too expensive, and at worst out of control. The line has run considerably over its original budget – a staggering €1.65 billion – paid for by Amsterdam's city council and the national government. The whole project will cost the city council over €900 million, not the estimated €317 million; and even if it keeps to the current schedule, it will still open six years later than originally projected. Part of the problem lies in the difficulties of digging beneath a city built on poles; time-consuming processes had to be invented to construct tunnels 40 metres (130 feet) deep. Although leaking walls and sinking old buildings temporarily stopped construction in 2009, everything now seems set for Amsterdam to get itself a proper A-train.

THE NEW SIDE

Compared to the Old Side, the New Side is much kinder and gentler. With the University of Amsterdam to hand, the focus is much more on the mind than the loins. Rhyming (nearly enough) with 'cow', the **Spui** is a charming square with a Friday book market and numerous bookshops and cafés. It caps the three main arteries that start down near the west end of Centraal Station: the middle-of-the-road walking and retail street Kalverstraat (which is called Nieuwendijk before it crosses the Dam), plus Nieuwezijds Voorburgwal and the Spuistraat.

A quiet backwater accessible via the north side of the Spui square or, when that entrance is closed, via Gedempte Begijnensloot (the alternating entrances are set up to appease residents), the **Begijnhof** is a group of houses built around a secluded courtyard and garden. It's one of the best known of the city's many *hofjes* (almshouses; *see p123* **Hidden Hofjes**).

Established in the 14th century, the Begijnhof originally provided modest homes for the Beguines, a religious and (as was the way in the Middle Ages with religious establishments for women) rather liberated sisterhood of unmarried ladies from good families, who, though not nuns and thus taking no formal vows, lived together in a close community and had to take vows of chastity. Since they did not have to take vows of poverty, the Beguines were free to dispose of their property as they saw fit, further ensuring

IN THE KNOW RELIGIOUS ART

While visiting the **Begijnhof** (*see left*), be sure to check out the beautiful painted stones on the wall behind the Houtenhuis, each of which depicts a scene from the Bible. Dating from the 17th and 18th centuries, these stones, once housed in the Rijksmuseum's vaults, were restored and installed here in 1961.

their emancipation as a community. They could, however, renounce their vows at any moment and leave – for instance, if they wanted to get married. The last sister died in 1971, while one of her predecessors never left, despite dying back in 1654. She was buried in a 'grave in the gutter' under a red granite slab that remains visible – and is often adorned with flowers – on the path.

Most of the neat little houses around the courtyard were modernised in the 17th and 18th centuries. In the centre stands the **Engelse Kerk** (English Reformed Church), built as a church around 1400 and given over to Scottish (no, really) Presbyterians living in the city in 1607; many became pilgrims when they decided to travel further to the New World in search of religious freedom. Now one of the principal places of worship for Amsterdam's English community, the church is worth a look primarily to see the pulpit panels, designed by a young Mondrian.

EXPLORE

Begijnhof.

Also in the courtyard is a **Catholic church**, secretly converted from two houses in 1665 following the complete banning of open Catholic worship after the Reformation. It once held the regurgitated Eucharist host that starred in the Miracle of Amsterdam, a story depicted in the church's beautiful stained-glass windows – there's an information centre next door. The wooden house at no.34, known as the **Houtenhuis**, dates from 1475 and is the oldest house still standing within the city. The Begijnhof is also very close to one of the several entrances to the **Amsterdam Museum**, which in turn is the starting point for the very informal walking tours **Mee in Mokum** (*see p53*).

The Spui square itself plays host to many markets – the most notable being the busy **book market** on Fridays – and was historically an area where the intelligentsia gathered for some serious alcohol abuse after a day's work on the local papers. The *Lieverdje*

Body Worlds: The Happiness Project. *See p78.*

(Little Darling) statue in front of the **Athenaeum Nieuwscentrum** store, a small, spindly and guano-smeared statue of a boy in goofy knee socks, was the site for wacky Provo 'happenings' that took place in the mid 1960s.

You can leave Spui by heading up Kalverstraat, Amsterdam's main shopping street, or Singel past Leidsestraat: both routes lead to the **Munttoren** (Mint Tower) at Muntplein. Just across from the **Bloemenmarkt**, the floating flower market, this medieval tower was the western corner of Regulierspoort, a gate in the city wall in the 1480s; in 1620, a spire was added by Hendrick de Keyser, the foremost architect of the period. The tower takes its name from when it minted coins after Amsterdam was cut off from its money supply during a war with England, Munster and France. There's a shop on the ground floor, **Jorrit Heinen Royal Delftware**, but the rest of the tower is closed to visitors. The Munttoren is prettiest when floodlit at night, though daytime visitors may hear its carillon, which often plays for 15 minutes at noon. From here, walk down Nieuwe Doelenstraat past the Hôtel de l'Europe (a mock-up of which featured in Hitchcock's *Foreign Correspondent*). Walk up Staalstraat and you'll end up at **Waterlooplein** (*see p142 and p146*).

Sights & Museums

★ Amsterdam Museum
Kalverstraat 92 (523 1822, www.amsterdam museum.nl). Tram 1, 2, 4, 5, 9, 14, 16, 24. **Open** 10am-5pm daily. **Admission** €11; €5-€8.25 reductions; free under-6s, IAmsterdam, MK. **No credit cards.** **Map** p58 B5 ⑬
A note to all those historical museums around the world that struggle to present their exhibits in an engaging fashion: head here to see how it's done. Amsterdam's historical museum is a gem – illuminating, interesting and entertaining. It starts with the very buildings in which it's housed: a lovely, labyrinthine collection of 17th-century constructions built on the site of a 1414 convent. You can enter it down Sint Luciensteeg, just off Kalverstraat, or off Spui, walking past the Begijnhof (*see p75*) and then through the grand Civic Guard Gallery, a small covered street hung with huge 16th- and 17th-century group portraits of wealthy burghers, as well as more modern works. And it continues with a computer-generated map of the area showing how Amsterdam has grown (and shrunk) throughout the last 800 years or so. It then takes a chronological trip through Amsterdam's past, using archaeological finds, works of art and some far quirkier displays to show the city's rise from fishing village to ecstasy capital.

NIEUWMARKT

The historic square is now a focus for festivities, markets and cafés.

The Nieuwmarkt is one of the city's oldest central squares, dominated by one of its oldest buildings, **De Waag**, whose origins may date from as long ago as 1425. Previously known as St Antoniespoort when it was part of the defensive medieval city wall, it was redubbed De Waag in the 17th century when it became the weighing hall (built in 1614) where merchants calculated the weight and subsequent value of grains and other goods arriving in Amsterdam by ship. It's easy to see why it's located here. Look north down the Geldersekade and you'll see the IJ; this canal used to be an unimpeded thoroughfare that led directly to the harbour.

De Waag has a fascinating history: while downstairs the weighing hall was bustling with trade, upstairs the city's medical guild was employed with another kind of business altogether – the cutting up of human bodies. The topmost tower was an anatomical theatre, where the city's physicians would perform dissections on executed convicts to describe to an audience of doctors, noblemen and laymen how the body functioned (or, at least, what was known at the time).

Tour guides like to tell visitors that this is where Rembrandt painted his famous group portrait, *The Anatomy Lesson of Dr Nicolaes Tulp* (1632), but that isn't strictly accurate. The tower that houses the anatomical theatre wasn't built until 1639, a full seven years after Tulp's commemorated lesson. Though there was probably a more informal dissection chamber in the building before that, Rembrandt would have painted the picture in his studio on Sint Antoniesbreestraat (*see p143* **Rembrandthuis**).

Today, the Waag is home to the Waag Society (557 9898, www.waag.org), an institute for art, science and technology, which surfs the interface between technology and culture, and organises events in the former anatomical theatre.

The market around De Waag has been a farmers' market since the city's Golden Age. It was a particularly popular trading spot for the city's Sephardic Jews, who had been migrating to this neighbourhood since the Spanish Inquisition. During World War II, the Nieuwmarkt was the site of far

De Waag

more grim business: rounding up Amsterdam's Jewish residents for deportation to the Nazi concentration camps. A popular fascist magazine, *De Waag*, was also published here.

More recently, in 1980, Nieuwmarkt was the site of riots when the city demolished housing to make way for the Metro. In 1991, it was saved by a citizens' committee from being irrevocably revamped by designer Philippe Starck.

These days, there's an outdoor market where all kinds of activities take place; on Saturdays, a farmers' market offers freshly baked artisan breads, cheeses and locally grown veg, along with antiques and crafts. There are occasional carnivals here (on Queen's Night), and on New Year's Eve it becomes detonation-central for fireworks displays. But most of the activity takes place around the square, in two dozen popular cafés and bars.

EXPLORE

Arti et Amicitiae

*Rokin 112 (623 3508, www.arti.nl). Tram
4, 9, 14, 16, 24.* **Open** noon-6pm Tue-Sun.
No credit cards. Map p58 C6 ➏
This marvellous old building houses a private
artists' society, whose initiates regularly gather in
the first-floor bar. Members of the public can climb
a Berlage-designed staircase to a large exhibition
space, home to some great temporary shows.

Body Worlds: The Happiness Project

*Damrak 66 (0900 8411 €0.45/min,
www.bodyworlds.nl). Tram 4, 9, 16, 24.*
Open 9am-6pm Mon-Wed, Sun; 9am-9pm
Thur-Sat. **Admission** €18; €12 6-18s; free
under-6s. **Map** p58 C3 ➏
People seem to love donating their bodies to be plas-
tinated for posterity. German anatomist Dr Gunther
von Hagens now has 13,000 such bodies touring the
world; since early 2014, 200 of these corpses are on
display in Amsterdam, to illustrate the relationship
between anatomy and happiness. *Photos p76.*

Koninklijk Paleis (Royal Palace)

*Dam (620 4060, info@dkh.nl for tours,
www.paleisamsterdam.nl). Tram 1, 2, 4, 5,
9, 13, 14, 16, 17, 24.* **Open** *July, Aug* 11am-
5pm daily. *Other months* varies. **Admission**
€10; €9 reductions; free under-18s, MK.
No credit cards. Map p58 B4 ➏
Designed along classical lines by Jacob van Campen
in the 17th century and built on 13,659 wooden piles
that were rammed deep into the sand, the Royal
Palace was originally built and used as Amsterdam's
city hall. The poet Constantijn Huygens hyped it as

'the world's Eighth Wonder', a monument to the
cockiness Amsterdam felt at the dawn of its Golden
Age (*see p236*). The city hall was intended as a
smugly epic 'screw you' gesture to visiting monarchs,
a subspecies of humanity the people of Amsterdam
had thus far happily done without. It was transformed into a royal palace during harder times, after
Napoleon had made his brother, Louis, King of the
Netherlands in 1808; this era can be traced through
the fine collection of furniture on display inside.

The exterior is only really impressive when
viewed from the rear, where Atlas holds his 1,000kg
(2,200lb) copper load at a great height. It's even
grander inside than out: the Citizens' Hall, with its
baroque decoration in marble and bronze that
depicts a miniature universe (with Amsterdam as its
obvious centre), is meant to make you feel about as
worthy as the rats seen carved in stone over the
Bankruptcy Chamber's door. The Palace became
state property in 1936 and the Dutch royal family
still use it when they feel the need to impress international guests.

Madame Tussaud's Scenerama

*Dam 20 (522 1010, www.madametussauds.nl).
Tram 4, 9, 14, 16, 24.* **Open** 10am-6.30pm
daily. **Admission** €22; €18 reductions; free
IAmsterdam. **Map** p58 B4 ➏
Craving some queasy kitsch factor? Waxy cheese-
textured representations from Holland's own Golden
Age of commerce are depicted alongside the Dutch
royal family, local celebs and global superstars.
Some of the models look like their subjects; some
don't. But while there's much campy fun to be had,
it comes at a price.

Koninklijk Paleis.

Madame Tussaud's Scenerama.

Nieuwe Kerk (New Church)

Dam (638 6909, www.nieuwekerk.nl). Tram 1, 2, 4, 5, 9, 16, 24. **Open** 10am-5pm daily, but hrs may vary. **Admission** €15; €5-€12 reductions; free under-6s, IAmsterdam. *Temporary exhibitions* varies. **No credit cards. Map** p58 B4 ❸

While the 'old' Oude Kerk in the Red Light District was built in the 1300s, the sprightly 'new' Nieuwe Kerk dates from 1408. It's not known how much damage was caused by the fires of 1421 and 1452, or even how much rebuilding took place, but most of the pillars and walls were erected after that time. Iconoclasm in 1566 left the church intact, though statues and altars were removed in the Reformation. The sundial on its tower was used to set the time on all the city's clocks until 1890. In 1645, the Nieuwe Kerk was gutted by the Great Fire; the ornate oak pulpit and great organ (the latter designed by Jacob van Campen) are thought to have been constructed shortly after the blaze.

Also of interest here is the tomb of naval hero Admiral de Ruyter (1607-76), who initiated the ending of the Second Anglo-Dutch war – wounding British pride in the process – when he sailed up the Medway in 1667, inspiring a witness, Sir William Batten, to observe: 'I think the Devil shits Dutchmen.' Poets and Amsterdam natives PC Hooft and Joost van den Vondel are also buried here. These days, the Nieuwe Kerk hosts organ recitals, state occasions and consistently excellent exhibitions, including World Press Photo (*see p35*).

Restaurants

★ Gartine

Taksteeg 7 (320 4132, www.gartine.nl). Tram 4, 9, 13, 14, 16, 17, 24. **Open** 8am-6pm Wed-Sun. **Main courses** €5-€20. **No credit cards. Map** p58 C6 ❽ **Tearoom**

Open only for breakfast, lunch and a full-blown high tea, Gartine is a testament to slow food, served by a friendly couple who grow their own veg and herbs in a greenhouse. Simple but marvellous.

Gebroeders Niemeijer

Nieuwendijk 35 (707 6752, www.gebroeders niemeijer.nl). Tram 1, 2, 5, 13, 17. **Open** 8.15am-6.30pm Tue-Fri; 8.30am-5pm Sat; 9am-5pm Sun. **Main courses** €4-€14. **Map** p58 B1 ❼ **Tearoom**

In stark contrast to the rest of the dingy shopping street it's on, Gebroeders Niemeijer is an artisanal French bakery and bright, light tearoom that serves breakfast and lunch. All the breads and pastries are made by hand and baked in a stone oven. Sausages come from local producers Brandt en Levie and cheeses from the city's best French cheese purveyor, Kef (Marnixstraat 192, www.kaasvankef.nl). Perfect.

Haesje Claes

Spuistraat 275 (624 9998, www.haesjeclaes.nl). Tram 1, 2, 5, 13, 17. **Open** noon-10pm daily. **Main courses** €16-€25. **Map** p58 B5 ❼ **Dutch**

In the heart of the city, between Dam Square and Spui, this beloved landmark is especially popular with tourists, though locals also come flooding in for traditional Dutch food, including *erwtensoep* (split-pea soup) and a great *stamppot* (potato mashed with greens). The service, however, is distinctly un-Dutch: friendly, available and fast. You can also order from the same menu at the utterly delightful brown bar next door at no.269, Café de Koningshut.

Kantjil & De Tijger

Spuistraat 291-293 (620 0994, www.kantjil.nl). Tram 1, 2, 5, 11. **Open** noon-11pm daily. **Rice table** €25-€32.50. **Map** p58 B6 ❼ **Indonesian**

Nieuwe Kerk.

EXPLORE

EXPLORE

For more than a quarter-century, this Jugendstil-styled brasserie has been serving well-cooked and authentic Indonesian 'rice table' (*rijsttafel* – though you can also buy à la carte). It's a good place to line one's belly before hitting the bars in the neighbourhood. For a more restrained meal costing less than a tenner, visit their nearby takeaway outlet, Kantjil To Go (Nieuwezijds Voorburgwal 342).

Société Wunderbar
Enge Kapelsteeg 3 (370 3448, www.societe wunderbar.com). Tram 14, 16, 24. **Open** 4pm-1am Tue-Thur; 4pm-3am Fri; 2pm-3am Sat; 2pm-10pm Sun. **Main courses** €20-€30. **Map** p58 C5 ⑫ Global
Wunderbar is a balancing act. It teeters between cocktail lounge and restaurant in concept, while the interior design juggles modern, vintage and industrial, and the menu covers everything from new American cuisine to Asian fusion. And it all works – especially the food. Book ahead.

Supperclub
Jonge Roelensteeg 21 (344 6400, www. supperclub.nl). Tram 1, 2, 5, 13, 17. **Open** 7.30pm-1am Mon-Thur, Sun; 7.30pm-3am Fri, Sat. **Set meal** *5 courses* €69 Mon-Wed, Sun; €90 Thur-Sat. **Main courses** (not Fri, Sat) €20. **Map** p58 B4 ⑰ Global
With its white decor, beds for seating, irreverent food combos that change weekly, and wacky acts, this arty and unique joint is casual to the point of being narcoleptic. Supperclub also has a cruise ship that trawls the local waters, as well as outposts in Dubai, Istanbul, San Francisco, LA and London.

D'Vijff Vlieghen
Spuistraat 294-302 (530 4060, www.vijff vlieghen.nl). Tram 1, 2, 5, 11. **Open** 6-10pm daily. **Main courses** €27-€32. **Set meal** €45.95 4 courses, €54.95 5 courses, €60.95 6 courses. **Map** p58 B6 ⑮ Dutch
'The Five Flies' achieves a rich Golden Age vibe – it even has a Rembrandt room, with etchings – but also works as a purveyor of over-the-top kitsch. The food is best described as poshed-up Dutch.

Bars

5&33
Martelaarsgracht 5 (820 5333, www.5and33.nl). Tram 1, 2, 4, 5, 9, 13, 16, 17, 24. **Open** 6.30am-1am Mon-Thur, Sun; 6.30am-2am Fri, Sat. **Map** p58 B1 ⑯
Red skull sculptures. Penis lamps. Projection curtains. It's very hard to do over-the-top in a tasteful and welcoming manner, but the insanely arty Art'otel (*see p283*) does just that with 5&33, its kitchen/bar/ library/lounge/art gallery, located just across from Centraal Station. Drop in for a coffee or a Horny Mule cocktail and decide how long you want to linger.

IN THE KNOW
DRINKING STRIPS

Patrol Spuistraat and Nieuwezijds Voorburgwal and you're sure to find a bar to match your mood. Starting at the north end of Spuistraat, you'll pass music venue **Bitterzoet** (no.2, *see p191*), straight-friendly gay bar **Prik** (no.109, *see p185*), arty magnet **Schuim** (no.189), squat hole **Vrankrijk** (no.216), punk hole the **Minds** (no.245), delightful 'brown bar' **Café de Koningshut** (no.269), the quite flashy **Café Dante** (no.320) — which used to be homebase for the nation's 'cuddle junkie' Herman Brood — followed by a range of choices around **Café Hoppe** (*see below*) on Spui square.

Looping back north on Nieuwezijds Voorburgwal, you'll encounter the kitsch and friendly **Café Diep** (no.256), American craft-beer joint **Beer Temple** (no.250) and charming former journo hangout **Scheltema** (no.242). OK, time for bed!

★ Belgique
Gravenstraat 2 (625 1974, www.cafe-belgique.nl). Tram 1, 2, 5, 16, 24, 25. **Open** 3pm-1am daily. **No credit cards.** **Map** p58 B3 ⑰
One of the city's smallest bars packs in eight beers on tap, plus another 50 bottled brews – mainly from neighbouring Belgium. They sometimes even manage to squeeze in an eight-piece bluegrass band. A gem of a pub, complete with dripping candles and hearty cheer.

Café de Dokter
Rozenboomsteeg 4 (626 4427, www.cafe-de-dokter.nl). Tram 1, 2, 4, 5, 9, 13, 14, 16, 17, 24. **Open** 4pm-1am Tue-Sat. **No credit cards.** **Map** p58 C6 ⑱
Definitely the smallest bar in Amsterdam at just a handful of square metres, the Doctor is also one of the oldest, dishing out the cure for whatever ails you since 1798. Centuries of character and all kinds of gewgaws are packed into the extremely compact space. Whisky figures large (there's a monthly special) and snacks include smoked *osseworst* (cured sausage) with gherkins. If it's too cosy, then head one block north to the similarly old-school De Engelse Reet (Begijnensteeg 4, 623 1777).

Café Hoppe
Spui 18-20 (420 4420, www.cafe-hoppe.nl). Tram 1, 2, 5, 9, 14, 16, 24. **Open** 8am-1am Mon-Thur, Sun; 8am-2am Fri, Sat. **Map** p58 B6 ⑱
The bon-vivant beer magnate Freddy Heineken (1923-2002) spent so much time in this ancient, woody watering hole that he ended up buying it.

What appealed to Fred most about the place is that it catered to everyone, from students wanting a cheap *biertje* through tourists enjoying the terrace to suits stopping by after work. And nothing much has changed. If you want something more evocative of a classic Parisian brasserie, try handsome Café Luxembourg next door.

★ Vleminckx

Voetboogsteeg 33 (624 6075, http://vleminckx desausmeester.nl). Tram 1, 2, 5. **Open** noon-7pm Mon, Sun; 11am-7pm Tue, Wed, Fri, Sat; 11am-9pm Thur. **No credit cards. Map** p58 C6 ③⓪
Chunky Belgian chips served with your choice of toppings. Opt for the *oorlog* ('war') version, where your chips are accompanied by a spicy peanut sauce, mayo and onions.

Coffeeshops

Abraxas

Jonge Roelensteeg 12-14 (625 5763). Tram 4, 9, 14, 16, 24. **Open** 10am-1am daily.
No credit cards. Map p58 B4 ③①
Located down a narrow alley, this lively shop is a tourist hotspot. Staff are friendly, the internet connection is free and chessboards are plentiful – as are the separate rooms connected by spiral staircases. It also has a healthy-sized drug menu, including half a dozen bio weeds and spacecakes.

De Dampkring

Handboogstraat 29 (638 0705). Tram 1, 2, 5. **Open** 10am-1am Mon-Thur; 10am-2am Fri, Sat; 11am-1am Sun. **No credit cards. Map** p58 C6 ③②

Known for its unforgettable (even by stoner standards) interior, the visual experience acquired from Dampkring's decor could make a mushroom trip look grey. Moulded walls and sculpted ceilings are painted deep auburn and laced with caramel-coloured wooden panelling – which made it the perfect location for the movie *Ocean's 12*. Equally trippy is the Dampkring Gallery (*see p99*).

Tweede Kamer

Heisteeg 6 (422 2236). Tram 1, 2, 5. **Open** 10am-1am Mon-Thur, Sun; 10am-2am Fri, Sat. **No credit cards. Map** p58 B6 ③③
Small and intimate, this sister shop of De Dampkring (*see left*) embodies the refined look and feel of old-jazz sophistication. Aided by a bakery around the corner, the spacecakes are sweet and lovely. The hash is highly regarded, but seating is extremely limited and the place is notorious for getting very crowded at peak times. If there's no room at Tweede Kamer, walk a dozen steps to Dutch Flowers (Singel 382, 624 7624).

Shops & Services

Albert Heijn

Nieuwezijds Voorburgwal 226 (421 8344, www.ah.nl). Tram 1, 2, 4, 5, 9, 13, 14, 16, 17, 24. **Open** 8am-10pm daily. **No credit cards. Map** p58 B4 ③④ **Food & drink**
The Dutch have a very close relationship with this, their biggest supermarket brand. The monopoly it holds on the city means you're always within a stone's throw of a 'Bertie': be it a regular store, an 'AH XL', or small 'AH To Go'.
Other locations throughout the city.

EXPLORE

5&33.

★ American Book Center

Spui 12 (625 5537, www.abc.nl). Tram 1, 2, 4, 5, 9, 14, 16, 24. **Open** noon-8pm Mon; 10am-8pm Tue, Wed, Fri, Sat; 10am-9pm Thur; 11am-6.30pm Sun. **Map** p58 C6 ⑤ **Books & music**

An Amsterdam institution since 1972, the American Book Center sells English-language books and magazines from the US and UK.

★ Athenaeum Nieuwscentrum

Spui 14-16 (bookshop 514 1460, news centre 514 1470, www.athenaeum.nl). Tram 1, 2, 4, 5, 9, 14, 16, 24. **Open** *Bookshop* 11am-6pm Mon; 9.30am-6pm Tue, Wed; 9.30am-9pm Thur; 9.30am-6.30pm Fri, Sat; noon-5.30pm Sun. *News centre* 8am-8pm Mon-Wed, Fri, Sat; 8am-9pm Thur; 10am-6pm Sun. **Map** p58 B6 ⑥ **Books & music**

The Athenaeum Nieuwscentrum stocks newspapers from all over the world, plus a wide choice of magazines, periodicals and tomes in many languages.

De Bierkoning

Paleisstraat 125 (625 2336, www.bierkoning.nl). Tram 1, 2, 5, 13, 14, 16, 17, 24. **Open** 11am-7pm Mon-Sat; 1-6pm Sun. **Map** p58 B4 ⑦ **Food & drink**

Named in honour of its location behind the Royal Palace, the 'Beer King' stocks a head-spinning 1,200 brands of beer from around the world, and a range of fine glasses to sup from.

Athenaeum Nieuwscentrum.

Bij Ons Vintage

Nieuwezijds Voorburgwal 150 (06 1187 1278 mobile, www.bijons-vintage.nl). Tram 1, 2, 5, 13, 14, 17. **Open** noon-7pm Mon; 11am-7pm Tue, Wed; 10am-9pm Thur; 10am-8pm Fri, Sat; noon-8pm Sun. **No credit cards**. **Map** p58 B3 ⑥ **Fashion**

This place is rammed with leather jackets, woollen hats, old Polaroid cameras and even some authentic 1960s ottomans. There's so much random gear here that you'll be struck with bargain-hunting fever. **Other location** Reestraat 13, Western Canal Belt.

★ Book Market at the Spui

Spui (no phone, www.deboekenmarktophetspui.nl). Tram 1, 2, 4, 5, 9, 13, 14, 16, 24. **Open** 10am-6pm Fri. **Map** p58 C6 ⑥ **Market**

Every Friday, the Spui square is filled with over 25 antiquarian booksellers covering all subjects and languages – it's a browser's paradise.

Concrete Image Store

Spuistraat 250 (625 2225, www.concrete.nl). Tram 1, 2, 5, 13, 14, 17. **Open** noon-7pm Mon-Wed, Fri, Sat; noon-9pm Thur; 1-6pm Sun. **Map** p58 B5 ⑥ **Gallery**

This shop/gallery's concept is more loose and humorous than rigidly concrete: a cross-fertilisation of street fashion, artist-made dolls, limited-edition shoes and exhibitions of photography and graphic design.

Copa Football Store

Prins Hendrikkade 20-B (620 1660, www.copa football.com). Tram 1, 2, 4, 5, 9, 13, 16, 17, 24. **Open** 11am-7pm Mon-Fri; 10am-6pm Sat; noon-6pm Sun. **Map** p58 B1 ⑥ **Gifts & souvenirs**

What happens when a footie obsessive starts a shop? He brings together an expanse of retro shirts, recycled bags, designer footballs, books, DVDs and even some functional football wear. Out front, he also parks his vintage Vespa covered with over 1,000 World Cup stickers. And he installs a special football chapel 'for those who have something to confess.'

Female & Partners

Spuistraat 100 (620 9152, www.femaleand partners.nl). Tram 1, 2, 5, 13, 17. **Open** 1-6.30pm Mon; 11am-6.30pm Tue, Wed, Fri; 11am-9pm Thur; 11am-6pm Sat; 1-6pm Sun. **Map** p58 A3 ⑥ **Sex shop**

It's fair to say that, in terms of the sex industry at least, Amsterdam is still predominantly a man's world. Female & Partners bucks the trend by welcoming women (and, yes, their partners) with an array of clothes, videos and toys.

Hay Amsterdam

Spuistraat 281 (370 8851, www.hay-amsterdam. com). Tram 4, 9, 14, 16, 24. **Open** noon-7pm Mon; 10am-7pm Tue-Fri; 10am-8pm Sat; noon-6pm Sun. **Map** p58 B6 ⑥ **Homewares**

THE BROWN STUFF

There's a new kind of coffeeshop – think bean, not weed.

Screaming Beans.

The Dutch played a fundamental role in establishing the global coffee market. In 1690, a cheeky Dutchman plucked away the coffee monopoly from the Arabs by smuggling a coffee plant out of Mocha, Yemen. It ended up in Amsterdam's **Hortus Botanicus** (*see p148*), where descendants of the original *Arabica* plant still survive. Some clones went off to Dutch colonies in Sumatra, Java, Ceylon (now Sri Lanka) and Suriname, where they flourished.

Now, more than three centuries later, Amsterdam is regaining its status as a java hub. The city is home to the European headquarters of Starbucks, although the US giant has so far been held in check by the ubiquitous local franchise, the Coffee Company. But it's the independent coffee houses – run by caffeine obsessives and popping up all over the place – that have added new-found energy and interest to the city's café scene.

Screaming Beans was one of the first to roast its own beans, at its Original Coffee Bar (Hartenstraat 12, 626 0966, www.screamingbeans.nl). A second location (1e Constantijn Huygensstraat 35, 616 0770) broadened the firm's repertoire to include highly rated French wines and cuisine. The two branches of **Two For Joy** (Frederiksplein 29, 330 6735; Haarlemmerdijk 182, 221 9552; www.two forjoy.nl) are more reminiscent of London coffeeshops, with their relaxed and international vibe, and wide choice of beans and techniques (filter, drip, Aeropress).

Espresso Fabriek provides a focal point for local baristas with its monthly Friday Night Bean Battle at its main location at the Westergasfabriek (Gosschalklaan 7, 486 2106, www.espressofabriek.nl).

Coffeeheads come to talk shop and admire the state-of-the-art equipment, a 3-group Kees van der Westen lever machine.

Located in the heart of the Red Light District, **KOKO Coffee & Design** (Oudezijds Achterburgwal 145, 626 4208, www.ilovekoko.com) combines coffee with art, design, retro furniture and quality browsing magazines. It is also worth a trip to Jordaan, for the Arabica Yellow Bourban coffee served at Brazilian lunch café **Cafezinho** (Tweede Laurierdwarsstraat 50, 221 9040, www.cafezinho.moonfruit.com). Those beans have travelled far, indeed – but now they're coming home to roast.

KOKO Coffee & Design.

EXPLORE

EXPLORE

PUBLIC RELIEF

Amsterdam's cutting-edge pissing policies.

Designers the world over have long watched how Amsterdam deals with public urination. After all, Schiphol Airport was the first to introduce the fly sticker on urinals, which gave men something to aim at, thereby keeping their stream more contained.

Back in 1998, 'wild pissing' – blokes pissing willy-nilly wherever – replaced dogshit as the population's main 'small grievance' in polls. Politicians began talking about the 'watering down' of civilisation's norms, and research by Amsterdam city council discovered that urine contamination had reached depths of between one and two metres in certain hotspots. Even more alarming in a city where the sparse number of ornate, bright green, cast-iron 19th-century public urinals are listed as monuments, some historical buildings were slowly getting slashed away through urine erosion. 'Wild Pissing Symposiums' (really, no shit) were held and 'A Plan of Action: Wild Pissing (1998-2005)' was formulated. Suggested solutions ranged from the distribution of stench-munching microbes to the employment of artists in designing self-cleaning piss-bowls.

The initial phase called for the obvious: implementing a €50 fine to those caught wild pissing. They also recommended the erection of more public toilets and a return to the 'Golden Age of the Urinoir', which ended in 1960 when the city fathers started to order their mass removal, suspiciously enough just as comprehensive maps of their locations and ratings began to appear in gay guidebooks to Amsterdam. As if to discourage such diligent charting, the new millennial urinal – the four-bowls-in-one, moulded grey plastic 'Rocket' – was chosen for its open design and ease of mobility, making it handy for use at festivals or over busy weekends. Some more high-tech 'Uri-liften' were permanently installed in the city's main nightlife squares – they rise as if by magic out of the ground on weekend nights.

A topic that gets consistently passed over is the age-old question of pissing rights for women. The sanisette – the French toilet cubicle that is already part of Paris's streetscape (and folklore, as stories circulate of children getting trapped in its overly enthusiastic self-cleaning system) –

was considered too expensive for mass implementation in Amsterdam.

But then market forces came to the rescue. The worldwide 'Where to Wee' app (www.wheretoweeapp.com), for example, can handily guide you to the nearest city public washroom. Then there's 2theloo (www.2theloo.com), which set up a 'restroom shop' on the pedestrianised shopping strip Kalverstraat (at no.126). You pay in coins and get a voucher for the same price to spend in partnered businesses. Some of the toilets even offer epic views.

Taking another approach, local artist Giny Vos created an installation piece, *The White Cube*, in a smelly alley, Nieuwezijds Armsteeg, which features a lit perspective-drawing of the living spaces behind the wall. It was meant to force pissers to show some respect for their environment. The alley still stinks. More effective, perhaps, are the slanted aluminium 'pee deflectors' placed in the corners of some alleys to bounce the piss back on to the pisser.

The latest in wee-inspired genius? The local water utility just began experimenting with harvesting pee from public urinals to use as fertiliser on the city's green roofs.

Inspired by the heyday of Scandinavian design in the 1950s and '60s, this Danish outfit offers modern and innovative furniture and home accessories – including designs by the Netherlands' own Scholten & Baijings. They also serve great coffee.

★ Hema
Kalverstraat 212 (422 8988, www.hema.nl). Tram 1, 2, 4, 5, 9, 13, 14, 16, 17, 24. **Open** 9am-7pm Mon-Wed, Fri, Sat; 9am-9pm Thur; 11am-6.30pm Sun. **Map** p58 C6 🞤 **Gifts & souvenirs**
A much-loved high-street institution, Hema is the place to check out when you need just about anything – clothes, towels, notebooks, soap dispensers, ring binders, those little bike lights – you name it.

Hemp Works
Nieuwendijk 13 (421 1762, www.hempworks.nl). Tram 1, 2, 5, 13, 17. **Open** 11am-7pm Mon-Wed, Sun; 11am-9pm Thur-Sat. **Map** p58 B1 🞥 **Fashion**
One of the first shops in Amsterdam to sell hemp clothes and products, and now one of the last, Hemp Works has had to diversify into seed sales; it's also been a Cannabis Cup-winner for its strain of the stinky weed.

Jorrit Heinen Royal Delftware
Muntplein 12 (623 2271, www.jorritheinen.com). Tram 4, 9, 16, 24, 25. **Open** 9.30am-6pm Mon-Sat; 11am-6pm Sun. **Map** p58 D6 🞦 **Homewares**
Souvenirs with provenance. Jorrit Heinen is an official dealer for Royal Delft and Makkum pottery, the bread and butter of the Dutch antiques trade. The stock here includes antiques too, with some pieces dating from the 17th century – for a price, of course.

Mark Raven
Nieuwezijds Voorburgwal 174 (330 0800, www.markraven.nl). Tram 1, 2, 5, 13, 14, 17. **Open** 10.30am-6pm daily. **Map** p58 A4 🞧 **Gifts & souvenirs**
This eponymously named artistic hub sells Raven's etchings in many guises – from canvases to T-shirts.

Marks & Spencer
Kalverstraat 226 (330 0080, www.marksandspencer.nl). Tram 4, 9, 14, 16, 24. **Open** 9am-7pm Mon-Wed, Fri, Sat; 9am-9pm Thur; noon-6pm Sun. **Map** p58 D6 🞨 **Department store**
After more than a decade's absence, the British food and clothing chain returned to Amsterdam in 2013 to a glowing response: the aisles were packed and within hours the sausages and crumpets had sold out. It was the talk of the expat town for weeks. Now it even looks like they might move to a larger location in 2015. So if you have an urge for some pre-packaged meals featuring the Brits' national food – Indian – or just feel it's time for some fresh underwear, look no further.

PGC Hajenius
Rokin 96 (623 7494, www.hajenius.com). Tram 4, 9, 14, 16, 24. **Open** noon-6pm Mon; 9.30am-6pm Tue-Sat; noon-5pm Sun. **Map** p58 C5 🞩 **Gifts & souvenirs**
A smoker's paradise (tobacco, not dope) for over 250 years, Hajenius offers cigarabilia from traditional Dutch pipes to own-brand cigars.

Postzegelmarkt
Nieuwezijds Voorburgwal, by no.280 (no phone). Tram 1, 2, 5, 13, 17. **Open** 10am-4pm Wed, Sat. **No credit cards. Map** p58 B5 🞪 **Market**
A specialist market for collectors of stamps, coins, postcards and commemorative medals.

Rituals
Kalverstraat 73 (344 9220, www.rituals.com). Tram 4, 9, 14, 16, 24. **Open** noon-6pm Mon, Sun; 10am-6pm Tue, Wed, Fri, Sat; 10am-9pm Thur. **Map** p58 C5 🞫 **Health & beauty**
A store integrating products for body and home. We all have to brush our teeth and do the dishes, so the shop is full of products to ritualise such daily grinds. **Other location** Leidsestraat 62, Southern Canal Belt (625 2311).

V&D
Kalverstraat 212-220 (0900 235 8363 €0.18/min, www.vd.nl). Tram 4, 9, 14, 16, 24. **Open** noon-7.30pm Mon; 10am-7.30pm Tue, Wed; 10am-9pm Thur; 10am-8pm Fri, Sat; noon-7pm Sun. **Map** p58 C6 🞬 **Department store**
V&D (short for Vroom & Dreesmann) mirrors the Dutch attitude: unpretentious and to the point. A national stalwart, this affordable chain store offers a little bit of something for everyone, be it a €35 frock or a €2 spatula. Its (usually heaving) La Place restaurant serves a range of organic treats.

Waterstones
Kalverstraat 152 (638 3821, www.waterstones.com). Tram 1, 2, 4, 5, 9, 14, 16, 24. **Open** 10am-6pm Mon; 9.30am-6.30pm Tue, Wed, Fri; 9.30am-9pm Thur; 10am- 6.30pm Sat; 11am-6pm Sun. **Map** p58 C6 🞭 **Books & music**
Thousands of books – mainstream and literary – plus newspapers, magazines, audio books, games and DVDs, all in English. The large children's section is delightful.
▶ *For details of book readings for kids, see p171.*

Weekday
Rokin 84 (623 0018, http://shop.weekday.com). Tram 14, 16, 24. **Open** noon-6.30pm Mon; 10am-6.30pm Tue, Wed, Fri, Sat; 10am-9pm Thur; noon-6pm Sun. **Map** p58 C5 🞮 **Fashion**
This glam former home of Dutch royalty was renovated using low-cost materials by this progressive yet affordable Swedish fashion retailer to sell its savvy selection of jeans and clothing for men and women.

EXPLORE

The Canals

EXPLORE

God may have made the water, but you can thank man for the canals. Keeping the sea and surrounding bog at bay are Amsterdam's 165 *grachten* (canals). Crossed by 1,400 bridges, they stretch for more than 75 kilometres (47 miles) around the city, and are, on average, three metres (ten feet) deep. The major canals and their radial streets are where the real city exists. What they lack in sights, they make up for with places for scenic coffee-slurping, quirky shopping, aimless walks and a spot of meditative gable-gazing.

Declared a UNESCO World Heritage Site in 2010, the *grachtengordel* (girdle, or belt, of canals) rings the centre of town, its waterways providing an attractive border between the tourist-laden centre and the gentler, artier, more 'local' outskirts. Here, we've grouped them into the Western Canal Belt and the Southern Canal Belt, which is, in fact, the order in which they were originally built.

Foam.

Don't Miss

1 Anne Frank Huis Insight into a personal and national history (p92).

2 Foam A photography museum worth snapping at (p104).

3 Stadsarchief Amsterdam The city's archives in a mystical building (p105).

4 Pathé Tuschinski Cinema Eye-melting castle to celluloid (p103).

5 Paradiso The world's premier 'pop temple' (p102).

From 1600 to 1650, during Amsterdam's Golden Age, the city's population ballooned four-fold, and it was obliged to expand once again. Construction began on the **Singel**, the city's original moat, and on the *grachtengordel* circling the city centre, the most elegant of the major canals. **Herengracht** (Lords' Canal) was where many of the ruling assembly had their homes. So that there would be no misunderstanding about status, Herengracht was followed further out by **Keizersgracht** (Emperors' Canal) and **Prinsengracht** (Princes' Canal). Immigrants were housed in the Jordaan.

When the canal belt was declared a UNESCO World Heritage Site, locals began to worry that Amsterdam might meet the same fate as Venice or Bruges, where tourism seems to dominate any other cultural character. However, excepting increased hordes of badly biking tourists, the vibe remains pretty much the same – whether it's during Gay Pride, the classical Canal Festival or the perhaps ill-advised annual Amsterdam City Swim. Indeed – while the waters look pretty, you're best advised to wash yourself in your hotel room. Otherwise, just enjoy the views…

CANAL CRUISING

Explore the city by water.

Stichting Battello.

During a sojourn in the city, Hans Christian Andersen wrote, 'The view from my window, through the elms to the canal outside, is like a fairy tale.' Canals are what people imagine when they think of 'Amsterdam', and they continue to enchant visitors today. Like any other city built on water, Amsterdam is best seen from a boat.

The tourist boats provide a doughty service, but they can't squeeze into the narrower waterways. Self-piloted hire boats are few and far between – in fact, only two outfits provide these: **Canal Motorboats** (Zandhoek 10A, 422 7007, www.canal motorboats.com) on Realeneiland; and **Boaty** (Jozef Israëlkade, between Ferdinand Bolstraat & 2e Van der Helststraat, 06 2714 9493 mobile, www.boaty.nl, closed in winter) on a dock outside Hotel Okura in De Pijp, which rents only silent electric motor boats. Boats from both firms have a capacity of six. If these don't suit, befriend a boating local or charter a tour.

Amsterdam also has its own gondola service, **Stichting Battello** (686 9868, 06 4746 4545 mobile, www.gondel.nl), and it's suitably unique. Not only will you glide silently along at an angle that reveals this city at its more picturesque, you'll also be chauffeured by one of two Guinness World Record holders: Hans, 'the tallest gondolier in the world', and Tirza, 'the only woman gondolier in the world'.

Such a ride will cost a group of up to six people around €140 an hour. You can bring along your own food or drink, or ask them to arrange refreshments for a reasonable price. The standard course is around the Jordaan, but you are welcome to stipulate your own route should you desire.

EXPLORE

The builders completed the Western Belt before finishing the grander Southern Belt. For ease of use, we also split our listings into these two sections. But when walking about, it's probably easier to just take it one canal at a time – after all, it's very easy to lose your sense of direction in such a circular town.

WESTERN CANAL BELT

Singel

One of the few clues to Singel's past as the protective moat that surrounds the city's wall is the **Torensluis** (Tower Gate) bridge that crosses it at Oude Leliestraat. It did indeed once have a lookout tower, and the space underneath was supposedly used as a lock-up for medieval drunks – but now it's home to very occasional art exhibitions and jazz nights (check the agenda at www.brug9.nl). On the bridge itself, a statue of the 19th-century writer Multatuli depicts his head forming as smoke from a bottle – a reference to the way he let the genie out of the bottle by questioning Dutch imperialism in such novels as *Max Havelaar* (1860). You can learn more about him at the nearby **Multatuli Museum**.

While you're wandering this canal, you may wish to contribute to the debate as to whether Singel 7 or Singel 166 is the smallest house in Amsterdam. In between, opposite Singel 38, is the Poezenboot ('Cat Boat', www.poezenboot.nl), an asylum for orphaned pussy cats. Always good for a snort is the **House with Noses** at Singel 116, although arty types might be a bit more interested in Singel 140-142. This was once the home of Banning Cocq, the principal figure of Rembrandt's *The Night Watch* (*see p131*). Further south, you'll find the town's poshest old-school sex club, **Yab Yum** (Singel 295, 624 9503, www.yabyum.com), which is now a museum where you can relive that glittery past when champagne flowed and décolletés were low.

The Canals

Starting at the western end of Herengracht, you'll reach a Vingboons building dating from 1638 at no.168, along with the architectural gem that is De Keyser's **Bartolotti House** (Herengracht 170-172, www.hendrickde keyser.nl). At Herengracht 366 is the **Bijbels Museum**. A few doors further south is the **Netherlands Institute of War, Holocaust & Genocide Studies** (Herengracht 380, 523 3800, www.niod.nl). This copy of a Loire mansion contains three kilometres of archives that include Anne Frank's diary, donated by her father Otto. For gentler thoughts, visit the

Felix Meritis Building.

Kattenkabinet (Cat Cabinet, Herengracht 297, 626 5378, www.kattenkabineet.nl).

Walking down Keizersgracht, you'll soon come to the **House with the Heads** (no.123), a pure Dutch Renaissance classic. The official story has these finely chiselled heads representing classical gods, but according to local folklore they are the heads of burglars, chopped off by a lusty maidservant. She decapitated six and married the seventh. Another true classic is at Keizersgracht 174, an art nouveau masterpiece by Gerrit van Arkels. A few paces down are the pink granite triangular slabs of the **Homomonument**, the world's first memorial to persecuted gays and lesbians.

Another key edifice is the **Felix Meritis Building** (Keizersgracht 324, www.felix. meritis.nl), a neoclassical monolith with the motto 'Happiness through merit' chiselled over its door. Nowadays, it's the European Centre for Art & Science and suffering an uncertain future due to subsidy cuts. Nearby is the equally epic home of the photography foundation **Huis Marseille**. This whole stretch was also the site of the legendary 'slipper parade', where the posh-footed rich strolled about every Sunday both to see and be seen. These days, those in the fashion know spend their time (and cash) in the surrounding stylish De 9 Straatjes (Nine Streets) – *see p97* **Dressed to the Nines**.

Named after William, Prince of Orange, Prinsengracht is the most charming of the canals, splitting as it does the posh ring from the more funky Jordaan. Pompous façades have been mellowed with shady trees, cosy cafés and

EXPLORE

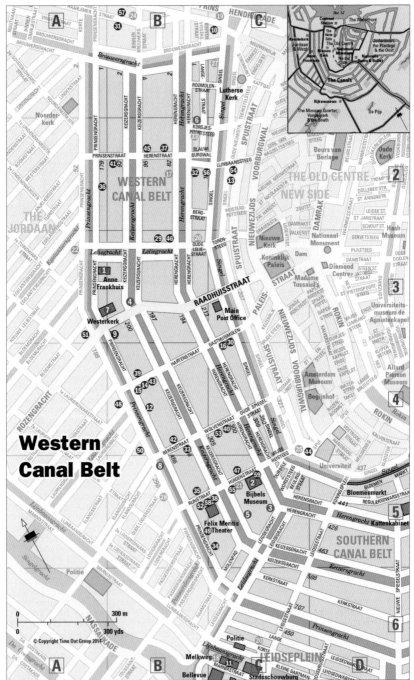

EXPLORE

Western Canal Belt

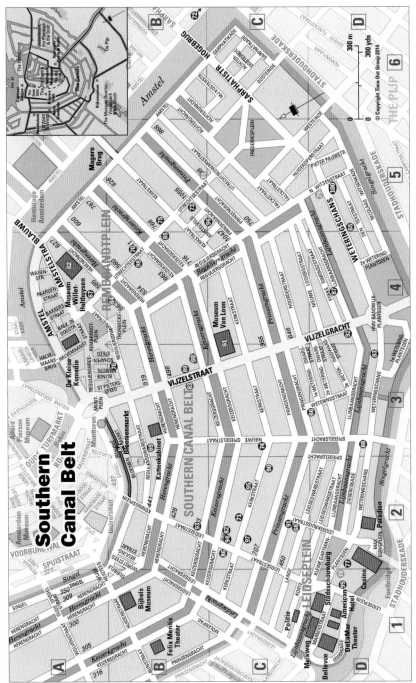

EXPLORE

some of Amsterdam's hipper houseboats. If you find yourself at the weekly **Noordermarkt** (*see p122*) or **Boerenmarkt** (*see p121*) in the Jordaan, then make sure you stop for coffee at the ever-popular **Papeneiland** (*see p121*). According to local legend, a tunnel used to run under the canal from here to a Catholic church located at Prinsengracht 7 at the time of the Protestant uprising.

On your way up Prinsengracht, you'll pass the **Anne Frank Huis** and the almost 400-year-old **Westerkerk**. Mari Andriessen's 1977 statue of Anne Frank stands nearby, at the corner with Westermarkt. Meanwhile, René Descartes fans – and if you think, therefore you probably are – can pay tribute to the great savant by casting an eye on his former house (Westermarkt 6). Further south is the **Woonboot Museum**.

Sights & Museums

★ Anne Frank Huis

*Prinsengracht 267 (556 7105, www.annefrank.nl).
Tram 13, 14, 17.* **Open** *July, Aug* 9am-10pm daily. *Apr-June, Sept, Oct* 9am-9pm Mon-Fri, Sun; 9am-10pm Sat. *Nov-Mar* 9am-7pm Mon-Fri, Sun; 9am-9pm Sat. **Admission** €9; €4.50 reductions; free under-9s, MK. **Map** p90 A3 ➊

During World War II, the young Jewish diarist Anne Frank and her family hid for two years behind a bookcase in the back annexe of this 17th-century canal house. On 4 August 1944, the occupants were arrested and transported to concentration camps, where Anne died with her sister Margot and their mother. Her father, Otto, survived, and decided that Anne's diary should be published. The rest is history: Anne's dream of becoming a best-selling author was fulfilled, with tens of millions of copies having since been printed in 70 languages. Today, more than a million visitors a year come to witness these sober unfurnished rooms. A new wing not only tells the story of Anne's family and the persecution of Jews, but also presents the difficulties of fighting discrimination of all types. Book ahead online to avoid the queues.

Bijbels Museum (Bible Museum)

*Herengracht 366 (624 2436, www.bijbels
museum.nl). Tram 1, 2, 5.* **Open** 10am-5pm Tue-Sat; 11am-5pm Sun. **Admission** €8; €4 reductions; free under-13s, IAmsterdam, MK.
No credit cards. Map p90 C5 ➋

Housed in a restored 17th-century Vingboons canal house, this museum aims to illustrate life and worship with archaeological finds, models of ancient temples and a splendid collection of Bibles from several centuries (including a rhyming Bible from 1271). You can also admire the splendid Jacob de Wit paintings, and the grand garden with biblical plants and a sculpture entitled *Apocalypse*.

Anne Frank Huis.

Het Grachtenhuis (Museum of the Canals)

*Herengracht 386 (421 1656, www.het
grachtenhuis.nl). Tram 1, 2, 5.* **Open** 10am-5pm Tue-Sun. **Admisssion** €12; €6 reductions; free under-5s, IAmsterdam. **Map** p90 C5 ➌

The building of Amsterdam's Canal Belt during the 17th-century Golden Age was one of the more ambitious urban expansion projects of all time. You get the full story through displays and an interactive 40-minute multimedia presentation.

Homomonument

*Westermarkt (no phone, www.homomonument.nl).
Tram 13, 14, 17.* **Map** p90 B3 ➍

Unveiled in 1987, Karin Daan's three-sectioned pink triangular monument to the memory of persecuted gays and lesbians was a world first. Flowers are often left on it for personal remembrance, especially during significant gatherings such as on World AIDS Day. For more information on gay and lesbian life in Amsterdam, visit the nearby Pink Point (www.pinkpoint.org) stall on Westermarkt. *See also pp180-189* **Gay & Lesbian**.

EXPLORE

Huis Marseille

Keizersgracht 401 (531 8989, www.huis marseille.nl). Tram 1, 2, 5. **Open** 11am-5pm Tue-Sun. **Admission** €8; €4 reductions; free under-17s, IAmsterdam, MK. **No credit cards. Map** p90 C5 ❺

The walls of this photography foundation might host the latest from contemporary hotshots such as Hellen van Meene, Guido Guidi or Naoya Hatakeyama; classic work by Bernd and Hilla Becher; or an overview of Rob Hornstra's impressive 'The Sochi Project'. Don't miss the DVDs and magazines in the 'media kitchen'.

FREE Multatuli Museum

Korsjespoortsteeg 20 (638 1938, www.multatuli museum.nl). Tram 1, 2, 5, 13, 17. **Open** 10am-5pm Tue; noon-5pm Sat, Sun; also by appt. **Admission** free. **Map** p90 B2 ❻

Just off Singel, this museum is dedicated to the satirical and anti-colonialist writer Eduard Douwes-Dekker (1820-87), aka Multatuli (meaning 'I have suffered much' in Latin), set in the house where he was born. The various literary artefacts pay testament to his credo: 'the human calling is to be human.' There's also a small library.

Westerkerk

Prinsengracht 277-279 (624 7766, tower 689 2565, www.westerkerk.nl). Tram 13, 14, 17. **Open** 10am-3pm Mon-Fri; 11am-3pm Sat. *Services* 10.30am Sun. **Admission** *Tower* €7.50. **No credit cards. Map** p90 A3 ❼

Before noise pollution, it was said that if you heard the bells of Westerkerk's tower, dating from 1631, you were in the Jordaan. The tower also offers a great view of this neighbourhood, provided you don't suffer from vertigo: the 85m (278ft) structure sways by 3cm (1.2in) in a good wind. The tower is emblazoned with a gaudy red, blue and gold 'XXX' crown; this was granted to the city in 1489 by the Holy Roman Emperor Maximillian in gratitude for treatment he received during a pilgrimage to Amsterdam. The triple-X came to be used by local traders – and later by local pornographers – to denote quality, and is now featured on the city's flag and coat of arms. It's thought that Rembrandt is buried in the church itself, although no one is quite sure where: Rembrandt died a pauper, and, as a result, is commemorated inside the building with a simple plaque. If queues for the tower are long, you can also enjoy expansive views

IN THE KNOW WHAT ARE YOU WAITING FOR?

To avoid the long queues at **Anne Frank Huis** (*see p92*), arrive first thing in the morning, after 7pm (in summer) or buy tickets online for a specified time slot.

at the Zuidertoren or the Ouderkerkstoren, which are both handled by the same office. Check the concert listings too. *Photo p94.*

Woonboot Museum

Prinsengracht, opposite no.296 (427 0750, www.houseboatmuseum.nl). Tram 13, 14, 17. **Open** *Mar-Oct* 11am-5pm Tue-Sun. *Nov-Feb* 11am-5pm Fri-Sun. Closed last 2wks Jan. **Admission** €3.75; €3 reductions, IAmsterdam. **No credit cards. Map** p90 B5 ❽

Aside from some discreet explanatory panels, a small slide show and a ticket clerk, the Hendrika Maria Houseboat Museum is laid out as a houseboat would be, to help visitors imagine what it's like to live on the water. It's more spacious than you might expect and does a good job of selling the lifestyle afforded by its unique comforts.

Restaurants

Bistro Bij Ons

Prinsengracht 287 (627 9016, www.bistro bijons.nl). Tram 13, 14, 17. **Open** noon-10.30pm Tue-Sun. **Main courses** €13.50-€18. **Map** p90 B3 ❾ **Dutch**

In the shadow of the Westerkerk, right near the Jordaan, two archetypal Amsterdam hostesses serve typical Dutch fare (think vegetable soup with meatballs, grandma's traditional *stamppot* mash, and warm apple pie) in a canal house restaurant with a living room vibe and watery views. A fun night out at a friendly price.

Bistrot Neuf

Haarlemmerstraat 9 (400 3210, www.bistrot neuf.nl). Tram 1, 2, 4, 5, 9, 13, 17, 24. **Open** noon-11pm daily. **Main courses** lunch €18-€22.50, dinner €25-€27.50. **Set meal** lunch €25 3 courses, dinner €44.50 3 courses. **Map** p90 C1 ❿ **French**

This elegantly designed bistro serves French cuisine alongside an extensive and well-thought-out wine list – the selection includes over 20 reasonably priced by-the-glass options for reds alone. The à la carte menu offers classics such as escargots in parsley and garlic butter, and other European dishes with a twist, such as duck with elderberry sauce. Finish with chocolate fondant or crème brûlée.

€ Eat at Jo's

Marnixstraat 409 (638 3336). Tram 1, 2, 5, 7, 10. **Open** noon-9pm Wed-Sun. **Main courses** €13-€15. **No credit cards. Map** p90 C6 ⓫ **Global**

Each day brings a different fish, meat and vegetarian dish to the menu of this cheap and tasty international kitchen. Star-spotters take note: whichever act is booked to play in the adjoining Melkweg (*see p192 and p197*) may very well chow down here beforehand, so keep your eyes peeled and autograph books to hand.

EXPLORE

Westerkerk. See p93.

Envy
Prinsengracht 381 (344 6407, www.envy.nl).
Tram 13, 14, 17. **Open** noon-3pm, 6-11pm daily.
Set meal €45 4 courses, €52.50 5 courses.
Map p90 B4 ⑫ **Italian**
A designer deli-cum-restaurant serving an arsenal of delicacies, which emerge from the streamlined refrigerators that line the walls, and from the able kitchen staff. The perfect place for those times when you want to try a bit of everything. A few doors down is sister establishment Vyne (Prinsengracht 411, 344 6408, www.vyne.nl), which is more of a wine bar, with a menu of quality nibbles.

★ € Greenwoods
Singel 103 (623 7071, www.greenwoods.eu).
Tram 1, 2, 5. **Open** 9.30am-5pm Mon-Thur;
9.30am-6pm Fri-Sun. **Main courses** €5-€10.
No credit cards. Map p90 C2 ⑬ **Café**
Service at this teashop is friendly but can be slow. Everything is freshly made, though – cakes, scones and muffins are baked daily on the premises – so it's understandable. In summer, sit on the terrace by the canal for the ultimate alfresco eating experience.
Other location Keizersgracht 465, Southern Canal Belt (420 4330).

Hartenkaas
Reestraat 19 (626 5271, www.hartenkaas.nl).
Tram 1, 2, 5. **Open** 9am-4pm daily.
Sandwiches €4.80. **No credit cards.**
Map p90 B4 ⑭ **Sandwiches**
This takeaway shop rates its sandwiches as the best in the city, and aside from its cockiness, the claim is close to the truth. A mere €4.80 and an ability to

choose from dozens of different toppings and tasty combinations is all you need for a hearty lunch while patrolling the Nine Streets shopping area.

★ Koffiehuis de Hoek
Prinsengracht 341 (625 3872, www.koffiehuis amsterdam.nl). *Tram 1, 7, 10.* **Open** 7.30am-4pm Mon-Fri; 9am-3.30pm Sat. **Sandwiches** from €2.50. **No credit cards. Map** p90 B4 ⑮ **Café**
A traditional Dutch sandwich and lunch (omelettes, pancakes and the like) outlet where all walks of life collide – from construction workers to the advertising folk of nearby agency KesselsKramer.

★ € 't Kuyltje
Gasthuismolensteeg 9 (620 1045, www.kuiltje.nl).
Tram 1, 2, 9, 24. **Open** 7am-4pm Mon-Fri; 10am-4pm Sat. **Sandwiches** €2-€6. **No credit cards.**
Map p90 C4 ⑯ **Sandwiches**
The wonderful and deeply filling world of Dutch *broodjes* (sandwiches) has its greatest champion in this takeaway, one of very few that still features proper home-prepared meat (including excellent roast beef) and fish salads in their buns, as opposed to the hugely unappealing factory-prepared products that have taken over the sandwich market. An awesome lunch every time.

Bars

★ 't Arendsnest
Herengracht 90 (421 2057, www.arendsnest.nl).
Tram 1, 2, 5, 13, 14. **Open** 2pm-midnight Mon-Thur, Sun; 2pm-2am Fri, Sat. **Map** p90 B2 ⑰

A temple to the humble hop, and set in a lovely canal house, the 'Eagle's Nest' sells only Dutch beer. Many of the customers are real-ale types, but even amateurs will enjoy the 350 standard and 250 seasonal brews, from cheeky house ale Herengracht 90 to Texelse Skuumkoppe. They serve excellent cheese and sausage snacks, but you can also opt for next door's Belgian restaurant, Lieve (Herengracht 88, 624 9635) – which is also happily beer-obsessed.

Bar Weber

Marnixstraat 397 (622 9910, www.hotelweber.nl). *Tram 1, 2, 5, 6, 7.* **Open** 7pm-3am Mon-Thur, Sun; 7pm-4am Fri, Sat. **No credit cards.** **Map** p90 C6 ⑱
Along with nearby sibling Bar Lux (Marnixstraat 403), Bar Weber offers a similar formula to students and the terminally hip who gather at these temples to pre-clubbing pleasure. There is no food or frippery, just booze, DJ-spun music and a party vibe. They've even expanded their line-up to include a seven-room boutique hotel – just in case you have to sleep it off.

Café Kobalt

Singel 2A (320 1559, www.cafekobalt.nl). *Tram 1, 2, 4, 5, 9, 13, 17, 24, 26.* **Open** 8am-1am Mon-Thur, Sun; 8am-3am Fri, Sat. **Map** p90 C1 ⑲
This rather sophisticated bar near Centraal Station is a great way to beat the train-delay blues. It has free Wi-Fi, round-the-clock food from breakfast to tapas to dinner, and any drink that you could name, from ristretto to champagne. DJs spin on Friday nights, while Sunday afternoons are dedicated to slinky live jazz shows.

Eijlders

Korte Leidsedwarsstraat 47 (624 2704, www.eijlders.nl). *Tram 1, 2, 5, 7.* **Open** 4.30pm-1am Mon-Wed; noon-1am Thur, Sun; noon-2am Fri, Sat. **No credit cards.** **Map** p90 C6 ⑳
Neon tat to one side, trendy Wendys to the other; Eijlders on Leidseplein is a cerebral alternative to both. A meeting place for the Resistance during the war, it now has a boho feel, with exhibitions, poetry nights and music – sometimes jazz, sometimes classical. Decor is handsome, with stained glass and dark wood.

De Pels

Huidenstraat 25 (622 9037, www.cafedepels.nl). *Tram 1, 2, 5.* **Open** 10am-1am Mon-Thur, Sun; 10am-3am Fri, Sat. **No credit cards.** **Map** p90 C5 ㉑
The Nine Streets are littered with characterful bars, and this one is a lovely old-style, tobacco-stained example that has an intellectual bent. In fact, De Pels can justifiably claim a prime spot in Amsterdam's literary and political legacy: writers, journalists and social activists often meet at this erstwhile Provo

hangout to chew the fat – although it's a nice spot in which to relax, whatever your mood.

★ De Twee Zwaantjes

Prinsengracht 114 (625 2729, www.cafe detweezwaantjes.nl). *Tram 1, 2, 5, 13, 14, 17.* **Open** 3pm-1am Mon-Thur, Sun; 3pm-3am Fri, Sat. **No credit cards.** **Map** p90 A3 ㉒
Oom-pah-pah, oom-pah-pah: that's how it goes at this salt-of-the-earth bar on the Jordaan side of the Prinsengracht. It's relatively quiet during the week, but weekends are real swinging singalong affairs, with revellers booming out tearjerkers about love, sweat and the Westerkerk. All together now: 'Op de Amster-dam-se grachten…'

Coffeeshops

★ Amnesia

Herengracht 133 (427 7874). Tram 13, 14, 17. **Open** 9.30am-1am daily. **No credit cards.** **Map** p90 B2 ㉓
You have to wonder at the choice of name, but Amnesia is a shop with swank decor, comfortable cushions and deep red walls. Located off the main tourist routes, it's often cool and quiet – though it occasionally fills up with locals. The pre-rolled joints are strong and smokeable. Summertime brings outdoor seating to the large, quiet canal street.

Barney's

Haarlemmerstraat 102 (625 9761, www.barneys. biz). Bus 18, 21, 22. **Open** 7am-1am daily. **No credit cards.** **Map** p90 B1 ㉔

Greenwoods.

EXPLORE

Renovated with some lovely old-fashioned apothecary paraphernalia, media screens showing specially filmed information videos and a vaporiser on every table, Barney's serves excellent organic bud worthy of the multiple High Times Cannabis Cup awards bestowed on it. If you're hungry or thirsty for alcohol, head a few doors down the road to sister locations Barney's Farm (no.98) or Barney's Uptown (no.105).

Dutch Flowers
Singel 387 (624 7624). Tram 1, 2, 5. **Open** 11am-11pm Mon; 10am-11pm Tue-Thur, Sun; 10am-2am Fri, Sat. **No credit cards.** **Map** p90 C4 ㉕
Squeezed on a little corner near the copious book and art sales on the Spui, this small shop has its decor slightly askew – even the CD rack. It's known for exceptional, high-grade hash, including pre-rolled joints. The large window up front offers a truly beautiful view of city life on an old, sloping street. Real Dutch flowers can be found at the Bloemenmarkt (*see p110*) – a kaleidoscope of an experience for stoned eyes.

Grey Area
Oude Leliestraat 2 (420 4301, www.greyarea.nl). Tram 1, 2, 5, 13, 14, 17. **Open** noon-8pm daily. **No credit cards.** **Map** p90 B3 ㉖
Run by two blokes living the modern American dream: open a stellar Amsterdam coffeeshop that offers some of the best weed and hash on the planet (try the Bubble Gum or Grey Mist Crystals). Also on offer are large glass bongs, a vaporiser and free refills of organic coffee. The owners are very affable and often more baked than the patrons; sometimes they stay in bed and miss the noon opening time.

Siberië
Brouwersgracht 11 (no phone, www.coffeshop siberie.nl). Tram 1, 2, 4, 5, 13, 17. **Open** 11am-11pm Mon-Thur, Sun; 11am-midnight Fri, Sat. **No credit cards.** **Map** p90 C1 ㉗
Friendly and mellow, Siberië offers internet access and plenty of board games, making it a cool place to while away any rainy day with great coffee or one of its 40 different loose teas (no nasty bags on a string here).
Other locations De Republiek, 2e Nassaustraat 1a, West (www.coffeeshopderepubliek.nl); De Supermarkt, Frederik Hendrikstraat 69, West (www.coffeeshopdesupermarkt.nl).

La Tertulia
Prinsengracht 312 (623 8503). Tram 7, 10. **Open** 11am-7pm Tue-Sat. **No credit cards.** **Map** p90 B5 ㉘
This mellow mother-and-daughter-run joint is decorated with plenty of plants, a little waterfall and lots of sunlight, which balances harmoniously with the all-bio buds and scrumptious weed brownies.

Two floors provide space for relaxation, quiet reading or gazing at the canal. Look for the seriously stoned Van Gogh painted outside.
▶ *For an eyeful of real-deal Van Gogh, visit the Van Gogh Museum (see p133).*

Shops & Services

Architectura & Natura
Leliegracht 22 (623 6186, www.architectura.nl). Tram 13, 14, 17. **Open** noon-6pm Mon; 10.30am-6.30pm Tue-Fri; 10am-6pm Sat. **Map** p90 B3 ㉙ **Books & music**
The stock at 'Architecture & Nature', which includes many works in English for monoglots, is exactly what you'd expect from its name: books on architectural history, landscape architecture, plant life, gardens and animal studies.

Brilmuseum/Brillenwinkel
Gasthuismolensteeg 7 (421 2414, www.brilmuseumamsterdam.nl). Tram 1, 2, 5, 13, 14, 17. **Open** 11.30am-5.30pm Wed-Fri; 11.30am-5pm Sat. **No credit cards.** **Map** p90 C4 ㉚ **Accessories**
Officially this 'shop' is an opticians' museum, but don't let that put you off. The fascinating exhibits feature glasses through the ages, and most of the pairs you see are also for sale to customers.

★ Caulils
Haarlemmerstraat 115 (412 0027, www.caulils. com). Tram 1, 2, 4, 5, 9, 13, 17, 24, 26. **Open** 11am-7pm Mon-Fri; 9am-6pm Sat. **Map** p90 B1 ㉛ **Food & drink**
Fervent foodies rate this delicatessen as the best shop in the country. Specialising in raw-milk cheeses, exotic cold cuts and singular wines, their selection is impeccably refined. Stock your picnic basket with class.

★ Deco Sauna
Herengracht 115 (623 8215, www.saunadeco.nl). Tram 1, 2, 5, 13, 17. **Open** noon-11pm Mon, Wed-Sat; 3-11pm Tue; 1-7pm Sun. **Admission** from €22.50. **No credit cards.** **Map** p90 B2 ㉜ **Health & beauty**
This beautiful art deco sauna provides facilities for a Turkish bath, Finnish sauna and cold plunge bath. There's also a solarium. Massages, shiatsu and beauty and skincare treatments are all available by appointment. Mixed bathing only.

Episode
Berenstraat 1 (626 4679, www.episode.eu). Tram 13, 14, 17. **Open** 11am-6pm Mon-Wed, Fri; 11am-8pm Thur; 10am-7pm Sat; noon-6pm Sun. **Map** p90 B4 ㉝ **Fashion**
In a basement on the Nine Streets, Episode's clean, concrete interior is brimming with men's and women's clothes that hail from the 1970s and '80s.

EXPLORE

DRESSED TO THE NINES

The best boutique booty in the Nine Streets.

It was a sign of the times. In 2013, Karl Lagerfeld saw fit to open his second flagship shop not in predictable PC Hooftstraat, but in the Nine Streets, a cluster of parallel streets connecting the city's three main canals between Raadhuisstraat/ Westermarkt and Leidsegracht. The affectionately dubbed 'Negens' is the shopping equivalent of Madonna: hot, happening and a sucker for a pair of fishnets. Luckily, there are also still shops dedicated to cheese, toothbrushes and doll repairs to keep things a bit real.

But back to fishnets: first stop has to be that vortex of vintage, **Laura Dols** (*see p99*). Loved by the city's darlings, this fashionable cavern positively glitters. For some bum-hugging denim, stop off at the **Spoiled** (*see p100*) Denim Bar for a cup of coffee and a chat about your 'problem areas'. The savvy guys at this bare-brick, loft-style store know their Levi's from their Citizens of Humanity and won't rest until your buns are cupped to perfection.

True Dutch style can be cashed in at **Hester van Eeghen** (Hartenstraat 37, 626 9212), the shop of the celebrated local shoe designer. Known for her way with leather, Hester loves a geometric shape or two and brash colours (the lime green inlay is a signature). Add a twist of Mexican flavour at **meCHICas** (Gasthuismolensteeg 11, 420 3092, www.mechicas.com), where local talent Debbie Verhagen designs trinkets 'with Dutch simplicity and South American flair'. **Exota** (Hartenstraat 10, 344 9390, www.exota.com) – not to be confused with stores that sell fluffy handcuffs and edible panties – is one for women and kids. Thick-knit bright scarves adorn the wooden shelves in winter, while paisley frocks with *Little House on the Prairie* appeal are a big draw in the summer.

Despite its bumbling name, **Relaxed at Home** (Huidenstraat 19, 320 2001) is a bright and airy store that's the sartorial equivalent of a cuddle – think thick nude scarves by Dutch stalwart Scotch & Soda. And while not officially part of the Nine Streets, **Rika Boutique** (Oude Spiegelstraat 9, 330 1112, www.rikaint.com) features the just-a-little-bit-rock'n'roll clothing and accessory designs of proprietor Ulrika Lundgren, along with labels such as LaLa Berlin and Alexander Wang.

In fact, if you haven't quenched your shopping thirst at the end of peering into every window of the Nine Streets, there are a few other Nine Street types of streets: connecting Herenstraat and Prinsenstraat in Western Canal Belt, and Hazenstraat in the Jordaan.

There's quite a masculine vibe – the military jackets and Levis are hard to beat – so this may not be the ideal spot for anyone looking for more of a '40s ladies' tearoom ambience.

Other location Waterlooplein 1, Jodenbuurt (320 3000).

Frozen Fountain

Prinsengracht 645 (622 9375, www.frozen fountain.nl). **Tram** 1, 2, 5, 7, 10. **Open** 1-6pm Mon; 10am-6pm Tue-Fri; 10am-5pm Sat; 1-5pm Sun. **Map** p90 C5 ❷ **Homewares**

The 'Froz' is a paradise for lovers of contemporary furniture. It stays abreast of innovative Dutch designers such as Piet Hein Eek, the maestro of furniture made with recycled wood; it also sells stuff by the non-Dutch likes of Marc Newsom, plus modern classics and photography.

Gerda's Bloemen en Planten (Gerda's Flowers & Plants)

Runstraat 16 (624 2912). **Tram** 1, 2, 5, 13, 14, 17. **Open** 9am-6pm Mon-Fri; 9am-5pm Sat. **Map** p90 B5 ❸ **Gifts & souvenirs**

Amsterdam's most inspired florist, Gerda's diminutive shop is full of fantastic blooms and has legendary window displays. If you're lucky, you'll spy sculptural bouquets on their way out the door.

★ I Love Vintage

Prinsengracht 201 (330 1950, www.ilove vintage.nl). **Tram** 13, 14, 17. **Open** 9.30am-6pm Mon-Sat. **Map** p90 A2 ❸ **Fashion**

There are few vintage stores that combine class (the silk Escada blazers are divine) with affordability (€1.99 for a pair of 1980s pearl earrings) and spot-on service. All in all, it's like stepping into your mum's dressing-up box, but everything fits and you won't resemble a bag lady on exiting.

JC Herman Ceramics

Herenstraat 10 (06 5794 5494 mobile, www. jcherman.org). **Tram** 13, 14, 17. **Open** noon-6pm Tue-Sat. **Map** p90 B2 ❸ **Homewares**

Herman Verhagen is one kickass potter. You can watch him in action in the back of his shop as he spins his self-designed ceramic and stoneware vases, bowls, pots and dinner sets – which end up in many homes and restaurants worldwide. Each week there's a new earthy selection on display. So wheel yourself over.

De Kaaskamer

Runstraat 7 (623 3483, www.kaaskamer.nl). **Tram** 1, 2, 5. **Open** noon-6pm Mon; 9am-6pm Tue-Fri; 9am-5pm Sat; noon-5pm Sun. **No credit cards. Map** p90 C5 ❸ **Food & drink**

De Kaaskamer offers over 200 varieties of domestic and imported cheeses, plus pâtés, olives, pastas and wines. Have fun quizzing the staff on the different cheese types and related trivia.

Frozen Fountain.

EXPLORE

Kramer/Pontifex

*Reestraat 18-20 (626 5274, http://sites.google.
com/site/pontifexkramer). Tram 13, 17.* **Open**
10am-6pm Mon-Sat. **No credit cards. Map** p90
B4 ❸ **Gifts & souvenirs**
Broken Barbies and battered bears are carefully
restored to health by Mr Kramer, a doctor for old-
fashioned dolls and teddies, who has practised
here for more than 25 years. In the same shop,
Pontifex is a traditional Dutch candle seller that
oozes old-world atmosphere.

★ Laura Dols

*Wolvenstraat 7 (624 9066, www.lauradols.nl).
Tram 1, 2, 5, 13, 14, 17.* **Open** 11am-6pm
Mon-Wed, Fri, Sat; 11am-9pm Thur; noon-6pm
Sun. **Map** p90 C4 ❹ **Fashion**
When Jean Paul Gaultier, Viktor & Rolf and Susan
Sarandon regularly pop into your store, you know
you're on to something good. This place is jam-
packed with 1950s-style wedding, ballroom and
Hollywood glitter gear.

Margriet Nannings

*Prinsenstraat 8 (620 7672, www.margriet
nannings.com). Tram 13, 14, 17.* **Open** 1-6pm
Mon; 10.30am-6pm Tue, Wed, Fri, Sat; 10.30am-
8pm Thur. **Map** p90 B2 ❶ **Fashion**
Dutch fashion designer Margriet Nannings is known
for her discreet and elegant tastes. Besides her own
range, she sells in-tune labels such as Comme des
Garçons, Paul Smith and Raf Simons, as well as a
selection of accessories and perfumes. The shop is
part of her mini-emporium on Prinsenstraat, which
includes another branch at no.15 and a menswear
shop at no.6.

Marlies Dekkers

*Berenstraat 18 (421 1900, www.marliesdekkers.
com). Tram 2.* **Open** 1-6pm Mon; 11am-6pm
Tue-Sat; noon-5pm Sun. **Map** p90 B4
❷ **Accessories**
Local lingerie designer Marlies Dekkers is already a
legend for having given women the world over stylish, understated underwear and swimwear. After
surviving bankruptcy in 2013, she continues to
provide truly dazzling gifts to stir the senses in her
sole shop in Amsterdam.

MK Jewelry

*Reestraat 9 (427 0727, www.mk-jewelry.com).
Tram 13, 14, 17.* **Open** 10.30am-5.30pm
Tue-Sat. **Map** p90 B4 ❸ **Accessories**
With a passion for gemstones, MK sells its own rustic yet elegant collection, along with brands such as
DoDo and Toywatch. Pressing your nose to the
immaculate windows you might be afraid of intrud-
ing, but you'll be glad you did. Once inside, all is
calm and relaxed, allowing the glitter of a million
reflected and refracted rays of light to work their
mesmeric magic. Prices start low.

★ Original Dampkring Gallery

Singel 395 (no phone). Tram 1, 2, 5. **Open**
11am-7pm Wed-Sun. **No credit cards.
Map** p90 C4 ❹ **Gifts & souvenirs**
Who knew that the glass-blowing of bongs had
turned into such a rich artform? This gallery associated with the Dampkring coffeeshop (*see p81*) is
breaking new ground in 'heady functional art', aka
borosilicate glass sculpture. They also feature an
exceptional selection of street art, including work by
local legends Laser 3.14, Hugo Mulder and mural
duo Telmo Miel. *Photos p100.*

Orson + Bodil/Alexander van Slobbe

*Herenstraat 38 (786 4474, www.orson-
bodil.com). Tram 13, 14, 17.* **Open** 11am-
6pm Tue-Fri. **Map** p90 B2 ❹ **Fashion**
Dutch fashion designer Alexander van Slobbe
gained international renown for his minimal and
modernist men's label SO. Since selling it in 2003,
he's focused on his women's line, orson + bodil.
Along with collaborations with Royal Tichelaar
Makkum and Puma, Van Slobbe also designed the
uniforms for the recently reopened Rijksmuseum.
His boutique is located just up the road from
Francisco van Benthum (no.13), his former protégé
and business partner.

★ Otherist

*Leliegracht 6 (320 0420, www.otherist.com).
Tram 7, 13, 14, 17.* **Open** noon-5pm Mon,
Sun; 11am-6.30pm Wed-Sat. **Map** p90 B3
❹ **Gifts & souvenirs**
If you are out to stock your own cabinet of curiosities
or looking for the ultimate unique gift, the Otherist
is one-stop-shopping heaven: glass eyeballs, 'vegan
mini-skulls', butterfly specimens, amulets, hip
flasks, medical posters and an ever-changing selection of other curiosa and handmade design items.
Indeed: embrace the 'other'. *Photos p101.*

Pâtisserie Pompadour

*Huidenstraat 12 (623 9554, www.pompadour-
amsterdam.nl). Tram 1, 2, 5, 7.* **Open** 10am-
6pm Mon-Fri; 10am-5pm Sat. **Map** p90 C5
❹ **Food & drink**
This fabulous *bonbonnerie* and tearoom – with
an 18th-century interior imported from Antwerp
– is likely to bring out the little old lady in anyone.
Its sibling also sports a decent tearoom serving
sublime sandwiches.
Other location Kerkstraat 148, Southern
Canal Belt (330 0981).

Raïnaraï

*Prinsengracht 252 (624 9791, www.rainarai.nl).
Tram 13, 14, 17.* **Open** noon-10pm Tue-Sun. **No
credit cards. Map** p90 B4 ❹ **Food & drink**
Mouth-watering North African fodder, from takeaway to an assortment of items no pantry should be

without. It's a self-proclaimed 'nomadic kitchen', so staff will come and cater wherever you please, although most people can't resist eating right on the premises as the food is so damn tasty. They also have a full-blown restaurant at the Westergasfabriek (Polonceaukade 40, 486 7109).

Ready to Fish

Prinsengracht 581 (330 9332, www.readyto fish.nl). Tram 1, 2, 5. **Open** noon-6pm Mon, Sun; 11am-6pm Tue-Sat. **Map** p90 B5 ⓵ **Fashion**
This gorgeous, airy shopping space is home to Dutch designer Ilja Visser's whimsical yet wearable clothing line. It has a real Alice in Wonderland feel, complete with sustainable chocolate that begs, 'Eat me.' Quite the catch.

Ron Mandos

Prinsengracht 282 (320 7036, www.ronmandos.nl). Tram 9, 13, 16, 17. **Open** noon-6pm Wed-Sat. **Map** p90 B4 ⓾ **Gallery**
In a spacious gallery, Mandos presents local and international contemporary artists, often with a slightly sentimental edge, and frequently with a few exhibitions running concurrently.

Simon Levelt

Prinsengracht 180 (624 0823, www.simon levelt.com). Tram 13, 14, 17. **Open** 10am-6pm Mon-Fri; 10am-5pm Sat; 1-5pm Sun. **Map** p90 A3 ⓾ **Food & drink**
Anything and everything to do with brewing and drinking, stocked in a remarkable old shop. The

premises date from 1839 and the place retains much of the original tiled decor.
Other locations throughout the city.

Skins Cosmetics

Runstraat 11 (528 6922, www.skins.nl). Tram 1, 2, 5, 7, 10. **Open** 1-7pm Mon; 11am-7pm Tue, Wed, Fri; 11am-8pm Thur; 10am-6pm Sat; noon-5pm Sun. **Map** p90 B5 ⓾ **Health & beauty**
The flagship store for Amsterdam's own skincare and fragrance empire has expanded its offering, and now includes cosmetics by REN, Dr Brandt, Leonor Greyl, Aveda and Le Labo. There's plenty of room in which to try the stock, and beauty services. Drop in to sample some RéVive, the skincare line containing anti-ageing 'miracle' ingredient EGF, or perfumes from some of today's greatest 'noses'.

Spoiled

Wolvenstraat 19 (626 3818, www.spoiled.nl). Tram 1, 2, 5, 13, 14, 17. **Open** noon-6pm Mon, Sun; 10am-6pm Tue, Wed, Fri, Sat; 10am-8pm Thur. **Map** p90 C4 ⓾ **Fashion**
Spoiled ups the ante at its fancy-pants location on the Nine Streets with loads of fashion, art, weird gadgets, designer toys, a hair salon and a jeans concept called Denim Bar, where one can throw back a drink while the staff relate all the news on the latest denim styles and brands. Contemporary labels to look out for include Tiger of Sweden, Cycle, Nudie, Freitag and Evisu, plus collections from Nike and Levi's.
▶ *For more on the fabulous Nine Streets, see p97* **Dressed to the Nines***.*

Original Dampkring Gallery. *See p99.*

EXPLORE

★ Totalitarian Art Gallery
Singel 87 (06 5369 3694 mobile, www.sovietart.com). Tram 1, 2, 5, 13, 14, 17. **Open** noon-6pm Thur-Sun. **Map** p90 C2 ⬛ **Gallery**
You'll be overwhelmed by the kitsch of history in this fascinating gallery, which has democratic tastes when it comes to totalitarian art – it covers the USSR, Nazi Germany and Communist China. There's paintings, photos, sculpture and advertising-cum-propaganda (it's such a fine line, after all). In 2013, the proprietor got into legal trouble for selling copies of Hitler's *Mein Kampf* and thereby renewing the discussion of whether or not the book should be banned. If you want something less edgy, just pick up a nice bust of Yuri Gagarin, the first man in space.

Van Ravenstein
Keizersgracht 359 (639 0067, www.van-ravenstein.nl). Tram 13, 14, 17. **Open** 1-6pm Mon; 11am-6pm Tue-Fri; 10.30am-5.30pm Sat; noon-5pm Sun. **Map** p90 C5 ⬛ **Fashion**
Van Ravenstein is a superb boutique with the best of the Belgian designers: Maison Martin Margiela, Ann Demeulemeester and Dries van Noten, among others. Don't miss the bargain basement for similarly stylish endeavours with less serious price tags.

★ Vega-Life
Singel 110 (620 4097, www.vega-life.nl). Tram 1, 2, 5, 13, 14, 17. **Open** 10am-6pm Tue-Fri; 10am-5pm Sat. **Map** p90 B2 ⬛ **Fashion**
This vegan lifestyle store has it all: clothing, footwear, books, vitamins, food and a friendly staff who will happily point you towards all the best animal-product-free shops and restaurants in town.

Vlaamsch Broodhuis
Haarlemmerstraat 108 (528 6430, www.vlaamsch broodhuys.nl). Tram 3 or bus 18, 21, 22. **Open** 8am-6.30pm Mon-Fri; 8am-6pm Sat; 9.30am-6pm Sun. **No cash**. **Map** p90 B1 ⬛ **Food & drink**
The name might be a bit of a mouthful, but it's worth a visit to wrap your gums around the tasty sourdough breads, fine French pastries and fresh salads, among other treats.
Other locations throughout the city.

De Witte Tandenwinkel
Runstraat 5 (623 3443, www.dewitte tandenwinkel.nl). Tram 1, 2, 5, 7, 10. **Open** 10am-5.30pm Tue-Fri; 10am-5pm Sat. **Map** p90 B5 ⬛ **Health & beauty**
The store that's armed to the teeth with brushes and toothpastes to ensure that your gnashers are pearly white when you most need them to shine.

Zipper
Huidenstraat 7 (623 7302, www.zipperstore.nl). Tram 1, 2, 5. **Open** noon-6pm Mon; 11am-6pm Tue, Wed, Fri, Sat; 11am-9pm Thur; 1-6pm Sun. **Map** p90 C5 ⬛ **Fashion**

Otherist. *See p99.*

EXPLORE

It may not be especially cheap, but the jeans, cowboy shirts, 1980s gear and '70s hipsters are definitely worth a gander; there's real treasure to be found on them there rails. **Other locations** Nieuwe Hoogstraat 8, Old Centre: Old Side (627 0353).

AROUND LEIDSEPLEIN

Leidseplein lies on the bottom of the 'U' made by the Canal Belt, and runs south from the end of Leidsestraat to the Amsterdam School-style bridge over Singelgracht and east towards the 'pop temple' **Paradiso** (*see p192 and p197*) to the **Max Euweplein** (a handy passage to Vondelpark; *see p128*) with its **Max Euwe Centrum** (Max Euweplein 30a, 625 7017, www.maxeuwe.nl) and giant chess set.

Artists and writers used to congregate on Leidseplein during the 1920s and '30s, when it was the scene of clashes between communists and fascists. During the war, protests were ruthlessly broken up by the Nazis and there's a commemorative plaque on nearby Kerkstraat. But thanks to the plethora of tourists drinking in pavement cafés, listening to buskers and soaking up the atmosphere – not to mention the huge variety of booze on offer – Leidseplein's latterday persona is more party town than party political.

The area has more theatres, clubs and restaurants than any other part of town. It's dominated by the **Stadsschouwburg** (*see p212,* the municipal theatre), multimedia center **Melkweg** (*see p192*) just around the corner, and by the cafés that take over the pavements during summer. This is when fire-eaters, jugglers, musicians and small-time con artists and pickpockets fill the square.

The café society associated with Leidseplein began with the opening of the city's first terrace bar, the Café du Théâtre, which, sadly, was demolished in 1877, 20 years before the final completion of Kromhout's **Eden Amsterdam American Hotel** (*see p281*). Opposite the American is a building, dating from 1882, that reflects Leidseplein's dramatic transformation: once grand, it's now illuminated by huge adverts and the new Apple flagship store. Just off the square, in the Leidsebos, is the more intriguing **Adamant**, a pyramid-like, hologram-effect sculpture that commemorated 400 years of the city's central diamond trade in 1986. Also, look out for a tiny 'sawing guy' sculpture by an anonymous artist in one of the trees.

SOUTHERN CANAL BELT
Around Rembrandtplein

Previously called Reguliersmarkt (Regular Market), this square was renamed in honour of Rembrandt in 1876; his statue – the oldest in the city – stands in the centre of the gardens, surrounded by more recent statues depicting *The Night Watch*, all gazing in the direction of the Jewish quarter. Though there's no longer a market, it's still the centre of commercial activity, with a wild profusion of neon lights, and a cacophony of music blaring out from the cafés, bars, restaurants and clubs on all sides. Unashamedly tacky, the square is home to a

Rembrandtplein.

Magerebrug. *See p104.*

variety of establishments, from the faded and fake elegance of the traditional striptease parlours to nondescript cafés, but there are a few exceptions to the air of tawdriness – places such as the grand café **De Kroon** (no.17), the art deco **Schiller** (no.24) and HL de Jong's crazily colourful dream-as-reality masterpiece, cinema **Pathé Tuschinski** (*see p176*).

Head west from here and you'll end up at Muntplein, by the floating flower market, **Bloemenmarkt**, at the southern tip of Singel. Over on the corner of the Amstel are some lively gay cafés and bars, and on the façade of Amstel 216, the city's freakiest graffiti. The 'House with the Bloodstains' was home to former mayor Coenraad van Beuningen (1622-93), whose brilliance was eclipsed by insanity. After seeing visions of fireballs and fluorescent coffins above the Reguliersgracht, he scrawled sailing ships, stars, strange symbols, and his and his wife's names – with his own blood – on the grey stone walls. Subsequent attempts to scrub off the stains have all proved futile. Or so the story goes…

From Rembrandtplein, walk south along the shopping and eating street Utrechtsestraat, or explore Reguliersgracht and Amstelveld.

The Canals

As the first canal to be dug in the glory days, Herengracht (named after the 'gentlemen' who initially invested in it) attracted the richest of merchants, and the southern stretch is where you'll find the most stately and overblown houses on any of Amsterdam's canals. The

Museum Willet-Holthuysen is a classic example of such a 17th-century mansion.

However, it's on the 'Golden Bend' – the stretch between Leidsestraat and Vijzelstraat – that things really get out of hand. By then, the rich saw the advantage of buying two adjoining lots so that they could build as wide as they built high. Excess defines the Louis XIV style of Herengracht 475, while tales of pre-rock 'n' roll exuberance are often told about no.527, whose interior was trashed by Peter the Great while he was here learning to be a ship's carpenter and picking up urban ideas for his dream city, St Petersburg.

Home to the **Stadsarchief Amsterdam**, the imposing Gebouw de Bazel building is round the corner on Vijzelstraat. Meanwhile, mischievous types annoy the mayor by mooring up on his personal dock before the official Herengracht 502 residence.

It's a similarly grand story on this southern section of Keizersgracht (named after Holy Roman Emperor Maximilian I). For evidence, pop into the **Museum van Loon** or photography museum **Foam**. But for an alternative view of this area, head to Kerkstraat, parallel to and directly between Keizersgracht and Prinsengracht. The houses here are less grand, but what they lack in swank they more than make up for in funkiness, with their galleries and shops only adding to the community feel. The pleasant oasis of Amstelveld helps, too, with **Amstelkerk** – the white wooden church that once took a break from sacred duties to act as a stable for Napoleon's horses – worth a look. Also stop for refreshment at **NEL** (Amstelveld 12, 626 1199, nelamstelveld.nl), which has perhaps the most scenic terrace in the city.

Head east along Kerkstraat and you'll find the **Magerebrug** ('Skinny Bridge'; *photo p103*), the most photographed bridge in the city and one said to have been built in the 17th century by two sisters living on opposite sides of the Amstel who wanted an easy way to get together for morning coffee. If you cross it and go down Nieuwe Kerkstraat, you'll get to the Plantage (*see p147*). Alternatively, turn right at Amstel and right again down Prinsengracht to see more grand canal houses and the **Pijpenkabinet** (Pipe Cabinet, Prinsengracht 488, 421 1779, www.pijpenkabinet.nl) and its 2,000-plus exhibits of all things tobacco – yes, tobacco.

Sights & Museums

★ Foam (Photography Museum Amsterdam)

Keizersgracht 609 (551 6500, www.foam.nl). Tram 16, 24. **Open** 10am-6pm Mon-Wed, Sat, Sun; 10am-9pm Thur, Fri. **Admission** €8; €5.50 reductions; free under-12s, IAmsterdam, MK. **No credit cards. Map** p91 B3 ⑩
Located in a tightly renovated canal house, this excellent museum displays a comprehensive array of talent, from rising stars (Ryan McGinley, Viviane Sassen) to big names (Weegee, Diane Arbus, Malick Sidibé and Richard Avedon). The café's food is a feast for the eyes as well as the stomach. Also check the website for details of exhibitions and pop-ups in other locations.

SERIOUSLY HOT STUFF
Where to find the best Indonesian cooking.

EXPLORE

Following Indonesian independence in 1949, 180,000 residents of the 'Spice Islands' emigrated to the Netherlands to become Dutch citizens. As a result, even Amsterdam's ubiquitous snackbars serve bastardised versions of Indonesian cuisine. Coming from an archipelago of more than 1,000 islands, with historical influences ranging from Chinese and Arabian to Portuguese and Dutch, Indonesian food mingles many cuisines with an almost infinite range of dishes.

To add to the confusion are the many Chin-Indo-Suri eateries, which serve cheap dishes that have taken on the tones of the many immigrants from China (often via Indonesia) and Surinam, another former colony whose Caribbean style is usually represented by the pancake-like roti. The usual dishes on offer at these places are satay, *gado-gado* (steamed veg and boiled egg served with rice and satay sauce), *nasi goreng* (onion-fried rice with meat, veg and egg) and *bami goreng* (the same but with noodles). While those are great for the monetarily challenged, all visitors should stretch their funds to visit an official purveyor of *rijsttafel* ('rice table') – a Dutch construct – a set meal that nobly tries to include as many dishes as possible.

While in days gone by, connoisseurs would have sent you to the Hague for the most authentic Indonesian restaurants, Amsterdam now offers ample choices of its own. There's **Tempo Doeloe** (*see p107*) and quirky **Coffee & Jazz** (Utrechtsestraat

113, Southern Canal Belt, 624 5851). Then there are the stellar cheap takeaways, such as **Toko Joyce** (Nieuwmarkt 38, Old Centre: Old Side, 427 9091, www.tokojoyce.nl) and **Sari Citra** (Ferdinand Bolstraat 52, De Pijp, 675 4102).

Top of the pile, however, is the relatively expensive **Blauw** (Amstelveenseweg 158-160, South, 675 5000, www.restaurant blauw.nl). The restaurant serves authentic dishes, but with a twist. Its 'rice table' is a feast for the well-walleted gods.

Blauw.

Museum van Loon

*Keizersgracht 672 (624 5255, www.museum
vanloon.nl). Tram 16, 24.* **Open** 11am-5pm Mon,
Wed-Sun. **Admission** €8; €6 reductions; free
under-6s, IAmsterdam, MK. **No credit cards**.
Map p91 C4 ⑤

Few interiors of Amsterdam's grand canal houses
have been preserved in anything approaching their
original state, but the former Van Loon residence is
one that has. Designed by Adriaan Dortsman, it was
originally the home of artist Ferdinand Bol. Hendrik
van Loon bought it in 1884 and it was opened
as a museum in 1973. The terrifically grand mid
18th-century interior and Louis XIV and XV decor
is a delight. So is the art. There's a collection of family portraits from the 17th to the 20th centuries; Ram
Katzir's striking sculpture *There*; and a modern art
show every two years.

Museum Willet-Holthuysen

*Herengracht 605 (523 1822, www.museumwillet
holthuysen.nl). Tram 9, 14.* **Open** 10am-5pm
Mon-Fri; 11am-5pm Sat, Sun. **Admission** €8;
€4-€6 reductions; free under-6s, IAmsterdam,
MK. **Map** p91 A4 ②

This 17th-century mansion was purchased in the
1850s by the Willet-Holthuysen family. When
Abraham, remembered as 'the Oscar Wilde of
Amsterdam', died in 1889, his wife Sandrina Louisa,
a hermaphrodite, left the house and its contents to
the city on the condition it was preserved and opened
as a museum. The family had followed the fashion
of the time and decorated it in the neo-Louis XVI
style: it's densely furnished, with an impressive collection of rare objets d'art, glassware, silver, fine
china and paintings – including a portrait of a rather
shocked-looking Abraham (taken on his honeymoon, perhaps?).

★ FREE Stadsarchief Amsterdam

*Vijzelstraat 32 (251 1511, www.stadsarchief.
amsterdam.nl). Tram 16, 24, 25.* **Open** 10am-
5pm Tue-Fri; noon-5pm Sat, Sun. **Admission**
free. **Map** p91 B3 ③

The city archives are located in an epic and decorative
1926 building that's shrouded in esoteric mystery.
The highly ornate structure was designed by architect
KPC de Bazel, a practitioner of Theosophy – a spiri-
tualist movement founded by the chain-smoking
Madame Blavatsky. The grand centrepiece is the
Treasure Room. As embellished as Tutankhamun's
Tomb, it displays the prizes of the collection. The
archives also host exhibitions and film screenings.
There is an excellent bookstore and café. *Photos p106.*

Tassenmuseum Hendrikje
(Museum of Bags & Purses)

*Herengracht 573 (524 6452, www.tassen
museum.nl). Tram 4, 9, 16, 24.* **Open** 10am-5pm
daily. **Admission** €9; €5.50-€7.50 reductions; free
under-13s, IAmsterdam, MK. **Map** p91 B4 ④

This museum is the world's largest collection of its
kind, with a total of over 4,500 exhibits: everything
from coin purses made of human hair to a Lieber
rhinestone collectible named 'Socks' after Hillary
Clinton's cat.

Restaurants

An

*Weteringschans 76 (624 4672, www.japans
restaurantan.nl). Tram 7, 10.* **Open** 6-10pm
Tue-Sat. **Main courses** €8-€19. **No credit
cards**. **Map** p91 D5 ⑤ **Japanese**

An serves some of the city's best Japanese cuisine –
sushi as well as starters, grilled dishes and several
vegetarian options. Staff are friendly and the place
is comfortable.

Buffet van Odette

*Prinsengracht 598 (423 6034, www.buffet-
amsterdam.nl). Tram 16, 24.* **Open** 10am-
9pm Mon, Wed-Sun. **Main courses** €7-€19.
Map p91 D3 ⑥ **Café**

A café that's so healthy it's sinful. Service is slow,
but the food is worth the wait, whether you choose
a hearty sandwich – made with bread from iconic
local bakery Hartog (Ruyschstraat 56, East, 665
1295) – a salad or a home-made cake. For breakfast,
opt for a croissant with butter or jam, or an omelette
– or both, when ordering a 'complete' breakfast,
including coffee/tea and juice.

George Deli

*Utrechtsestraat 17 (330 0171, www.cafe
george.nl). Tram 4, 9, 14.* **Open** 9am-9pm
Mon-Sat; 9am-8pm Sun. **Main courses** €5-€10.
Map p91 A4 ⑦ **American**

'Serving everyday food' and an all-day breakfast –
including eggs benedict – George knows how to start
your day right. It's on Rembrandtplein, on an indoor
balcony above an outlet of locally sourced supermarket Marqt (*see p136*). George also has two more
brasserie-like offerings: Café George (Leidsegracht,
Western Canal Belt, 626 0802) and George WPA
(Willemsparkweg 74, Amsterdam South, 470 2530).

Japan Inn

*Leidsekruisstraat 4 (620 4989, www.japaninn.nl).
Tram 1, 2, 5, 7, 10.* **Open** 5-11pm daily. **Main
courses** €10-€35. **Map** p91 C2 ⑧ **Japanese**

Japan Inn offers both quality and quantity. The fresh
sushi and sashimi are served from the open kitchen
and are hits with students (who dig the quantity)
and Japanese tourists (who come for the quality).

Lion Noir

*Reguliersdwarsstraat 28 (627 6603, www.lion
noir.nl). Tram 1, 2, 5.* **Open** 11.30am-1am Mon-
Thur; 11.30am-3am Fri; 6pm-3am Sat; 6pm-1am
Sun. **Main courses** €22-€24. **Map** p91 B3
⑨ **French**

EXPLORE

Stadsarchief Amsterdam. See p105.

EXPLORE

The emphasis at Lion Noir is firmly on meat, with hearty but not overwhelming mains including top-notch foie gras and duck breast medallions. The velvet and artfully weather-beaten leather furnishings, stuffed birds and (yes) ornamental dog skeletons, combined with the genetically perfect staff, give the impression of an Abercrombie & Fitch shoot curated by Tim Burton.

€ Loekie
Utrechtsestraat 57 (624 3740, www.loekie.net). Tram 4. **Open** *9am-6pm Mon, Tue, Thur-Sat; 9am-1pm Wed.* **Sandwiches** €5-€8. **No credit cards. Map** p91 B4 **70 Sandwiches**
Loekie isn't quite as cheap as some other sandwich shops, and you'll have to queue, but a french stick with Italian fillings makes for an excellent meal. Fine quiche, cheesecake and tapenade too.

Los Pilones
Kerkstraat 63 (320 4651, www.lospilones.com). Tram 1, 2, 5, 11. **Open** *4pm-midnight daily.* **Main courses** €12-€18. **Map** p91 C2
71 Mexican
A splendid Mexican cantina with an anarchic bent, Los Pilones is run by three young and friendly Mexican brothers, one of whom does the cooking, so expect authentic food rather than standard Tex-Mex

fare. There are over 180 – yes, 180 – tequilas on offer, so don't be surprised if the evening ends in a blur. **Other locations** 1e Anjeliersdwarsstraat 6, The Jordaan (620 0323); Geldersekade 111, Old Centre: Old Side (776 0210).

La Rive
InterContinental Amstel Amsterdam, Professor Tulpplein 1 (520 3264, www.restaurantlarive. com). Tram 7, 10 or Metro Weesperplein. **Open** *6.30-10.30pm Mon-Sat; 5-9pm Sun.* **Main courses** €52-€80. **Set meal** €95 5 courses, €115 7 courses. **Map** p91 B6 **72 French**
Although Bord'Eau at hotel De l'Europe (*see p278*) is the proud owner of two Michelin stars, La Rive at the InterContinental Amstel Amsterdam (*see p284*), with one star, overshadows the hotel competition, with superb regional French cuisine without the excessive formality that can too often mar such places. For the perfect meal when money is no object.

Segugio
Utrechtsestraat 96 (330 1503, www.segugio.nl). Tram 4, 6, 7, 10. **Open** *6-11pm Mon-Sat.* **Main courses** €19-€31. **Set meal** €49.50 4 courses. **Map** p91 B5 **73 Italian**
Best. Risotto. Ever. A delightful variety of fresh ingredients and flavour combinations embellish and

embolden this most luxurious of dishes. There are
pastas, soups, meat and fish dishes on offer too.
In fact, this Italian restaurant has all the elements
to make the perfect lingering meal for both foodies
and romantics.
▶ *Can't get a table? There's plenty more great
Italian action at Toscanini (see p119) and
Yam-Yam (see p119).*

€ Stach Food

*Nieuwe Spiegelstraat 52 (737 2220, www.
stach-food.nl). Tram 7, 10.* **Open** 8.30am-
10pm Mon-Sat; 9am-9pm Sun. **Main courses**
€3.50-€8. **Map** p91 C3 ⓱ **Sandwiches**
A healthy takeaway shop on the antique and art
gallery strip. Sandwiches, salads and full meals –
with a tiny coffee bar in the back.
Other locations Haarlemmerstraat 150, Western
Canal Belt (737 2626); Van Woustraat 154, De Pijp
(754 2672).

Tempo Doeloe

*Utrechtsestraat 75 (625 6718, www.tempodoeloe
restaurant.nl). Tram 7, 10.* **Open** 6-11.30pm
Mon-Sat. **Main courses** €19.50-€42. **Rice table**
€27.50-€37.50. **Map** p91 B5 ⓱ **Indonesian**
This cosy and rather classy Indonesian restaurant
(heck, it even has white linen) is widely thought to
serve the city's best and spiciest *rijsttafel* ('rice
table'), a local speciality, and not without good reason. It's best to book ahead; if you turn up on the off-
chance and find the place full, try the much cheaper
and more casual Rice & Spice Asian Deli and tea bar
across the way (Utrechtsestraat 98A, 752 9772,
www.riceandspice.nl) as a tasty plan B.

★ € Van Dobben

*Korte Reguliersdwarsstraat 5-9 (624 4200,
www.eetsalonvandobben.nl). Tram 4, 9, 14,
16, 24.* **Open** 10am-9pm Mon-Wed; 10am-1am
Thur; 10am-2am Fri, Sat; 11.30am-8pm Sun.
Main courses €3.25-€8. **No credit cards**.
Map p91 B3 ⓱ **Dutch**
A *kroket* is the national version of a croquette: a
melange of meat and potato with a crusty, deep-fried
skin, best served on a bun with lots of hot mustard.
This 1945-era late-nighter is the uncontested champion of *kroket* shops.

€ Wagamama

*Max Euweplein 10 (528 7778, www.wagamama.nl).
Tram 1, 2, 5, 7, 10.* **Open** noon-10pm Mon-Thur,
Sun; noon-11pm Fri, Sat. **Main courses** €9-€15.
Map p91 D2 ⓱ **Asian**
Amsterdam has three branches of the popular quick
'n' cheap Asian chain that originated in London. You
may not fancy lingering in the minimalist canteen
setting, but you certainly can't fault the speedy serv-
ice or the tasty noodle dishes and soups.
Other locations Zuidplein 12, Zuid (620 3032);
Amstelstraat 8, Southern Canal Belt (320 0310).

Lion Noir. *See p105.*

EXPLORE

Bloemenmarkt. See p110.

Bars

De Balie
Kleine Gartmanplantsoen 10 (553 5151,
www.debalie.nl). Tram 1, 2, 5, 7, 10.
No credit cards. Map p91 D1 ⑦
Theatre, new media, photography, cinema and literary events sit alongside lectures, debates and discussions about social and political issues at this
influential centre for the local intelligentsia. Throw
in a café too, and you've got healthy food for both
mind and body.

Café Kale
Weteringschans 267 (622 6363, www.cafekale.nl).
Tram 7, 10, 16. **Open** 11am-1am Mon-Thur; 11am-
2am Fri, Sat; noon-11pm Sun. **Map** p91 D5 ⑦
If you're burnt out by Albert Cuyp market, you can
do far worse than recover at this smart locals' café.
Although it calls itself a 'real brown bar', the styling
is colourful and modern. Food is far from old-
fashioned, with griddled vegetables and chorizo putting in regular appearances. Rembrandtplein and
Leidseplein are both within walking distance.

Door 74
06 3404 5122 mobile, www.door-74.com.
Tram 4, 16, 24. **Open** 8pm-3am Mon-Thur,
Sun; 8pm-4am Fri, Sat.
'Exclusivity' may be a dirty word in Amsterdam's
strenuously egalitarian bar scene, but rather than
using inflated prices, long queues or grumpy door-
men as its filter, Door 74 employs secrecy –
and rewards in-the-know trendies with excellent
cocktails mixed by some of the best barmen in the
business. To make a reservation (and discover the

location), leave a text message or voicemail with
name, number of people, time and date, and your
phone number.

Ludwig
Reguliersdwarsstraat 37 (625 3661, www.bar
ludwig.com). Tram 1, 2, 5. **Open** 6pm-1am Wed,
Thur, Sun; 6pm-3am Fri, Sat. **Map** p91 B2 ⑧
Insanely hip at times, Ludwig is named for the bi-
curious Bavarian 'fairytale king' famed for his wild
parties. The place serves his legacy well, from the
industrial kitsch interior to the gay-friendly (but not
exclusive) party programme. Design bells and whis-
tles come courtesy of illustrator Parra and his crew.

Onder de Ooievaar
Utrechtsestraat 119 (624 6836, www.onder
deooievaar.nl). Tram 4. **Open** 10am-1am Mon-
Thur; 10am-3am Fri, Sat; 10.30am-1am Sun.
No credit cards. Map p91 B5 ⑧
Onder de Ooievaar achieves a great deal by not trying all that hard. What you get is an uncomplicated
venue for an evening's carousing among a mixed
bunch of trendies, locals and the odd visitor.
Highlights include 't IJ beer on tap, the downstairs
pool table (a genuine rarity in Amsterdam bars) and
the lovely Prinsengracht-side terrace for when you
fancy an alfresco tipple.

Shops & Services

Art Unlimited
Keizersgracht 510 (624 8419, www.artunlimited.
com). Tram 1, 2, 5. **Open** noon-6pm Mon, Sun;
10.15am-6pm Tue, Wed, Fri, Sat; 10.15am-7pm
Thur. **Map** p91 C2 ⑨ **Gifts & souvenirs**

WHERE TO SPEND IT

Amsterdam's shopping districts – the cheat sheet.

DAMSTRAAT
A street at war with its former self, Damstraat is still failing to jettison the sleaze and change into a boutique-lined oasis. Alas, its proximity to the Red Light District means that the countless laddish types out on the town can impinge on this otherwise lovely area.

THE JORDAAN
Tiny backstreets laced with twisting canals, cosy boutiques, lush markets, bakeries, galleries, restful old-fashioned cafés and bars. The Jordaan captures the spirit of Amsterdam like nowhere else in the city. The 'hood is also handily cut in half by furnishings- and design-rich street Rozengracht.

LEIDSESTRAAT
Connecting Koningsplein and Leidseplein, Leidsestraat is peppered with fine shoe shops and more high-street shops, but you'll still have to dodge trams to shop there. Cyclists: note that bikes aren't allowed along this strip.

MAGNA PLAZA
Right behind Dam Square, this architectural treat was once a post office. Its subsequent reincarnation as a five-floor mall is beloved by tourists, although the locals are somewhat less keen.

NINE STREETS
The small streets connecting Prinsengracht, Keizersgracht and Herengracht in between Raadhuisstraat and Leidsegracht offer a very diverse mix of boutiques, antiques shops and a good range of quirky speciality stores (*see p97* **Dressed to the Nines**).

KALVERSTRAAT & NIEUWENDIJK
Kalverstraat and its scruffier extension Nieuwendijk are where the locals come for their consumer kicks. Shops here are largely unexciting – mainly high-street stores – yet they still get insanely busy on Sundays. Still, it's pedestrian-only, so you can forget the dreaded bikes and focus on the tills; just make sure you follow the unwritten law of keeping left as you cruise up or down the street.

HAARLEMMERSTRAAT/ HAARLEMMERDIJK
Forming the northern border of Western Canal Belt and the Jordaan, these connected streets have bloomed into a remarkable culinary/boutique destination.

PC HOOFTSTRAAT
Amsterdam's elite shopping strip has had a rocky ride in the last few years, but with a new infusion of designer shops embracing both established and up-and-coming names, things are looking better all the time.

DE PIJP
This bustling district is notable mainly for the Albert Cuypmarkt and its ethnic food shops, but more fashion boutiques are filling the continually gentrifying gaps.

SPIEGELKWARTIER
Across from the Rijksmuseum and centred on Spiegelgracht, this area is packed with antiques shops selling real treasures at suitably high prices. Dress for success and keep your nose in the air if you want to fit in with the big-spending locals here.

EXPLORE

Damstraat.

The most comprehensive collection of international photographs and posters in the Netherlands, and the largest collection of postcards in Western Europe. The typography posters are good for tourists seeking a unique memento.

BioMarkt

Weteringschans 133 (638 4083, www. biomarkt.nl). Tram 6, 7, 10. **Open** 8am-8pm Mon-Sat; 11am-7pm Sun. **Map** p91 D3 ㉝ **Food & drink**

The largest health food supermarket in the whole of Amsterdam. You'll find everything here, from organic meat, fruit and vegetables (delivered fresh daily) to quite surprisingly tasty sugar-free chocolates, and organic wine and beer.

Bloemenmarkt (Flower Market)

Singel, between Muntplein & Koningsplein. Tram 1, 2, 4, 5, 9, 14, 16, 24. **Open** 9am-5.30pm Mon-Sat; 11am-5.30pm Sun. **No credit cards.** **Map** p91 B3 ㉞ **Market**

This fascinating collage of colour is the world's only floating flower market, with 15 florists and garden shops (although many also hawk cheesy souvenirs these days) permanently ensconced on barges along the southern side of Singel. The plants and flowers usually last well and are good value. *Photo p108.*

Concerto

Utrechtsestraat 52-60 (623 5228, www. concerto.nl). Tram 9. **Open** 10am-6pm Mon-Wed, Fri, Sat; 10am-9pm Thur; noon-6pm Sun. **Map** p91 B4 ㉟ **Books & music**

Head to this sprawling row of connected shops to pick up classic Bach recordings, obscure Beatles items, or even that fave Diana Ross album that got nicked from your party. There are also second-hand 45s and new releases at decent prices. But mainly musos come from afar to browse the savvy selection of CDs and DVDs that cover almost every musical genre.

Eichholtz

Leidsestraat 48 (622 0305, www.eichholtz deli.nl). Tram 1, 2, 5. **Open** 10am-6.30pm Mon; 9am-6.30pm Tue, Wed, Fri, Sat; 9am-9pm Thur; noon- 6pm Sun. **Map** p91 C2 ㊱ **Food & drink**

IN THE KNOW
REFINED SHORTCUT

To avoid the bustle of shopping artery Leidsestraat, take the art and antique gallery route of Spiegelgracht and Nieuwe Spiegelstraat to connect between the Old Centre and the Museum District. Much more refined…

Beloved of expats, this is the place where Yanks can get their hands on chocolate chips, homesick Brits can source Christmas puddings and sentimental Australians can score Vegemite.

Galerie Akinci

Lijnbaansgracht 317 (638 0480, www.akinci.nl). Tram 7, 10, 16, 24. **Open** 1-6pm Tue-Sat. **Map** p91 D4 ㊲ **Gallery**

Part of a row of connected galleries, Akinci thrives on surprising its visitors, hosting exhibitions that employ every contemporary art medium, with a slightly political aesthetic and a bent towards feminist interpretations.

Galerie Alex Daniëls – Reflex Amsterdam

Weteringschans 89A (627 2832, www.reflex amsterdam.com). Tram 7, 10. **Open** 10am-6pm Tue-Sat. **Map** p91 D3 ㊳ **Gallery**

Alex Daniëls is a second-generation gallerist from Amsterdam who presents art and photography that is contemporary, accessible and often linked to the world of fashion – think Araki, David LaChapelle and local legend Erwin Olaf. The gallery provides a nice contrast to the antiques in nearby Spiegelkwartier.

Independent Outlet

Vijzelstraat 77 (421 2096, www.skateboards amsterdam.nl). Tram 4, 16, 24. **Open** 1-6pm Mon, Sun; 11am-6pm Tue, Wed, Fri, Sat; 11am-9pm Thur. **Map** p91 B3 ㊴ **Accessories**

This is the place for customised skateboards, Vans shoes and labels such as Fred Perry, plus a great selection of punk imports.

Lambiek

Kerkstraat 132 (626 7543, www.lambiek.nl). Tram 4, 16, 24. **Open** 11am-6pm Mon-Fri; 11am-5pm Sat; 1-5pm Sun. **Map** p91 C2 ㊵ **Books & music**

Lambiek, founded in 1968, claims to be the world's oldest comic shop and has thousands of books from around the world; its on-site cartoonists' gallery hosts regular exhibitions and the openings bring together the tight-knit local scene.

Luk's Schoenmakerij

Leidsekruisstraat 2 (623 1937). Tram 1, 2, 5, 7, 10. **Open** 9am-5.30pm Tue-Fri; 9am-5pm Sat. **No credit cards. Map** p91 C2 ㊶ **Repairs**

Reliable and speedy shoe repairs.

Mail & Female

Nieuwe Vijzelstraat 2 (623 3916, www.mail female.com). Tram 7, 10, 16, 24, 25. **Open** 11am-7pm Mon-Sat; 1-6pm Sun. **Map** p91 D4 ㊷ **Sex shop**

The Netherlands' oldest mail-order shop for saucy toys and clothes, for and by women, also has a friendly walk-in outlet. Passionate!

Penelope Craft Boutique.

Onitsuka Tiger

*Leidsestraat 27 (528 6183, www.onitsukatiger.
com). Tram 1, 2, 5.* **Open** noon-6pm Mon, Sun;
10am-6pm Tue, Wed, Fri, Sat; 10am-9pm Thur.
Map p91 B2 🔢 **Accessories**

Flagship store for the iconic Japanese trainer brand
Onitsuka Tiger, which continues to make waves the
world over. Should your favourite pair not be on the
shelves, staff will happily order it for you.

Paul Warmer

*Leidsestraat 41 (427 8011, www.paulwarmer.
com). Tram 1, 2, 5.* **Open** 1-6pm Mon; 10am-
6pm Tue, Wed, Fri, Sat; 10am-9pm Thur; noon-
6pm Sun. **Map** p91 C2 🔢 **Accessories**

Fashionista heaven: refined footwear for men and
women. Gucci, Roberto Cavalli and Emillio Pucci are
among the upmarket designers represented.

Penelope Craft Boutique

*Kerkstraat 117 (06 1427 7733 mobile,
www.penelopecraft.com). Tram 16, 24.* **Open**
11am-6pm Tue-Sat. **Map** p91 C2 🔢 **Homewares**

The handmade revival is green, slow, eco and cool.
Penelope Craft Boutique satisfies that crafting urge
with all manner of ribbons, buttons, yarns, needles
and inspiration. Weekly craft nights and workshops
keep the local crafting scene fresh and fun. Crafters
of the world unite!

Plantenmarkt (Plant Market)

Amstelveld (no phone). Tram 4, 16, 24.
Open 9.30am-4pm Mon. **No credit cards**.
Map p91 C5 🔢 **Market**

Despite a general emphasis on plants, pots and
vases, the Plantenmarkt also has cut flowers for sale.
Each spring, the house plants go on sale, while the
later months of the year burst into colour with the
transient glory of garden annuals.

Powders

*Kerkstraat 56 (06 8140 4069 mobile).
Tram 1, 2, 5.* **Open** 8am-9.45pm daily. **No
credit cards**. **Map** p91 C2 🔢 **Dry-cleaner**

Washing and dry-cleaning at a central location.

Salon de Lingerie

*Utrechtsestraat 38 (623 9857, www.salonde
lingerie.nl). Tram 4, 9, 14, 16, 24.* **Open** 1-6pm
Mon; 10am-6pm Tue-Fri; 10am-5pm Sat; noon-
5pm Sun. **Map** p91 B4 🔢 **Accessories**

Find sultry lingerie brands such as Lise Charmel
(adored by the really quite attractive Dutch super-
model Doutzen Kroes), Eprise, Simone Perele and
Freya, and the kind of staff who can determine if
you've been wearing the wrong-sized bra for a decade.

Tesselschade: Arbeid Adelt

*Leidseplein 33 (623 6665, www.tesselschade-
arbeidadelt.nl). Tram 1, 2, 5, 7, 10.* **Open**
11am-5.30pm Tue-Fri; 10am-5pm Sat.
Map p91 D1 🔢 **Homewares**

Absolutely everything at Tesselschade is sold on a
non-profit basis by Arbeid Adelt ('Work Ennobles'),
an association of Dutch women dating from the 19th
century. There are plenty of toys and decorations,
as well as more utilitarian household items such as
tea cosies and decorated clothes hangers.

Uliveto

*Weteringschans 118 (423 0099, www.uliveto.
net). Tram 6, 7, 10.* **Open** 11am-8pm Mon-
Fri; noon-6pm Sat, Sun. **No credit cards**.
Map p91 D5 🔢 **Food & drink**

Uliveto is a superb Italian deli that – along with the
usual wines, pastas and fruity olive oils for dipping
bread – has an irresistible takeaway selection of ten-
der roasted seasonal vegetables, grilled fish, rack of
lamb and polenta, plus ricotta cheesecake.

EXPLORE

Jordaan & West

When Amsterdam was extended in the 17th century, the Jordaan emerged as an area designated for the working classes and smelly industries; it also provided a haven for victims of religious persecution, including Huguenots and Jews. In keeping with the original residents' modest financial circumstances, the houses are mostly small and densely packed, at least when compared to dwellings along the swankier canals. The area is now a higgledy-piggledy mixture of old buildings, modern social housing and the occasional eyesore. Despite this, property is highly desirable, and although locals are mainly proud, community-spirited Jordaaners, the nouveaux riches have moved in and the 'hood is gentrifying. Still, the folk of the Jordaan share a fierce sense of identity, which is known across the nation, and a uniquely laid-back lifestyle.

Noordermarkt.

Don't Miss

1 Noordermarkt Old-world flea market, every Monday morning (p122).

2 Brouwersgracht The most scenic canal in Amsterdam? Or is it Prinsengracht? (p114).

3 Westelijke Eilanden Historical harbour 'hood with quirks (p114).

4 Westergasfabriek Industrial past, artistic future (p116).

5 De Nieuwe Anita The most relaxed club in the world (p197).

NORTH OF ROZENGRACHT

The area north of Rozengracht is easy to get pleasantly lost in. Little lanes and alleys link the already quiet main streets in a mazy haze, and it's no surprise that such a chilled atmosphere incorporates some of the city's best cafés: **'t Smalle** (Egelantiersgracht 12), for example, set on a small canal, where Peter Hoppe (of Hoppe & Jenever, the world's first makers of gin) founded his distillery in 1780. (The Japanese have built an exact replica of 't Smalle in Nagasaki's Holland Village.)

Between scenic coffees or decadent daytime beers, check out the specialist shops tucked away on the adorable side streets. Some of the city's best outdoor markets can also be found nearby: Monday morning's bargainous **Noordermarkt**, and Saturday's paradise of organic produce **Boerenmarkt**, are held around the **Noorderkerk**, the city's original Calvinist church, built in 1623. Adjacent to the Noordermarkt is the equally bargain-packed **Westermarkt**, while another general market fills Lindengracht on Saturdays. For those wishing to add a pinch of culture to their grocery shopping, the Noorderkerk holds concerts every Saturday afternoon at 2pm (mid September to mid June) as well as evening performances (see p204).

Between **Brouwersgracht** and the blisteringly scenic **Westelijke Eilanden**, more quirky shopping opportunities can be found on **Haarlemmerstraat** and its westerly extension, **Haarlemmerdijk**. Though not officially part of the Jordaan, this strip and its alleys share an ambience.

Head east towards Centraal Station past **West Indische Huis** (Herenmarkt 93-97). This home to the famous West Indies Trading Company (WIC) stored the silver that Piet Hein took from the Spanish after a sea battle in 1628, and was the setting for such dubious decisions as selling all of Manhattan for 60 guilders, and running the slave trade between Africa and the Caribbean. Today, it's a popular venue for events and wedding receptions. Heading west, Haarlemmerdijk ends at **Haarlemmerplein**, where you'll see the imposing Haarlemmerpoort city gate, built in 1840. Behind it is wonderful **Westerpark** (see p116 **Floodlights on Westerpark**), connecting to the happening arts complex **Westergasfabriek**.

Sights & Museums

Bibliotheca Philosophica Hermetica

Bloemstraat 15 (625 8079, www.ritmanlibrary.nl). Tram 13, 17. **Open** 1.30-5pm Mon; 10am-12.30pm, 1.30-5pm Tue-Fri. **Admission** €5. **No credit cards. Map** p115 C4 ❶

The Bibliotheca Philosophica Hermetica holds more than 20,000 manuscripts and volumes of Christian-Hermetic tradition. You'll find that it's the perfect place for fact-checking *The Da Vinci Code* or discovering small but illuminating exhibitions. Guided tours (€10) are also available.

Museum Het Schip

Spaarndammerplantsoen 140 (418 2885, www.hetschip.nl). Bus 22. **Open** 11am-5pm Tue-Fri. Guided tours every hr. **Admission** €7.50; €5 reductions; free IAmsterdam, MK. **No credit cards.**

Just north of Westerpark, Spaarndammerplantsoen features three monumental public housing blocks designed by Michel de Klerk, the most expressionist of which is known as Het Schip (The Ship). Museum Het Schip is one of the finest examples of the Amsterdam School architectural movement, and a must-see for architecture students the world over. The carefully designed interior is quite an experience to behold, and exhibitions investigate the importance of public housing in Amsterdam, and the cultural-historical value of the Amsterdam School (see p251 **School of Rock**).

Restaurants

De Aardige Pers

2e Hugo de Grootstraat 13 (400 3107, www.samanrestaurant.nl). Tram 10. **Open** 4-11pm daily. **Main courses** €10-€15. **No credit cards. Map** p115 A5 ❷ Persian

Located just west of the Jordaan, on an emerging culinary boulevard, 'The Nice Persian' is aptly named. Enjoy Iranian cuisine served family-style and with family grace, such as delicious lamb with *sabzi* (green herbs), or chicken in walnut and pomegranate sauce. A surprising experience for anyone not versed in this rich culinary culture.

IN THE KNOW ISLAND LIFE

Just north of the Jordaan are the **Westelijke Eilanden** (the 'Western Islands' of Realeneiland, Prinseneiland and Bickerseiland). These artificial islands were created in the 17th century to sustain maritime activity. Although there are now trendy warehouse flats, artists' studios and a yacht basin – where once shipyards, tar distillers, and fish salters and smokers were based – the area still remains the best place for a scenic stroll evocative of seafaring times. After admiring the yellow submarine moored on Bickerseiland, unwind at the **Blaauwhooft** café (Hendrik Jonkerplein 1, 623 8721, www.blaauwhooft.nl).

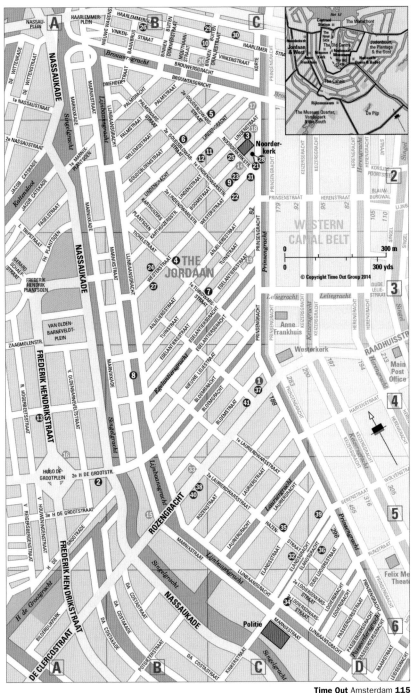

FLOODLIGHTS ON WESTERPARK

A gas of a neighbourhood – complete with art park.

North Sea Jazz Club.

EXPLORE

A few short decades ago, the Westerpark neighbourhood was known for its squatters and drugs. It's now an alluring 'hood, close to the Jordaan, that's unified by the monumental **Westergasfabriek**, a former gas works turned arts park.

Back in the 1960s, when the Netherlands switched over to natural gas, a 14.5-hectare coal gas company site on the western edge of the city became obsolete. It remained a somewhat rundown storage centre until the 1990s, when it was zoned for use as a cultural park. Designed by American landscape architect Kathryn Gustafson, it's a clever example of urban reuse.

The former energy plant is now a thriving park with walking and running trails, a babbling brook, a wading pool for kids, playing fields for football and other sports, tennis courts and outdoor gyms. The buildings now house cultural destinations: an intimate art-house cinema (**Het Ketelhuis**, *see p176*); large and small performance venues; dance clubs; daycare centres; and a slew of restaurants, bars and cafés. The most surprising reworking? A giant gas tank in the middle of the one-time factory complex has been transformed into a party/events location called the Gashouder.

The new **North Sea Jazz Club** (*see p201*) is an initiative from the organisers of the world-renowned North Sea Jazz Festival. For something more urban, there's **MC Theater** (*see p197*) and its soul-food restaurant **Toko MC** (Polonceaukade 5, 475 0425, tokomc.nl). Alternatively, try **Pacific Parc** (Polonceaukade 23, 488 7778, www.pacificparc.nl), which regularly features nasty but nice rock 'n' roll bands.

For edgy eats, **Proef** (Gosschalklaan 12, 682 2656, www.proefamsterdam.nl) is home to 'eating designer' Marije Vogelzang, who presents sharing plates with a whimsy that will make you smile: salads are served in teacups and soup in mason jars. For something more down to earth, check out the sun-kissed patios of **WestergasTerras** (Klönneplein 4-6, 684 8496, www.westergasterras.nl) or 'nomadic restaurant' **Rainarai** (www.rainarai.nl). If it's the third Sunday of the month, you can explore the stalls of the excellent **NeighbourFood Market** (www.neighbourfoodmarket.nl).

There are also some standout eateries in the adjoining neighbourhood, including **Café-Restaurant Amsterdam** (*see p117*) and Italian restaurant/deli **Bella Storia** (Bentinckstraat 28, 488 0599, www.bellastoria.info).

★ Bordewijk

*Noordermarkt 7 (624 3899, www.bordewijk.nl).
Tram 3, 10 or bus 18, 21, 22.* **Open** 6.30-
10.30pm Tue-Sat. **Main courses** €24-€29.
Map p115 C2 **❸** French
Come here to sample some of the city's finest original
food and palate-tingling wines in a stylish designer
interior. The service and atmosphere are both
relaxed, and the kitchen is very reliable.

Café-Restaurant Amsterdam

*Watertorenplein 6 (682 2666, www.cradam.nl).
Tram 10.* **Open** 10.30am-midnight (kitchen
closes 10.30pm) Mon-Thur, Sun; 10.30am-1am
Fri, Sat (kitchen closes 11.30pm). **Main courses**
€7-€22. Dutch
This spacious monument to industry just west of the
Jordaan pumped water from the coast's dunes for
around a century. Now it pumps out honest Dutch
and French dishes, from *kroketten* to caviar, under
a mammoth ceiling and floodlights rescued from the
old Ajax stadium. It's a truly unique – and child-
friendly – experience.

€ Comestibles Kinders

*Westerstraat 189 (622 7983, www.broodje
kinders.nl). Tram 3, 10 or bus 18, 21.*
Open 7am-5pm Mon-Sat; 8am-4pm Sun.
Sandwiches €2.40-€3.50. **Map** p115 B3
❹ Sandwiches
The best sandwich shop in the Jordaan? Decide
over a 'Bolgeri' with chicken fillet, bacon, pesto, let-
tuce, mayo and some secret herbs for a mere €2.40.
There's also a happy rainbow of other options.

Duende

*Lindengracht 62 (420 6692, www.cafe-duende.nl).
Tram 3, 10.* **Open** 5-11pm Mon-Fri; 4-11pm
Sat, Sun. **Tapas** €4-€15.50. **Map** p115 C1
❺ Spanish
Get a real taste of Andalucia with the fine tapas
dished up at Duende. Be prepared to share your table
with an amorous couple or, perhaps, one of the flamenco dancers who might offer you a free lesson
before getting up to stamp and strut. Flamenco performances happen at 10.30pm on the first Saturday
of the month.

G's Really, Really Nice Place

*Goudsbloemstraat 91 (no phone, www.really
niceplace.com). Tram 3, 10.* **Open** 6pm-2am
Thur, Fri; 10.30am-7pm Sat, Sun. **Main courses**
€9-€18. **Map** p115 B2 **❻** Café
Resembling a Hipstamatic version of a 'brown café'
(all letterpress fonts and vintage crockery), G's is a
bar that serves superlative brunch on weekends and
hosts quirky pop-up events. They also mix a crack-
ing bloody mary – a food group in itself, according
to the owner. Hours can vary and extra events can
happen spontaneously, so check ahead on the website and book ahead via email.

La Oliva Pintxos y Vinos

*Egelantiersstraat 122-124 (320 4316,
www.laoliva.nl). Tram 3, 10.* **Open** noon-
10pm Mon-Wed, Sun; noon-11pm Thur-Sat.
Main courses €22.50-€26.50. **Map** p115 C3
❼ Spanish
From yuppies to genuine Spaniards, many praise La
Oliva's authentic food and tapas, as well as the rich
selection of wines by the glass. If it's too busy (and
there's a good chance it will be), there are plenty of
other restaurants along this strip, recently nicknamed 'Little Italy'.

Semhar

*Marnixstraat 259-261 (638 1634, www.
semhar.nl). Tram 10.* **Open** 4-10pm Tue-
Sun. **Main courses** €15-€18. **Map** p115 B4
❽ Ethiopian
A great spot to sample the spicy, vegetarian-friendly
food of Ethiopia, including *injera* (a type of sourdough pancake), best accompanied by a beer. Ideal
after an afternoon spent wandering the Jordaan.

SLA

*Westerstraat 34 (789 3019, www.ilovesla.com).
Tram 3, 10.* **Open** 11am-9pm Mon, Sat, Sun;
noon-9pm Tue-Fri. **Main courses** €7.50-€9.
No cash. Map p115 C2 **❾** Salads
'Sla' means salad. And, indeed, they are organic
health freaks here – but in a relaxed and tasty way.
Try one of their 'favourites' (grilled organic chicken
with cauliflower, broccoli and red quinoa, perhaps)
or create your own personalised salad. To maintain
balance, forgo the juices for a locally produced beer
from Brouwerij 't IJ.

SLA.

EXPLORE

Other locations Ceintuurbaan 149, De Pijp (789 3080).

★ Small World Catering
Binnen Oranjestraat 14 (420 2774, www.small worldcatering.nl). Bus 18, 22. **Open** 10.30am-7pm Tue-Fri; 10.30am-6pm Sat; noon-6pm Sun. **Main courses** €7.50-€10. **No credit cards**. **Map** p115 C1 ⑩ **Café**
The home base for this catering company is this tiny deli with a lovely proprietor. As well as superlative coffee and fresh juices, there are salads, lasagne and excellent sandwiches.

★ Toscanini
Lindengracht 75 (623 2813, www.restaurant toscanini.nl). Tram 3, 10. **Open** 6-10.30pm Mon-Sat. **Main courses** €18-€26. **Set meal** €47.50 6 courses. **Map** p115 C2 ⑪ **Italian**
The invariably excellent food at this popular spot is prepared in an open kitchen. Expect the likes of Sardinian sheep's cheese with chestnut honey and black pepper, or beef tenderloin with rosemary and lardo di colonnata. Book in advance if you want to ensure a table.
▶ *If you don't want to make an evening of it, or are looking for something cheaper, nearby Capri (Lindengracht 63, 624 4940) has fine pizza.*

Vlaming
Lindengracht 95 (622 2716, www.eetcafe vlaming.nl). Tram 3, 10. **Open** 6pm-midnight Tue-Thur; 6pm-1am Fri, Sat. **Main courses** €13.50-€20. **Map** p115 B2 ⑫ **Dutch/Global**
Whether it's for the North Sea-size burger or Asian-inspired tuna steaks, regulars keep returning to this cosy and neighbourly 'eating café' in the heart of the Jordaan. Their second outlet is roomier, more brasserie-like and open seven days a week, but its menu lacks the burger. Book ahead.
Other locations Prinsengracht 193a, Western Canal Belt (427 2063).

★ Yam-Yam
Frederik Hendrikstraat 88-90 (681 5097, www.yamyam.nl). Tram 3, 10. **Open** 6-10pm Tue-Sat; 5.30-10pm Sun. **Main courses** €10-€18. **No credit cards**. **Map** p115 A4 ⑬ **Italian**
Unequalled and inexpensive pastas and pizzas (cooked in a wood oven) in a hip and casual atmosphere: no wonder Yam-Yam is a local favourite. It's certainly worth the trip west of the Jordaan, but be sure to book in advance.

Bars

Café Hegeraad
Noordermarkt 34 (624 5565). Tram 3, 10 or bus 18, 21, 22. **Open** 8am-1am Mon-Thur; 8am-3am Fri, Sat; 9am-1am Sun. **No credit cards**. **Map** p115 C2 ⑭

Toscanini.

The polar opposite – geographically as well as figuratively – of minimalist Proust (*see p121*) and its neighbour Finch, this gabled building with leaded windows has probably been a café for as long as the Noorderkerk church that it looks on to has been standing. Be careful not to spill your drink on the carpeted tables.

★ Café Soundgarden
Marnixstraat 164-166 (620 2853, www.cafe soundgarden.nl). Tram 10, 13, 17. **Open** 1pm-1am Mon-Thur; 1pm-3am Fri; 3pm-3am Sat; 3pm-1am Sun. **No credit cards**. **Map** p115 B5 ⑮
A dirty old rockers' bar where musos, journos and everyone else who refuses to grow up gets smashed in one big, sloppy mêlée. The soundtrack is composed from the entire back catalogue of classic alternative pop, often from DJs and bands, and sometimes accompanied by (inexpert) dancing. Bliss. At the back is a surprisingly restful terrace, where boats can moor when it's time for a break from touring the canals. There's also pool, pinball and a good range of beer.

IN THE KNOW CITY FARM

Just a few minutes by bicycle from Westergasfabriek, you'll come across a friendly neighbourhood farm in the middle of a sheep field. The volunteer-run **Buurtboerderij Ons Genoegen** (Spaarndammerdijk 319, 337 6820, www.buurtboerderij.nl) has a lovely café and organises assorted events throughout the year. Perfect for when the big, bad city just gets too much.

PAINTING THE TOWN

Street art has come of age in Amsterdam.

Amsterdam has a very active street-art scene, visible on almost every corner, in many shapes and sizes, from free-hand graffiti to stencils, sculptures, tags and stickers. Although it's illegal to mark public and private buildings, the city's famous liberalism makes it somewhere that writers (as they're called in graff parlance) love to tag. Even though the city spends around €350,000 a year on cleaning monuments and municipal buildings, and fines street vandals, that's a pittance compared to other cities. And there are plenty of legal walls – aka 'Halls of Fame' – the sites of painting jams where artists collaborate on a stretch of concrete or an entire building.

One of the more prolific practitioners is **Laser 3.14**. Dubbed Amsterdam's very own 'guerrilla poet', his words of wisdom are dotted all over town. No building site is safe from his aerosol and post-modern one-liners (in English). 'Swallowed by your own introspective vortex,' and 'She fears the ghouls that reside in her shadow,' are just two cryptic examples.

Many old-school graffiti artists – such as **Morcky**, **Boghe**, **Hugo Mulder (DHM)**, **Ottograph**, **Juice**, **Delta** and **Shoe** – long ago crossed over to creating design work and/or exhibiting in galleries worldwide. The latest local making a splash is Swiss-born **Bustart**, who specialises in paper posters depicting introspective animals.

Arguably the most prolific and well-known local street artists are **The London Police (TLP)**. These two British men have put their own stamp on the streets of the world with their 'lads': deceptively simple-looking, black and white blob characters, which first appeared on electricity boxes around town, but later found their way into galleries. One of their murals is beside the street art-friendly gallery **GO** (Prinsengracht 64, 422 9580, www.gogallery.nl). Not far away, next to a school yard across from Tuinstraat 172, is another huge mural, a collaboration between primary schoolkids and the illustrator/designer **Parra**. Local artists **Jeroen Koolhaas** and **Dre Urhahn** regularly jet to Brazil to work with schoolchildren to paint whole favelas with bright primary colours. Never have slums looked so funky. Check out www.favelapainting.com.

Original Dampkring Gallery (*see p99*) hosts regular street-art exhibitions, and sells work by the likes of Laser 3.14. There's more street art on show at **Henxs** (St Antoniebreestraat 136-138, 638 9478, www.henxs.com), but you might also come face to face with the artists themselves, as this is where they stock up on spray cans and markers (if not from the spray paint stand at nearby Waterlooplein flea market). The shop is hard to miss: the sticker-covered front porch is a kind of who's who of the Amsterdam street scene. Meanwhile, bar **Hannekes Boom** (*see p156*) hosts painting events in the summer, and there's lots to see at the former shipyard **NDSM** (*see p158* **Northern Lights**), long the place for street artists to practise their trade.

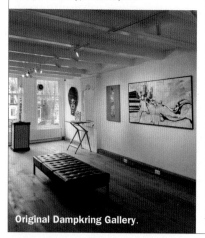

Original Dampkring Gallery.

Hugo's Bar & Kitchen

Hugo de Grootplein 10 (751 6633, www.bar hugo.nl). Tram 3, 10. **Open** 5pm-1am Mon-Thur; 5pm-3am Fri, Sat; noon-11pm Sun. **Map** p115 A4 ⑯

Just west of Jordaan, a former Moroccan veg shop with an industrial makeover is now a bar-restaurant where cocktails reign supreme. Try their signature concoction, Hugo the Great: special rum, chartreuse, sage, pepper, honey, lime and St-Germain elderflower liqueur. They also have an inventive and reasonably priced French-inspired menu – crab salad with sherry, beetroot and mandarin, for instance – and serve brunch on Sundays until 9pm.

Papeneiland

Prinsengracht 2 (624 1989, www.papeneiland.nl). Tram 3, 10 or bus 18, 21, 22. **Open** 10am-1am Mon-Thur, Sun; 10am-2am Fri, Sat. **No credit cards. Map** p115 C1 ⑰

This beautiful Delft-tiled bar is a wonderful spot for a drink and a chinwag. A definite talking point is the café's fascinating history: apparently, a tunnel runs under the canal, which, when Catholicism was outlawed in the 17th century, secretly delivered worshippers to their church opposite. It certainly explains the bar's name: Pope's Island.

Proust

Noordermarkt 4 (623 9145, www.proust.nl). Tram 3, 10 or bus 18, 21, 22. **Open** 9am-1am Mon; 5pm-1am Tue-Fri, Sun; 9am-3am Sat. **Map** p115 C2 ⑱

Still trendy after all these years, and great for a market pit stop or to kickstart a bar crawl. The interior is pared down in style – as are the punters. If it's full, try Finch next door; on warm days, both bars' terraces merge into one convivial whole to create an atmosphere that is pure Amsterdam.

★ 't Smalle

Egelantiersgracht 12 (623 9617, www.t-smalle.nl). Tram 13, 14, 17. **Open** 10am-1am Mon-Thur, Sun; 10am-2am Fri, Sat. **No credit cards. Map** p115 C3 ⑲

This is one of the most scenic terraces on one of the prettiest canals, so it's no surprise that waterside seats are snared early in the day – patience is essential. It's very cute inside too, with gleaming brass fixtures harking back to the heady drinking days of the 18th century, when it was the Hoppe distillery.

★ Vesper Bar

Vinkenstraat 57 (846 4458, www.vesperbar.nl). Bus 18, 22. **Open** 8pm-1am Tue-Thur; 5pm-3am Fri, Sat. **Map** p115 B1 ⑳

You know you're in the hands of a good bartender when, instead of offering you a cocktail menu, he simply asks, 'What do you feel like?' Vesper's talented team serve old-fashioned classics and modern interpretations or anything you fancy, in classy and charming surroundings. Wine and beer take a back seat to the hard stuff, but, like everything at this intimate bar, both are sourced from small-scale and carefully selected producers.

Shops & Services

★ Boerenmarkt

Noordermarkt (no phone). Tram 3, 10 or bus 18, 21, 22. **Open** 9am-4pm Sat. **No credit cards. Map** p115 C2 ㉑ **Market**

Every Saturday, the Noordermarkt (*see p122*) turns into an organic farmers' market. Singers or medieval musicians sometimes perform alfresco, making the whole experience feel more like a cultural day trip than a grocery run.

▶ *Serene Saturday concerts take place at nearby Noorderkerk (see p114).*

DAK 77

Westerstraat 77 (688 7788, www.daklocal foods.nl). Tram 3, 10 or bus 18, 21, 22. **Open** 10.30am-8pm Mon-Fri; 9.30am-9pm Sat. **Map** p115 C2 ㉒ **Food & drink**

DAK specialises in food and drink from local producers, so come here for prime treats from the likes of stellar organic caterer Streep, sausage kings Brandt & Levie or brewery Oedipus (which produces a hoppy ale called Momma – but don't read too much into it). You can also pop by for a coffee or an Italian meal and some fine wine.

Delicious Food

Westerstraat 24 (320 3070, www.deliciousfood.nl). Tram 3, 10 or bus 18, 21, 22. **Open** 9.30am-6.30pm Mon-Fri; 9am-6pm Sat. **No credit cards. Map** p115 C2 ㉓ **Food & drink**

Organic produce has reached the self-contradictory pinnacle of urban-rustic chic at this fancy health-food store – a useful place if you're buying in bulk.

DAK 77

EXPLORE

Moooi.

Distortion Records
Westerstraat 244 (627 0004, www.distortion.nl).
Tram 3, 10. **Open** 11am-6pm Tue, Wed, Fri;
11am-9pm Thur; 10am-6pm Sat. **No credit
cards. Map** p115 B3 **㉔ Books & music**
A tiny store with a chaos of vinyl (and some CDs),
from 1970s punk rock, jazz, funk, soul, Latin and
soundtracks, through lo-fi, indie, noise, garage and
industrial, to '80s and '90s indie, electro, hip hop and
reggae, ending up in break beats and house for those
with more dancefloor-oriented interests.

Flesch Records
*Noorderkerkstraat 16 (622 8185). Tram 3,
10 or bus 18, 22.* **Open** 10am-4pm Mon;
1-5pm Tue-Fri; 10am-6pm Sat. **Map** p115 C2
㉕ Books & music
Sheer genius: if sales sometimes lag in the world of
rare vinyl, antique radios and classic record players
and needles, don't whine – just start selling a selection of fruit and veg on the side. You may also want
to cast your eye over Flesch's equally eccentric
neighbour: Donald E Jongejans (no.18, 624 6888,
open 11am-6pm Mon, Sat), a vintage eyewear specialist that sells unused frames dating from the mid
1800s to the present day.

Jutka & Riska
*Haarlemmerdijk 143 (06 2466 8593 mobile,
www.jutkaenriska.nl). Bus 18, 22.* **Open** 10.30am-
7pm Mon-Wed, Fri-Sun; 10.30am-9pm Thur.
No credit cards. Map p115 B1 **㉖ Fashion**
This kooky store (there are Barbie dolls lurking all
over the place) stocking a mix of 'old, new, borrowed
and blue' fashion prides itself on its extensive range
of reasonably priced 1950s, '60s and '70s frocks.
Most cost under €50. There's also second-hand

Sonia Rykiel, vintage Yves Saint Laurent blazers
and some colourful one-off pieces from the store's
Jutka & Riska label.
Other locations Bilderdijkstraat 194,
Oud West (618 8021).

Moooi
*Westerstraat 187 (528 7760, www.moooi.com).
Tram 3, 10.* **Open** 10am-6pm Tue-Sat.
Map p115 B3 **㉗ Homewares**
A former school has been transformed into a Dutch
design hub and the studio of design star Marcel
Wanders – inventor of the iconic Knotted Chair, and
also responsible for the Andaz Amsterdam (*see
p282*) hotel. On the ground floor, step into his stylish
store, Moooi, the showroom for his work and the
portfolios of other creatives such as Studio Job, Piet
Boon and Jurgen Bey. But don't come here expecting
to find any bargains.

★ Noordermarkt
*Noordermarkt (no phone). Tram 3, 10 or bus
18, 21, 22.* **Open** 7.30am-1pm Mon. **No credit
cards. Map** p115 C2 **㉘ Market**
North of Westermarkt, Noordermarkt is frequented
by the serious shopper. The huge stacks of (mainly
second-hand) clothes, shoes, jewellery and hats need
to be sorted with a grim determination, but there are
real bargains to be had. Arrive early or the best stuff
will probably have been nabbed.
▶ *An organic farmers' market is held here on
Saturdays; see p121 Boerenmarkt.*

Papabubble
*Haarlemmerdijk 70 (626 2662, www.papa
bubble.nl). Bus 18, 22.* **Open** 1-6pm Mon,
Wed-Fri; 10am-6pm Sat. **Map** p115 C1
㉙ Food & drink
Touch, smell and ask about the world of freestyle
swirly candy making. They'll even make you a customised business card out of just water, sugar and
glucose. In short: make your dream candy a reality.
Other locations Staalstraat 16,
Old Centre: Old Side.

Store Without A Home
*Haarlemmerdijk 26 (no phone, www.store
withoutahome.nl). Bus 18, 22.* **Open** 1-6pm
Mon; 10am-6pm Tue-Sat. **No cash. Map**
p115 C1 **㉚ Homewares**
It must bode well for the local economy: pop-ups are
putting down permanent roots (*see p167* Collector
and *p167* Hutspot Amsterdam). From cloud-shaped
lights to cushions embroidered with birds, everything in this interiors trove is guaranteed to make
your apartment happier.

Westermarkt
*Westerstraat (no phone). Tram 3, 10 or bus 18,
21, 22.* **Open** 9am-1pm Mon. **No credit cards.**
Map p115 C2 **㉛ Market**

EXPLORE

A Monday market selling all sorts of stuff. The people packing the pavement are proof of the reasonable prices and range of goods, including new watches, pretty (and not so pretty) fabrics and cheap clothes. ▶ *Don't forget to visit the neighbouring (mainly second-hand) Noordermarkt; see left.*

ROZENGRACHT & FURTHER SOUTH

Once a canal, the now filled-in Rozengracht scythes through the heart of the Jordaan in unappealing fashion. Rembrandt lived at no.184 from 1659 until his death a decade later – there is a plaque on the first floor. While you're here, look up at the gable of Rozengracht 204 to spy an iron stickman wall anchor, or consider visiting some of the many galleries (*see p124* **Art Throb**).

South of Rozengracht is notable for the **Antiek Centrum Amsterdam** antiques market. Elandsgracht 71-77 is where the labyrinthine Sjako's Fort was said to have once stood. Sjako is often referred to as the 'Robin Hood of Amsterdam', though while he was happy stealing from the rich, he usually neglected to give to the poor. Still, he had style: not many burglars go about their business dressed in white and accompanied by henchmen clad in black. In 1718, his 24-year-old head ended up spiked on a pole where the Shell Building now stands, but local anarchist bookstore **Fort van Sjako** (Jodenbreestraat 24, Jodenbuurt, 625 8979, www.sjakoo.nl), and a shrine in the window of the building that replaced his fort keep his name alive – though, sadly, a local historian recently proved the story of Sjako was almost completely myth.

Restaurants

Balthazar's Keuken

Elandsgracht 108 (420 2114, www.balthazar skeuken.nl). Tram 7, 10. **Open** 6-11pm Wed-Sat. **Set meal** €32.50 3 courses. **Map** p115 C5 ㉜ **Mediterranean**
This tiny restaurant is always packed tight, so you really need to book ahead to make sure of enjoying its excellent set menu of meat or fish dishes.

Bars

Struik

Rozengracht 160 (625 4863), Tram 10, 13, 14, 17. **Open** 5pm-1am Mon-Thur; 3pm-3am Fri, Sat; 3pm-1am Sun. **No credit cards. Map** p115 B5 ㉝

HIDDEN HOFJES

A stroll around the city's compact courtyards.

It's widely claimed that the name 'Jordaan' derives from the French *jardin* (garden) via the French Huguenots who migrated to the neighbourhood in the 17th century. Peek behind the grand houses and apartment blocks that flank the nearby canals and you'll see why: there's a multitude of tranquil residential courtyards, known in Dutch as *hofjes* (almshouses). Originally built by charitable patrons during the Middle Ages for elderly women and the vulnerable, these oases now form some of the most desirable spots to live, providing the luxury of verdant seclusion within a busy and vibrant city. Private tours (*see pp50-53*) can be arranged, but wandering them on your own preserves the tranquil feel. The best known are the **Raepenhofje** (Palmgracht 28 38), **Venetiae** (Elandsstraat 106-136), **Sint Andrieshofje** (Egelantiersgracht 107-114), **Karthuizerhof** (Karthuizerstraat 21-31), **Suyckerhofje** (Lindengracht 149-163), **Claes Claesz Hofje** (1e Egelantiersdwarsstraat 3) and, oldest by far, the **Lindenhofje** (Lindengracht 94-112).

Remember that the art of *hofje*-hopping is a gamble, because entrances are sometimes locked in deference to the residents. Take a chance and you may be surprised by the delights inside, but don't peer through the windows – that's just rude.

ART THROB

Crossing a river of Jordaan art.

You could easily spend a whole holiday trawling the 40-odd galleries in the Jordaan. Occupying former homes or shops, they're pleasantly compact spaces, best visited in the afternoon from Wednesday to Saturday.

Galerie Gabriel Rolt (Elandsgracht 34, 785 5146, www.gabrielrolt.com) is a great starting point: it's one of the more respected galleries in town, with an international selection of intriguing artists, such as Abner Preis and photography duo Adam Broomberg and Oliver Chanarin. From here, head west and turn right into Hazenstraat, which contains many galleries and is also an excellent artery from which to dart left and right to visit others.

Witzenhausen Gallery (Hazenstraat 60, 644 9898, www.witzenhausengallery.nl), an internationally minded 'white box' with an outpost in New York, features often-terrific new work by acclaimed artists such as Alvaro Barrios and Hendrik Kerstens, as well as emerging artists. On the next corner, **Stigter van Doesburg** (Elandstraat 90, 624 2361, www.stigtervandoesburg.com) has an impressive roster of artists including Tjebbe Beekman, Irene Fortuyn and miniaturist Saskia Olde Wolbers. Cross a bridge and turn right to find canalside **Torch** (Lauriergracht 94, 626 0284, www.torchgallery.com), which has built a quirky reputation by exhibiting the likes of Jake and Dinos Chapman, Anton Corbijn and Richard Kern.

Returning to Hazenstraat, the next left leads to **Annet Gelink Gallery** (Laurierstraat 187-189, 330 2066, www.annetgelink.com) – she's seen by many artists as the most desired contemporary-art dealer of the moment. Why? Simple: her stable of hot, young international up-and-comers, including David Maljkovic, Barbara Visser, Erik van Lieshout and Ryan Gander. And she has plenty of space and light to lavish on them. Take the next right off Hazenstraat to reach **Stedelijk Museum Bureau Amsterdam** (Rozenstraat 59, 422 0471, www.smba.nl). It's often hipper than its mothership, with subversive shows by locally based rising stars.

On the north side of Rozengracht is **Galerie Fons Welters** (Bloemstraat 140, 423 3046, www.fonswelters.nl). Doyen of the Amsterdam art scene, Fons Welters

Galerie Fons Welters.

likes to 'discover' local talent and has shown remarkable taste in the fields of photography and installation, providing a home for Dutch artists Jennifer Tee and Berend Strik. A visit here is worth it for the Atelier van Lieshout entrance alone.

Paul Andriesse (Leliegracht 47, 623 6237, www.paulandriesse.nl) is one of the original gallerists in the Jordaan district, but has been moving around a lot recently – and will likely do so again in 2014. Currently he's just over the Prinsengracht in the Southern Canal Belt, where he shows top-tier artists such as Marlene Dumas, Thomas Struth and the curious Austrian twin sisters Christine and Irene Hohenbüchler, along with newcomers.

Then there's the even more curious **KochxBos Gallery** (1e Anjeliersdwarsstraat 36, 681 4567, www.kochxbos.nl), back in the Jordaan and further north. It specialises in work from the dark sides of 'low-brow' artists such as Ray Caesar, Mark Ryden and Tim Biskup – art for those who like their hot rods ablaze, their punk snotty and their films in the Lynchian tradition.

If you are fascinated by what lies behind closed doors, then visit **Open Ateliers Jordaan** (www.openateliersjordaan.nl) in late May, when around 60 artists' studios open their doors to the public.

A chilled bar for creatives who like their music cool and their design street. The friendly neighbourhood café vibe is enhanced by budget-priced daily dinner specials. Later on, the DJ kicks in. They also have a larger sister operation up the street, Brandstof (Marnixstraat 357, 422 0813, www.bar-brandstof.nl).

Shops & Services

★ Antiek Centrum Amsterdam

Elandsgracht 109 (624 9038, www.antiekcentrumamsterdam.nl). Tram 7, 10, 17. **Open** 11am-6pm Mon, Wed-Fri; 11am-5pm Sat, Sun. **Map** p115 C6 ❷ **Market**

The 70-plus stalls here deal mainly in antiques, with plenty of collectors' items; you'll find everything from pewter to paintings, and glassware to gold. It's easy to get lost in the quiet premises and find yourself standing alone by a stall crammed with antiquated clocks ticking eerily away.

Chocolátl

Hazenstraat 25a (no phone, www.chocolatl.nl). Tram 3, 10, 12. **Open** 11am-6pm Tue-Sat; 1-5pm Sun. Hours may vary in winter. **Map** p115 C5 ❸ **Food & drink**

Regarding their shop as a 'chocolate gallery', the folks behind Chocolátl are evangelical about artisanal, single-origin chocolate from around the globe – along with chocolate-friendly teas, coffees and beer. All in all, a very sweet operation.

HJ van de Kerkhof

Elandsgracht 43 (623 4084, www.kerkhofpassementen.com). Tram 7, 10, 17. **Open** 11am-5pm Tue-Sat. **No credit cards**. **Map** p115 D5 ❸ **Accessories**

Tassel maniacs go wild at this well-stocked haberdashery. A sea of shakeable frilly things, lace and rhinestone banding, and much more besides.

Kitsch Kitchen

Rozengracht 8-12 (462 0051, www.kitschkitchen.nl). Tram 13, 14, 17. **Open** 10am-6pm Mon-Sat; noon-5pm Sun. **Map** p115 C4 ❸ **Homewares**

A Mexican *mercado* with a twist. Even the hardiest opponents of tat will love the ultra-colourful culinary and household objects, including crockery, oilcloths, bike-seat covers and paper banners.

★ SPRMRKT

Rozengracht 191-193 (330 5601, www.sprmrkt.nl). Tram 13, 14, 17. **Open** noon- 6pm Mon; 10am-6pm Tue, Wed, Fri, Sat; 10am- 8pm Thur; 1-6pm Sun. **Map** p115 B5 ❸ **Fashion**

A whopping 450sq m (4,850sq ft) store – that's pretty big for Amsterdam – of exceptionally cool duds. The prize is the shop-within-the-shop, SPR+, featuring picks from Maison Martin Margiela, Rick Owens and others.

Tenue de Nîmes

Elandsgracht 60 (320 4012, www.tenuedenimes.com). Tram 7, 10. **Open** noon- 6pm Mon, Sun; 10am-6pm Tue, Wed, Fri, Sat; 10am-8pm Thur. **Map** p115 D5 ❸ **Fashion**

Aptly named after the spiritual home of denim (a rustic French town called Nîmes), this boutique-cum-photography gallery features bare brick walls adorned with denim-covered beams, antiquated Singer sewing machines and limited-edition Raw Cannondale bicycles. The shop's selection of edgier brands, including Momotaro, Acne and Rag & Bone, is second to none.

Other locations Haarlemmerstraat 92-94, Western Canal Belt (331 2778).

De Vegetarische Slager

Rozengracht 217 (423 4199, www.vegetarianbutcher.com). Tram 10, 13, 14, 17. **Open** 8.30am-7.30pm Mon-Fri; 8.30am-7pm Sat; 11am-7pm Sun. **Map** p115 B5 ❹ **Food & drink**

'The Vegetarian Butcher' sells killer pea-based chicken, bacon and other 'meats' that grab your taste buds without involving any killing – plus other vegan/vegetarian meals and ingredients. Hugely popular, this deli/takeaway/supermarket seems set to go international.

Wegewijs

Rozengracht 32 (624 4093, www.wegewijs.nl). Tram 13, 14, 17. **Open** 8.30am-6pm Mon-Fri; 9am-5pm Sat. **No credit cards**. **Map** p115 C4 ❹ **Food & drink**

The Wegewijs family opened this shop more than a century ago. On offer are around 50 foreign and more than 100 domestic varieties of cheese, including *graskaas*, a grassy-tasting cheese that's available in summer. You're allowed to try the Dutch varieties before you buy.

OUD WEST

Between Westerpark and the Museum Quarter & Vondelpark lies Oud West. While mostly a residential area, the shopping streets De Clercqstraat, Kinkerstraat and, especially, hipster strip Jan Pieter Heijestraat are all worth a wander. Outdoor market **Ten Katemarkt** (9am-6pm Mon-Sat) provides the district's heart – along with econo food, clothes and cafés. One of the market's cross-streets, Bellamystraat, is regarded by many as one of the cuter streets in the city with its tiny but lush front yards. In late 2014, Oud West will develop into more of a going-out hub with the opening of **De Hallen** (Bellamyplein, www.tramremisedehallen.nl). This former tram depot and 19th-century monument is being turned into a 'centre for media, fashion, craft and culture', complete with hotel, shops, cinema, TV studios, library, food court and daycare.

EXPLORE

Museums, Vondelpark & Zuid

Over a century ago, the area now known as the Museum Quarter was still outside the city limits. Towards the end of the 19th century, the city expanded rapidly and the primarily upper-class city fathers decided to erect a swanky neighbourhood between the working-class areas to the west and south. The area's heart lies in Museumplein, the city's largest square; it's a cultured, expensive part of town.

Oud Zuid, Amsterdam's own golden monument to the good life, is located just a stroll through the city's central green space, the Vondelpark. Stretching out in a ring beneath it is Nieuw Zuid (New South); further south is Amstelveen with the beautiful Amsterdamse Bos forest.

Concertgebouw.

Don't Miss

1 Rijksmuseum Lose yourself in the nation's 'treasure house' (p130).

2 Vondelpark Chill out on the grass – bongos optional (p128).

3 Van Gogh Museum Everyone's favourite earless genius (p133).

4 Stedelijk Museum How modern do you want your art? (p130).

5 Concertgebouw The best classical venue on the planet? (p203).

Vondelpark.

EXPLORE

THE MUSEUM QUARTER

The centre of the Museum Quarter is **Museumplein**, the city's largest square, bordered by the **Rijksmuseum**, the **Stedelijk Museum of Modern Art**, the **Van Gogh Museum** and the **Concertgebouw** (*see p203*). Developed in 1872, Museumplein served as a location for the World Exhibition of 1883, and was then rented out to the Amsterdam ice-skating club between 1900 and 1936. During the Depression, the field was put to use as a sports ground, and during World War II, the Germans built bunkers on it. In 1953, the country's 'shortest motorway', Museumstraat, cut it in two. The more recent additions of grass, a wading pool (that gets transformed into a skating rink in winter), a skate ramp, café and a wacky extension to the Van Gogh Museum helped boost it a bit. But now, with both the Stedelijk and the Rijksmuseum reopened, the square is back to being an essential destination for visitors.

As you might expect in such seriously highfalutin cultural surroundings, property in this area doesn't come cheap – and the affluence is apparent. **Van Baerlestraat** and, especially, **PC Hooftstraat** are as close as Amsterdam gets to Rodeo Drive, offering solace to the kind of ladies who would otherwise be lunching.

While you're in the area, it's worth visiting nearby **Roemer Visscherstraat**. This road, which leads to Vondelpark, is notable not for its labels but for its buildings. Each of the houses from nos.20 to 30 represents a different country and all are built in the appropriate 'national' architectural style: thus Russia comes with a miniature dome; Italy has been painted pastel pink; and Spain's candy stripes have made it one of the street's favourites.

Vondelpark

Vondelpark – named after the city's best-known poet, Joost van den Vondel, whose controversial play *Lucifer* caused the religious powers of the 17th century to crack down hard on those who engaged in what was termed 'notorious living' – is the most central of the city's major parks. Its construction was inspired by the large development of the Plantage, which had formerly provided the green background for the leisurely walks of the rich. The original ten acres opened in 1865, and were designed in the 'English style' by Zocher, with the emphasis on natural landscaping. The park has actually sunk some two to three metres since it was first built – some larger trees are in fact 'floating' on blocks of styrofoam or reinforced with underground poles. ·

IN THE KNOW QUEUE HOPPING

Do yourself a favour and get to museums early: the queues in the afternoon can get frustratingly long, and the galleries unbearably busy. You can avoid the main queues for certain museums altogether if you buy your tickets in advance online or have an IAmsterdam card; check websites for details.

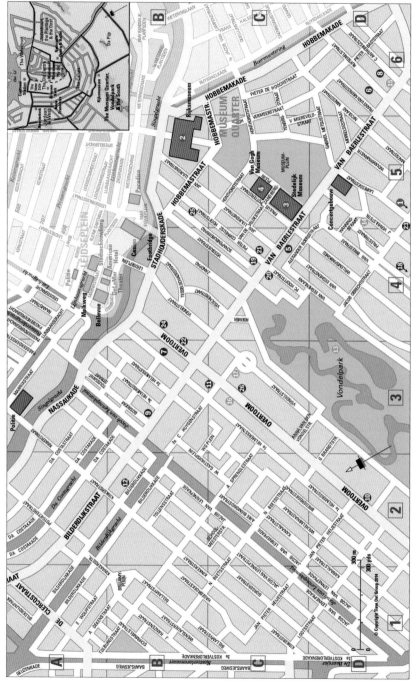

EXPLORE

There are several ponds and lakes in the park plus a number of play areas and cafés, including **'t Blauwe Theehuis** (Round Blue Teahouse) and the **Groot Melkhuis** (which hosts a creative workshop for kids in its huge playground on Wednesday afternoons in summer). Keep your eye out for a huge Picasso sculpture in the middle of the park, and the wild parakeets that were accidentally released in 1976 and have spread across the city. Around the corner – and providing a unique place for coffee – is the epic **Hollandsche Manege** (*see p253*), a wooden version of the Spanish Riding School in Vienna.

Vondelpark gets insanely busy on sunny days and Sundays, when bongos abound, dope is toked and football games take up any space that happens to be left over. Hundreds of rollerbladers meet here weekly for the Friday Night Skate (www.fridaynightskate.com), then skate through the city for more than 20 kilometres (12.5 miles). The **Vondelpark Openluchttheater** (*see p205*), a festival of free open-air performances (films, plays, concerts), takes place throughout the summer.

The south-western end of the park runs along Amstelveenseweg, a varying culinary strip very much worth cruising. For example, **Ron Gastrobar** (Sophialaan 55, 496 1943, www.rongastrobar.nl) is named after local entrepreneurial celebrity chef Ron Blaauw, who put his two Michelin stars on the line by coming up with a simpler, more affordable menu of 25 no-nonsense back-to-basics mains costing €15 each. If that's busy, there are a lot of other options too.

For decades, Vondelpark, and especially its rose garden, has also been a notorious midnight meet-up spot for gay men looking for some frisky risk-taking, but it wasn't until 2008 that the Amsterdam district council proclaimed a new set of rules announcing the official 'toleration' of public sex in the park. 'As long as other people in the park don't feel disturbed, then there is no problem with it,' said one pragmatic politician. According to the 'house rules', enjoying a garden romp is only permitted after dark, and condoms must be cleared away to keep the surrounds tidy. Police officers cannot interrupt the fun unless participants are causing a public nuisance, such as broadcasting their enjoyment too noisily or appearing too close to a public path. Some people see it as an example of Dutch pragmatism: take a problem and deal with it without alarm or fear. Others see it as a way to attract the wrong kind of tourists. Nearby residents seem indifferent: 'I've only ever noticed drunk people in the park. It's actually quite disappointing – I haven't noticed anything quite that exciting,' said one.

Sights & Museums

Electrische Museumtramlijn Amsterdam

Amstelveenseweg 264 (673 7538, www. museumtramlijn.org). Tram 16 or bus 15, 62. **Open** Easter-Oct 11am-5.30pm Sun. **Tickets** (return) €5; €3 4-11s. **Map** p129 D5 ❶

Both the pride and raison d'être of the Electric Tramline, based in a beautiful 1915 railway station, is its rolling stock. Colourful antique streetcars, gathered from several cities, make their way along a special 7km (four-mile) line that heads south from the station through the surprisingly rural Amsterdamse Bos. Trams depart every 20-30 minutes, Sundays only. The station also houses a fine café, Macy's.

★ Rijksmuseum

Museumstraat 1 (674 7000, www.rijksmuseum.nl). Tram 2, 5, 7, 10, 12. **Open** 9am-5pm daily. **Admission** €15; free under-19s, MK. **Map** p129 B5 ❷

The Rijksmuseum reopened to much fanfare in 2013 after a decade of renovation (*see p131* **The 'Museum of the Netherlands'**). Originally designed by PJH Cuypers and opened in 1885, the nation's 'treasure house' is home to 40 Rembrandt and four Vermeer paintings – and holds up a mirror to Centraal Station, built by the same architect. The collection was started when William V began to acquire pieces just for the hell of it, and has been growing ever since. Besides Rembrandt's *The Night Watch* and Vermeer's *Kitchen Maid* and *Woman Reading a Letter*, it also has works by the likes of Frans Hals, Jacob de Wit and Ferdinand Bol. There's also a wealth of Asian and decorative arts on display, including 17th-century furniture, intricate silver and porcelain, and 17th- and early 18th-century dolls' houses. All this plus temporary exhibitions and the museum's freely accessible garden, filled with Dutch Golden Age gateways and architectural fragments. There's also an outpost at Schiphol Airport. And don't miss the museum's excellent website; book tickets online to avoid the queues.

▶ *Visit the Rembrandthuis museum to see the world's largest collection of the master's sketches; see p143.*

★ Stedelijk Museum of Modern Art

Museumplein 10 (573 2911, www.stedelijk.nl). Tram 2, 5, 12. **Open** 10am-6pm Mon-Wed, Fri-Sun; 10am-10pm Thur. **Admission** €15; €7.50 reductions; free under-19s, IAmsterdam, MK. *Temporary exhibitions varies.* **No credit cards** (except shop). **Map** p129 C5 ❸

After roaming homeless for years, the Stedelijk Museum – Amsterdam's go-to institution for modern and contemporary art – returned to its revamped haunt in 2012 (*see p132* **New Look, New Direction**). The museum has an amazing and diverse collection to draw from. Pre-war highlights

THE 'MUSEUM OF THE NETHERLANDS'

After a controversial, decade-long rebuild, the Rijksmuseum reopens.

EXPLORE

The numbers are impressive: 2,500 visitors per hour come and try to absorb the 8,000 works of art spread over 80 rooms that cover 12,000 square metres (129,000 square feet) of exhibition space dedicated to the Netherlands' cultural history since AD 1100. The only drawback is that it took the **Rijksmuseum** (*see p130*) ten years of rebuilding to make this happen. But since its reopening in 2013, the locals have (mostly) stopped quibbling. After all, in addition to Rembrandt's *The Night Watch* and an impressive selection of Vermeers, the museum also has a badass biplane from 1917 suspended from its ceiling.

The €375 million renovation, undertaken by Spanish architects Cruz y Ortiz, united the two halves of the museum by linking its two courtyards via an underground passage. A century of whitewash was removed and the original 19th-century frescoes painstakingly recreated. The end result is simply stunning – and earned the architects the prestigious Abe Bonnema Prize.

British historian Simon Schama waxed lyrical: 'What has been done with the museum is less a restoration with some fancy contemporary design than the inauguration of a curatorial revolution. When you see those early Rembrandts or the great mannerist *Massacre of the Innocents* of Cornelis van Haarlem with its ballet of twisting rumps, you will also encounter, as would those who would first have seen them, the silver, weapons and cabinets that were the furniture of the culture that made those pictures possible.'

While most visitors are equally impressed, the media hype about the museum seems to suggest that the city is going through an arts renaissance. In fact, smaller and more grassroots operations – the ones that may produce the Rembrandts and Vermeers of the future – have experienced massive cutbacks (*see p134* **Culture Slash**).

A four-hour documentary, *The New Rijksmuseum*, followed the decade's worth of logistics and bureaucracy behind the project. The film tested the patience of international audiences, who were flabbergasted by not only the intricacies of Dutch cultural politics but also the power of Amsterdam's cyclists. Indeed, 'Tunnelgate' – referring to the vaulted cycle passage that goes through the museum – was another typically local issue. The museum's original plan was to close the tunnel to bicycles, but the local government stepped in (after much goading by the Dutch Bicycling Union and the public) to keep it open. So enjoy the art, but do keep an eye out for those passing cyclists while you're standing in line.

EXPLORE

NEW LOOK, NEW DIRECTION

Can the revamped Stedelijk holds its own in the international art world?

Eight years is a long time to wait for a bath, in anyone's book. In 2012, the **Stedelijk Museum of Modern Art** (*see p130*) reopened to give Amsterdam back its world-class modern-art collection, which covers everything from Mondrian to Emin. It now has an eye-catching new extension – the 'bathtub', as the locals soon dubbed it – made of shiny composite fibre more commonly used for the hulls of yachts. Architects Benthem Crowel created the extension, which hulks over the rather ho-hum original 1895 building. It also provides a very grand entrance that faces Museumplein square instead of the street. Inside, the contrasts come together in presenting the best of the Stedelijk's collection of 90,000 objects.

The highlights are a very mixed bag indeed: Roy Lichtenstein's *As I Opened Fire*, Gilbert & George's Shit Pictures, Henri Matisse's *La perruche et la sirène*, Christian Friedrich's video work *Untitled*, Jean Tinguely's kinetic sculptures, Jeff Koons' *Ushering in Banality*, Kazimir Malevich's *Suprematist Painting (Eight Red Rectangles)*, Anselm Kiefer's *Innenraum*, Diane Arbus's photograph *A Jewish Giant at home with his parents in the Bronx, NY*, Edward Kienholz's aromatic installation *The Beanery*, and the list goes on...

You'll also find work by local heroes such as video artist Aernout Mik and painter Marlene Dumas. And there is also an excellent display of 2,000 design objects – including a complete bedroom by Gerrit Rietveld from 1926 – which provide evidence of why the Netherlands remains at the vanguard of international design.

With American curator Ann Goldstein at the helm, the reopened museum hoped to be able to play with the big boys of international art – such as London's Tate Modern, Bilbao's Guggenheim and Paris's Pompidou Centre – but many rate this ambition as absurd since those museums' annual budgets dwarf that of the Stedelijk.

Then there's Goldstein herself. In August 2013, she announced she was leaving a year before the end of her five-year term because she considered her work to be done. However, as the museum's first foreign director, she had problems from the beginning fitting in with the bureaucratic complexities of local politics. She was also widely criticised for not learning Dutch and not being communicative enough – as well as leaning too heavily on West Coast minimalism. As of press time, it was not yet clear who would fill her shoes.

No matter – the Stedelijk is still a world-class collection worth immersing oneself in.

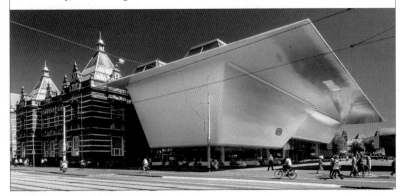

include works by Cézanne, Picasso, Matisse and Chagall, plus a collection of paintings and drawings by the Russian constructivist Kasimir Malevich. Among post-1945 artists in the collection are minimalists Donald Judd, Barnett Newman and Frank Stella, pop artists Roy Lichtenstein, Sigmar Polke and Andy Warhol, abstract expressionists Karel Appel and Willem De Kooning, and conceptual artists Jan Dibbets, Jeff Koons and Bruce Nauman.

★ Van Gogh Museum
Paulus Potterstraat 7 (570 5200, www.vangogh museum.nl). Tram 2, 3, 5, 12. **Open** 10am-6pm Mon-Thur, Sat, Sun; 10am-10pm Fri. **Admission** €15; free under-18s, IAmsterdam, MK. *Temporary exhibitions* varies. **Map** p129 C5 ❹
As well as the bright colours of his palette, Vincent van Gogh is known throughout the world for his productivity, and that's reflected in the 200 paintings and 500 drawings that form part of the permanent exhibition based in the Rietveld building. In addition to this collection, there are also examples of his Japanese prints and works by the likes of Toulouse-Lautrec that add perspective to Van Gogh's own artistic efforts. Temporary exhibitions focusing on Van Gogh's contemporaries and his influence on other artists are assembled from both the museum's own extensive archives and private collections. It's also worth noting that Friday evenings often feature lectures, concerts and films. To avoid the queues, book online or try visiting around noon or late afternoon. *Photo p135.*
▶ *For the museum's special activities for kids, see p172.*

Restaurants

€ Bagels & Beans
Van Baerlestraat 40 (675 7050, www.bagels beans.nl). Tram 3, 5, 12. **Open** 8am-5.30pm Mon-Fri; 8.30am-5.30pm Sat, Sun. **Main courses** €3-€8. **Map** p129 C4 ❺ Café
An Amsterdam success story, this branch of B&B has a wonderfully peaceful back patio. It's perfect for an economical breakfast, lunch or snack; sun-dried tomatoes are employed with particular skill, elevating the humble sandwich to the status of something far more sublime and satisfying. **Other locations** throughout the city.

Le Garage
Ruysdaelstraat 54-56 (679 7176, www.restaurant legarage.nl). Tram 3, 5, 12, 16. **Open** noon-11pm Mon-Fri; 6-11pm Sat, Sun. **Main courses** €17.50-€32.50. **Map** p129 D6 ❻ French
Don your glad rags to blend in at this fashionable brasserie, which is great for emptying your wallet while you watch a selection of aging Dutch glitterati do exactly the same. The authentic French regional cuisine – and 'worldly' versions thereof – is pretty good.

€ Hap Hmm
1e Helmerstraat 33 (618 1884, www.hap-hmm.nl). Tram 1, 7, 10. **Open** 4.30-8pm Mon-Fri. **Main courses** €7-€12. **No credit cards. Map** p129 B3 ❼ Dutch
Hungry but hard up? You need some of the Dutch grandma cooking served in this canteen with a living-room feel. 'Yummy Bite', as the name translates, will happily pack your empty insides with meat and potatoes for not much more than €7.

I Kriti
Balthasar Floriszstraat 3 (664 1445, www. ikriti.nl). Tram 3, 5, 12, 16. **Open** 5-10pm daily. **Main courses** €15-€24. **Map** p129 D6 ❽ Greek
Eat and party Greek style in this evocation of Crete, where a standard choice of dishes is lovingly prepared. Bouzouki-picking legends drop in on occasion and pump up the frenzied atmosphere, further boosted by plate-lobbing antics. Nearby, De Greikse Taverna (Hobbemakade 64-65, 671 7923, www.degrieksetaverna.nl) may lack plate-smashing atmosphere but competes on taste.

Pastis
1e Constantijn Huygensstraat 15 (616 6166, www.pastisamsterdam.nl). Tram 1, 12. **Open** 4pm-1am Mon-Fri; 9am-3am Sat; 10am-1am Sun. **Main courses** €17.50-25. **Map** p129 B3 ❾ Brasserie
This Pastis may not be in New York's meatpacking district, but this neighbourhood favourite sure packs a punch when it comes to brasserie classics from caesar salad to crème brûlée. Generous opening hours make it the perfect choice for a very easy Sunday morning indeed.

★ € De Peper
Overtoom 301 (412 2954, www.depeper.org). Tram 1. **Open** 6pm-1am (kitchen 6-8.30pm) Tue, Thur, Fri, Sun. **Set meal** €7-€10 2 courses. **No credit cards. Map** p129 D2 ❿ Vegetarian
The cheapest and best vegan food in town is to be found in the artistic 'breeding ground' OT301 (*see p194*). De Peper is a collectively organised, non-profit project combining culture with cooking – and

EXPLORE

there's usually a DJ to aid digestion. But do book ahead on the day that you plan to visit (call 4-7pm).

▶ *While you're here, check out the film menu for some interesting documentaries or perhaps an old Hollywood classic. See p179.*

€ De Peperwortel
Overtoom 140 (685 1053, www.peperwortel.nl). *Tram 1, 7, 10.* **Open** noon-9pm daily. **Main courses** €8.50-€15.50. **No credit cards.** **Map** p129 C3 ⓫ Global
One could survive for weeks eating nothing except takeaways from Riaz (*see below*) and this traiteur, the fabulous 'Pepper Root'. It serves a wide range of dishes, embracing Dutch, Mexican, Asian and Spanish cuisines.

★ € Riaz
Bilderdijkstraat 193 (683 6453, www.riaz-amsterdam.nl). *Tram 3, 7, 12, 17.* **Open** noon-9pm Tue-Sat; 3-9pm Sun. **Main courses** €6-€20. **No credit cards.** **Map** p129 B2 ⓬ Surinamese
Amsterdam's finest Surinamese restaurant is where Ruud Gullit scores his rotis when he's in town.

Bars

★ 't Blauwe Theehuis
Vondelpark 5 (662 0254, www.blauwetheehuis.nl). *Tram 1, 2, 3, 5, 12.* **Open** 9am-5pm Mon-Fri; 9am-8pm Sat, Sun (hours extended on sunny weekends). **Map** p129 D3 ⓭

One of the few local landmarks that allows you to nestle inside with a beer, HAJ Baanders' extraordinary 1930s teahouse – a sort of UFO/hat hybrid that landed itself in the middle of Vondelpark – is a choice spot for fair-weather drinking with its huge surrounding terrace. In summer, there are DJs and barbecues, although it's a romantic spot for dinner and drinks all year round.

Café Welling
Jan Willem Brouwerstraat 32 (662 0155, www.cafewelling.nl). *Tram 2, 3, 5, 12, 16.* **Open** 4pm-1am Mon-Thur; 4pm-2am Fri; 3pm-2am Sat; 3pm-1am Sun. **Map** p129 D5 ⓮
Just behind the Concertgebouw, brownish Welling offers plenty of choice in the beer department – plus excellent, locally produced *jenever*. The welcoming atmosphere is in contrast to many of the other, overpriced, posh spots near here. Be charmed by the regulars, who often come in carrying their instruments.

Café Wildschut
Roelof Hartplein 1-3 (676 8220, www.cafe wildschut.nl). *Tram 3, 5, 12, 24.* **Open** 9am-1am Mon-Thur; 10am-2am Fri, Sat; 10am-midnight Sun. **Map** p129 D6 ⓯
A stunning example of Amsterdam School architecture (*see p251* **School of Rock**), this elegant semi-circular place puts the 'grand' into grand café and drips with nouveau detail. Drink and food choices mirror the upmarket surroundings, as does the clientele, which includes flush locals, loud yuppies and art-weary tourists in desperate need of refuelling.

CULTURE SLASH
Public funding cuts hit the Dutch arts world.

The Netherlands has long had a generous attitude towards subsidising cultural initiatives. But in 2011, the then right-leaning government slashed arts funding by €200 million – a drastic 25 per cent – to take effect at the start of 2013.

Of course, some argue that subsidies breed a certain laziness, as well as 'cultivate mediocracy'. And certainly there were many cases where the fat could be trimmed. However, the cuts came with much rhetoric about the elitist and parasitic ways of the arts world (aka 'the hobbies of the left'). This rhetoric echoed the thoughts of the anti-Muslim Freedom Party leader and failed filmmaker Geert Wilders, who then enjoyed veto power in the frail coalition government under PM Mark Rutte. There was also little time for some 40 arts organisations – including four orchestras,

a dozen dance/theatre companies and a range of art galleries – to react to the cuts and try to find alternative sources of funding.

Many believe this 'clear cutting' will permanently damage the country's much lauded cultural scene. The larger, more established institutions generally kept their funding and the smaller initiatives are often driven by goodwill anyway, so it was the medium-sized outfits that suffered most. And it's these organisations that play a vital role in connecting the low with the high – and thereby helping raise the stature of future Van Goghs and Rembrandts.

But what's done is done and now organisations are scrambling to come up with new, more entrepreneurial, paradigms in which they can continue to exist. Stay tuned…

Van Gogh Museum. *See p133.*

EXPLORE

Gollem's Proeflokaal

*Overtoom 160-162 (612 9444, www.cafe
gollem.nl). Tram 1, 3, 12.* **Open** 4pm-1am
Mon-Thur; noon-3am Fri, Sat; noon-1am Sun.
No credit cards. Map p129 C3 ⑯
A simply outstanding place to get sozzled, this dark
and cosy Belgian beer specialist offers more than 150
bottled brews – including 42 abbey beers and 14 trap-
pist – and 21 on tap, from easy-drinkers to demonic
head-pounders such as Delirium Tremens. The helpful menu lists the strengths of the suds for those
erring on the side of caution. There's also a pubby
food menu. There's another more elfish and ancient
branch at Raamsteeg 4, on the New Side.

Proeflokaal Butcher's Tears

*Karperweg 45 (06 5390 9777 mobile, www.
butchers-tears.com). Tram 16.* **Open** 4-9pm
Wed-Sun. **No credit cards.**
This small brewery opened a 'tasting local' in
2013. *See p150* **What's Brewing?**

Coffeeshops

Tweedy

*2e Constantijn Huygensstraat 76 (618 0344).
Tram 1, 2, 3, 5, 12.* **Open** 11am-11pm daily.
No credit cards. Map p129 C3 ⑰
The relocated interior of a 1970s Dutch commuter
train is sprawled throughout the shop, with fat red
vinyl booths, train tables and overhead luggage
racks dotted here and there. Expect prices to slightly
outweigh quality; but some may find the convenience
of being able to have a toke just before admiring

the Vondelkerk church next door and proceeding to
Vondelpark to be well worth it.

Shops & Services

2

*Cornelis Schuytstraat 27 (845 2626, www.
2-amsterdam.nl). Tram 2.* **Open** noon-6pm
Mon; 10am-6pm Tue-Sat; noon-5pm Sun.
Map p129 D4 ⑱ **Fashion**
If Cornelis Schuytstraat were on the Monopoly
board, the Ferillis family would be taking over. After
the massive success of '1', their menswear shop on
the same strip, '2' marks the family's foray into womenswear. Occupying a former florist, it serves chic
brands such as American Retro and Lala Berlin.
Other location Cornelis Schuytstraat 27
(671 5239, www.1-amsterdam.nl).

Azzurro Due

*PC Hooftstraat 138 (671 9708, www.azzurro
fashiongroup.nl). Tram 2, 3, 5, 12.* **Open** 1-6pm
Mon; 10am-6pm Tue, Wed, Fri, Sat; 10am-10pm
Thur; noon-6pm Sun. Map p129 C4 ⑲ **Fashion**
If you've got the urge to splurge, this is as good a
spot as any, with saucy picks from Alexander Wong,
3.1 Phillip Lim, Chloé and Stella McCartney.

★ Blue Blood

*PC Hooftstraat 142 (676 6220, www.blue
bloodbrand.com). Tram 2, 3, 5, 12.* **Open**
1-6pm Mon; 10am-6pm Tue-Wed, Fri; 10am-
8pm Thur; 10am-5.30pm Sat; noon-5.30pm Sun.
Map p129 C4 ⑳ **Fashion**

EXPLORE

The home of local denim label Blue Blood Jeans has all the lovely aspirational gear any upwardly mobile trendster could ever want, all under one perfectly curated roof. Expect own-brand denim and scooter helmets, as well as make-a-statement Antik Batik frocks.

▶ *Amsterdam can be considered a denim capital. Two other local brands have shops very nearby: G-Star Raw (PC Hooftstraat 24-28) and Denham (Hobbemastraat 8). There's also Gsus, with three stores (Westerstraat 158, The Jordaan; NZ Voorburgwal 182, Old Centre: New Side; Koningsplein 8, Old Centre: New Side).*

Four
PC Hooftstraat 127 (679 224, www.f-o-u-r.com). Tram 2, 3, 5, 12. **Open** 1-6pm Mon, Sun; 10am-6pm Tue, Wed, Fri, Sat; 10am-8pm Thur. **Map** p129 C4 ㉑ **Fashion**
The first clothing store in Amsterdam that can be transformed into a pop-up club complete with monster sound system, this fourth venture from Azzurro

Fashion Group – stocking everything from street style to Francisco van Benthum – has raised the bar for experiential shopping.

Friday Next
Overtoom 31 (612 3292, www.fridaynext.com). Tram 1, 3, 12. **Open** noon-6pm Mon; 9am-6pm Tue-Fri; 10am-5pm Sat; noon-5pm Sun. **Map** p129 B3 ㉒ **Fashion**
A concept store with a difference: it has a stellar café serving sandwiches, coffee and salads. But they also stand out on interiors boulevard Overtoom for their highly personal and varied selection of furnishings, jewellery, clothing and accessories – from the funky owl patterns of ShulzWorks to cast-off crockery of Esther Derkx.

Lairesse Apotheek
Lairessestraat 40 (662 1022, www.delairesse apotheek.nl). Tram 3, 5, 12, 16, 24. **Open** 8.30am-6pm Mon-Fri; 10am-5pm Sat. **Map** p129 D5 ㉓ **Pharmacy**
One of the largest suppliers of alternative medicines in the country, chemist Marjan Terpstra wanted her shop to reflect her speciality. Designed by Concrete, the shop is out of the way if you're just popping in for haemorrhoid cream, but the interior is so inspiring it should be on any design junkie's must-see list.

Marqt
Overtoom 21 (820 8292, www.marqt.com). Tram 1, 2, 3, 5, 7, 12. **Open** 9am-9pm daily. **No cash**. **Map** p129 B4 ㉔ **Food & drink**

Four.

SNACK ATTACK

From chips to street-food festivals, this is the best fast food in town.

You know street food is gaining in street cred when Robert Kranenborg, perhaps Amsterdam's most acclaimed chef, has a truck selling coal-grilled burgers around town (see www.thrillgrill.nl for the schedule). Other budget-priced snacks include rolled 'pizzas' from Turkish bakeries, Dutch *broodjes* (sandwiches) from bakers and butchers, and the spicier Surinamese *broodjes* from 'Chin-Indo-Suri' snack bars (*see p104* **Seriously Hot Stuff**).

Fast food can tell you a lot about the tastes of a nation. You must – yes, you really must – try raw herring. It's best between May and July when the *nieuw* (new) catch hits the stands. These newcomers don't need any extra garnish like onions and pickles, since their flesh is at its sweetest – thanks to the high fat content that the herring was planning to burn off in the arduous business of breeding. There's a quality fish stall or shop around most corners, which also provides smoked eel and other fishy sandwich fillings. And they're as cheap as chips (or, at least, a lot cheaper than sushi).

Speaking of chips, the best are the chunky Belgian ones (*Vlaamse frites*), double-fried to ensure a crispy exterior and creamy interior. Enjoy them along with your pick of toppings, such as *oorlog* ('war'): mayo, spicy peanut sauce and onions. **Vleminckx** (*see p81*) and **Manneken Pis** (Damrak 41, near Centraal Station) are two of the best places to eat them.

The local term for a greasy snack – *vette hap* – translates literally as 'fat bite', which says a lot for the honesty of the Dutch. At the ubiquitous **FEBO**, you can put your change into the glowing vending machine and, in return, get a hot hamburger, *bamibal* (a deep-fried noodle ball of vaguely Indonesian descent), or a *kaas soufflé* (a cheese treat). The most popular choice is the *kroket*, a melange of meat and potato with a deep-fried skin, best served on a bun with hot mustard. **Van Dobben** (*see p107*), a 1945-vintage late-night venue just off Rembrandtplein, is the uncontested champion when it comes to the *kroket*, though you can find a more refined shrimp version at nearby bakery **Holtkamp** (Vijzelgracht 15, 624 8757).

The move towards unpretentious and straightforward cooking is also seen in the rise of street food stalls and food vans. Sadly, thanks to local bylaws, these mobile operations are usually only allowed at festivals, including the hugely popular **Rollende Keukens** (*see p37*). A similar venture, **Kanen bij Ten Kate** (www.kanenbij tenkate.nl), was launched in 2013 on Ten Katemarkt in Amsterdam West. Every Thursday between 4pm and 9pm (as long as the weather allows), a posse of food trucks and some long tables create a convivial atmosphere. Keep your eye out for 'The Kitchen of the Unwanted Animal', which serves such delicacies as *krokets* made from swans harvested in the name of keeping Schiphol Airport safe for jets. Meanwhile, there are active efforts to change the law so that street food can return to where it belongs: the street.

EXPLORE

Amsterdam's newest organics market focuses on fresh produce, meat and fish sourced from local and regional farmers and independent producers. It also sells great fresh bread from Brood bakery and pizzas from De Pizza Bakker. Products are predominately fair trade too.

Other locations Utrechtsestraat 17, Southern Canal Belt; Haarlemmerstraat 165, Western Canal Belt; Wolvenstraat 22, Western Canal Belt.

Meyer Schoenen

PC Hooftstraat 45 (664 3355, www.meijers schoenen.com). Tram 2, 3, 5, 12. **Open** 10am-6pm Mon-Wed, Fri; 10am-9pm Thur; 10am-5.30pm Sat; 1-5pm Sun. **Map** p129 B5 ㉕ **Accessories**
Meyer has put the craftsmanship of its handmade men's and women's shoes first since 1934 with . Old-school classiness.

Pied-à-Terre

Overtoom 135-137 (627 4455, www.piedaterre.nl). Tram 1, 3, 12. **Open** 1-6pm Mon; 10am-6pm Tue-Wed, Fri; 10am-9pm Thur; 10am-5pm Sat. **Map** p129 C3 ㉖ **Books & music**

Brimming with travel books, international guides and more than 65,000 maps, Pied-à-Terre is an absolute must-visit for adventurous types.
▶ *For inspiration on places to visit, browse our Escapes chapter; see pp216-229.*

NIEUW ZUID

Nieuw Zuid (New South) is bordered to the north by Vondelpark, to the east by the Amstel and to the west by the **Olympisch Stadion** (www.olympisch-stadion.net). Constructed for the 1928 Olympic Games, the area is noted for its Amsterdam School glory (*see p251* **School of Rock**). The New South was planned by Hendrik Berlage and put into action by a variety of Amsterdam School architects, who designed both private and public housing for the area. It's the former that's given the New South what character it has, most notably around Apollolaan and Beethovenstraat.

The few visitors tend to be here on business, especially around the **World Trade Center**

THE SERPENT'S TALE

Don't overlook this gem of a modern-art museum.

The marvellous **CoBrA Museum of Modern Art** includes masterpieces by the avant-garde artists of the original CoBrA movement, as well as new work by contemporary artists whose aesthetic sensibilities in some way adhere to the movement's values. Though the movement was relatively short-lived, beginning in 1948 and ending in 1951, it produced some of the Netherlands' most enduring names in 20th-century art, such as Constant, Corneille and Karel Appel.

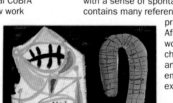

An acronym for Copenhagen, Brussels and Amsterdam – the cities from which the key artists of the movement hailed – CoBrA was the northern European artistic response to the destruction and chaos of World War II. The CoBrA artists created a style unimpeded by academic traditions, marked by vibrant colours and typically created with a sense of spontaneity. The work contains many references to so-called primitive art from Africa and 'naïve' work made by children or untrained artists, using purely emotive imagery and experimental forms.

The museum itself, a beautiful airy space with an abundance of natural light and a view over a swan-dotted canal bordered by weeping willows, was founded in 1995 with a mission to become the definitive exhibition space and archive for artwork and documentation about the movement. Its permanent collection contains about 300 paintings, sculptures and works on paper, as well as archived documents from the CoBrA era.

Zuidas.

and the steadily rising modern-architecture neighbourhood of **Zuidas**. The controversial Noord-Zuidlijn Metro is set to link this district with the centre of town and Amsterdam Noord. East of here is another staple of Amsterdam business life: the ugly **RAI Exhibition & Congress Centre**, which holds numerous trade fairs, conventions and a range of public exhibitions throughout the year.

However, in between the RAI and the WTC lies one of Amsterdam's most beautiful parks. Extended and renovated in 1994, **Beatrixpark** is a wonderfully peaceful place, very handy if you want to avoid the crowds in town on a summer's day. The Victorian walled garden is worth a visit, as is the pond, complete with geese, black swans and herons. Amenities include a wading pool and play area for kids. Nearby, housed in a circular ex-church, is the highly regarded **Restaurant As** (Prinses Irenestraat 19, 644 0100, www.restaurantas.nl); it's known for rearing its own pigs.

Further south still, **Amstelpark** was created for a garden festival in 1972, and today offers recreation and respite to locals in the suburb of Buitenveldert. A formal rose garden and rhododendron walk are among the seasonal spectacles, and there's also a labyrinth, pony rides and a children's farm, plus tours on a miniature train.

AMSTELVEEN

Of all the southern suburbs, Amstelveen is the most welcoming to the casual visitor. Though the **CoBrA Museum** helps, the main attraction here is the **Amsterdamse Bos**, a mammoth planned wood that's treasured by locals yet neglected by visitors. Providing work for 20,000 unemployed people during the Depression, this forestation project

started in 1934, and the last tree was planted in 1967. With its 137 kilometres (85 miles) of footpaths, 51 kilometres (32 miles) of cycle paths, 50 bridges, 150 indigenous species of trees and over 200 species of birds, the Amsterdamse Bos is one of the largest city parks in Europe. The eight-square-kilometre (three-square-mile) site sprawls beautifully, and comes with a great many attractions in case the tranquillity isn't enough.

The man-made Bosbaan is used for rowing, fishing and, in freezing winters, a spot of ice-skating. Other attractions include a visitor centre (**Bezoekerscentrum Amsterdamse Bos**), play areas, a horticultural museum, jogging routes, a buffalo and bison reserve, the Fun Forest tree-top climbing park (Apr-Oct), a bike-hire centre (Mar-Oct), a watersports centre, stables and a picnic area. There's also a great goat farm selling cheese, milk and ice-cream.

Sights & Museums

FREE Bezoekerscentrum Amsterdamse Bos
Bosbaanweg 5, near Amstelveenseweg (545 6100, www.amsterdamsebos.nl). Bus 170, 172. **Open** noon-5pm Tue-Sun. **Admission** free.
The visitor centre recounts the history and use of the Amsterdamse Bos. Its mock woodland grotto, which can turn from day to night at the flick of a switch, is wonderful for kids.

CoBrA Museum of Modern Art
Sandbergplein 1 (547 5050, www.cobra-museum.nl). Tram 5 or Metro 51 or bus 142, 170, 172. **Open** 11am-5pm Tue-Sun. **Admission** €9.50; €3.50-€6 reductions; free under-6s, MK. **No credit cards** (except shop). *See p138* **The Serpent's Tale**.

Jodenbuurt, Plantage & Oost

The area now known as Jodenbuurt is the city's old Jewish quarter. It was a lively Jewish hub up to World War II, when the Nazis concentrated the Jewish population of the Netherlands here before deportation. Many houses left empty after the war were torn down to make way for the new metro and contemporary buildings – it's now a peculiar mix of old and new. The Plantage, by contrast, is lush with verdant spaces. As the city expanded in the 19th century, it became one of Amsterdam's first suburban developments, with elegant villas and wide streets. The often forgotten frontier that is Oost and its Oosterpark emerged in the late 19th century and currently rates as one of the city's up-and-coming areas.

Waterlooplein.

Don't Miss

1 Joods Historisch Museum Dig deep into A'dam's Jewish past (p143).

2 Waterlooplein Market Flea market matrix (p146).

3 Artis Royal Zoo Frolic with flamingos (p147).

4 Brouwerij 't IJ Beer brewed in the shadow of a windmill (p151).

5 Hortus Botanicus It's green and it's peaceful (p148).

Hermitage Amsterdam.

JODENBUURT

Just off the Nieuwmarkt, **Sint Antoniesbreestraat** is home to assorted shops, bars and cafés, along with the modern yet tasteful council housing designed by local architect Theo Bosch. In contrast, there's the Italian Renaissance-style **Pintohuis** at no.69, which was grandly remodelled in the late 17th century by Isaac de Pinto. A Jewish refugee who had fled the inquisition in Portugal, de Pinto became one of the main investors in the immensely lucrative Dutch East India Company.

Across the street, pop through the bizarre skull-adorned entrance between nos.130 and 132 to enter the restful square, formerly a

graveyard, near the **Zuiderkerk** (South Church). Designed by master builder Hendrick De Keyser and built between 1603 and 1614, the Zuiderkerk was the first Protestant church to appear after the Reformation. Three of Rembrandt's children were buried here, and the church was painted by Monet during a visit to the Netherlands. Crossing over the bridge at the end of Sint Antoniesbreestraat, you'll arrive at **De Hogeschool voor de Kunsten** (Arts Academy) on the left and the **Rembrandthuis** on the right. Immediately before this, though, a few steps down to the right lead to **Waterlooplein Market** – a dream destination for bargain-hunters if you're a patient shopper.

Nearby, you'll find the 19th-century **Mozes en Aäronkerk** (Waterlooplein 205), built on Spinoza's (*see p62*) birthplace. This former clandestine Catholic church is almost situated above the much chirpier children's playground **TunFun** (*see p173*), which runs below Mr Visserplein square, in a former underpass. Dominating Waterlooplein is the **Nationale Opera & Ballet** (*see p204 and left* In the Know), an important opera and ballet venue for the city. Also nearby are the **Hermitage Amsterdam** and the **Joods Historisch Museum**.

By the **Portuguese Synagogue** on Mr Visserplein, look out for the Jonas Daniël Meijerplein site. Here, Mari Andriessen's bronze *Dockworker* statue, erected in 1952, commemorates the February Strike of 1941 – a protest against Jewish deportations that began among workers in the city's shipyards.

IN THE KNOW THE STOPERA

The Muziektheater, rebranded as **Nationale Opera & Ballet** in 2014 (*see p204*), has been the long-time home of the Nederlands Opera and the Nationale Ballet. It shares the building with the Stadhuis (City Hall). Standing on the site of a former Jewish ghetto, this controversial €136m civic headquarters-cum-opera house was designed by Wilhelm Holzbauer and Cees Dam. Locals protested against the city's decision to tear down the original 16th- and 17th-century residences, and a riot ensued in 1982 – which is why the theatre is still known as the 'Stopera'.

Sights & Museums

Hermitage Amsterdam
*Amstel 51 (530 8755, www.hermitage.nl).
Tram 9, 14 or Metro Waterlooplein.* **Open**
10am-5pm daily. **Admission** €15; €5-€12
reductions; free under-6s, IAmsterdam, MK.
Map p144 B4 ❶
The Amsterdam outpost of St Petersburg's
Hermitage museum opened in 2009. Set in a former
19th-century hospital with a 17th-century courtyard,
the building has two vast exhibition spaces, a concert hall and a restaurant. The museum mounts two
exhibitions a year, borrowing items from the three-
million-strong collection of its prestigious Russian
parent. The Hermitage's riches owe much to the
collecting obsession of Peter the Great (1672-1725),
who came to Amsterdam to learn shipbuilding and
the art of building on waterlogged ground – the
latter knowledge he applied to his pet project, St
Petersburg. Peter befriended local doctor Frederik
Ruysch, perhaps the greatest ever anatomist and
preserver of body parts and mutants in jars. Ruysch
enjoyed constructing ghoulish collages with gall and
kidney stones piled up into landscapes; dried veins
woven into lush shrubberies and testicles crafted
into pottery. The scenes were animated with dancing
foetus skeletons. However, most exhibitions here are
of a more genteel nature: Rembrandt, French
Impressionists or archaeological discoveries found
along the Silk Route.

★ Joods Historisch Museum (Jewish Historical Museum)
*Nieuwe Amstelstraat 1 (531 0310, www.jhm.nl).
Tram 9, 14 or Metro Waterlooplein.* **Open**
11am- 5pm daily. Closed Jewish New Year &
Yom Kippur. **Admission** (includes Portuguese
Synagogue and Hollandse Schouwburg) €12;
€3-€6 reductions; free under-13s, IAmsterdam,
MK. **No credit cards. Map** p144 B3 ❷
Housed in four former synagogues in the old Jewish
quarter, the Jewish Historical Museum is packed
with religious items, photographs and paintings
detailing the rich history of Jews and Judaism in the
Netherlands throughout the centuries. There's also
an excellent children's wing (*see p171*), with interactive exhibits on different aspects of Jewish culture,
while temporary exhibitions exploring Jewish life,
history and culture often use interviews, film footage
and photos to bring their themes to life.
▶ *For an intimate insight into a Jewish family's
life in hiding, visit the Anne Frank Huis; see p92.*

Portuguese Synagogue
*Mr Visserplein 3 (531 0380, www.portuguese
synagogue.nl). Tram 9, 14 or Metro
Waterlooplein.* **Open** *Apr-Oct* 10am-5pm Mon-
Thur, Sun; 10am-4pm Fri. *Nov-Mar* 10am-4pm
Mon-Thur, Sun; 10am- 2pm Fri. Closed Yom
Kippur. **Admission** (includes Joods Historisch

Museum and Hollandse Schouwburg) €12; €3-
€6 reductions; free under-13s, IAmsterdam, MK.
No credit cards. Map p144 B3 ❸
Inaugurated in 1675, architect Elias Bouwman's
mammoth synagogue is one of the largest in the
world, and was reputedly inspired by the Temple of
Solomon. It is built on wooden piles, and surrounded
by smaller annexes (including offices, archives and
one of the world's oldest libraries). The synagogue
holds occasional concerts and candlelit events.

Rembrandthuis
*Jodenbreestraat 4 (520 0400, www.rembrandt
huis.nl). Tram 9, 14 or Metro Waterlooplein.*
Open 10am-6pm daily. **Admission** €12.50;
€4-€10 reductions; free under-6s, IAmsterdam,
MK. **Map** p144 A3 ❹
Rembrandt bought this house for 13,000 guilders
(then a massive sum) in 1639, at the height of his
career. Sadly, the free-spending artist went bankrupt

Joods Historisch Museum.

EXPLORE

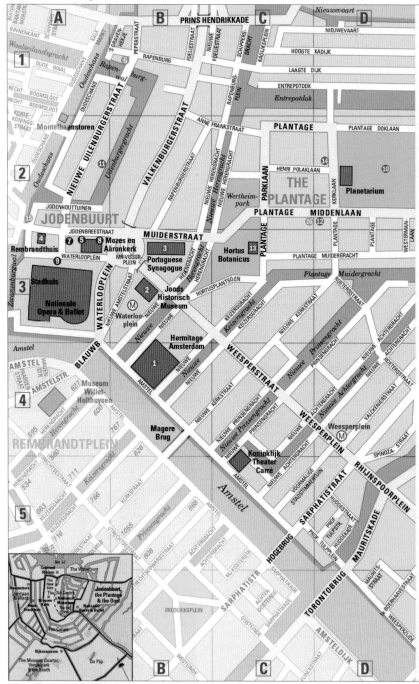

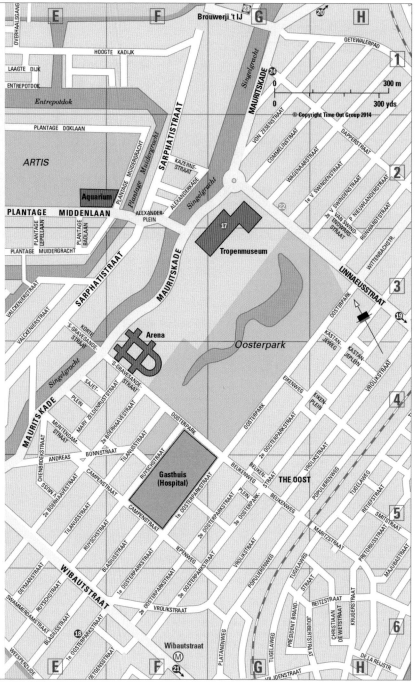

290 Square Meters.

in 1656 and was forced to move to a smaller house (Rozengracht 184). It's now a museum, whose faithfully reconstructed interiors were based on the room-by-room inventory of his possessions that was made when he went bankrupt. Knowing it's a mock-up does add a slightly unreal air to proceedings, though. The museum also contains a remarkable collection of Rembrandt's etchings, which show him at his most experimental.

▶ *If it's Rembrandt's paintings you're interested in, the Rijksmuseum holds one of the largest collections of his work in the world; see p130.*

Restaurants

Woo Bros

Jodenbreestraat 144 (428 0488, www.restaurant woobros.nl). Tram 9, 14 or Metro Waterlooplein. **Open** 4pm-1am Tue-Sun. **Main courses** €3.50-€22.50. **Map** p144 A3 ❺ **Asian**

With a menu of small dishes (three per person is about right for a full meal) that switches seamlessly from Japanese to Indonesian, Vietnamese to Thai, to Chinese and back (Peking duck sits alongside sushi), Woo Bros offers fusion perfection in quirky, low-lit surroundings.

Bars

Hiding in Plain Sight

Rapenburg 18 (06 2529 3620 mobile, www.hps amsterdam.com). Bus 22, 48. **Open** 6pm-1am Mon-Thur; 6pm-3am Fri, Sat. **Map** p144 B1 ❻

Given this speakeasy-style cocktail bar's proximity to the ancient docks where sailors would snog their goodbyes before embarking on treacherous journeys, it's appropriate that it offers liquid danger in the form of a concoction called 'The Walking Dead'. Based on the potent Zombie, HPS's secret

recipe is served (and then set on fire) in a giant glass skull. Bar-imposed limit: one per night. Reservations are recommended.

Shops & Services

290 Square Meters

Houtkopersdwarsstraat 3 (419 2525, www.290sqm.com). Tram 9, 14 or Metro Waterlooplein. **Open** 11am-6pm Tue-Sat. **Map** p144 A3 ❼ **Fashion**

In its former space, this shop/agency/gallery's claim to fame was that it was the first place in the world where people could purchase customised Nikes. Now occupying larger premises (an ex-bank vault), it offers a spectrum of goods, from bikes to fashion, limited-edition books and scents.

Out of the Closet

Jodenbreestraat 158 (620 6261, www.outofthe closet.org/nl). Tram 9, 14 or Metro Waterlooplein. **Open** 10am-7pm Mon-Sat; noon-6pm Sun. **Map** p144 A3 ❽ **Fashion/homewares**

This is the first outlet in Europe of the US chain of thrift shops that donates all profits to providing healthcare to AIDS patients. Besides clothes and furniture, the store offers free advice and HIV tests.

Waterlooplein

Waterlooplein (no phone). Tram 9, 14 or Metro Waterlooplein. **Open** 9am-5pm Mon-Sat. **No credit cards**. **Map** p144 A3 ❾ **Market**

Amsterdam's top tourist market is basically an enormous flea market with the added attraction of loads of new clothes too (admittedly, gear can be a bit pricey and, at many stalls, a bit naff). Bargains can be found, but they may well be hidden under piles of cheap 'n' nasty toasters and down-at-heel (literally) shoes.

THE PLANTAGE

South-east of Mr Visserplein lies the largely residential area known as the Plantage. The attractive Plantage Middenlaan winds past the **Hortus Botanicus**, passes close to the **Verzetsmuseum**, runs along the edge of **Artis Royal Zoo** and heads towards the marvellous **Tropenmuseum**.

In the late 19th and early 20th centuries, Amsterdam was a major world diamond centre, and most of the rocks were cut and sold in and around this area. The headquarters of the diamond cutters' union, designed by Hendrik Berlage as a far more outward expression of socialism than his Stock Exchange (aka **Beurs van Berlage**, see p62), still exist on Henri Polaklaan as **De Burcht** (www.deburcht.nl), an events location that also runs occasional tours of the epic interior. Other extant buildings – such as the **Gassan**, the Saskiahuis and the Coster – also act as reminders that the town's most profitable trade was once based here. However, the spectre of World War II reappears at the **Hollandse Schouwburg**, while the **Verzetsmuseum** documents the Dutch Resistance. Look out too for Van Eyck's **Moedershuis** (Plantage Middenlaan 33), built as a refuge for young, pregnant women.

The Plantage is still a wealthy part of town, with graceful buildings and tree-lined streets, although its charm has somewhat faded over the years. The area has seen extensive redevelopment; if you wander down Entrepotdok, you can admire the delicate balancing act between the new and the old, with post-hippie houseboats and good views of Artis providing a charming contrast to the new apartment buildings.

Sights & Museums

★ Artis Royal Zoo

Plantage Kerklaan 38-40 (0900 27 84 796, €0.25/min, www.artis.nl). Tram 9, 14. **Open** *Summer* 9am-6pm daily. *Winter* 9am-5pm daily. **Admission** €19.95; €16.50 reductions; free under-3s. **No credit cards. Map** p144 D2 ⑩

The first zoo in mainland Europe (and the third oldest in the world) provides a relaxing day out for children and adults. It's so chilled here that if the weather is nice, you're allowed to stay beyond closing time. On special occasions they even give gay animal tours – those pink flamingos are outlandish! Along with the usual animals (of all sexual orientations), Artis has an indoor 'rainforest' for nocturnal creatures and a 120-year-old aquarium with a simulated canal, complete with eels and bike wrecks. Further attractions include a planetarium, a geological museum and, for kids, a petting zoo and playgrounds. In summer, the zoo extends Saturday

Out of the Closet.

opening hours until sunset and hosts special events and tours; see below **In the Know**. *Photo p148.*

FREE Gassan Diamond

Nieuwe Uilenburgerstraat 173-175, (622 5333, www.gassan.com). Tram 9, 14 or Metro Waterlooplein. **Open** 9am-5pm daily. **Admission** free. **Map** p144 A2 ⑪

Amsterdam is famous for its diamond trade, something it owes largely to the Jewish population in and around the Jodenbuurt area. Of the many sparkler shops, Gassan Diamond comes out on top with an epic building that once housed 357 polishing machines, when it was the biggest diamond processing plant in the world. Get in the mood by upgrading from the free tour to one that includes champagne. But remember: falling in love with a piece of compressed carbon is the easy part – working out how you're going to pay for it may prove to be trickier. They also have a showroom on Dam Square in the Old Centre (Rokin 1-5, 624 5787).

FREE Hollandsche Schouwburg

Plantage Middenlaan 24 (531 0310, www. hollandscheschouwburg.nl). Tram 9, 14 or

---

IN THE KNOW NIGHT OWLS

From June to August, **Artis Royal Zoo** (*see left*) stays open until sunset every Saturday. Known as 'ZOOmeravonden', these extended summer evenings bring a roster of free activities, such as face-painting for kids, live music and zookeeper talks (in Dutch, but worth watching nevertheless). You can even bring a picnic and dine alfresco with the animals.

EXPLORE

EXPLORE

Artis Royal Zoo. *See p147.*

Metro Waterlooplein. **Open** 11am-5pm daily. **Admission** donations accepted (or as part of admission to Joods Historish Museum or Portuguese Synagogue). **Map** p144 D2 ⑫
In 1942, this grand theatre became a main point of assembly for around 80,000 of the city's Jews before they were taken to the transit camp at Westerbork. It is now a monument with a small but impressive exhibition and a memorial hall displaying 6,700 surnames by way of tribute to the 104,000 Dutch Jews who were exterminated.
▶ *For details of guided walks exploring the city's World War II history; see pp50-53.*

★ Hortus Botanicus
Plantage Middenlaan 2A (625 9021, www. dehortus.nl). Tram 9, 14 or Metro Waterlooplein. **Open** 9am-5pm daily. **Admission** €8; €1-€5 reductions. **No credit cards. Map** p144 C3 ⑬
The Hortus has been a peaceful oasis since 1682, although it was set up more than 50 years earlier when East India Company ships brought back tropical plants and seeds to supply doctors with medicinal herbs (as well as coffee plant cuttings, one specimen of which continued to Brazil to kickstart the South American coffee industry). Highlights include a massive water lily, the *Victoria amazonica*, which blooms only once a year, and the oldest potted plant in the world, a 300-year-old cycad, on display in the 1912 palm greenhouse. Other conservatories maintain desert, tropical and subtropical climates, and a butterfly greenhouse sets hearts of all ages aflutter. Round out your visit in the organic café.

★ Verzetsmuseum (Museum of the Dutch Resistance)
Plantage Kerklaan 61 (620 2535, www. verzetsmuseum.org). Tram 9, 14. **Open** 11am-5pm Mon, Sat, Sun; 10am-5pm Tue-Fri. **Admission** €8; €4.50 reductions; free under-7s, IAmsterdam, MK. **No credit cards. Map** p144 D2 ⑭
The Verzetsmuseum is one of Amsterdam's most illuminating museums, and quite possibly its most moving. It tells the story of the Dutch Resistance through a wealth of artefacts: false ID papers, clandestine printing presses, illegal newspapers, spy gadgets and an authentic secret door behind which Jews once hid. The engaging presentation is enhanced by the constant use of personal testimonies. Regularly changing temporary exhibitions explore various wartime themes and modern-day forms of oppression, and there's a small research room as well. All in all, an excellent enterprise.

Bars

Café de Sluyswacht
Jodenbreestraat 1 (625 7611, www.sluyswacht.nl). Tram 9, 14 or Metro Waterlooplein. **Open** 12.30pm-1am Mon-Thur; 12.30pm-3am Fri, Sat; 12.30pm-7pm Sun. **Map** p144 A2 ⑮
Listing crazily, this wooden-framed bar has been pleasing drinkers for decades, though the building itself has been around since 1695, when it began life as a lock-keeper's cottage. It's snug and warm inside, while outside commands great views of Oude Schans – making it suitable for boozing in both balmy and inclement weather. An excellent place for a sneaky sundowner.

Eik & Linde
Plantage Middenlaan 22 (622 5716, www. eikenlinde.nl). Tram 7, 9, 14. **Open** 11am-1am Mon-Thur; 11am-2am Fri; 2pm-2am Sat. **No credit cards. Map** p144 C2 ⑯
'The Oak & Lime Tree' is an old-fashioned, family-run neighbourhood café-bar. Local memorabilia on the walls, including posters from radio shows that were held on the premises, give it historical appeal; low prices, Dutch snacks, soups and sandwiches, and a laid-back air make it user-friendly.

OOST

South of Mauritskade is Amsterdam Oost (East), where the hotel complex **Arena** (*see p288*) is located along the edge of a former graveyard that was long ago transformed into **Oosterpark**. Wild ducks swim on the lake, grey herons nest here, and the park also has a Speaker's Corner, for anyone wishing to have a rant. Near the corner of Oosterpark and Linneausstraat is the spot where filmmaker Theo van Gogh was murdered by an Islamic extremist in 2004, after making a film deemed to be offensive to Muslims. A sculpture, *The Scream*, was unveiled in the park in 2007 in his memory.

The **Tropenmuseum** and **Dappermarkt** are the area's main tourist draws. Here too, though, the famous **Studio/K** (*see p179*) offers hip parties, savvy films and a terrific café with an expansive terrace, while Javastraat is dotted with ethnic shops. Meanwhile, Linnaeusstraat should satisfy all your café-lingering needs – if you dare venture into the wildly over-the-top brown cafe **Ruk & Pluk** (no.48, 665 3248) for some real local flavour.

Further out, the **Brouwerij 't IJ**, a brewery beside a windmill in the Indische Buurt (Indonesian neighbourhood), is a good place to stop and sip a beer. Further east, you'll find neglected green gem **Flevopark** with its ancient Jewish cemetery and stellar **Distilleerderij 't Nieuwe Diep** (Flevopark 13, 465 0222, www. nwediep.nl, open Apr-Aug 3-8pm Tue-Sun, Sept-Mar 3-6pm Tue-Sun), an old mill house and now a distillery and tasting-house pumping out Dutch *jenever* and other liquors. With views over a pond from the picnic tables and a nice selection of bar snacks, this is the perfect place to stop and smell the flowers – and the fermenting grains.

EASTERN PROMISE
The art of reinvention in Oost.

Studio/K

For the last decade or so, the city council has been trying to encourage artists and creative types to invade Oost – with one crucial hub being cinema/club/café **Studio/K** (*see p179*). This approach follows tried and tested urban development logic: artists improve the profile of an area, then the yuppies rush in.

Two of the city's hottest clubs make themselves at home here, located in two former newspaper offices. The **Volkskrantgebouw** (Wibautstraat 150, www.volkskrantgebouw.nl) was launched in 2007 as a new concept, with a group negotiating to take over the building and fill it with creative industries and artists. The icing on the cake is **Canvas** (*see p194*), a rooftop café/restaurant/cocktail bar/club on the seventh floor, with a stellar view of the city. After extensive renovations, the complex was due to reopen in mid 2014 with a revamped club and an 'arts hotel'.

However, Canvas is the lo-fi little brother compared to the operation across the street. Nightclub **Trouw Amsterdam** (*see p194*) continues to combine progressive programming and good food – plus it's just been given a 24-hour licence, but only until 1 January 2015 when it has to find a new location.

Then there are the artistic initiatives. **De Service Garage** (Cruquiusweg 79, 06 4130 7367 mobile, www.deservice garage.nl) – a former garage – organises expansive exhibitions while also providing studio space for eight artists. In sharp contrast, **PS Project Space** (Madurastraat 72, 337 6254, www.psprojectspace.nl) is tiny but oftens features major rising international stars. Another example is **Stichting outLINE** (Oetewalerstraat 73, 06 1213 0916 mobile, www.outline amsterdam.nl); once part of the local hospital, this beautiful 19th-century chapel-like structure in a quiet *hofje* (almshouse) is now an artistic meeting place. The former patients' rooms are artists' studios and the main space – an airy, elegant room – hosts six to eight solo shows a year.

Trouw Amsterdam.

EXPLORE

Sights & Museums

Tropenmuseum

Linnaeusstraat 2 (568 8200, www.tropen museum.nl). Tram 9, 14 or bus 22. **Open** 10am-5pm Tue-Sun. **Admission** €12.50; €4-€8 reductions; free under-6s, IAmsterdam, MK. **Map** p145 G2 ⓱

Visitors to this handsome building get a vivid glimpse of daily life in the tropical and subtropical parts of the world – a strange evolution for a museum that was originally erected in the 1920s to glorify Dutch colonialism. Exhibits (which range from religious items and jewellery to washing powder and vehicles) are divided by region, including South-east Asia, Oceania, West Asia, North Africa, Latin America and a series called Man and Environment. Temporary shows, covering everything from Bollywood to Death, are also consistently excellent. There's an engaging array of books and souvenirs in the shop, and the restaurant offers tasty global eats and a terrace with a view. Children are made welcome too: a special branch of the museum, the Tropenmuseum Junior, is aimed at six- to 13-year-olds and has some inspired exhibitions of its own. There are also hands-on craft activities at the

WHAT'S BREWING?

Amsterdam's microbrewery scene is growing.

For decades, **Brouwerij' t IJ** (*see p151*) in Oost ruled the roost when it came to locally brewed golden elixirs. But now it's got some competition from other home-grown microbreweries. In the Old Centre, **Bierfabriek** (*see p68*) offers home-brewed beers including red ale Rosso and dark porter Nero, as well as some of the finest roast chicken in town. Just be wary on Friday nights when the joint gets taken over by the post-work crowd attracted to the 'tap tables' (booking essential), where you can pour your own beer.

For more hipster-flavoured brews, try **Proeflokaal Butcher's Tears** (*see p135*) in Amsterdam South, where you can indulge in their rather strong and evocatively named beers, including Green Cap, Raggle Taggle, Misery King and Witchfinder. There are also coffees, Dutch ciders, international beers and wines and, on occasion, snacks. They also organise concerts, hot-sauce tastings and other special events.

And who says that psychiatric patients and alcohol shouldn't mix? Brewery and shop **De Prael** (*see p68*) in the heart of the Red Light District is proving all the critics wrong. Originating 15 years ago in an industrial estate on the outskirts of town, De Prael was set up on the basis of its owners' background in mental healthcare and love of brewing to the sound of quirky local songs. By establishing De Prael as a 'social firm', with commercial objectives, they were able to invest all the earnings back into the foundation. Currently they employ 70 staff, all of whom have a psychiatric condition: 80 per cent are schizophrenic, and the others suffer from borderline personality disorders. Yes, there

Brouwerij' t IJ.

are plenty of jokes, but the rules are simple: no drinking on the job and be on time.

All the beers from the De Prael brewery share their names with old-fashioned tears-in-your-beers singers. For instance, Mary is named after Mary Servaes (aka the Zangeres Zonder Naam, 'Singer Without a Name') and as a *tripel*, its high alcohol content makes it as robust as the lady herself. Johnny, a blond beer, is named after the fair-haired Johnny Jordaan; Heintje is as fresh and fruity as Hendrik (Hein) Simons was reputed to be.

Afterwards, you can perhaps keep up the theme by going for dinner at **Freud** (Spaarndammerstraat 424, Amsterdam West, 688 5548, www.restaurant freud.nl), a restaurant run by former psychiatric patients.

EXPLORE

weekend (in Dutch); subsidy cuts threatened their existence in 2013, but now they seem set to continue for the foreseeable future.

Restaurants

Beter & Leuk
Eerste Oosterparkstraat 91 (767 0029, www.beterenleuk.nl). Tram 3. **Open** noon-5pm Mon; 10am-5pm Tue-Sat; 11am-4pm Sun. **Main courses** €4.50-€18.50. **Map** p145 E6 ⓲ **Café**
A breakfast-slash-lunch-slash-boutique café with a mission summed up by its name, which means 'Better & Nice'. Decoration is minimal and the kitchen open to view. The menu – including eggs, croissants, homemade granola, sandwiches, salads and cakes – is scribbled on a blackboard and hand-written on brown paper. The monthly Sunday vegan brunch is popular.

★ De Kas
Kamerlingh Onneslaan 3 (462 4562, www. restaurantdekas.nl). Tram 9. **Open** noon-2pm, 6.30-10pm Mon-Fri; 6.30-10pm Sat. **Set meal** lunch €39 2 courses, dinner €49.50 3 courses. **Map** p145 H3 ⓳ **Global**
In Park Frankendael, way out to the east, is this renovated 1926 greenhouse. It's now a posh and peaceful restaurant that inspires much fevered talk among local foodies. The international menu changes daily, based on whatever goodies were harvested that morning.

Pompstation Bar & Grill
Zeeburgerdijk 52 (692 2888, www.pompstation.nu). Tram 14. **Open** *Grill* 6-10.30pm Tue-Sat; 5-10pm Sun. *Bar* 5pm-1am Tue-Thur; 5pm-3am Fri, Sat; 5pm-midnight Sun. **Main courses** €16-€45. **Map** p145 H1 ⓴ **European**
Located in a water-pumping station with lofty 18m (60ft) ceilings and tall, narrow windows (the pumps, now in the cellar, are still in use), this Zeeburg spot combines a bar and spacious restaurant. Its gastronomic USP is its selection of high-quality meat: rib-eye, tenderloin, rump steak and hamburgers. There's also a respectable choice of seafood dishes and a smattering of vegetarian options too.

Rijsel
Marcusstraat 52b (463 2142, www.rijsel.com). Tram 3. **Open** 6-10pm Tue-Sat. **Main courses** €18-€23. **Map** p145 F6 ㉑ **French/Belgian**
Housed in a former *huishoudschool*, which was one of the domestic science institutions blamed for the general decline of the Dutch kitchen, you'll find frugality only in terms of the decor at Rijsel. The busy dining room is overseen by amiable staff. Specialising in the best rotisserie chicken, like, ever, Rijsel has established itself as another delicious reason to head East.

Dappermarkt.

Bars

De Biertuin
Linnaeusstraat 29 (665 0956, www.debiertuin.nl). Tram 9. **Open** 11am-1am Mon-Thur, Sun; 11am-3am Fri, Sat. **Map** p145 G2 ㉒
The 'Beer Garden' does indeed have a wide selection of beers, as well as some of the city's most highly regarded grilled chicken. The proprietors also run other student- and hipster-friendly restaurant-bars in Oost, including the more appropriately liquor-soaked Bukowski (Oosterpark 10, 370 1685, www.barbukowski.nl).

Brouwerij 't IJ
Funenkade 7 (528 6237, www.brouwerij hetij.nl). Tram 10. **Open** 2-8pm daily. **No credit cards.** Map p145 G1 ㉓
Set at the base of the Gooyer windmill, this famous pub is where wares from the adjoining award-winning local brewery, 't IJ, can be sampled. The interior is pretty bare (still looking like the municipal baths it once was) and seating minimal, so if the weather permits, head outside to the pavement tables. The standard range includes pale Plzen, British-style IPA and darker, stronger Colombus. *See also p150* **What's Brewing?.**

Shops & Services

Dappermarkt
Dapperstraat (no phone). Tram 3, 10, 14. **Open** 9am-6pm Mon-Sat. **No credit cards.** **Map** p145 G1 ㉔ **Market**
Dappermarkt is a locals' market at heart: prices don't rise to match the number of visitors. It sells all the usual market fodder, along with piles and piles of cheap clothes.

Waterfront & Noord

Amsterdam's historic wealth owes a lot to the city's waterfront, where goods were unloaded, weighed and prepared for storage in the area's warehouses. During Amsterdam's trading heyday in the 17th century – documented nicely in the Scheepvaartmuseum – most maritime activity was centred east of Centraal Station, along Prins Hendrikkade and on the artificial islands east of Kattenburgerstraat. At the time, the harbour and its arterial canals formed a whole with the city itself. A reduction in commerce slowly unbalanced this unity, and the construction of Centraal Station late in the 19th century served as the final psychological cleavage, blocking both the city's view of the harbour and its own past. But now eyes are once again focused north across the IJ river, thanks to the new EYE film museum and the emerging nightlife hub around the former Shell buildings.

OBA.

Don't Miss

1 EYE This film museum defines the new view on Noord (p159).

2 NDSM Former shipyard, now arts haven (p158).

3 OBA Take in the view from the wonderful public library (p156).

4 Tolhuistuin A new, much anticipated cultural venue (p159).

5 Barco Relaxing canal barge with drinks, food and music (p156).

EXPLORE

CENTRE

If you walk east along the IJ riverfront from behind Centraal Station, you'll come to the famous **Muziekgebouw** (*see p203*). This epicentre of modern music, also home to the **Bimhuis** (*see p201*), comes appended with studios, rehearsal spaces and exhibition galleries. There's also a grand café and a restaurant with a charming terrace that overlooks the scenic wateriness of the IJ. Its neighbour is the glass, wave-shaped passenger terminal for luxury cruise ships. And if you continue heading eastwards, you will discover the modern architecture of the trendy Eastern Docklands (*see p256* **Along the Waterfront**).

Alternatively, still heading east from Centraal Station – but this time in front of it – you'll pass Amsterdam's vast central library, **OBA (Openbare Bibliotheek Amsterdam)**, which has spectacular views from its restaurant. Equally ambitious is its neighbour, the city's music school, **Conservatorium van Amsterdam**. De Architekten Cie designed the building according to Japanese *engawa* principles: the hallways are on the exterior to maximise soundproofing for the practising students, yet also create a transparency that invites passers-by in to listen to a recital. More views can be had from the rooftop of the **NEMO Science Center**; a striking green building resembling a sinking ship, it dominates the horizon. Across the water from NEMO is the grand structure of the recently reopened **Nederlands Scheepvaartmuseum**, one of the world's finest nautical museums.

Sights & Museums

FREE ARCAM
Prins Hendrikkade 600 (620 4878, www. arcam.nl). Bus 22. **Open** 1-5pm Tue-Sat. **Admission** free. **Map** p155 D3 ❶

IN THE KNOW LOCK STOP

When cycling to Durgerdam (*see p222*) or Marken (*see p219*), it's always worth stopping at the ancient **Café 't Sluisje** (Nieuwendammerdijk 297, 636 1712, www.cafehetsluisje.nl), with its terrace straddling a lock system in Nieuwendam, the oldest part of Amsterdam Noord. On Sundays in July and August (at noon, 2pm and 4pm), you and your bike can catch the historic ferry *IJveer XIII*, leaving from Pier 14 from behind Centraal Station.

The gallery at the Architecture Centrum Amsterdam is obsessed with the promotion of Dutch contemporary architecture, from the early 20th-century creations of the world-famous Amsterdam School to more modern designs. It organises forums, lectures, its own series of architecture books, and exhibitions in its fresh 'silver snail' location.

Mediamatic Factory
VOC-kade 10 (638 9901, www.mediamatic.net). Tram 10. **Open** varies. **Admission** varies. **Map** p155 C4 ❷
Located some distance easterly, near urban beach and club Roest (*see p156*), Mediamatic Factory is a project/exhibition space and hydroponic farm in an ancient warehouse. It's home to an inspired multimedia team, who pop up all over the place with all sorts of inspired projects. Recently, they set up a *tosti* factory to create and sell grilled cheese sandwiches from scratch – grain was harvested and a cow fattened. Who knows what they'll get up to next…

Museum 't Kromhout
Hoogte Kadijk 147 (627 6777, www.kromhout museum.nl). Bus 22, 42, 43. **Open** *May-Sept* 10am-3pm Tue; noon-4pm 1st & 3rd Sun of mth. *Oct-Apr* 10am-3pm Tue. **Admission** €5; €3 under-15s. **No credit cards. Map** p155 D4 ❸
Dating from the 18th century, this is the oldest remaining original shipyard still in use. The nostalgic museum is full of old ship engines – some of which can still burst to life – and an original 19th-century workshop.

★ Nederlands Scheepvaartmuseum (National Maritime Museum)
Kattenburgerplein 1 (523 2222, www. hetscheepvaartmuseum.nl). Bus 22. **Open** 9am-5pm daily. **Admission** €15; €7.50 reductions; free under-5s, IAmsterdam, MK. **Map** p155 D3 ❹
Dutch nautical history is rich and fascinating, so it follows that the country should boast one of the world's finest nautical museums – second only, say experts, to London's National Maritime Museum. And it's even better since renovations in 2011. Marvel at the models, portraits, boat parts and other naval ephemera, housed in a wonderful building built 350 years ago by Daniel Stalpaert. Don't miss the large replica of an 18th-century East India Trading Company (VOC) ship, with costumed 'sailors'.

★ NEMO Science Center
Oosterdok 2 (531 3233, www.e-nemo.nl). Bus 22, 48. **Open** 10am-5pm Tue-Sun. *School holidays* 9am-6pm daily. **Admission** €15; free under-4s, IAmsterdam, MK. **Map** p155 D3 ❺
NEMO has built a strong reputation as a child-friendly science museum. It eschews exhibits in favour of all manner of hands-on trickery, gadgetry

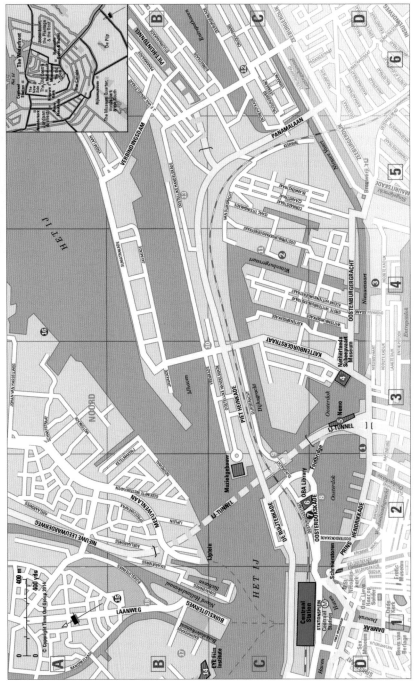

EXPLORE

and tomfoolery: you can play DNA detective games, blow mega soap bubbles or explode things in a 'wonderlab'. Watch the online animated film *Growing Pains*, which was produced for its Teen Facts exhibit, and you'll discover how pleasantly busy NEMO is. In addition, Renzo Piano's mammoth copper-green structure is a true eye-pleaser. The rooftop café is a lovely place in which to while away an afternoon reading and relaxing – that is, if it's not being used as a virtual beach or for a jazz festival.

FREE OBA (Openbare Bibliotheek Amsterdam)
Oosterdokskade 143 (523 0900, www.oba.nl).
Tram 1, 2, 4, 5, 9, 13, 14, 16, 17, 24.
Open 10am-10pm daily. **Admission** free.
Map p155 C2 ⑥
One of Europe's largest public libraries, this big city landmark opened on 07-07-07. Designed by Dutch architect Jo Coenen, the building treats arriving visitors to a soaring view up to its seventh floor café-restaurant, which, in turn, offers a spectacular view over Amsterdam. The interior, with walnut floors and white walls and shelves, is eminently low-key; colour comes from the free books and the mixed bag of people using the free Wi-Fi – or the polyester study 'pods' (an ideal spot for a nap). The place was much praised when it opened, though critics have posed pertinent questions such as, 'Where exactly are all the books?'

Restaurants

&Samhoud Places
Oosterdokskade 5 (260 2094, www.samhoud places.com). Tram 1, 2, 4, 5, 9, 13, 14, 16, 17, 24. **Open** *Restaurant* 7pm-1am Wed, Thur, Sat; noon-1am Fri; 2-7pm Sun. *Lounge* noon-1am Wed-Fri; 2pm-1am Sat; 2-7pm Sun. **Main courses** *Restaurant* €45-€125. *Lounge* €6.50-€35. **Set meal** *Restaurant* €129.50 4 courses, €169.50 7 courses. **Map** p155 D2 ⑦ **Global**
Moshik Roth is one cheeky chef: in 2013, he hoaxed the media with the idea that he was opening a DNA restaurant. He's also insanely popular as a TV chef in Israel. And this, his collaboration with 'caring capitalist' Salem Samhoud, is one of the most insanely popular (and expensive) high-end restaurants in town – complete with two Michelin stars. Alternatively, you can settle in the lounge for a cocktail and a rather more affordable tomato burger.

Bars

★ Barco
Oosterdokskade 10 (626 9383, www.cafe barco.nl). Tram 1, 2, 4, 5, 9, 13, 14, 16, 17, 24. **Open** 4pm-1am Mon-Thur; 4pm-3am Fri, Sat; 4pm-midnight Sun. **Map** p155 D2 ⑧
A repurposed canal barge moored at Oosterdok, across from the public library, Barco has 360-degree

Barco.

city views, affordable food including tapas, bands performing in the hold ('a band on a ship!') and a sun-trap terrace. You'll feel pretty damn smug to have discovered it.

Hannekes Boom
Dijksgracht 4 (419 9820, www.hannekesboom.nl). Tram 26. **Open** 11am-1am Mon-Thur, Sun; 11am-3am Fri, Sat. **Map** p155 C2/3 ⑨
With a huge terrace and a view of the harbour, the Boom rates as one of the city's hottest hot spots – even though it was made of scrap lumber. Not only street-art-friendly, it's also a treat for children as there's plenty of space to play, plus painting workshops.

Pakhuis de Zwijger
Piet Heinkade 179 (788 4433, www. dezwijger.nl). Tram 26. **Open** 9am-11pm Mon-Fri. **Map** p155 B3 ⑩
This great IJ-side café is a gateway to the cutting edge. A former warehouse now houses assorted media, creative and cultural organisations, and provides a platform for readings, workshops and all kinds of events – check the website for the latest programme. Innovation is key, and particularly inspired are VJ visionaries Beamlab and street-fashion guerrillas Streetlab.

Roest
Jacob Bontiusplaats, entrance on Czar Petersstraat 213 (308 0283, www.amsterdamroest.nl). Tram 10, 26 or bus 43. **Open & admission** varies. **Map** p155 C4 ⑪
Named 'rust' as a nod to its industrial setting, Roest has plenty of middle-of-nowhere, graffiti-covered credentials. Its line-up of ever-changing themed parties, not to mention the expansive outdoor terrace and sandy beach, manage to keep even the most

fickle trendsters entertained. They also regularly throw larger parties in the massive industrial Van Gendthallen across the way.

EASTERN DOCKLANDS

Further east are **Java-eiland and KNSM-eiland**, man-made peninsulas originally built as breakwaters for the Eastern Docklands. The largely residential Java-eiland may, at first glance, look like a dense designer prison, but it's a nice spot for a watery stroll. At Azartplein, it meets KNSM-eiland, named after the Royal Dutch Steam Company located here until 1977. Squatters, artists and urban nomads took over the area in the 1980s, but were ordered to move out in the '90s. The entire area was then reshaped into a modern residential district, based on a 1988 blueprint by Dutch architect/urban planner Jo Coenen. Many of the old buildings were preserved. While plans initially called for a rather exclusive neighbourhood, the city mandated that a significant portion of the homes were to be rented, to attract a more diverse population.

Nevertheless, with its waterside bars and eateries and trendy shops, the area is looked upon as an upmarket neighbourhood. For more, *see p256* **Along the Waterfront**.

Sights & Museums

Persmuseum (Press Museum)

Zeeburgerkade 10 (692 8810, www. persmuseum.nl). Bus 22, 65. **Open** 10am-5pm Tue-Fri; noon-5pm Sun. **Admission** €4.50; €3.25 reductions; free under-13s, IAmsterdam, MK. **No credit cards. Map** p155 C6 ⑫
The Press Museum covers the 400-year history of magazine and newspaper journalism in Amsterdam and the Netherlands. The temporary exhibitions usually focus on graphics, cartoons, photography or specific magazines.

Bars

Koffiehuis KHL

Oostelijke Handelskade 44 (779 1575, www. khl.nl). Tram 10, 26. **Open** noon-10pm Tue-Sun. **No credit cards. Map** p155 B5 ⑬

WATERSIDE EATS

More options for waterfront dining.

Amsterdam's outer watery edges are home to some expansive eating hotspots.

Blijburg

Muiderlaan 1001, IJburg (416 0330, www.blijburg.nl). Tram 26. **Open** varies. **Main courses** €8-€22. **No credit cards**.
Being 25km (15 miles) from the sea, Amsterdam was no one's choice for a beach holiday – until sand was tipped on the artificial islands of IJburg. The vast expanse of sand and adjoing freshwater lake are being exploited for their surreal beach-like properties by restaurant/bar Blijburg – with barbecues, bands and DJs.

Harbour Club

Cruquiusweg 67, Zeeburg (767 0421, www.theharbourclub.nl). Tram 10. **Open** 11am-1pm Mon-Thur, Sun; 11am-2am Fri, Sat. **Meals served** noon-11pm Mon-Fri, Sun; 5-11pm Sat. **Main courses** €20-€45.
Thousands of square metres of pure glam, contained in a former wine warehouse on the IJ riverfront, Harbour Club brings Ibiza to these rainy climes. Featuring a restaurant with sushi room, bar, club and terrace, this is *the* place to see and be seen.

REM Eiland

Haparandadam 45-2, Houthavens (688 5501, www.remeiland.com). Bus 22, 48. **Open** noon-10pm daily. **Main courses** €18.
A former pirate TV station in the North Sea, this ocean platform was brought to the outer reaches of the western harbours to be reborn as a posh restaurant with compelling views that blend well with the fruits de mer. But a drink is fine too.

Zomer Restaurant

Vuurtoreneiland (www.vuurtoreneiland.nl).
'Lighthouse Island' is a wonderfully quiet island the size of a couple of footie fields across from the fishing town of Durgerdam. A 2013 contest for how to best use the island produced 300 ideas (including a brothel). But the winner was an organic, locally sourced 'summer restaurant', which is set to open in May 2014. It will operate on Thursday to Saturday evenings and Sunday afternoons, when things will be family-oriented. There are also plans for a hotel of 'hay huts' and a winter restaurant. Bookings, complete with ferry arrangement, can only be made online.

EXPLORE

EXPLORE

NORTHERN LIGHTS

Industrial hinterland becomes arty enclave.

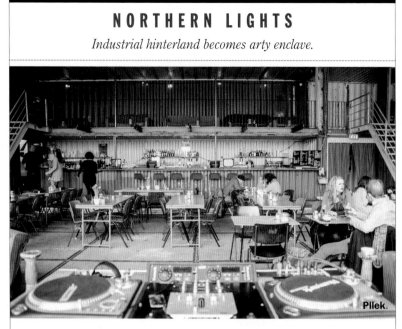

Pllek.

A 20-minute free ferry ride from Centraal Station, the former shipyard **NDSM-werf** (www.ndsm.nl) sports a wonderful and unique post-apocalyptic vibe that's ideal for parties, concerts and wacky theatre festivals such as **Over het IJ** (*see p38*). One hall forms the country's largest cultural incubator, with over 100 studios for artists, theatre companies and other creative professionals. The interior walls of this Kunststad ('art city', as it's now known) give the feeling of an expressionist film set, with parts covered in Banksy-like graffiti and an LED McDonald's sign hanging beside a large-scale chalk drawing of a child crying.

Nearby, **Nieuw Dakota** (Ms van Riemsdijksweg 41b, 331 8311, www.nieuwdakota.com) is part of a mini gallery row presenting contemporary work from both national and international artists. The surrounds include arty student accommodation made out of containers, and a 'clean energy' exhibition. NDSM also hosts a huge **flea market** every first weekend of the month; check www.ijhallen.nl for details.

As ground zero for Dutch subculture, NDSM has attracted some big players. TV network MTV set up its Benelux headquarters in a wildly revamped former woodwork factory; Greenpeace moved its offices here (handy for parking their boat *Sirius*); and even the iconic Dutch department store HEMA is headquartered here, complete with a flagship shop (NDSM-straat 12) to test new products and services. Plus there's plenty more in the planning – including a high-end mini-hotel in the crane formerly used to drag ships to dry dock (*see p287* **Small and Suite**).

To complete the picture of an alternative area where hippie ideals meet high tech, visit the **Noorderlicht Café** (NDSM Plein 102, 492 2770, www.noorderlichtcafe.nl), which offers a flower-child scene: there's a campfire, lounge music, strings of colourful lights and a terrace. Built, appropriately enough, out of shipping containers, **Pllek** (TT Neveritaweg 59, 290 0020, www. pllek.nl) is an urban beach hotspot that includes a deep skateboard pool. And right by the ferry pier in a former petrol station, **Pont Station** (MS Van Riemsdijkweg 28, 633 0224, www.pontstation.nl) peddles organic greasy snacks.

Recycling has indeed come a long way – and what's described above is only the tip of the post-industrial iceberg.

The beautiful, light-flooded interior harks back to the days in the early 20th century when this was a canteen serving staff of the Royal Holland Lloyd shipping line. Now it's a café-cum-meeting space serving the local community, with plenty to attract new visitors. There's art on the walls and regular live music to lift the spirits.

AMSTERDAM NOORD

The industrial expanse of Noord, once the city's engine house, is evolving into one of Amsterdam's hippest enclaves. But there was a time when the area was right off the map – in centuries past, the land on the other side of that big, watery body called the IJ was mainly the place where the remains of freshly executed criminals were hung on display. Once that practice stopped, there was very little of interest to pull short-term visitors northwards – except perhaps the lure of cycling routes towards such scenic fishing villages as Volendam and Marken (see pp216-229 **Escapes & Excursions**), or the trip on the free ferry from the back of Centraal Station.

But with the impending Noord-Zuidlijn Metro link (see p74 **Old Station, New Hub**) aiming to unite this once isolated area with the rest of the city, plus the various accompanying, and suitably ambitious, redevelopment plans, things are changing very quickly. Witness the gentrifying former shipyards NDSM (see p158 **Northern Lights**), film institute **EYE**, new music and culture venue **Tolhuistuin** (see p198) and upcoming nightlife (see p193 **24-Hour Party Town**).

Sights & Museums

★ EYE
IJPromenade 1 (589 1400, www.eyefilm.nl). Ferry from Centraal Station to Buiksloterweg. **Open** *Exhibitions* 11am-6pm Mon-Thur, Sat, Sun; 11am-9pm Fri. *Café-restaurant* 10am-1am Mon-Thur, Sun; 10am-2am Fri, Sat. **Map** p155 B1 ⓬
The former Filmmuseum was reincarnated in 2012 as EYE, in a new building directly across from Centraal Station. You can't miss it: it's an angular white structure that looks as if it might take flight. If you still haven't taken the free ferry, please do so immediately – the view from the excellent café-restaurant alone is worth your while. Exhibitions cover directors such as Federico Fellini, Stanley Kubrick or local hero Johan van der Keuken, with related programming taking place in the cinemas. Downstairs, there are pods in which you can surf through the history of Dutch film. EYE is also the new home for other noble film-related initiatives, such as the annual animation festival Klik! (www.klikamsterdam.nl).

Restaurants

Café Modern
Meidoornweg 2 (494 0684, www.modern amsterdam.nl). Ferry from Centraal Station to Buiksloterweg. **Open** 7-11pm Mon-Sat. **Set meal** €40 4 courses. **Map** p155 B1 ⓯ **Global**
By day, this old bank building is brunch spot Jacques Jour (www.jacquesjour.nl). By night, under the name Café Modern, this roomy and wittily designed space is a globe-trotting restaurant serving a set menu (one easily adapted for vegetarians); do book in advance. Upstairs is boutique hotel Sweet Dreamz (www.sweetdreamz.nl).

★ Hotel de Goudfazant
Aambeeldstraat 10h (636 5170, www.hotel degoudfazant.nl). Ferry from Centraal Station to IJplein. **Open** 6-10pm Tue-Sun. **Main courses** €18. **Set meal** €30.50 3 courses. **Map** p155 A4 ⓰ **Global**
Deep in the north and deeper still within a warehouse, this is post-industrial dining at its best. Yes, it's about the location, but the food, from French dishes to pizza, is excellent and affordable.

Bars

Coffee Virus
A Lab Building, Overhoeksplein 2 (06 1650 2531 mobile, www.thecoffeevirus.nl). Ferry from Centraal Station to Buiksloterweg. **Open** 9am-5pm Mon-Fri. **Map** p155 B1 ⓱
The former Shell Laboratories is now A Lab (www.a-lab.nl), a hub for multidisciplinary creatives. The Coffee Virus is the cosy public lunch room in the lobby, where the futurists of tomorrow meet up over coffee and sandwiches.

Ot en Sien
Buiksloterweg 27 (636 8233). Ferry from Centraal Station to Buiksloterweg. **Open** noon-1am Mon-Thur, Sun; noon-3am Fri, Sat. **No credit cards**. **Map** p155 B1 ⓲
This little bar (the oldest in Noord) feels like it's in the heart of the countryside. It has no pretensions, just friendly service and a fantastic range of Dutch and Belgian beers, including La Trappe Quadrupel.

Shops & Services

For clothes and cheap food, visit the local open-air markets on **Mosplein** (9am-6pm Wed-Sat) and **Buikslotermeerplein** (noon-6pm Mon; 8am-5pm Tue-Sat). The 'alternative furniture boulevard', Papaverweg, has two terrific vintage furniture shops at nos.46-48: midcentury modern furniture dealer **Neef Louis** (486 9354, www.neeflouis.nl) and rustic-inspired vintage shop **Van Dijk en Ko** (684 1524, www.vandijkenko.nl).

EXPLORE

De Pijp

Not exactly a treasure trove of historical sights, De Pijp is rooted firmly in the present. Well over 150 different nationalities keep its global village vibe alive, and many niche and upmarket restaurants and bars have flourished here in recent years. The gentrification process is firmly under way as the construction of the Metro's controversial Noord-Zuidlijn (*see p74*) continues pretty much directly beneath bustling Ferdinand Bolstraat.

Originally a late 19th-century working-class neighbourhood, today the Pijp is home to a mix of halal butchers, Surinamese, Spanish and Turkish delicatessens, and restaurants offering authentic Syrian, Moroccan, Thai, Pakistani, Chinese and Indian cuisines. This makes it one of the best areas in town to buy tasty snacks and street-food treats, the many ingredients for which are almost always bought fresh from the single largest daily market anywhere in the Netherlands: Albert Cuypmarkt.

EXPLORE

Sarphatipark.

Don't Miss

1 **Albert Cuypmarkt** A neigbourhood-defining street market (p166).

2 **Sarphatipark** Have a picnic in your friendly local park (p162).

3 **Albine** Cheap and cheerful Chinese-Surinamese restaurant (p162).

4 **Hutspot Amsterdam** A department store for pop-ups (p167).

5 **Twenty Third Bar** Posh cocktails with a view (p166).

De Pijp is the best known of Amsterdam's working-class quarters to be built in the late 19th century. Harsh economics saw the construction of long, narrow streets, which probably inspired the change in name from the official, double-yawn-inducing 'Area YY' to its appropriate nickname, 'the Pipe'. Because rents were high, many tenants were forced to sublet rooms to students, who then gave the area its bohemian character.

That said, the many Dutch writers who lived here in the late 19th and early 20th centuries helped add to the alternative atmosphere. These included such luminaries as Heijermans, De Haan and Bordewijk, who most famously described World War I Amsterdam as a 'ramshackle bordello, a wooden shoe made of stone.' Many painters had studios here too – people like Piet Mondrian, who once lived in the attic of Ruysdaelkade 75, where he began formulating de Stijl while enjoying a view of the decidedly old-school **Rijksmuseum** (*see p130*).

And, of course, the area was packed with brothels and drinking dens. In the basement of Quellijnstraat 64 (now a neighbourhood centre), the Dutch cabaret style – distinguished by witty songs with cutting social commentary for lyrics – was formulated by Eduard Jacobs, and continues to live on through the likes of Freek de Jonge, Hans Teeuwen and Najib Amhali.

At the turn of the 20th century, De Pijp was a radical socialist area. The place has lost much of its bite since those days and many families with children have fled to suburbia. Still, the number of cheap one- and two-bedroom places, combined with the reasonably central location, makes the area very attractive to students, young single people and couples, and De Pijp has the densest gay population in Amsterdam.

During the last half century, many immigrants have found their way to De Pijp, setting up shops and restaurants and so inspiring the general economic upswing of the area. De Pijp now houses a mix of nationalities and their cuisines. Thanks to these low-priced exotic eats, it's easily the best place in the city for quality snacking treats, especially around **Albert Cuypmarkt**, the hub around which De Pijp turns. This market attracts thousands of customers every day, and spills merrily into the adjoining roads: the junctions of Sweelinckstraat, Ferdinand Bolstraat and 1e Van der Helststraat, north into the lively Gerard Douplein, and south towards Sarphatipark.

EXPLORING THE AREA

From Albert Cuypstraat, if you cross Ferdinand Bolstraat you'll find a cluster of fine, cheap Chinese-Surinamese-Indonesian restaurants.

After passing the former diamond factory turned boutique hotel, **Sir Albert** (*see p289*), you'll discover that diamond turns to ruby around the corner on **Ruysdaelkade**, De Pijp's very own mini red-light district. Enjoy the sight of steaming, hooter-happy motorists caught in their own traffic gridlock while you lounge casually around an otherwise restful canal.

Head away from the water (and the red lights) a few blocks along 1e Jan Steenstraat and you'll soon run across De Pijp's little green oasis: **Sarphatipark**, designed and built as a miniature Bois de Boulogne by the slightly mad genius Samuel Sarphati (1813-66). Aside from building the Amstel hotel and the Paleis voor Volksvlijt, Sarphati showed philanthropic tendencies as a baker of inexpensive bread for the masses, and as initiator of the city's rubbish collection. The centrepiece fountain comes complete with a statue of Sammy himself.

After your stroll in the park, wander north up 1e Van der Helststraat towards **Gerard Douplein**. This little square, with its cafés, coffeeshops, chip shops and authentic Italian ice-cream parlour, turns into one big terrace during the summer, and is hugely popular with the locals. **Heinekenplein**, the U-shaped open-air gathering of cafés, Indian restaurants and Irish pubs just by the **Heineken Experience**, is a suntrap in summer months, and often houses one-off cinema screenings and the occasional music festival.

Sights & Museums

Heineken Experience

Stadhouderskade 78 (523 9666, www.heineken experience.com). Tram 7, 10, 16, 24. **Open** 11am-7.30pm Mon-Thur; 11am-8.30pm Fri-Sun. Last ticket sale 2hrs before closing. **Admission** €18; €14 reductions. **Map** p163 B2 ❶
Heineken stopped brewing here in 1988, but kept the building open for tours and marketing. The 'experience' is spread across four levels and 18 attractions, and includes multiple interactive displays, a mini brewery and a 'stable walk', where visitors can see Heineken's iconic shire horses. And where else could you take a virtual reality ride from the perspective of a Heineken bottle? Plus you get three cold ones at the end. But if it's just green hoodies you're after, head straight to the Heineken brand store (Amstelstraat 31, Southern Canal Belt, www.heinekenthecity.nl).

Restaurants

€ Albine

Albert Cuypstraat 69 (675 5135). Tram 16, 24. **Open** 10.30am-10pm Tue-Sun. **Main courses** €5-€14.50. **No credit cards**. **Map** p163 C2 ❷ Asian

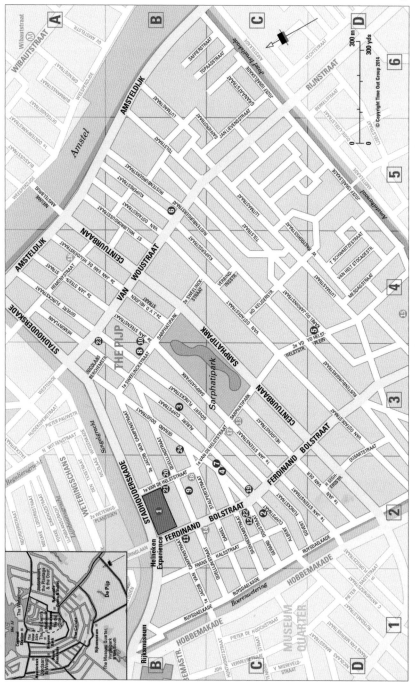

Bags packed, milk cancelled, house raised on stilts.

You've packed the suntan lotion, the snorkel set, the stay-pressed shirts. Just one more thing left to do — your bit for climate change. In some of the world's poorest countries, changing weather patterns are destroying lives.

You can help people to deal with the extreme effects of climate change. Raising houses in flood-prone regions is just one life-saving solution.

Climate change costs lives.
Give £5 and let's sort it *Here & Now*

www.oxfam.org.uk/climate-change

Be Humankind ⊗ **Oxfam**

One in a whole row of cheap Suri-Chin-Indo spots located in De Pijp, Albine – where a Chinese influence predominates – gets top marks for its lightning service and reliable vegetarian or meat meals with roti, rice or noodles. If you need a fix on a Monday, sister restaurant New Albine, a few doors down at no.49, is open seven days a week.

€ Bazar
Albert Cuypstraat 182 (675 0544, www.bazar amsterdam.nl). Tram 16, 24. **Open** 11am-midnight Mon-Thur, Sun; 11am-1am Fri, Sat. **Main courses** lunch €5-€10, dinner €15-€16. **Map** p163 B3 ❸ **North African**
This former church, now an Arabic-kitsch café, is one of the glories of Albert Cuypmarkt. Sticking to the winning formula set by its Rotterdam mothership, its menu lingers in North Africa.

Butcher
Albert Cuypstraat 129 (470 7875, www.the-butcher.com). Tram 4, 16, 24. **Open** noon-midnight Mon, Tue, Sun; 11am-midnight Wed-Sat. **Main courses** €9-€12. **Map** p163 C2 ❹ **Burgers**
Never mind the hush-hush 'invite only' club upstairs, it's all about the burgers at this chic-but-spare joint. About a dozen versions are on offer, from the aptly titled The Daddy (250g prime Aberdeen Angus beef) to the Veggie Delight. Note, closing time is flexible. At no.48, Burgermeester (www.burgermeester.eu) is an outlet of a citywide healthy burger chain.

District 5
Van der Helstplein 17 (770 0884, www.district5. nl). Tram 3. **Open** 5.30-10.30pm daily. **Main courses** €8.50-€19. **Map** p163 D4 ❺ **Italian**
Here you'll find a good, fairly priced daily menu of authentic Italian cooking (including a long list of pizzas), plus a sublime house wine. The outdoor patio is a lovely spot in summer.

Firma Pekelhaaring
Van Woustraat 127 (679 0460, www. pekelhaaring.nl). Tram 16, 24. **Open** 10am-midnight daily. **Main courses** €17.50-€24.50. **Map** p163 B5 ❻ **European**
Meat and fish dominate the menu here – the grilled mackerel is divine – although vegetarians will be happy with the creative pasta dishes. Desserts are also exemplary: the whole peach encased in almond cake and served with lavender cream makes a trip here worthwhile.

French Café
Gerard Doustraat 98 (470 0301, www.the frenchcafe.nl). Tram 16, 24. **Open** 5-10pm Mon-Sat. **Main courses** €16.50-€28. **Map** p163 C2 ❼ **French**
This charming and highly lauded brasserie in the heart of De Pijp offers upscale French fare, such as

terrine of guinea fowl and duck liver, and *côte de boeuf* with *pommes fondantes. Bon appétit!*

Little Collins
Eerste Sweelinckstraat 19 (673 2293, www. littlecollins.nl). Tram 3, 4. **Open** 10.30am-4pm Wed; 10.30am-10pm Thur, Fri; 9am-4pm Sat, Sun. **Main courses** €6-€13.50. **Map** p163 B3 ❽ **Brasserie**
Brunch dishes at this Aussie-run bar-restaurant range from wholesome own-made muesli to roast pork belly to a gut-busting 'big one': homemade sausage with bacon, eggs and all the trimmings. Whatever you choose, wash it down with a spicy bloody mary. Dinner is served Thursday and Friday.

★ Mamouche
Quellijnstraat 104 (670 0736, www.restaurant mamouche.nl). Tram 3, 12, 24. **Open** 5pm-1am Mon-Thur, Sun; 5pm-3am Fri, Sat. **Main courses** €18.50-€23.50. **Map** p163 B2 ❾ **North African**
In the heart of multicultural De Pijp, this is a Moroccan restaurant with a difference: it's posh, stylish (in a sexy, minimalist sort of way) and provides groovy background music that's best described as 'North African lounge'.

★ Le Restaurant
2e Jan Steenstraat 3 (379 2207, www.le restaurant.nl). Tram 3, 4. **Open** 7-10pm Tue-Sat. **Set dinner** €78.50 5 courses. **No credit cards. Map** p163 B3/4 ❿ **French**
Acclaimed chef-patron Jan de Wit returned home after a two-Michelin star restaurant adventure in Vreeland. His formula is simple: five courses inspired by French cuisine and what's in season, changing on a monthly basis. It earned him the first 10/10 review from feared local critic, the late Johannes van Dam.

De Taart van m'n Tante
Ferdinand Bolstraat 10 (776 4600, www. detaart.com). Tram 16, 24. **Open** 10am-6pm daily. **Cakes** €4-€8. **No credit cards. Map** p163 B2 ⓫ **Tearoom**
'My Aunt's Cake' started life as a purveyor of over-the-top cakes (which it still makes) before becoming the campest tearoom in town. In a glowing pink

EXPLORE

IN THE KNOW STREET ART

Take a look at the street signs in De Pijp, and you'll notice that most of the blocks are named after famous 17th-century painters. Jan Steen, Ferdinand Bol, Gerard Dou and Frans Hals – whose street, Frans Halsstraat, is very pretty, and rich with cafés and bars – are just a few of the artists honoured.

space filled with mismatched furniture, it's particularly gay-friendly (note the Tom of Finland cake).

€ Warung Spang-Makandra

Gerard Doustraat 39 (670 5081, www.spang makandra.nl). Tram 7, 10, 16. **Open** 11am-10pm Mon-Sat; 1-10pm Sun. **Main courses** €4.50-€10. **No credit cards. Map** p163 C2 ⑫
Indonesian
An Indonesian-Surinamese restaurant where the Indonesian influence always comes up trumps with the excellent Javanese *rames* (rice platter). Great for a takeaway, though its relaxed vibe and beautiful dishes may encourage you to linger.

Bars

Café Krull

Sarphatipark 2 (662 0214, www.cafekrull.com). Tram 3, 4, 16, 24. **Open** 9am-1am Mon-Thur, Sun; 9am-3am Fri, Sat. **Map** p163 C3 ⑬
Light from the windows floods this delightful locals' café, which is busy at all hours, with laptop holders taking advantage of the free Wi-Fi, parents treating their offspring to a hot chocolate, and – later on – imbibers of every stripe chatting happily. The outdoor picnic tables are a dream in summer.

Kingfisher

Ferdinand Bolstraat 24 (671 2395, www.kingfishercafe.nl). Tram 16, 24. **Open** 10am-1am Mon-Thur; 10am-3am Fri, Sat; noon-1am Sun. **No credit cards. Map** p163 B/C2 ⑭
The bar that began the gentrification of De Pijp is now one of the old guard, but its sleek-with-a-twist-of-kitsch chic (glossy red walls, American fridges) still sets the agenda for other young pretenders in the area, as does its loungey feel, cocktails and world-fusion snacks menu. The hip clientele has aged gracefully along with the watering hole, but makes room for a dash of new blood.

Twenty Third Bar

Ferdinand Bolstraat 333 (678 7111, www. okura.nl). Tram 16, 24. **Open** 6pm-1am Mon-Thur, Sun; 6pm-2am Fri, Sat. **Map** p163 D4 ⑮

ALBERT CUYPMARKT

Find everything you need (and more) at the city's biggest street market.

For those willing to navigate south, **Albert Cuypmarkt** (*see p167*) is a worthy source of multicultural gems. Just outside the historic centre, this busy market is definitely one for the locals or those keen to break free of the *grachts*. A 19th-century development for the working class, it's now populated by Dutch, Moroccan, Surinamese, Vietnamese and Turkish stallholders. You'll find everything from walls of veg, Turkish flatbread, fresh *stroopwafels* (the gooey, syrupy Dutch treat) and edam cheese to Vietnamese *loempias* being hawked loudly. And to bring an edge of class to the affair, in 2013 a new organic food market began on side street 1e Sweelinckstraat every Wednesday.

Besides the regular market tat – nylon lingerie that errs on the porno side, knock-off perfumes (Guggi Envy, anyone?), cringe-worthy CDs and a whole spectrum of textiles, from faux Andy Warhol prints to tan-coloured corduroy – one of the biggest draws to dear old Albert are the florists selling ten white roses for €4 or bunches of tulips for €2.50.

While it's easy to get distracted by all the stalls, it's worth checking out the nearby shops and cafés. For example, the charming and helpful **Fourniturenwinkel Jan De Grote Kleinvakman** (Albert Cuypstraat 203a, 673 8247) – which translates as 'Haberdashery Shop Jan the Big Small Craftsman' – has everything you need to keep your wardrobe in good repair. You can also check if the concept behind **Trust** (Albert Cuypstraat 210, 737 1532) is still making business sense: you pay what you want for their fine selection of coffees, soups, salads and sandwiches. Don't they know how the marketplace works?

On the 23rd floor of Hotel Okura (*see p289*), this cocktail bar offers fantastic views of the Pijp and the compact Amsterdam School architecture of the Rivierenbuurt. Be prepared to pay for the view – and the 17 different varieties of champagne on offer. If you're particularly flush, try the hotel's stellar and expensive Japanese restaurant Yamazato (678 7450, www.yamazato.nl).

Wijnbar Boelen & Boelen
1e Van der Helststraat 50 (671 2242, www.wijnbar.nl). Tram 3, 4, 16, 24. **Open** 4pm-midnight Tue-Thur, Sun; 4pm-1am Fri, Sat. **Map** p163 B2 ⑯
Many people come here for the Frenchified food, but, as the name implies, the wine is the star at this compact yet airy bar on the edge of De Pijp's main nightlife strip. Dozens are available by the glass, more by the bottle, and prices range from pocket-friendly to splurge. The emphasis is on Old World wine, but there are also good selections from the Antipodes and the Americas.

Coffeeshops

Katsu
Eerste van der Helststraat 70 (no phone, www.katsu.nl). Tram 3, 16, 24. **Open** 11am-11pm Mon-Thur; 11am-midnight Fri, Sat; noon-11pm Sun. **No credit cards. Map** p163 C3 ⑰
This little treasure offers a giant selection of various strains of hash and weed at a wide and fair range of prices – quite possibly the best selection in town, in fact. The interior is pleasantly green, with plenty of leafy potted plants, and a crowd of older locals.

★ Yo-Yo
2e Jan van der Heijdenstraat 79 (664 7173). Tram 3, 4. **Open** noon-7pm Mon-Sat. **No credit cards. Map** p163 A4 ⑱
Located on a leafy street near Sarphatipark and the Albert Cuypmarkt, this relaxed spot lacks the commercialism and crowds found in more central shops. The herb is all-organic, as is the coffee.

Shops & Services

★ Albert Cuypmarkt
Albert Cuypstraat (no phone). Tram 4, 16, 24. **Open** 9am-6pm Mon-Sat. **No credit cards. Map** p163 C2 ⑲ **Market**
Amsterdam's largest general market sells everything from pillows to prawns at great prices. The clothes tend to be run-of-the-mill cheapies. *See p166* **Albert Cuypmarkt**.

Collector
1e van der Helststraat 1d (623 3229, www.thecollector.com). Tram 7, 10, 16, 24. **Open** noon-6pm Wed, Fri, Sat; noon-8pm Thur. **Map** p163 B2 ⑳ **Fashion**

At the back of Suzette van Dam's cavern of boho womenswear and trinkets, housed in a former photographer's studio, a sign reads: 'F*ck It, Let's Go To New York'. But she draws her style inspiration from time spent at the London College of Fashion, and she's the first Dutchie to stock bags from Anya Hindmarch. Nearby is another well-curated fashion store: Charlie + Mary (Gerard Doustraat 84, www.charliemary.com) and its excellent in-house café, the Proud Otter.

Dirk van den Broek
Marie Heinekenplein 25 (673 9393, www.lekkerdoen.nl). Tram 16, 24. **Open** 8am-9pm Mon-Sat; 10am-9pm Sun. **Map** p163 B2 ㉑ **Food & drink**
Suddenly fashionable – its red bags are now must-haves for the town's designer lemmings and have even been spotted on the arms of the fashion ratpack overseas – Dirk remains cheaper than Albert Heijn. Choice may have improved, but it's not the most glam of supermarkets.
Other locations throughout the city.

★ Duikelman
Ferdinand Bolstraat 66-68 (671 2230, www.duikelman.nl). Tram 7, 10, 16. **Open** 9.30am-6pm Tue-Fri; 9.30am-5pm Sat. **Map** p163 C2 ㉒ **Homewares**
Offering over 10,000 culinary tools – from ladles to truffle raspers – Duikelman is the place for professional cooks. They've recently taken over a couple of other spaces across the street: head to Gerard Doustraat 54 for cookbooks and porcelain, or next door to that if you want to admire their stoves.

Hutspot Amsterdam
Van Woustraat 4 (223 1331, www.hutspot amsterdam.com). Tram 4. **Open** 10am-7pm Mon-Sat; noon-6pm Sun. **Map** p163 A4 ㉓ **Market**
A new concept: a permanent place for pop-ups. Hutspot brings together 50 creatives dealing in all sorts of things, from furniture to sausages. Everything is for sale and the selection changes every month. Browse and snack happy. In fact, the concept has proved such a success, they've opened a second, larger location in the Jordaan (Rozengracht 204-210, 370 8708).

Poptasi
Gerard Doustraat 103 (753 1871, www.poptasi.com). Tram 4, 16, 24. **Open** 10am-5pm Tue-Sat. **Map** p163 B3 ㉔ **Food & drink**
All extravagant wallpaper and cartoon-punk iconography, Amsterdam's only macaron specialist looks like what might have resulted had Tim Burton and David LaChapelle co-directed the movie *Chocolat*. Inventive flavours such as salted caramel, liquorice and Bounty (chocolate and coconut) mean the place tastes as good as it looks.

EXPLORE

Arts & Entertainment

Children

Amsterdammers love hanging out with their children. And they love transporting their kids in tank-like cargo bikes (*bakfietsen*) – so beware, especially on Wednesday afternoons when school finishes at noon and the number of child-friendly activities is staggering. Check out the *Jeugd* (youth) or *Kind* (child) sections in Amsterdam's free magazines and newspaper listings. The city's scale and numerous sights make it a pleasure to walk around, even for those with smaller legs. Nappy-changing facilities, however, are few and far between: the best bets are department stores or the public library. A trip on the canals is a must for all ages. Alternatively, head north by taking one of the free IJ ferries from behind Centraal Station. And if you're thinking about hiring bikes, the *bakfiets* is indeed great for loading your pre-pedalling offspring.

ANIMAL FUN

Viewing the horses on display at Amsterdam's riding school, the **Hollandsche Manege** (Vondelstraat 140, 618 0942, www.dehollandschemanege.nl), near Vondelpark, is free, but paying for lessons (available daily) is worth it – parents can relax in the beautiful café while their offspring trot around contentedly in the yard below.

Young kids will love any of the 17 or so children's farms that are dotted around the city; check www.goudengids.nl under 'Kinderboerderijen' for one near you. Further afield is the free **Ridammerhoeve Goat Farm** (Nieuwe Meerlaan 4, Amsterdamse Bos, 645 5034, www.geitenboerderij.nl), where kids can pet and feed the goats, pigs, hens and horses while parents purchase some excellent-quality cheese. For something a little larger, head to **Artis Royal Zoo** (*see p146*) – enjoyable even on a wet day.

BABYSITTING

Oppascentrale Kriterion
624 5848, https://oppascentralekriterion.nl. **Rates** €7/hr; additional charge Fri, Sat.

Administration charge €5 per booking.
Annual membership €25. **No credit cards**.
This reliable babysitting outfit uses students, all of whom are over 18 and have been carefully vetted. Advance booking is advised; you'll need to register first online or by phone.

CREATIVE ARTS

★ Groot Melkhuis
Vondelpark 2, Museum Quarter (612 9674, www.grootmelkhuis.nl). Tram 2, 3, 5, 12. **Open** 10am-6pm daily. **No credit cards**. **Map** p316 G15.
This self-service café in Vondelpark (with free Wi-Fi) has a great play area. On Wednesday afternoons, the *kinderatelier* (children's studio, 2-4pm, €5) invites kids to play in an artistic way.

Keramiekstudio Color Me Mine
Roelof Hartstraat 22, Museum Quarter (675 2987, www.colormemine.nl). Tram 3, 5, 12, 24. **Open** 11am-6pm Tue-Sat; 1-5pm Sun. **Rates** vary. **Map** p315 L16.
Fun with ceramics, mosaics and good old-fashioned finger painting. Staff are happy to advise little ones suffering an early onset of artist's block. Tots under six must be accompanied by an adult.

ARTS & ENTERTAINMENT

Het Kinderkookkafe

Vondelpark 6b, Museum Quarter (625 3257, www.kinderkookkafe.nl). Tram 1, 2, 3, 5, 12.
Open *Help Yourself Bar* 10am-5pm daily.
Rates vary. **No credit cards. Map** p316 F15.
Kids can make pizza and sausage animals and decorate cupcakes under guidance at the DIY bar, while parents relax and enjoy the fruits of their offspring's labour. Other courses run in school holidays.

FILM

Most children's films are dubbed, but an 'OV' after the title means it's showing in its original language. In autumn there are two film festivals of interest to kids (*see p178* **Festival Fever**): **Cinekid** offers quality films from around the globe, while **Klik!** specialises in animated fare.

LIBRARIES

★ OBA (Openbare Bibliotheek Amsterdam)

For listings, see p156.
As well as having English-language books, a play area, changing rooms and a great roof-top restaurant, Amsterdam's spectacular central library hosts a multitude of events for kids, including regular story-reading sessions in English.
▶ *English bookshop Waterstones also holds regular readings for kids; see p85.*

MUSEUMS

Amsterdam's museums are either highly interactive, extraordinarily life-like or the real thing. Experience life on a houseboat at the **Woonboot Museum** (*see p93*); watch pianos play themselves at the **Pianola Museum** (Westerstraat 106, The Jordaan, 627 9624, www.pianola.nl); or catch a ride on the antique **Electrische Museumtramlijn** (www.museumtramlijn.org) to the Amsterdamse Bos.

Below, we list child-specific activities at major museums. Also ask about kids' audio tours, 'treasure hunt' leaflets and the like.

CoBrA Museum

For listings and full review, see p139.
Every Sunday between 11am and 2pm, the CoBrA hosts its *kinderatelier* (children's studio), where kids can paint and draw under the guidance of a teacher. It includes a special tour of the museum.

Joods Historisch Museum

For listings and full review, see p143.
Guided tours for youngsters take place in the main museum, while the special children's museum allows youngsters to follow the life of a Jewish family, partake in Hebrew workshops and get creative with special activities.
▶ *The Anne Frank Huis is one of the city's most evocative sites; see p92.*

ARTS & ENTERTAINMENT

OBA.

★ NEMO Science Center
For listings and full review, see p154.
This science museum is completely dedicated to blowing kids' minds.

Rijksmuseum
For listings and full review, see p130.
The nation's treasure house offers a variety of workshops related to colour, etching, digital cartooning, photography and even stop-motion animation.

Stedelijk Museum
For listings and full review, see p130.

Amsterdam's main modern-art museum offers family workshops and tours related to the current temporary exhibition – for example, how to make a suprematist composition à la Malevich or a modern Dutch design object à la Marcel Wanders.

Van Gogh Museum
For listings and full review, see p133.
This popular museum hosts a bevy of children's activities, such as a weekend workshop themed to the current exhibition, including a tour and painting time. English tours are available with advance group bookings. There's also a children's audio tour.

STATE OF PLAY
A primer of fun for the little ones.

Play! Amsterdam is an ingenious guidebook listing Amsterdam's best playgrounds, from lone pieces of climbing equipment to large-scale playgrounds. Written and published by Becky Russell, the book came about when Russell found herself at the start of the summer break one year with two young children and no plans. Bored of their usual playgrounds, they decided to seek out some new spots. Consequently, Russell decided to create a book of her findings.

Turns out that there are 414 ways for kids to have gratis fun in Amsterdam. Becky's top three are the **Het Woeste Westen** (Westerpark, www.woeste westen.nl, tram 10 or bus 21, 48, 60), which, with its combination of space,

high grass, wild flowers, canals and tunnels, recaptures what it's like to grow up in the country. The 'rough playground' at the corner of Jan van Galenstraat and **Willem de Zwijgerlaan** (Bos en Lommer, tram 12, 14) has challenging equipment that's suitable for all, including a rope bridge, wobbly bridge and high tube slide down a large hill. A green oasis in an otherwise concrete neighbourhood, **Speeltuin Wittenburg** (Fortuinstraat 4, Waterfront, bus 22, 43) also appeals to all, but the high climbing frame with balance beams and bridges is particularly suited to 'big adventurers'.
Play! Amsterdam (and the Android app) is available via www.playamsterdam.nl.

PARKS

Vondelpark (*see p128*) is very popular, but you'll find at least one good park per district. With its city farm, water adventure park and swimming area (summer only), ex-gasworks **Westergasfabriek** (*see p213*) entertains the young and young-at-heart. **Amstelpark** (*see p139*) promises hours of fun with a miniature train and a maze. Take the whole day to explore the **Amsterdamse Bos** (*see p139*); the goat farm and pancake house are sure to be a hit.

PLAY

★ TunFun

Mr Visserplein 7, Jodenbuurt (689 4300, www. tunfun.nl). Tram 9, 14 or Metro Waterlooplein. **Open** 10am-6pm daily. **Admission** €8.50 1-12s; free adults. **No credit cards. Map** p313 M9.

An urban recycling success, this cavernous indoor playground used to be an underpass. Huge soft-play constructions provide endless joy for those under 12, with ball pools for tiny tots and full-on jungle gyms for more adventurous older kids.

SWIMMING & SPORTS

Indoor pools **Marnixbad** (Marnixplein 1, Jordaan, 524 6000, www.hetmarnix.nl), **De Mirandabad** (De Mirandalaan 9, Zuid, 252 4444) and the spectacular art nouveau **Zuiderbad** (Hobbemastraat 26, Museum Quarter, 252 1390), and outdoor pools **Brediusbad** (Spaarndammerdijk 306, West, 684 6984) and **Flevoparkbad** (Zeeburgerdijk 630, Oost, 692 5030) are all good for kids. But if you don't want to get disoriented in a crowd of wet nudists, then it's good to call ahead for the best time for kids. **Vondelpark** (*see p128*) and **Westergasfabriek** (*see p213*) offer outdoor water areas in the summer.

Drier activities include the massive **Klimhal Amsterdam**, the biggest indoor climbing centre in the Netherlands, featuring different walls and 'mountains' to suit kids from six years up. With two pistes and real snow, **Snowplanet** (which may change its name to SnowWorld due to a 2014 buyout) is almost like the real thing, and there are even introductory sessions for three- to four-year-olds. For something a little closer to the ground, kids will go crazy for the indoor carting track at **Race Planet for Kids**, where they can play with pedal cars, electric F1 cars and more.

★ Klimhal Amsterdam

Naritaweg 48, Sloterdijk (681 0121, www.klimhal amsterdam.nl). Tram 12 or Metro or NS rail Sloterdijk. **Open** 5-11pm Mon, Tue, Thur; 2-10.30pm Wed; 4-11pm Fri; 9.30am-10.30pm Sat;

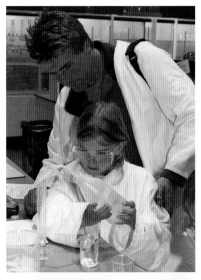

NEMO Science Center.

IN THE KNOW SHIP AHOY

For a proper pirate experience, visit the VOC-Schip *Amsterdam*. This replica of an 18th-century Dutch East India Company cargo ship, complete with 'real' sailors, forms part of the newly renovated **Scheepvaartmuseum** (*see p154*).

9.30am-11pm Sun. **Admission** €12.75; €9.50-€10 reductions; €6 equipment hire. **No credit cards**.

Race Planet for Kids

Herwijk 10, Sloterdijk (611 1120, www.race planet.com). Tram 17 then bus 82. **Open** varies. **Admission** from €17.50 under-12s; €19.50 adults.

★ Snowplanet

Recreatieschap Spaarnwoude, Heuvelweg 6-8, Velsen-Zuid (025 554 5848, www.snowplanet.nl). Tram 17 then bus 82. **Open** 9am-11pm daily. **Admission** from €10/hr; €7.50 equipment hire.

THEATRE & MUSIC

Both the **Jeugdtheater De Krakeling** (Nieuwe Passeerdersstraat 1, Western Canal Belt, reservations 624 5123, www.krakeling.nl) and **Het Nederlands Marionettentheater** (Jacob Obrechtstraat 28, Museum Quarter, 692 8031, www.nederlandsmarionettentheater.nl) offer language-no-problem puppet and mime performances for kids; check websites for programmes. Amsterdam's pre-eminent venue for classical music, the **Concertgebouw** (*see p203*), regularly programmes children's concerts, featuring multidisciplinary elements such as film to engage the senses.

OUTSIDE AMSTERDAM

Set in a forest, the enormous **Efteling** amusement park is packed with state-of-the-art thrills, traditional rides, fairy-tale characters, and even talking rubbish bins. Featuring more than 700 scale models of the Netherlands' most famous sights, the miniature city of **Madurodam** is a wonderland (especially when they're lit up from within on summer evenings). In the beautiful nature reserve of Berg en Bos, the expansive **Apenhaul** is home to all manner of primates that are free to roam the grounds – as are visitors. All are within a hour's travel from Amsterdam.

For other attractions out of town, *see pp216-229* **Escapes & Excursions**.

★ Apenheul

JC Wilslaan 21, Apeldoorn (055 357 5757, www.apenheul.nl). **Open** *July, Aug* 10am-6pm daily. *Apr-June, Sept, Oct* 10am-5pm daily. Closed Nov-Mar. **Admission** €19.75; €17.50 reductions; free under-3s.

Efteling

Europalaan 1, Kaatsheuvel, Noord Brabant (0900 0161, www.efteling.com). **Open** *July, Aug* 10am-8pm Mon-Fri, Sun; 10am-midnight Sat. *Apr-June, Sept, Oct* 10am-6pm daily. *Nov-Mar* 11am-6pm daily. **Admission** €34.50; free under-4s.

Madurodam

George Maduroplein 1, The Hague (070 416 2400, www.madurodam.nl). **Open** *July, Aug* 9am-9pm daily. *Apr-June* 9am-8pm daily. *Sept, Oct* 9am-7pm daily. *Mar* 9am-6pm daily. *Jan, Feb, Nov, Dec* 11am-5pm daily. **Admission** €15.50; €10.50-€13.50 reductions; free under-3s. **No credit cards**.

ARTS & ENTERTAINMENT

Madurodam.

Film

The Dutch are not major global players when it comes to film. Director Alex van Warmerdam's dry, dark *Borgman* (2013) was the first Dutch film to compete for the Palme d'Or at Cannes since 1975. But you may recognise Dutch household names such as *Game of Thrones* actress Carice van Houten and *Control* director Anton Corbijn. And then there are the transplants, such as directors Steve McQueen (*12 Years a Slave*) and Peter Greenaway (*Nightwatching*).

The city is home to some of Europe's most beautiful mainstream cinemas (including deco delight Pathé Tuschinski), a fine crop of arthouse institutions and film festivals aplenty. But the real news is film institute EYE, newly relocated and reaching for the celluloid stars.

CINEMAS

First-run

Movies
Haarlemmerdijk 161, Jordaan (638 6016, www.themovies.nl). Tram 3 or bus 18, 21, 22. **Tickets** €9.50-€12; €70 10-visit card. **Screens** 4. **No credit cards. Map** p311 E6.
The oldest cinema in Amsterdam to remain in regular use, the Movies has been circulating celluloid since way back in 1912, and still exudes a genteel atmosphere of sophisticated elegance. The excellent adjoining restaurant serves decent set dinners, with the cost (from €24.50) including film admission.
▶ *The Movies is one of the hosts of the brilliant annual Cinekid Amsterdam film festival – see p178 Festival Fever.*

Pathé ArenA
ArenA Boulevard 600, Zuidoost (0900 1458 premium rate, www.pathe.nl). Metro Bijlmer ArenA. **Tickets** €8-€12.50. **Screens** 14.
This multi-screen complex is one of the best places to enjoy those guilty-pleasure blockbusters with little chance of bumping into someone you know, because of its peripheral location way out by the Ajax stadium. Styled with all the finesse of a big brick house, it nonetheless has comfortable seating and the only IMAX screen in Amsterdam – unquestionably the best place to catch 3D movies.

Pathé City
Kleine-Gartmanplantsoen 15-19, Southern Canal Belt (0900 1458 premium, www.pathe.nl). Tram 1, 2, 5, 6, 7, 10. **Tickets** €9-€11.50. **Screens** 7. **Map** p314 J12.
Once the cinematic equivalent of a used-car salesman, this former multiplex received a long-overdue reinvention in 2010 as an arthouse/mainstream hybrid, with the emphasis firmly on quality programming. It's perfect for a date, with a grown-up theatrical vibe (think velvet curtains) and a wine bar.

Pathé de Munt
Vijzelstraat 15, Southern Canal Belt (0900 1458 premium rate, www.pathe.nl). Tram 4, 9, 14, 16, 24. **Tickets** €7.50-€10. **Screens** 13. **Map** p314 K10.
This is central Amsterdam's monster multiplex. In its favour are huge screens and comfortable seating. And now that the City (*see above*) has gone upmarket, this is the place for big-budget Hollywood kicks.

Pathé Tuschinski

★ Pathé Tuschinski

Reguliersbreestraat 26-34, Southern Canal Belt (0900 1458 premium rate, www.pathe.nl). Tram 4, 9, 14, 16, 24. **Tickets** €9-€11.50. **Screens** 6. **Map** p315 L11.

This extraordinary cinema is named after Abraham Tuschinski, who was Amsterdam's most illustrious cinematic entrepreneur. Built in 1921 as a 'world theatre palace', the decor is an arresting clash of rococo, art deco and Jugendstil, which can make it hard to keep your eyes on the silver screen. Glittering premières take place to road-blocking effect. If you're more 'in the red' than red carpet-ready, check out the morning screenings.

Arthouses

Cinecenter

Lijnbaansgracht 236, Western Canal Belt (623 6615, www.cinecenter.nl). Tram 1, 2, 5, 7, 10. **Tickets** €6.50-€10. **Screens** 4. **No credit cards. Map** p314 H12.

Tucked discreetly away from the madding bustle of nearby Leidseplein, this snug, artsy and student-friendly cinema is home to a cosmopolitan array of

IN THE KNOW
ACCESS ALL AREAS

A fictional town called **Cineville** (www.cineville.nl) brings together 12 arthouse and repertory cinemas in Amsterdam – plus another dozen or so cinemas across the country – which between them screen around 100 films a week. A pass costing €19 a month provides access to them all.

films. The trendy yet welcoming bar is the perfect arena for a little post-film debate, should you emerge from the screening to find it's raining. That's if you even need an excuse.

★ EYE

IJpromenade 1, Noord (589 1400, www.eyefilm.nl). Ferry from Centraal Station to Buiksloterweg. **Tickets** €7.50-€10. **Screens** 4.

The most important centre of cinematography in the Netherlands by a country mile, EYE specialises in major retrospectives and edgier contemporary fare. The annual summer programme typically features an exhaustive array of screenings, talks and exhibitions dedicated to the celebration and reassessment of showbiz lynchpins, with past examples including nouvelle vague director Jean-Pierre Melville. A lesser-known function of the place is its loving programme of celluloid restorations. *Photo p179.*

Filmhuis Cavia

Van Hallstraat 51-52, West (681 1419, www.filmhuiscavia.nl). Tram 10 or bus 21. **Tickets** €4. **Screens** 1. **No credit cards.**

Blink and you'll miss this one. Housed in the amiable seclusion of a once-squatted school above a gym, the left-of-mainstream Filmhuis Cavia specialises in obscure, queer and/or political pictures. You can also rent the place out for a film-themed party of your own; ideal if you consider yourself an armchair revolutionary.

Het Ketelhuis

Haarlemmerweg 8-10, Westerpark (684 0090, www.ketelhuis.nl). Tram 10 or bus 21. **Tickets** €7.50-€9.50. **Screens** 3. **No credit cards. Map** p311 D6.

Once of little interest to non-Dutch-speaking film fans (it used to specialise in un-subtitled homegrown movies), the Ketelhuis now screens interesting international art films alongside the Netherlands' finest flicks. The revival of the Westergasfabriek and regular festivals haven't hurt its popularity among cinematically minded Amsterdammers, and the staff here are among the friendliest in town.

▶ *For more details on the Westergasfabriek and all the goodies it has to offer, see p116 Floodlights on Westerpark.*

Kriterion

Roetersstraat 170, Oost (623 1708, www. kriterion.nl). Tram 7, 10 or Metro Weesperplein. **Tickets €7.50-€9.50. Screens 2. No credit cards. Map p313 O9.**

Founded in 1945 by a group of Resistance-fighter undergraduates, this cinema continues to be run by a bunch of students – to great success. The programme is made up of quality films, first-runs as well as contemporary classics, while the Movies that Matter series guarantees thought-provoking discussions. The Kriterion's sneak previews are almost always sold out, and the convivial bar usually facilitates much post-film analysis.

Rialto

Ceintuurbaan 338, De Pijp (676 8700, www. rialto film.nl). Tram 3, 12, 24. **Tickets €9-€10. Screens 3. No credit cards. Map p315 N14 F6.**

De Pijp's neighbourhood cinema, the Rialto offers an eclectic mix of arty features, documentaries, classics, festivals and kids' fare. It broadens the mix with frequent avant-garde film premières, as well as regular introductory talks about films chosen by guest speakers. Disabled access is good too. Be warned, though, as the foreign films here rarely have subtitles other than Dutch ones.

De Uitkijk

Prinsengracht 452, Southern Canal Belt (223 2416, www.uitkijk.nl). Tram 1, 2, 5, 7, 10. **Tickets €8-€9. Screens 1. No credit cards. Map p314 J12.**

This charming hole-in-the-wall cinema shows select arthouse flicks for a discerning audience, plus a smattering of mainstream and foreign-language gems that may have escaped your attention first time around.

FORGET THE CINEMA

Vexed by the multiplex? Try these alternative film venues.

The trend for showing films any place but in the buildings specifically designed for that purpose is booming in Amsterdam, but it wasn't always so. 'About five years ago, I decided Amsterdam was in dire need of an underground film scene,' says American and long-time Amsterdam resident Jeffrey Babcock. These days, the film connoisseur – hundreds of DVDs line the walls of his apartment – curates several indie nights around the West, including the packed weekly **Cinemanita** gatherings in the cavernous space at the back of hipster hangout **De Nieuwe Anita** (*see p179*). Hardly any of his choices have been screened in the Netherlands before. Notions such as profit or star power are of no concern, and other non-commercial criteria can prevail. 'Every film I show has something unique and valuable,' explains Babcock. 'To me, cinema is about ideas and creativity, about life.'

And sometimes cinema is also about Jacuzzis. In March 2014, 21 hot tubs, 21,000 litres of water, 150 bathrobes, many bottles of cava and two cinema screens were due to be employed for the city's first **Hot Tub Movie Club** (HTMC, www.hottubmovieclub.nl) in the Machinegebouw at Westergasfabriek. It's enough to make Hugh Hefner jealous.

The no less casual **Shortcutz** (www.shortcutznetwork.com/project/ amsterdam) takes place in the rather more rarefied surrounds of **De Kring** (Kleine Gartmanplantsoen 7, 623 6985, www.kring.nl), a private members' club for artists. At free weekly screenings on Tuesdays, local filmmakers – both amateur and professional – can show their latest short-film creations – and receive critical feedback. Every year, the best short films are celebrated at an awards ceremony at **EYE** (*see p176*).

Meanwhile, various squatty initiatives also hold screenings, such as former bomb shelter **Vondelbunker** (www.vondelbunker.nl) – with everything from weird B-movies to docs that inspire activism. **Joe's Garage** (www.joesgarage.nl) in Oost, which has regular Sunday screenings, even asks people to make contact if they have a film they want to share with an audience.

'It proves that people are interested in seeing something different from Pathé blockbusters,' says Babcock. And it also shows that you don't necessarily need an expensive marketing scheme.'

ARTS & ENTERTAINMENT

Multimedia centres

16cc

Kadijksplein 16, Waterfront (627 0236, www.16cc.nl). Bus 22, 42, 43. **Tickets** €7.50. **Screens** 1. **Map** p313 N7.

Located on a scenic square with many other eating and drinking options nearby, 16cc is a delightful café – with a small cinema in the basement – that looms large on the city's cultural scene with its quirky programming of alternative film, photography, music, art and literature.

De Balie

Kleine-Gartmanplantsoen 10, Southern Canal Belt (553 5100, www.debalie.nl). Tram 1, 2, 5, 7, 10. **Tickets** €7-€9.50. **Screens** 2. **No credit cards.** **Map** p314 J12.

A temple to high culture, De Balie is a bar, theatre and debating ground, and plays host to several left-field film festivals and expertly curated cinematic curiosities. Look out for Cineville Talkshow, often your first chance to see an upcoming release, with a little heated (quite often Dutch) debate thrown in for good measure.

FESTIVAL FEVER

If you screen it, they will come.

Delve into Amsterdam's bulging calendar of film festivals and a plethora of intriguing alternatives to the regular mainstream fare soon appear. The festival season kicks into gear at the end of January with the annual **International Film Festival Rotterdam** (www.filmfestivalrotterdam.com) – the largest film festival, and one of the largest cultural events, in the country. Lasting 12 days and using venues across nearby Rotterdam, IFFR specialises in arthouse fare and exotic films, with a traditionally strong helping of esoteric Asian flicks, and plenty of directors showing up for Q&As.

The **Africa in the Picture** (www.africa inthepicture.nl) festival is somewhat sporadic but usually takes place at the beginning of the year, giving the emerging African film scene a much needed, and much deserved, platform by organising screenings, discussions and parties, which are then taken on tour across the country.

Also something of a moveable feast in terms of venue and time of year is **Roze Filmdagen** (www.rozefilmdagen.nl), literally Amsterdam's 'pink film days', a ten-day showcase of queer-minded flicks from around the world. For the time being, it seems to have settled into the wonderful Westergasfabriek venue MC Theater (*see p116*), in mid March. Look out for promo posters in town – they're wonderfully witty.

April brings the **Imagine Film Festival** (www.imaginefilmfestival.nl), which caters to both gorehounds and kids with a line-up of fantasy, sci-fi and horror films. Gory and ghoulish appearances notwithstanding, the crowds and crew are a good-natured bunch and the festival has grown large enough to offer some intriguing flicks while maintaining a cosy atmosphere for allcomers.

Even Amsterdam nights can get sultry in August, so get comfortable at one of the open-air screens that litter the city. The one at Stenen Hoofd, Westerdoksdijk, devotes several nights to showing the unreleased gems of the year at free after-dark festival **Pluk de Nacht** (www.plukdenacht.nl).

The kids are all right during October's autumn holiday, when the five-day **Cinekid** (www.cinekid.nl), the largest child-oriented film festival on the planet, has its annual play date. It involves some 500 productions, from feature films to TV series to interactive installations. MediaLab lets four- to 14-year-olds experience movie-making through play, workshops and installations, guided by industry experts. Key venues are the Movies cinema and the Westergasfabriek culture centre.

Punching way above its weight, **Amsterdam Film Week** (www.amsterdam filmweek.com), at the end of October, has the ability to snag all sorts of star names. In 2013, Susan Sarandon was guest of honour and award-winning director Steve McQueen dropped by to pick up the public's prize for *12 Years a Slave*. As well as retrospectives, the festival includes sneak previews, award-winners and indie faves.

For five fun-packed days in November, Amsterdam becomes the animated capital of Europe, courtesy of the brilliant **Klik! Amsterdam Animation Festival** (www.klik amsterdam.nl), geared towards the young, the old and every cartoon-lover in between.

The biggest documentary festival in the world also touches down at the end of November in the form of the **International Documentary Filmfestival Amsterdam** (www.idfa.nl), with intimate Q&As and workshops from the best in the biz.

EYE. *See p176.*

Filmhuis Griffioen
Uilenstede 106, Amstelveen (598 5100, www.filmhuisgriffioen.nl). Tram 5. **Tickets** €5-€8. **Screens** 1.
A small student-run cinema on the campus of the Free University, this is a cheap and eminently enjoyable place in which to check out the films you missed in their first run – even if you missed them by a decade or so (think *Magnolia* and other turn-of-the-20th-century awards magnets).

Melkweg
Lijnbaansgracht 234a, Western Canal Belt (531 8181, www.melkweg.nl). Tram 1, 2, 5, 7, 10. **Tickets** €8 (incl membership). **Screens** 1. **Map** p314 H12.
For a venue famed primarily for its musical appeal, the Melkweg hosts a surprisingly broad array of quality cinema, from foreign-language festival fodder to music-video nights, although the racket that comes through the floor when there's a band playing elsewhere in the building might distract you from your flick. Rather than grumbling about noise pollution, it helps if you go with the flow and consider this a free sample.
▶ *The Melkweg also hosts plenty of great club nights and gigs.*

De Nieuwe Anita
Frederik Hendrikstraat 111, West (no phone, www.denieuweanita.nl). Tram 3, 10, 14. **Tickets** €3. **Screens** 1. **No credit cards**. **Map** p311 E10.

This former squat is a buzzing hive of hipster activity. Aside from the live performances, laid-back lounging nights and (but of course!) impromptu hair salons that crowd the eclectic schedule here, Monday evenings feature staggeringly obscure but highly enjoyable films (*see p177* **Forget the Cinema**), often with a lengthy intro from the Anita's voluble curator.

OT301
Overtoom 301, Vondelpark (779 4913, www.ot301.nl). Tram 1. **Tickets** from €4. **Screens** 1. **No credit cards**. **Map** p316 F15.
A former Dutch film academy transformed by squatters into a cultural 'breeding ground', OT301 has a radio station, vegan restaurant De Peper (*see p133*) and a charming 80-seat cinema that shows unusual films ranging from activist documentary to double and even triple bills of arthouse classics. Screenings typically happen on Tuesdays and Sundays, and the volunteers who work here are generally happy to hear programme suggestions.

Studio/K
Timorplein 62, Oost (692 0422, www.studio-k.nu). Tram 7, 14. **Tickets** €6-€9. **Screens** 2. **No credit cards**.
The 'K' here might stand for 'kooky', sometimes veering into the realms of the pleasantly 'kitsch'. Screening mostly alternative and non-commercial films, the venue also has a theatre, club and a café/gallery, which makes it the ideal venue for festivals. The restaurant, with good vegetarian options, offers a dinner and film deal for €21.

Gay & Lesbian

Some say that Amsterdam has lost ground as a 'gay capital' since it hosted the world's first gay wedding in 2001. Is Amsterdam Gay Pride now something that comes but once a year? Or is Amsterdam simply the world's first integrated, post-gay city, where anything goes? Whatever conclusions you draw, you'll certainly have fun getting there. Amsterdam remains keen to broadcast its credentials as a haven for liberalism and open-mindedness. It has an impressive track record when it comes to gay rights: homosexuality was decriminalised in 1811, the first gay/lesbian bar opened in 1927 (Café 't Mandje, still open today – *see p60*), and one of the first gay rights organisations, the COC Nederland, was founded in Amsterdam in 1946, at a time when much of the rest of the world considered homosexuality an illness. Today, there's still plenty to party about.

THE SCENE TODAY

After a couple of years of serious hand-wringing about whether or not Amsterdam still deserved its 'gay capital' title, the city seems to be getting back on track. Local political parties have tried hard to make Amsterdam gay-friendly. Meanwhile, Amsterdam Gay Pride has gone the way of many others by embracing corporate sponsorship – some major companies and banks even have their own floats to make sure spectators get the message (the main message being that they're keen to emphasise their employee diversity).

Until very recently, the scenes for gay men and women were quite separate and they'd only get together on big occasions such as Queen's Day (now King's Day), Pride or one-off parties like the mighty Love Dance. Now there are an increasing number of mixed bars and club nights. The gay clubbing scene is on the up, reinvigorated by a wealth of young talent and plenty of fresh faces. A word of warning, though: free condoms aren't universal on the scene, and a range of STDs – including HIV –

are on the rise, with barebacking as popular and controversial here as in any other big city.

INFORMATION

Gay & Lesbian Switchboard
623 6565, www.switchboard.nl.
Affiliated with the umbrella organisation Schorer, this band of sympathetic and knowledgeable volunteers has been giving advice for years. You can ask them about anything, from HIV risk factors to the best new bars, and they speak perfect English.

Homomonument
Westermarkt, Western Canal Belt. Tram 13, 14, 17. **Map** p312 G9.
Unveiled in 1987, Karin Daan's three-sectioned pink triangle – symbolising past, present and future – was a world first. It's also a place to celebrate and to be proud: on King's Day and Pride it gets annexed to the open-air disco and market.

★ IHLIA
6th floor, Openbare Bibliotheek Amsterdam, Oosterdokskade 143, Waterfront (523 0837,

www.ihlia.nl). **Open** *Exhibitions* 10am-10pm daily. *Information* noon-5pm Mon-Thur. **Map** p313 L6. The spectacular view is reason enough for journeying up to the sixth floor of Amsterdam's amazing public library, but this archive of LGBT-related materials, from biographies to condom packets, is Europe's largest.

★ **Pink Point**
Westermarkt, Western Canal Belt (428 1070, www.pinkpoint.org). Tram 13, 14, 17. **Open** 10am-6pm daily (reduced hrs in winter). **Map** p312 G9.
Queer queries? Need to know which party to go to? Looking for political pamphlets? Or just a gay postcard or a street map? Head to this kiosk near the Homomonument, and its friendly and chatty staff.
▶ *For information about gay and lesbian matters, and HIV, see Resources pp293-297.*

MEDIA
Print

Most lesbigay printed matter is in Dutch, but it's good to know that a fair chunk is bilingual, including **Gay & Night** (www.gay-night.nl), **Gay News** (www.gaynews.nl) and **Amsterdam Gay Map** (http://guide.gayamsterdam.com/maps), all of which are published monthly. The standard of English can be decidedly dodgy, but they're free, and available in bars around the city. Amsterdam-published **Butt** (www.buttmagazine.com) looks like a low-rent porn mag (and there are plenty of sexy pictures among its pink pages), but pulls off some of the most interesting interviews of any gay publication, with the likes of Edmund White, Rufus Wainwright and

THE QUEER YEAR
A seasonal guide to gay and lesbian events.

For a full guide to the city's annual events, *see pp34-43* **Diary**.

SPRING
It's been something of a moveable feast for a while, but the **Roze Filmdagen** (*see p178* **Festival Fever**) – a week-long celebration of LGBT film, both international and home-grown – seems to have settled into March for the time being. The opening and closing night parties are especially popular.
While most of the town turns bright orange during **Koningsdag** (King's Day, 27 April; *see p39* **The Queen, um, King of All Parties**), pockets of Amsterdam are a shocking shade of pink as queers and dykes ostensibly celebrate King Willem-Alexander's birthday. Festivities focus on the memorial Homomonument (*see p180*) and the Amstel.
The Homomonument itself is at the centre of a more sombre commemoration on **Herdenkingsdag** (Remembrance Day, 4 May), when victims of Nazi persecution are remembered with flowers and speeches. The following day, **Bevrijdingsdag** (Liberation Day), sees a huge party with plenty of dancing at the monument.
There are a couple of biennial film festivals: **CinemAsia** (www.cinemasia.nl) in April, which started out as the Queer & Asian Film Festival and remains lesbian-run to this day; and transgender celebration **TranScreen** (www.transcreen.org) in May.

AIDS Memorial Day in late May remembers victims around the world with songs, music, candles and speeches. It takes place at the Dominicus Church in Spuistraat.

SUMMER
The biggest event of the summer is, of course, **Amsterdam Gay Pride**. Gradually taking over the entire first week of August, this all-encompassing event includes cultural and sporting activities, but at its heart it's really just one enormous party. The main attraction is the floating parade on the Saturday – *see p187* **A Straight Guide to Gay Pride**.

AUTUMN
In October, a darker, more intimate party takes place. **Leather Pride** is celebrated with FF, rubber and other menu-only parties in the main leather bars. To top it off, there's a huge Get Ruff! party where, as the name suggests, guys come to have all kinds of unfeasibly pervy fun behind closed doors.

WINTER
World AIDS Day on 1 December is marked with **Love Dance** at Paradiso (*see p197*), a massively popular AIDS-benefit party with DJs, performances and fashion shows. The fundraising festivities are now spilling out into other gay and gay-friendly venues (see www.worldaidsnight.com for details).

ARTS & ENTERTAINMENT

Eagle Amsterdam.

Marc Jacobs. **Fantastic Man** (www.fantastic man.com), from the same stable, is a very influential 'gentleman's style journal' that, if not strictly gay, is doused in homosexual sensibility.

If you can read some Dutch, check out the local edition of **Winq** (www.winq.com), the global gay glossy with brains, published from a canal house in the Red Light District. *Winq* recently fused with the long-running lifestyle/ news digest **De Gay Krant**. **PS**, *Het Parool's* Saturday supplement, also has pink listings.

Also in Dutch is **Zij aan Zij** (www. zijaanzij.nl), a general lesbian glossy; back copies of the mag are available online. Online magazine and shop **La Vita** (www.la-vita.nl) offers a similarly bland diet. Both have national listings, but in Dutch only. The most exciting lesbian publication is **Girls Like Us** (GLU, www.glumagazine.com), an English-language quarterly with a side order of top-quality parties that has injected hope into the city's dowdy dyke scene. Expect a mixture of chatty interviews, fashion-driven shoots and ephemera dug from dusty old archives.

TV & Radio

MVS Gay Station – TV
www.mvs.nl. Through Salto TV: channels 39+, 616MHz. **Times** 10-11pm Sat; 9-10pm Sun.
The lesbian and gay community media company covers all aspects of gay life, from visiting porn stars to retired hairdressers, and all points in between. Usually in Dutch but with English-language items; some programmes are also online.

MVS Gay Station – Radio
www.mvs.nl. 106.8 FM, 103.3 on cable.
Times 7-8pm Fri; 6-8pm Sat.
News, features, interviews and music with a gay twist. The shows are usually in Dutch, but there are regular exceptions.

Pinq Radio
www.pinqradio.com.
Run by a ragtag array of volunteers and nightlife notables, Pinq Radio has been streaming online since 2008. Broadcast from Amsterdam's best gay parties, it's a way of sharing in the fun, even if you can't be there in person. Local style guru Ruud van der Peijl and his friend Bas Andrea have an often hilarious live show, Sphincter Radio (4-6pm Wed).

WHERE TO STAY

The **Gay & Lesbian Switchboard** (*see p180*) has details of gay- and lesbian-friendly hotels. Those listed below are mostly gay-run. For more hotels, *see pp276-289.*

Amistad
Kerkstraat 42, Southern Canal Belt (624 8074, www.amistad.nl). Tram 1, 2, 5. **Rates** €60-€158 double. **Map** p314 J12.
Run by the very friendly Johan, Joost, Mike and Rick, this hip hotel shines like the pages of a trendy magazine. Rooms are cosy, and the breakfast area on the ground floor doubles as a gay internet lounge every day after 1pm. The lounge is open to non-residents.

Anco Hotel
Oudezijds Voorburgwal 55, Old Centre: New Side (624 1126, www.ancohotel.nl). Tram 4, 9, 14, 16, 24. **Rates** (incl breakfast) €99-€145 double; €45 dorm bed. **Map** p312 K8.
Minutes away from the Zeedijk and Warmoesstraat, the Anco has double, single and three- to four-bed dorm rooms, and a studio. All come with TV, free gay adult channel and free Wi-Fi. There are some new rooms and a brand-new kitchen.

Golden Bear
Kerkstraat 37, Southern Canal Belt (624 4785, www.quentingoldenbear.nl). Tram 1, 2, 5.
Rates €72-€114 double. **Map** p314 J12.

The first gay hotel in town, the Golden Bear has spacious and comfortable rooms, though not all are en suite. Single rooms have double beds.

★ ITC Hotel
Prinsengracht 1051, Southern Canal Belt (623 0230, www.itc-hotel.com). Tram 4. **Rates** €75-€125 double. **Map** p315 M11.
Situated on a quiet stretch of Prinsengracht that's convenient for the gay hotspots, the ITC Hotel has 20 charming rooms. Free internet access and friendly staff help ensure that guests have a pleasant stay.

BARS & CLUBS

The gay scene is concentrated in a handful of areas in the Old Centre. Getting between them is easy and quick, though each has its own identity. Entry to clubs and bars is free unless stated otherwise.

Warmoesstraat

The long and narrow **Warmoesstraat** is the oldest street in town. It's just around the corner from the red-lit headquarters of the oldest profession. Packed in the tourist season, it's full of cheap hostels and eateries, coffeeshops, bars and sex shops aimed at backpackers. It's also the street with leather/sex bars, a gay porn cinema/shop, and a gay hotel, the **Anco** (*see p182*), just minutes away. **Getto** (*see p187*) provides a warm haven to rest and eat. Be aware that junkies and drug sellers think tourists are easy prey, so act streetwise.

Argos
Warmoesstraat 95 (331 3752, www.argosbar. com). Tram 4, 9, 16, 24. **Open** 10pm-3am Mon-Thur; 10pm-4am Fri, Sat; 7pm-3am Sun. **No credit cards. Map** p312 K8.
'No perfume', it says at the door. Argos, the most venerable leather/fetish bar in town, likes men to smell like men. Expect friendly staff, porn on a big screen and hot clientele of all ages, some of whom just come for the basement darkroom with cabins and a sling for less sedate entertainment.

Eagle Amsterdam
Warmoesstraat 90 (06 4787 7614 mobile, www.theeagleamsterdam.com). Tram 4, 9, 16, 24. **Open** 10pm-4am Mon-Thur, Sun; 10pm-5am Fri, Sat. **No credit cards. Map** p312 K8.
Known for its reputation – sexy and friendly punters, but dirty toilets and unfriendly staff – this men-only cruise bar with 35 years of history can get absolutely packed. The downstairs darkroom is always action-filled, as is the upstairs area late at night; it has some cosy benches should you want to get intimate and a pool table complete with adjustable sling above it.

Warehouse
Warmoesstraat 96 (no phone, www.warehouse-amsterdam.com). Tram 4, 9, 16, 24. **Open** 11pm-4am Thur, Sun; 11pm-5am Fri, Sat. **Map** p312 K8.
In 2013, the people behind the infamous Rapido (*see p186*) club night at Paradiso opened their own gay dance club – where women are also welcome. Once home to the Cockring and its legendary darkrooms, the site has been revamped with industrial flourishes, a big dancefloor, and an excellent light and sound system. The focus is now on the tunes, and keeping things fun and unpretentious. Elements (on Thursday) sticks to tribal and funky house. Fun Fridays are energetic, with DJs such as Sharon-O-Love and Saeed Ali. On Saturdays, Deviate shakes things up with a changing roster of DJs. And Sundays form a NightShift under DJs Dikky Vendetta and Manmachine.

Zeedijk

Once full of junkies, this notorious street just off Nieuwmarkt and running all the way to Centraal Station has been cleaned up, and is now full of Asian eateries, bars and restaurants. Still, stay on guard as it's no country lane.

De Barderij
Zeedijk 14 (420 5132, www.barderij.com). Tram 4, 9, 16, 24. **Open** 4pm-1am Mon-Thur, Sun; 4pm-3am Fri, Sat. **No credit cards. Map** p312 K7.
This no-frills bar attracts older gays and straight locals who all enjoy the living room-like atmosphere. Before you know it, you're chatting and boozing with the unpretentious guys until the early hours. It also organises meals and variety shows.

★ Queen's Head
Zeedijk 20 (420 2475, www.queenshead.nl). Tram 4, 9, 16, 24. **Open** 4pm-1am Mon-Thur, Sun; 4pm-3am Fri, Sat. **No credit cards. Map** p312 K7.
A fun, attitude-free bar (and clientele), with a great view over the canal at the back. Tuesday is bingo night and Sundays are for Netherbears. It also hosts special parties on – not surprisingly – Queen's Day (now King's Day), plus skin nights, football nights (most usually during the World Cup), Eurovision Song Contest night and so on.

Rembrandtplein

Not just the main drag for commercial nightlife and tourist hotspots, **Rembrandtplein** is also home to many of Amsterdam's gay and lesbian bars. Although just a few minutes' stroll from Reguliersdwarsstraat, the scene here is much more light-hearted and camp. There are also a couple of reasons for lesbians

ARTS & ENTERTAINMENT

to visit: bar **Vive la Vie** (*see p189*) and windowless dance cupboard **Club Roque** (Amstel 178, www.clubroque.nl), which is a funny old mixture of sweat and karaoke, though it can be a laugh if you're in the right frame of mind.

Halvemaansteeg is a short lane of brash, loud bars full of male punters of all ages (with the odd lesbian and straight girl to leaven the mix). They're attitude-free, and will burst into a Eurovision singalong at the drop of a feather boa. Round the corner on the Amstel are a few more bars that blast out cheesy hits.

Amstel 54
Amstel 54 (06 2955 7092 mobile). Tram 4, 9, 14. **Open** 4pm-3am Mon-Thur, Sun; 4pm-4am Fri, Sat. **No credit cards. Map** p315 L10.
Previously known on the scene as Amstel Taveerne, this place has a solid spot in local gay history. It has always maintained a vibe of old-fashioned friendliness and over-the-top gayness. The charming old-school pink interior and Sunday's Lady Galore's Drag Night still help keep the dream alive.

Chez Rene
Amstel 50 (420 3388, www.chez-rene.nl). Tram 4, 9, 14. **Open** 6pm-3am Mon-Thur, Sun; 6pm-4am Fri, Sat. **No credit cards. Map** p315 L10.
A relaxed 'brown café' styled pub that attracts attitude-free lesbian and gay customers. A well-timed happy hour between 11pm and midnight often inspires getting down and dancing in a cheesefest sort of way. If you're out for a night on the razzle with your gang, nearby bars Hotspot (Amstel 102) and Rouge (Amstel 60) are similarly jaunty joints.

Entre Nous
Halvemaansteeg 14 (06 1392 6453 mobile). Tram 1, 2, 4, 5, 9, 14, 16, 24. **Open** 9pm-3am Wed-Thur, Sun; 9pm-4am Fri, Sat. **No credit cards. Map** p315 L10.
Although it looks slightly terrifying from the outside – put that down to the blacked-out windows – on the inside, this 'brown café' is actually pretty fluffy, full of younger gay guys with a thirst for cheap music and good fun. Many local gay folk flit between this place and the Montmartre, opposite.

★ Lellebel
Utrechtsestraat 4 (427 5139, www.lellebel.nl). Tram 9, 14, 20. **Open** 8pm-3am Mon-Thur, Sun; 8pm-4am Fri, Sat. **No credit cards. Map** p315 L10.
A tiny drag bar where the cross-dressing clientele provide all the entertainment themselves. Though most people will be in drag, admirers and friends are welcome, and the atmosphere is friendly. Tuesday is karaoke, Thursday is karaoke and cocktails, and Monday is DJ request night.

Reguliersdwarsstraat

Once unquestionably the gayest stretch of street in Amsterdam, **Reguliersdwaarsstraat** had its heyday in the 1990s, when practically every other bar on the miniature strip between Koningsplein and Vijzelstraat was broadly painted with the pink brush. Following the demise of its most iconic venues, there's much talk of a city-aided renaissance, but in tough economic times it remains to be seen what form that will take. Currently, there seems to a move towards more mixed crowds, as exemplified by **Ludwig** (*see p108*). There are also enough other stalwarts and small-scale new initiatives to keep the place ticking over.

Club NYX
Reguliersdwarsstraat 42 (no phone, www.club nyx.nl). Tram 1, 2, 4, 5, 9, 16, 24. **Open** 11pm-4am Thur; 11pm-5am Fri, Sat (until 9am 1st Sat of mth). **No credit cards. Map** p314 K11.
'Gay Street' stalwart Club Exit has been reborn as mixed Club NYX, named for the Greek goddess of the night. Three floors offer distinct sounds and vibes – making liberal use of graffiti, glitter and concrete – and a toilet DJ keeps the party going while you wash your hands at a giant pink phallus.

Lunchroom Downtown
Reguliersdwarsstraat 31 (789 0554, www. lunchroomdowntown.nl). Tram 1, 2, 4, 5, 9, 16, 24. **Open** 10am-6pm Mon-Fri, Sun; 10am-7pm Sat. **No credit cards. Map** p314 K11.
It took them a decade or two to change the name from Coffeeshop Downtown to avoid people coming in looking for cannabis. It's always been about sandwiches, cakes, drinks and international mags here. You might need the latter – service can be slow when the place is busy. Ah well, there's always the hunky, dressed-to-a-T guys to look at in this tiny multi-level hangout. In summer, the lovely and popular terrace sometimes attracts straight couples from the nearby Flowermarket, who soon realise their mistake.

Reality Bar
Reguliersdwarsstraat 129 (639 3012, www. realitybar.nl). Tram 1, 2, 4, 5, 9, 16, 24. **Open** 8pm-3am Mon-Thur, Sun; 8pm-4am Fri, Sat. **No credit cards. Map** p315 L10.
One of the few bars in town where black and white gay guys regularly meet and mingle, Reality Bar is always popular during happy hour (8.30-10pm). Things pump up later on, when ferociously uptempo Latin and Surinamese music gets the crowd moving.

Taboo
Reguliersdwarsstraat 45 (775 3963, www.taboo bar.nl). Tram 1, 2, 4, 5, 9, 16, 24. **Open** 5pm-3am Mon-Thur; 5pm-4am Fri; 4pm-4am Sat; 4pm-3am Sun. **Map** p314 K11.

Club NYX.

The latest venture from Brendan van de Ruit, formerly manager of the now-defunct Club Exit, Taboo is hoping to breathe some life back into an ailing district. In some ways, it's just another gay bar – it plays Cher, and is festooned in rainbows – but what the place lacks in mould-breaking sparkle, it makes up for in decent prices and a double happy hour (6-7pm, 1-2am). A pub crawl often departs from Taboo on Saturdays at 8pm.

Kerkstraat

Home to pioneering cradle of filth **Club Church** and kink shop **Black Body** (*see p188*), this quiet street off busy Leidsestraat sure is gay. It even has a few gay hotels, yet it's less posing pink than other areas.

★ Club Church
Kerkstraat 52 (no phone, www.clubchurch.nl). Tram 1, 2, 5, 7, 10. **Open** 8pm-1am Tue, Wed; 10pm-4am Thur; 10pm-5am Fri, Sat; 4pm-4am Sun. **Admission** €5-€10; 10-visit card €75. **Map** p314 J12.
This deceptively cavernous venue is more than a little progressive, and it's been a long time since Amsterdam has seen the opening of a gay venue where sex is so unambiguously on the agenda. Erotic theme nights run the full gamut of (mostly male) pervy possibility, from naked parties to fisting to the women-friendly Horenbal, where those 'dressed for trade' are offered free bubbly. A highlight is Thursday's Blue (*see p186*) hosted by local drag legend and scene-maker Jennifer Hopelezz. Several of the city's fetish parties have also migrated here from smaller venues in the Red Light District. To top it all, Church features a bar with Greek-style columns, a stage perfect for drag-queen acts, a great sound and light system, and various dark, dark chambers.

De Spijker
Kerkstraat 4 (341 7366). Tram 1, 2, 5. **Open** 4pm-1am Mon-Thur, Sun; 4pm-3am Fri, Sat. **No credit cards. Map** p314 J11.
This small boozer used to be a theatre in its previous life. Punters still liven things up and it can become rather crowded and rowdy. The diverse clientele ranges from cute young guys to older muscle men and a few women, and all mingle happily. On the downside, the pool table always seems to be occupied.

Other Areas

Mankind
Weteringstraat 60, Southern Canal Belt (638 4755, www.mankind.nl). Tram 7, 10, 16, 24. **Open** noon-11pm Mon-Sat. **No credit cards. Map** p314 K12.
A quiet locals' bar tucked down a side street near the Rijksmuseum, and the antiques shops and art galleries of Spiegelstraat. It also provides delicious sandwiches and a cheap dish of the day. Come summer, the canalside patio is perfect to catch some sun, read the international magazines or simply watch the world go by.

★ Prik
Spuistraat 109, Old Centre: New Side (320 0002, www.prikamsterdam.nl). Tram 1, 2, 5, 13, 17. **Open** 4pm-1am Tue-Thur, Sun; 4pm-3am Fri, Sat. **No credit cards. Map** p312 H8.
'Queer or not – Prik is certainly hot.' Indeed. True to the bar's slogan, this popular meeting point succeeds in attracting a diverse crowd, which enjoys its movie nights, delicious snacks and groovy sounds. The sporadic speed-dating events held here are a particularly fun way to infiltrate the local scene. After a night here – perhaps, Monday, when pints are a mere €3 – you might be tempted to squeeze yourself into one of those saucy T-shirts.

Web
Sint Jacobsstraat 6, Old Centre: New Side (623 6758, www.thewebbaramsterdam.com). Tram 1, 2, 3, 5. **Open** 1pm-1am Mon-Thur, Sun; 1pm-2am Fri, Sat. **No credit cards. Map** p312 J7.
Cheap booze and sexy bartenders, cheesy/classic dance tracks, Wednesday sex-shop vouchers lottery, Sunday snack afternoon – such ingredients make this men-only leather/cruise bar heave with a crowd of all ages. The upstairs darkroom is hygienic, and the numerous cubicles almost resemble those at a gym – perfect to act out that locker-room porn fantasy you've always dreamed of.

ONE-OFF CLUB NIGHTS

★ Blue
For full listings, see p185 **Club Church.**
Open 10pm-4am Thur. **Admission** €5.
Even the club most dedicated to gay sex parties is reflecting the mixing of local scenes. Hosted by the balloon-butted Jennifer Hopelezz, Blue attracts the full spectrum: gay, lesbian, straight, bears, hipster beards, drag queens and your dear old mom. Plus wacky acts and cheap drinks.

Danserette
Akhnaton, Nieuwezijds Kolk 25, Old Centre: New Side (624 3396, www.danserette.nl). Tram 1, 2, 5, 13, 17. **Open** Sat; check website for dates. **Admission** varies. **Map** p312 J7.
This occasional Saturday-nighter at Akhnaton is for those who aren't afraid to mouth the words to Madonna hits. Also on the decks are classic disco classics and recent chart tunes. They also produce the more moveable fest Club Danserette.

F*cking Pop Queers
www.ultrasexi.com.
This once-monthly club night is now more of a mobile event: possibly to Las Vegas in the US, or back home for New Year's Eve at Paradiso. It's the place where young fashion gays can dance around their designer bags. Practise your pout beforehand – the party's Facebook page is as much of an event as the night itself.

Furball
www.furball.nl.
This hirsute heaven for hairy men and their smooth admirers has been held at various venues around town, but seems to have settled into Club Church (*see p185*). It's a great dance night, sometimes with a theme. There's no dress code, no darkroom, just plenty of sweaty hairy guys, in all shapes, sizes and ages, having a furry old time.

Rapido
www.clubrapido.com.
Very popular – but irregular – club night where shirtless muscle marys dance and flirt to pumping

house tunes. Their nights at Paradiso (*see p197*) are legendary, and they have also set up new venue the Warehouse (*see p183*). Check out the website for the latest dates, and also to have a peek at the online magazine.

★ Spellbound
www.spellbound-amsterdam.nl.
Held at OCCII (*see p198*), this cheap 'Queer Underground Dance Party' is popular with a non-scene crowd. Its success is easily explained by the heavy beats of techno, acid and dub, performances and the snug bar.

★ De Trut
Bilderdijkstraat 165, West (612 3524, www.trutfonds.nl). Tram 3, 7, 12, 17. **Open** 10pm-4am Sun. **Admission** €2. **No credit cards. Map** p316 F12.
If you don't want the weekend to end, head to this alternative dance night in a former squat. It's cheap, it's crowded, it's fun and it's been running for 30 years. Arrive early, certainly before 11pm, or you may have to queue for a long time.

(Z)onderbroek
For full listings, see p185 **Club Church.**
Open 10pm- 5am Fri, 1st Sat of mth; 8pm-4am Sun. **Admission** €10; €5 Sun.
A men-only dance party with an underwear-only dress code. Tank tops are tolerated, but only just.

Sex Parties

Despite the controversial closure in 2010 of sleaze behemoth Cockring – reborn in 2013 as the much less greasy dance club the Warehouse (*see p183*) – gay visitors will have no difficulty finding relief. That's largely thanks to the opening of **Club Church** (*see p185*), a multi-level perve paradise hosting everything from regular FF parties to the occasional Twink Sex Orgy. Meanwhile, 'erotic café' **Sameplace** (Nassaukade 120, Oud West, 475 1981, www.sameplace.nl) goes gay every Monday night between 8pm and 1am.

RESTAURANTS

A good rule of thumb: if a place is brand spanking new or has spectacular decor, it's sure to attract the homo food-nerd herds. The eateries listed below are gay-run or have significant numbers of gay diners.

Bar Huf
Reguliersdwarsstraat 43 (303 9561, www.barhuf.nl). Tram 1, 2, 5. **Open** 4pm-1am Mon-Thur, Sun; 4pm-3am Fri, Sat. *Meals served* 4pm-midnight daily. **Main courses** €12-€17. **Map** p314 K11.

Simple, quality ingredients come together at this late-night newcomer with a clean, industrial look. Enjoy everything from burgers to cheese fondue, sea bass and sausages (from local producers Brandt en Levie) – and a great wine list too. The name refers to Dutch photographer Paul Huf, who took an iconic shot of four 1960s Dutch football stars, including Johan Cruijff, in a hilariously homoerotic pose. Sister establishment Bar Paul, a cosier, updated 'brown café', is a few doors down at no.41.

Garlic Queen
Reguliersdwarsstraat 27, Southern Canal Belt (422 6426, www.garlicqueen.nl). Tram 1, 2, 5. **Open** 5pm-midnight Wed-Sun. **Meals served** 5-11pm Wed-Sun. **Main courses** €18.50-€20.50. **Map** p314 K11.

Portraits of the real queen, Beatrix, smile down on the metaphorical queens (as well as a wide range of other diners) chowing down in this camp temple to the stinking rose. Every dish contains at least one clove of the stuff – one contains 60 – though spoilsports can order any garlic-free.

★ Getto
Warmoesstraat 51, Old Centre: Old Side (421 5151, www.getto.nl). Tram 4, 9, 16, 24. **Open** 4pm-1am Tue-Thur; 4pm-2am Fri, Sat; 4pm-midnight Sun. *Meals served* 6-11pm Tue-Sun. **Main courses** €10-€15. **Map** p312 K7.

Cheap, cheerful, tasty and filling: that's what the food is like at this sparkly diner at the back of the thoroughly mixed lesbian and gay bar/lounge. On Wednesday nights, all burger dinners (a house

A STRAIGHT GUIDE TO GAY PRIDE
It's party time, whatever your sexual orientation.

Taking place during the first week of August, **Amsterdam Gay Pride** (www.amsterdamgaypride.nl) may be one of the lesbian and gay community's most anticipated annual events, but the extended weekend of crowded street parties, parades, vibrant drinking and noise draws thousands of spectators – straight and gay alike – all eager to join in.

The festival offers thousands of distractions, running the A to Z of camp: androgyny, barely clad boys, flirtation, leather, lesbians, muscle marys, PVC poseurs, and, of course, theatrics. They all take part in a genuinely non-stop playground. Then there's the dizzying array of affiliated events: street parties, more street parties, singalongs, performances and Pride's apex, the awesome Canal Parade – the world's only floating Pride – along the Prinsengracht and Amstel canal on Saturday afternoon (2-6pm).

Canals spill over with topless mermaids, half-naked firefighters, Marilyn Monroe lookalikes, pole dancers, gladiators, beauty queens, angels and wrestlers all waving from around 100 different boats. This watery showcase draws thousands of onlookers – estimates put them at 350,000, and no one's clocking who's gay and who ain't. Then there are the politicians who hitch rides on the boats in the name of scoring gay-cred points.

Everyone puts in overtime, cultivating the following day's hangover – although they've probably drunk their way through the first

one, as the celebrating technically starts on Friday. Or Thursday, depending on who you ask. The closing party takes place on late Sunday afternoon on Rembrandtplein, with a huge number of Dutch musicians, DJs and those with energy left to keep partying.

Like Queen's Day (or King's Day, as it's now called), when the city's population doubles and crams into the centre of the city, Pride is terribly Amsterdam. It's relaxed, tolerant, positive, outrageous and definitely worth celebrating.

speciality) cost just €10. Combined with the week-day, two-for-the-price-of-one cocktail happy hour, this is the ideal place for an inexpensive date.

Hemelse Modder
Oude Waal 11, Old Centre: Old Side (624 3203, www.hemelsemodder.nl). Tram 1, 2, 4, 5, 9, 13, 16, 17, 24 or Metro Nieuwmarkt. **Open** 6pm-midnight daily. *Kitchen* 6-10pm daily. **Set meal** €33.50 3 courses, €39.50 5 courses. **Map** p313 L7.
This restaurant located on a handsome canal has for years been a favourite with members of the pink community, who come for its up-to-date menu and friendly service. Try their namesake chocolate dessert 'Heavenly Mud'.

FILM & THEATRE

The first Wednesday of the month is Gay Classics night at **Pathé de Munt** (*see p175*), where you get a drink – pink champagne – thrown in with your ticket, plus a two-for-one voucher for a local watering hole after the show. **De Balie** (*see p178*) regularly presents lesbigay films of a more socially aware nature, while the **Rialto** (*see p177*) cinema has a gay and lesbian summer season, when it screens the best films from the previous year. For film festivals, *see p181* **The Queer Year**.

The **Queen's English Theatre Company** (www.qetc.nl) gives the queer eye to classic English-language plays a couple of times a year; its productions of Alan Bennett plays have been particularly well received, both at the CREA theatre (Nieuwe Achtergracht 170, Old Centre: Old Side, 525 1400, www.crea.uva.nl) and at the Edinburgh Festival.

Vrolijk.

SHOPS & SERVICES

Although legendary gay book shop Intermale closed down a few years ago, **Vrolijk** is still going strong. The **American Book Center** (*see p82*) has a well-stocked gay section. **Waterstones** (*see p85*) doesn't have a dedicated gay range, but it does carry the major British gay titles.

★ Cuts 'n' Curls
Korte Leidsedwarsstraat 74, Southern Canal Belt (624 6881, www.cutsandcurls.nl). Tram 1, 2, 5, 7, 10. **Open** 10am-8pm Tue-Fri; 10am-4pm Sat. **Map** p314 J12.
This hairdressers' offers butch and basic haircuts with a sensitive side: many of the shampoos and conditioners are vegan-friendly.

Gays & Gadgets
Spuistraat 44, Old Centre: New Side (330 1461, www.gaysandgadgets.com). Tram 1, 2, 5, 13, 14, 17. **Open** 11am-7pm Mon-Sat; noon-7pm Sun. **Map** p312 H7.
A dazzling and demented array of camp nonsense and household objects, most of it made in China. If a willy or boobs can't be incorporated into the design proper, you can bet your bottom dollar it can be dipped in pink paint or accessorised with a sparkly boa, which is why sections of Gays & Gadgets look like Paris Hilton has chucked her guts there.

★ Vrolijk
Paleisstraat 135, Old Centre: New Side (623 5142, www.vrolijk.nu). Tram 1, 2, 5, 13, 14, 17. **Open** 11am-6pm Mon-Wed, Fri, Sat; 11am-9pm Thur; noon-6pm Sun. **Map** p312 J9.
The best international selection of rose-tinted reading, whether fiction or fact – plus CDs, DVDs, guides and the best gifts you'll find in town. It also has a second-hand section, and sells a good range of gay T-shirts, condoms and cheeky gifts.

Leather/Rubber/Sex Shops

Whether you're in need of a tattoo, a piercing, some kinky toys or a complete leather outfit, Amsterdam's 'Leather Lane', Warmoesstraat, is where to find it. **Mr B** (Warmoesstraat 89, 788 3060, www.misterb.com) sells anything from a cheap cockring to expensive chaps. It also does tattoos and piercings (there's a female piercer too), plus DVDs and tickets for all the big gay events. At the Amsterdam branch of **RoB** (Warmoesstraat 71, 422 3000, www.rob.eu), you can pick up a wristband or a full complement of leather/rubber gear, before hitting the bars. Make your rubber fantasies come true at **Black Body** (Kerkstraat 173, 626 2553, www.blackbody.nl). **Drakes** (Damrak 61, 627 9544, www.drakesdirect.com) is a 'sex

Nieuwezijds Sauna.

boutique' and porn cinema. Women with a dirty mind should head to sex shop **Female & Partners** (*see p82*). **Demask** (Zeedijk 64, 423 3090, www.demask.com) is fun for all.

SAUNAS

Nieuwezijds Sauna
Nieuwezijds Armsteeg 95, Old Centre: New Side (331 8327, www.saunanieuwezijds.nl). Tram 1, 2, 5. **Admission** €18 incl 1st drink; €14 under-27s. **Map** p312 J7.
At the end of 2013, after much sweaty anticipation, the city's first new cruising sauna in years opened in a former bingo hall. Slings, sex cabins, darkrooms and glory holes add some dirt to an otherwise glistening clean and elegant operation.

Thermos
Raamstraat 33, Western Canal Belt (623 9158, www.thermos.nl). Tram 1, 2, 5. **Open** noon-8am Mon-Fri; noon Sat-8am Mon. **Admission** €15; €10 reductions. **Map** p314 H12.
Quite busy during the week and absolutely packed at weekends, this four-level sauna (one of the largest of its kind in Europe) offers it all: a tiny steam room, large dry-heat room, darkroom, porn cinema, private cubicles, bar, hairdresser, masseur, gym and small roof terrace. And for those who want to heat, meet and 'greet', then eat, there's a restaurant too.

THE LESBIAN SCENE

The nightlife scene for lesbians isn't brilliant, but it's been worse, and at the moment there's a fair variety of bars and one-off club nights to satisfy most tastes. However, there is less

variety than on the men's scene and, given the lack of any genuinely mixed bars (apart from **Getto**, *see p187*), that's reason enough for lesbians to gird their loins and go to the men's bars – in particular to **Blue** (*see p186*). Apart from a few strictly men-only places (generally sex clubs), women are welcome everywhere – though they will, of course, be in the minority.

Flirtation
www.flirtation.nl.
The biggest lesbian night in the country – currently housed in Panama (*see p194*) and taking place every few months or so – this extravaganza claims to attract more than 1,000 women a pop. The secret of its success? Themed parties where dressing up is encouraged, a playlist of house, and a 'keep 'em hungry for more' policy.

Garbo for Women
Strand West, Stavangerweg 900, Houthavens (www.garboforwomen.nl). Bus 22, 48. **Open** 6pm-2am 3rd Sat of mth. **Admission** €6.
A space for gay and bisexual ladies to socialise and strut their stuff to tunes by DJ SOL and others. This laid-back meet near Westerpark occasionally incorporates free tango workshops.

★ Girlesque
www.girlesque.nl.
Perhaps the most invigorating development of late on the lesbian scene has been the rise of girl-oriented burlesque. Formed in 2007 by Bianca Morel, the Girlesque collective hops between various club nights and larger events such as Lovedance and Pride, delivering high-end titillation and a refreshing dose of glamour to a mixed crowd.

★ Saarein
Elandstraat 119, Jordaan (623 4901, www. saarein.info). Tram 7, 10. **Open** 4pm-1am Tue-Thur; 4pm-2am Fri; noon-2am Sat; 1pm-1am Sun. **No credit cards. Map** p316 G11.
This hardy perennial 'brown café' of the lesbian scene is particularly popular at weekends. The women it attracts tend to be slightly older, but young bucks certainly make an appearance. The only lesbian pool table in town resides in the basement.

★ Vive la Vie
Amstelstraat 7, Southern Canal Belt (624 0114, www.vivelavie.net). Tram 4, 9, 14. **Open** 4pm-3am Mon-Thur, Sun; 4pm-4am Fri, Sat. **Map** p313 L10.
In business for almost 35 years, this small, basic bar just off Rembrandtplein is run by Mieke Martelhoff and partner Rosemary. The walls are lined with pictures of female Hollywood icons; under the watchful gaze of Elizabeth Taylor, a varied bunch of lesbians (and their friends) drink and dance to mainstream and Dutch hits. It gets packed late on Saturdays.

ARTS & ENTERTAINMENT

Nightlife

After years of offering so-so clubbing, Amsterdam has once more become a great place for creatures of the night, thanks in part to local folks being motivated to organise their own events in obscure places, as well as several locations finally receiving extended-hours licences. It's enjoyably eclectic: you can find anything from minimalist grooves to maximum noise.

Meanwhile, when it comes to music gigs, there has definitely been something of a renaissance in recent years. Amsterdam has long been established as one of the world's most important ports of call for international musicians, in virtually every imaginable genre (but especially jazz); but these days it's got a very lively home-grown music scene too. And whatever you're seeking, it'll be readily available within close proximity to the Canal Belt.

Clubs

The age of the massive and extravagant club is over, even if the torch is being kept somewhat alive by newcomer **Air**. More with the times, **Trouw Amsterdam** continues its progressive programming, in an odd post-industrial setting and with a new 24-hour licence. It's just this kind of grassroots operation, run by a group of like-minded friends, that has taken on the mega-clubs of yesteryear. At the cosiest end of the scale are **Bitterzoet** and **Club Up**, which go for funky quality over capacity. Similar vibes

can be found further afield at **Studio/K** (*see p149*), **Canvas** and **Roest** (*see p156*), which also throws larger parties in the massive industrial Van Gendthallen.

And Amsterdam's nightlife seems set to become even more diverse. There are scuzzy venues for students and rockers, meat markets for stags, and cutting-edge clubs for hipsters. Note that concerts at rock, pop and jazz venues often run into club nights. Plus there are two annual mega-dance events: **5 Days Off** (*see p35*) in March and **Amsterdam Dance Event** (*see p42*) in October.

In general, clubbing here is really no different from clubbing in any large international city. All venues have bouncers, so show up on time and with a mixed crowd to increase your chances of getting in. Storing your coat in the cloakroom might cost, as might using the toilets (typically €1-€1.50), but in many clubs outside the city centre they're free. The Dutch aren't great tippers at the bar – ten per cent is considered generous. Almost no one will actually be inside a club before midnight: people are either at home or in a bar loosening up. For gay and lesbian clubs, *see pp180-189* **Gay & Lesbian**.

IN THE KNOW
NARCOTIC NO-NOS

Clubbers can still smoke weed and hash (in designated smoking areas), but it's unwise to solicit anything stronger, as undercover cops are putting in appearances at larger techno parties across the city. Plus, what you think you're buying is not likely to be what you'll get.

Old Centre

★ Bitterzoet

Spuistraat 2 (421 2318, www.bitterzoet.com).
Tram 1, 2, 5. **Open** 8pm-3am Mon-Thur, Sun;
8pm-4am Fri, Sat. **Admission** €5-€17.50.
No credit cards. Map p312 H7.
Cool, casual and cosy, Bitterzoet has been around for
over a decade. The key to success is booking clubnight people, bands and DJs who do it more for the
passion than the fame. Hip hop, street art, alternative
rock, Afrobeat or broken beats may define particular
nights – or be all mashed up together in a single
night. Next door, at no.4, sibling De Goudvis Club
(737 2121, www.degoudvisclub.nl) serves global
street food.

Disco Dolly

Handboogstraat 11 (620 1779, www.discodolly.nl).
Tram 1, 2, 4, 5, 9, 14, 16, 24. **Open** 9pm-4am
Mon-Thur, Sun; 9pm-5am Fri, Sat. **Admission**
free-€10. **No credit cards. Map** p312 K10.
Until recently, this was home to the city's student
meat-market dance club, Dansen bij Jansen. Disco
Dolly is attempting to find a broader audience, yet
doesn't stray too far – expect fairly commercial
disco, funk and house. If you do feel a bit old, try sister night bar Bloemenbar, next door at no.15.

Winston Kingdom

Warmoesstraat 131 (623 1380, www.winston.nl).
Tram 1, 2, 5, 9, 13, 14, 16, 17, 24. **Open**
9pm-4am Mon-Thur, Sun; 9pm-5am Fri, Sat.
Admission €4-€10. **No credit cards.**
Map 312 J8.
An intimate venue that attracts a mixed crowd with
its alternative rock and indie-tronica. Bands, from

IN THE KNOW BEACH BARS

Once a wonderful secret, the beach clubs
at **Bloemendaal aan Zee** – an hour-long
bus ride from Amsterdam – now lure
clubbers by the thousands each summer
weekend. Seven different bars (open
May to October) offer music, fashion
and fabulous fixtures and fittings. There's
a venue to suit everyone, from kooky
Woodstock through chic Bloomingdale
to Ibiza-like Republiek.

---

garage and folk to funky hip hop and ska, perform
daily, followed by alternative DJs. Cheeky Monday
brings relief to yet another working week with jungle and drum 'n' bass.
▶ *On the same site, the Winston Hotel (see p281)*
is renowned for its arty rooms, decorated by local
artists and companies.

Canals

Air

Amstelstraat 16 (820 0670, www.air.nl).
Tram 4, 9, 14. **Open** 11pm-4am Thur; 11pm-5am
Fri, Sat; 11.30pm-4am Sun. **Admission** €9-€15.
No credit cards. Map p313 L10.
Like a phoenix from the ashes, a new club has risen
in the same location as legendary club iT. The musi-
cal offerings are varied, and the crowd mixed. De
Nachtbar on Thursday delivers a creative, arty,
interactive time where house and funk prevails;
Friday often has more of a techno feel; on Saturday,
it's all a bit more commercial.

ARTS & ENTERTAINMENT

Roest. *See p156.*

Melkweg.

Club Abe

Amstelstraat 30 (845 7872, www.clubabe.com).
Tram 4, 9, 14. **Open** 10pm-4am Mon, Sat;
11pm-3am Thur; 5pm-4am Fri; 8pm-2am Sun.
Admission free-€35. **Map** p313 L10.
Newcomer Abe is a very high-end club/lounge that
strives for an international vibe of exclusivity and
maturity (if you look younger than 27, you'll have
trouble getting in). You'll find sophisticated cocktails
and sounds; think jazzy soul and deep house. The
colour scheme takes in purple, deep green and gold –
the last, along with safes and a wall of bills, reflect
the building's past as a bank.

Club Up/De Kring

*Korte Leidsedwarsstraat 26 (623 6985, www.club
up.nl). Tram 1, 2, 5, 7, 10.* **Open** 11pm- 4am
Thur; 11pm-5am Fri, Sat. **Admission** €6-€15.
No credit cards. Map p314 J12.
Club Up is an intimate venue with a great sound system, connected via a corridor to artists' members'
club De Kring. If you can, visit when both areas are
accessible, since De Kring provides the laid-back
atmosphere that the often packed, discotheque-like
ballroom of Club Up lacks. DJs spin disco, techno
and house.

Escape

Rembrandtplein 11 (622 1111, www.escape.nl).
Tram 4, 9, 14. **Open** 11pm-4am Thur, Sun;
11pm-5am Fri, Sat. **Admission** €5-€16.
No credit cards. Map p313 L10.

With a capacity of 2,000, this is about as big as clubbing gets in central Amsterdam. Ever since club
night Chemistry left, the place has vanished from
the national spotlight, resurfacing instead as a venue
for a younger, more mainstream crowd. Queues still
form on Saturday and Sunday evenings, and the
bouncers are wary of groups of tourists, so squeeze
into a slinky T-shirt, slap on some hair product and
get in line early.

Jimmy Woo

Korte Leidsedwarsstraat 18 (626 3150,
www.jimmywoo.com). Tram 1, 2, 5, 7, 10.
Open 11pm-4am Thur-Sun. **Admission**
€10-€20. **Map** p314 J12.
Amsterdam has never seen anything quite so luxu-
riously cosmopolitan as Jimmy Woo's. Marvel at the
lounge filled with a mix of modern and antique furniture, and confirm for yourself the merits of the
bootylicious light design and sound system. If you
have problems getting inside, try the equally hip and
happening Chicago Social Club (Leidseplein 12, 530
7303, www.chicagosocialclub.nl), next door.

Melkweg

Lijnbaansgracht 234a (531 8181, www.melkweg.nl).
Tram 1, 2, 5, 7, 10. **Open** 11pm-5am Fri;
midnight-5am Sat. **Admission** €5- €32.
Membership (compulsory) €4/mth; €25/yr.
No credit cards. Map p314 H12.
This one-time dairy (the name translates as 'Milky
Way') and former hippie haven offers a galaxy of
stellar programming in its two main halls. It can get
ridiculously crowded, but it's great value and down-
to-earth – with a little bit of everything thrown into
the mix. Watch out for Saturday's hip hop-flavoured
Encore, plus the Kill All Hipsters nights with indie-
tronica. Four times a year, the amazing Helemaal
night opens the doors to all the building's spaces,
including the impressive Rabo hall that is shared
with the Stadsschouwburg.

Paradiso

For listings, *see p197.*
An Amsterdam institution, this large former church
is a safe clubbing bet, with a trusty formula of live
show followed by a DJ from around 11pm. Saturdays
pull in a youngish, up-for-it crowd, while midweek
Noodlanding ('Emergency Landing') is particularly
good for an alternative, indie feel. It's also a popular
music venue for 'intimate' concerts by international
superstars and lesser-known names.

Studio 80

Rembrandtplein 17 (www.studio-80.nl). Tram 4, 9,
14. **Open** 10pm-4am Wed, Thur, Sun; 11pm-5am
Fri, Sat. **Admission** free-€12. **No credit cards**.
Map p313 L10.
In the middle of Rembrandtplein's neon glitz and ice-
cream-eating crowds lurks this ex-radio studio, a
black pearl waiting to be discovered. Dirty disco,

24-HOUR PARTY TOWN

Could Amsterdam become the city that never sleeps?

For years, locals complained that Amsterdam's nightlife was dead. City by-laws forced clubs and pubs to close early; underground parties were vigorously monitored and shut; even finding food in the wee hours proved difficult. You might occasionally get lucky with a decent after-party, but in general the only option after 4am or 5am on weekends was home – from where you can contact the beer taxi (www.biertaxiamsterdam.nl, 06 223 100 66 mobile) to get a late-night delivery – which, incidentally, always remains an option...

For a proper nightlife scene, Rotterdam was generally deemed the place to go. But then, in 2003, the new role of 'night mayor' (*nachtburgemeester*) was introduced to Amsterdam – a concept swiped from, yes, Rotterdam. Though not an official government post, the successive mayors worked to rebuild bridges of communication between the nocturnal souls and the daytime politicians. One message was clear: people wanted a late-night scene that was low-key and laid-back, rather than big, bold and trendy. They also wanted longer opening hours.

Finally, in 2013, five drinking and dining zones (with more to follow) were given 24-hour licences. This momentous occasion has been seen as a belated antidote to the growing conservatism of society. Some felt

(some still feel) the city was becoming a victim of overly zealous legislation: smoking had been banned, mushrooms had been banned, coffeeshops were closing; what next, beer?

The five zones cover the various bars and clubs located in the arts complex Westergasfabriek (*see p116* **Floodlights on Westerpark**); club **Trouw Amsterdam** (*see p194*); and three locations in up-and-coming Amsterdam Noord directly across from Centraal Station. These are **De Overkant** (www.deoverkant.com), an old industrial complex currently used for one-off events; **Tolhuistuin** (*see p198*), which occupies the former pavilion and gardens of the abandoned Shell company office complex; and the **Shell Tower**, a late 1960s high-rise on the same site. This will become the true focal point once it's been renovated into **A'dam** (www.adamtoren.nl). Scheduled for completion at the end of 2015, it will feature a hotel, artists' and recording studios, panoramic dining in a revolving restaurant, and the highest dancefloor in the city.

The 24-hour licences won't mean venues will be constantly open, selling alcohol round the clock. Some may opt to serve breakfast to unwinding clubbers, or launch a new exhibition at dawn – but at least the city can now experiment with the possibilities. So fasten your seatbelts...

deep electronic acid and gritty hip hop are shown off at very reasonable prices. The city's most progressive techno and minimal crowds find their home here, and have no trouble bringing disc-spinning or synthesiser-wielding friends from as far afield as Berlin and Barcelona.

Sugar Factory
Lijnbaansgracht 238 (627 0008, www.sugar factory.nl). Tram 1, 2, 5, 7, 10. **Open** midnight-5am Thur-Sat; 11pm-5am Sun. **Admission** €5-€17. **No credit cards. Map** p314 H12.
This 'night theatre' club has found its niche as a place where performance meets clubbing, catering to both beat freaks and more traditional music fans at the same time. Resident DJs and club nights liven up the week, while Wicked Jazz Sounds brighten Sunday evenings, with musicians and sometimes even a big band. Occasional alternative rock bands are booked here by the Melkweg (*see p192*).

Jordaan & West

Westerunie
Klönneplein 4-6, Westergasfabriek (684 8496, www.westerunie.nl). Tram 10. **Open** varies Fri, Sat. **Admission** varies.
Occupying an old factory building in cultural park Westergasfabriek, Westerunie consists of a larger space and the more intimate Westerliefde. For larger events, they can use another, even bigger, hall nearby. Fridays usually focus on a particular genre from years past (disco or old-school rave, say). Saturdays tend to have one-offs by the better party organisers around town, such as ExPornStar and the people behind the Loveland festival.

Museums, Vondelpark & Zuid

★ OT301
Overtoom 301 (412 2954, www.ot301.nl). Tram 1. **Open** varies Fri, Sat. **Admission** €5-€10. **No credit cards. Map** p316 F15.
This multipurpose venue offers cheap bottled beer and a wildly varying programme, including Haunted Science drum 'n' bass nights, Matjesdisco ('Mullet Disco' – dress accordingly) or a savvy selection of bands and DJs from alternative-minded Subbacultcha! (*see p198* **In the Know**). OT301 is also a key film venue (*see p179*).

Jodenbuurt, Plantage & Oost

Canvas
Wibautstraat 150 (716 3817, www.canvas7.nl). Tram 3 or Metro Wibautstaat. **Open** varies. **Admission** €5-€9.
Let's see what Canvas does to keep the underground scene fresh yet relaxed, when it reopens in 2014 after extensive renovations. In the past, the diverse programme has ranged from cutting-edge electronica through hip hop to club house and live jazz. Sitting atop a former newspaper building, it also sports some of the best views in town – along with the most hilarious toilet attendants. During the day, it operates as a café and cocktail bar. See p149 **Eastern Promise**.

★ Trouw Amsterdam
Wibautstraat 127 (463 7788, www.trouw amsterdam.nl). Tram 3 or Metro Wibautstaat. **Open** varies. **Admission** €10-€18. **No credit cards.**

OT301.

Brought to you by the creative forces behind the fondly remembered Club 11, Trouw also features a Mediterranean restaurant and De Verdieping art gallery – plus a 24-hour party licence. Expect experimental electronica, underground dance music and innovative vibes. Note: they're due to shut in early 2015, but will likely move the party elsewhere. *See p149* **Eastern Promise**.

Waterfront & Noord

Panama
Oostelijke Handelskade 4 (311 8686, www.panama.nl). Tram 26. **Open** 8pm-4am Thur; 11pm-5am Sat, Sun. **Admission** €10-€20.
Nightlife anchor Panama opened way back in 2001 on what was a deserted strip, now transformed with high-rise offices, steep rents and the shiny Muziekgebouw (*see p203*). Most nights mix up-and-coming Dutch DJs with big international names, such as Ferry Corsten and Sander Kleinenberg. Also look out for the regular lesbian-friendly club night Flirtation. In the same location is Spanish restaurant Mercat (344 6424, www.mercat.nl).

Comedy

While the Dutch have their own cultural history of hilarity, thanks in large part to their own very singular take on the art and practice of cabaret, stand-up is a fairly recent import to the Netherlands in general and Amsterdam in particular. However, it's become more popular in recent years, and shows usually feature a mix of international and local acts, often performing in English.

VENUES

Toomler (Breitnerstraat 2, South, 670 7400, www.toomler.nl) usually programmes Dutch stand-up, but also organises English-language nights and festivals on occasion.

★ Boom Chicago
Rozentheater, Rozengracht 117, Jordaan (217 0400, tickets 0900 266 6244, www.boom chicago.nl). Tram 10, 13, 14, 17. **Tickets** €12-€22.50. **Map** p311 10F.
This American improv troupe is one of Amsterdam's biggest success stories, with alumni including Seth Meyers (*Saturday Night Live*) and Jason Sudekis (*30 Rock*). Several different shows, all in English, run seven nights a week (winter is slightly quieter), featuring a mix of audience-prompted improvisation, rehearsed sketches, full-blown themed shows and guest comedians from around the world – coupled with dinner options. They also organise excellent boat tours, give improv classes and have a fine bar in Bar 117. In short, a genuine cultural movement in an unexpected form.

IN THE KNOW LAUGHS ON TAP

Shot of Improv is **Boom Chicago**'s (*see below*) late-night Saturday show, starting at 10.30pm. Take advantage and stock up on booze during the preceding happy hour (9.30-10pm). And if the improvisers like any of your suggestions and use one or more of them to create an hilarious scene, you might even get a bonus beer.

Comedy Café Amsterdam
Max Euweplein 43-45, Southern Canal Belt (638 3971, www.comedycafe.nl). Tram 1, 2, 5, 7, 10. **Tickets** €5-€16. **Map** p314 J13.
The Comedy Café has been doing a decent job of bringing stand-up to a wider Amsterdam audience by usually offering shows in a mind-boggling blend of Dutch and English. Mondays and Tuesdays are open-mic nights; on Wednesdays comics try out new material; Sundays are reserved for Loco Toko Picture Show (English-language improv). Shows start at 9pm daily, with an extra slot at 11.30pm on Saturday.

Comedy Theatre
Nes 110, Old Centre: Old Side (422 0033, www.comedytheater.nl). Tram 4, 9, 14, 16, 24. **Tickets** free-€15. **Map** p312 K9.
Hyping itself as the 'club house' for comedians, this former tobacco factory on a peaceful theatre street combines acerbic, politically hard-hitting material with more straightforward stand-up. Expect local legends such as Javier Guzman and international acts such as Tom Rhodes or Lewis Black. Bigger acts (Eddie Izzard) also appear, but in larger venues. Wednesday's open podium has free admission. Call ahead to make sure that at least some of the acts are English-speaking.

Music

On any given night in Amsterdam, you can be sure to find something to suit your aural taste, from the classy jazz of improv drummer Han Bennink and saxophonist hero Benjamin Herman of the New Cool Collective, to the ex-squat punks the Ex, who jam with Ethiopian roots musicians. Alternatively, drink and dance to the hip-hop orchestra of Kyteman, or enjoy the eastern European party sounds of the Amsterdam Klezmer Band. Or get goose bumps from poetry-fuelled alternative folksters Spilt Milk. The more musical genres you throw into the mix (think heavy metal, art rock, Frisian fado), the longer the list of Dutch musical innovators gets.

Alongside the home-grown talent are a plethora of international acts. Amsterdam is

ARTS & ENTERTAINMENT

Mulligans.

firmly established as a crucial port of call on the international touring circuit, thanks to such iconic venues as **Paradiso** and **Melkweg**. And with new locations such as **North Sea Jazz Club**, **Tolhuistuin** and **People's Place** (www.peoplesplaceamsterdam.nl), the future looks bright indeed. It's also worth keeping your eyes peeled for what's happening in Haarlem, Utrecht or Rotterdam – you could be a 15- to 60-minute train ride away from your favourite band.

TICKETS & INFORMATION

Many of the larger venues sell tickets via their own website. Otherwise, the main ticket retailers are **Ticketmaster** (www.ticket master.nl) and **Uit Amsterdam** – online at www.amsterdamsuitburo.nl, or in person at their Ticketshop (Leidseplein 26, Southern Canal Belt, open 10am-5pm daily). The **Last Minute Ticket Shop** (www.lastminuteticket shop.nl) shifts tickets at half their face value from 10am, for musical and theatrical events showing that night. It has outlets at the central library OBA (*see p156*) and in the main Amsterdam Tourist Board office (*see p297*), across from Centraal Station.

Uit Amsterdam's free monthly magazine *Uitkrant* (pronounced 'out-krant') is available in theatres, bars, bookshops and the Uit Amsterdam Ticketshop. *A-mag*, a new English-language listings magazine published six times a year by the city tourist organisation, is found in many hotels for free and is also sold at tourist offices and in newsagents.

ROCK & POP
Old Centre

Bitterzoet
For listings, *see p191*.
This busy, comfy and casual bar doubles as a music venue and club. Both bands and DJs tend to embrace the jazzy, alternative, world and urban side of sound.

De Brakke Grond
For listings, *see p68*.
This Flemish cultural centre and general artists' hangout regularly presents a variety of contemporary music from Belgium – which has an alternative music scene that has long been the envy of the Netherlands.

'Skek
Zeedijk 4-8 (427 0551, www.skek.nl). Tram 4, 9, 14, 16, 24 or Metro Nieuwmarkt. **Open** 4pm-1am Mon; noon-1am Tue-Thur, Sun; noon-3am Fri, Sat. **Admission** free. **No credit cards. Map** p312 K7.
Run by the same student organisation as the Kriterion (*see p177*) cinema, the focus at this bar-restaurant is on value and quality. While students lap up the discounts, music-lovers will appreciate the regular singer-songwriter and jazz gigs.

Winston Kingdom
For listings, *see p191*.
Part of a weird and wonderful hotel complex, the Winston is where artistic decadence collides with rock 'n' roll grime. Evenings offer new talent, both local and international, followed by a club night (included in the entry price).

a rare sense of grandeur, with multiple balconies and stained-glass windows peering down upon the performers. The smaller venue upstairs is a great place to catch new talent before the big time. Both are wonderfully intimate; bands feed off the surroundings, making for some special nights. Most gigs are followed by club nights.

Paradiso also books shows in other locations, such as Tolhuistuin (*see p198*); De Duif, an ancient and beautiful church that's perfect for mellower artists; and People's Place (Stadhouderskade 5/6, near Vondelpark, www.peoplesplaceamsterdam.nl), a small, flexible space with a superlative soundsystem that's a hotspot for the coolest music. *Photo p198.*

Jordaan & West

MC Theater
Polonceaukade 5, Westergasfabriek (606 5050, www.mctheater.nl). Tram 10. **Open** varies. **Admission** varies.
This venue dedicated to urban arts – whether it's clubbing, live music, comedy, theatre, dance – has an eye for the globally up-and-coming, from musician Seun Kuti (son of Fela) to American hip hop artist Jonwayne. The Afrovibes Festival focuses on contemporary South African art and music, while Electric Avenue presents the latest in electronica.

★ De Nieuwe Anita
Frederik Hendrikstraat 111 (no phone, www.denieuweanita.nl). Tram 3, 10, 14. **Open** varies. **Admission** varies. **No credit cards**. **Map** p311 E10.
A fixture in Amsterdam's subculture, DNA has become a sparkling promoter of fresh talents in the world of independent rock and electronica. Programming is sporadic and based on good relations with understanding neighbours; check the website first before heading out. It also operates as a cinema (*see p179*).

★ Pacific Parc
Polonceaukade 23, Westergasfabriek (488 7778, www.pacificparc.nl). Tram 10. **Open** 11am-1am Mon-Thur; 11am-3am Fri, Sat; 11am-11pm Sun. *Shows* usually 11pm/midnight. **Admission** free.

Canals

★ Melkweg
For listings, *see p192*.
Melkweg acts as a home away from home for music of all styles, and draws a suitably eclectic crowd. Its two decent-sized concert halls – the Max room has a capacity of up to 1,500 – offer a full programme year round. It also has an excellent cinema, gallery and a café, and book more intimate shows across the street at Sugar Factory (*see p194*).

★ Mulligans
Amstel 100 (622 1330, www.mulligans.nl). Tram 4, 9, 14, 16, 24. **Open** *Bar* 4pm-1am Mon-Thur; 4pm-2am Fri; 2pm-3am Sat; 2pm-1am Sun. *Shows* 9pm Wed; 9.30pm Thur; 10pm Fri, Sat; 7pm Sun. **Admission** free. **No credit cards**. **Map** p313 L10.
You'll find Irish pubs in every major European city, but only a handful are as much fun as Mulligans. The formula is a familiar one; the music on offer ranges from traditional Celtic acts to modern-day rock and pop singers and songwriters. The open session on Sundays is great for musos and onlookers.

★ Paradiso
Weteringschans 6-8 (626 4521, www.paradiso.nl). Tram 1, 2, 5, 7, 10. **Open** 11.30pm-4am Wed, Thur; midnight-5am Fri; 11.30pm-5am Sat. **Admission** from €6. **Membership** (compulsory) €3.50/mth; €25/yr. **No credit cards**. **Map** p314 J13.
A cornerstone of the Amsterdam nightlife scene, this former church is in such high demand that it often hosts several events in one day. The main hall has

IN THE KNOW
CULTURAL BEACON

Music isn't the sole remit at the **Melkweg** (*see p192 and left*): the complex is also home to a cinema (*see p179*), an art gallery and a café, Eat at Jo's. It also shares a state-of-the-art theatre space with neighbour Stadsschouwburg Amsterdam. Don't miss this key venue in the centre of the city.

ARTS & ENTERTAINMENT

Paradiso.
See p197

While its sprawling terrace attracts moms and baby buggies by day, bar-restaurant Pacific Parc attracts the nastier yet compelling aspects of rock 'n' roll by night. Local DJs such as Bone, Mappe, Stuka and Pete Slovenly generally spin on Thursdays to Saturdays, and international badass bands touring the dives of Europe are often asked to complete the line-up. Crazed, pelvic-thrust-based dancing generally ensues.

Museums, Vondelpark & Zuid

OCCII
Amstelveenseweg 134 (671 7778, www.occii.org). Tram 1, 16, 24. **Open** 9pm-2am Mon-Thur, Sun; 10pm-3am Fri, Sat. **Admission** €3-€7. **No credit cards**.
Formerly a squat, this friendly volunteer-run bar and concert hall is tucked away at one end of Vondelpark. While its squat-scene days may be over, the legacy remains: the roster offers touring underground rock, experimental and reggae acts, plus adventurous local bands.

OT301
For listings, *see p194*.
Music varies from underground acts to established names, but tends to be on the less commercial side of things. If you don't like the music, it also has a radio station, vegan restaurant and arthouse cinema to keep you entertained.

IN THE KNOW SCENE-MAKERS

Fans of alternative music should follow the good work of **Subbacultcha!** (www.subbacultcha.nl), which specialises in booking all the best up-and-coming underground guitar and electronica bands. Membership – €8 a month – gives you free access to all their shows and events.

Vondelbunker
Vondelpark 8 (no phone, www.schijnheilig.org). Tram 3. **Open** varies. **Admission** free. **Map** p314 H14.
This 1947 bomb shelter, located under a bridge that crosses Vondelpark, is temporary home to Schijnheilig, an activist collective that transforms abandoned places into free arenas for expression. Activities include squatting info nights, film screenings and bands – usually of the more punky variety.

Waterfront & Noord

Barco
For listings, *see p156*.
This bar-restaurant on a boat often features local bands – from punk 'tude to Latin grooves.

Café Pakhuis Wilhelmina
Veemkade 576 (419 3368, www.cafepakhuis wilhelmina.com). Tram 26 or bus 42. **Open** varies Wed-Sun. **Admission** €5-€8.
Wilhelmina is still often overlooked by casual music lovers. Is it the club's IJ location? The absence of bouncers? Or the cheap bottles of beer? Regardless, don't miss it if your heart lies with today's left-field music scene of alternative bands, cover bands and Hardrockkaraoke.

★ Tolhuistuin
Tolhuisweg 5 (763 0650, www.tolhuistuin.nl). Ferry from Centraal Station to Buiksloterweg. **Open** varies. **Admission** varies.
IThis new arts complex in Noord should be open for the business of culture by summer 2014. These former Royal Dutch Shell buildings and gardens have already been used for a summer festival and as a base for various creative companies since 2009. Now, with a 24-hour licence, they'll feature an indoor music venue (to be programmed by Paradiso; *see p197*), a massive restaurant with views over the IJ, and various gallery spaces and dance studios.

COUNTRY MUSIC

A round-up of the Netherlands' best annual music festivals.

Come summer, the Dutch club scene slows down – though it's really more of a sideways step. Amsterdam's urban beaches, such as **Blijburg** (*see p157*) and **Roest** (*see p156*), begin to host more shows and some crazy parties, and music festivals take place across the country. Even better, many are completely free. Below are the major events (in chronological order); check www.festivalinfo.nl for a full list and line-ups. For music festivals in Amsterdam itself, *see pp34-43*.

Eurosonic Noorderslag
www.eurosonic-noorderslag.nl.
Date mid Jan.
A rare midwinter shindig, this four-day international industry showcase in Groningen is for those seriously into the rock and pop scenes. The emphasis is on acts expected to make an impact across Europe in the coming year.

Where the Wild Things Are
www.wtwta.nl. **Date** Mar.
With the motto 'real beds, real bands', this new weekend festival takes place at Center Parcs de Eemhof in Zeewolde. It's an intimate affair (only 4,000 tickets) aimed at a more mature crowd. Loud guitars, adventurous pop and experimental electronica rule the roost.

Pinkpop
www.pinkpop.nl. **Date** May/June.
Attracting a slightly younger and poppier crowd than Lowlands (*see right*), Pinkpop is somewhat less adventurous than its indie sister. Still, there are plenty of big names in the worlds of pop, rock, dance and metal at the three-day event at Megaland, in Landgraaf.

★ Parkpop
www.parkpop.nl. **Date** late June.
Loads of European cities claim to hold the largest free festival. The Hague's Parkpop is the Dutch contender: organisers usually expect 300,000 to 500,000 visitors for this family-type affair. Expect some surprisingly big names, Dutch acts and upcoming urban outfits across the event's three side-by-side stages.

Metropolis
www.metropolisfestival.nl.
Date early July.
For the last quarter-century, Rotterdam's Zuiderpark has become an alternative-music honeypot for one day every summer. Bands such as Radiohead, the Black Keys and the Strokes played here before they become household names. And, get this – admission is free.

North Sea Jazz
www.northseajazz.nl.
Date mid July.
This three-day mega-event, a favourite with Dutch and other jazz fans, stages around 180 acts, including some big names. Drawing almost 25,000 visitors per day, it's held in the Ahoy complex in the south of Rotterdam – not the most attractive of locations, but it does allow space for further growth.

Lowlands
www.lowlands.nl. **Date** mid Aug.
Holland's largest alternative-music festival takes place over a long weekend, attracting up to 60,000 young hipsters each day to see assorted bands, theatre acts and street performers. Good weather isn't crucial – all the important stages are inside huge tents.

Crossing Border
www.crossingborder.nl.
Date Nov.
Based in the Hague, this gathering puts words before melody. Crossing Border offers a stimulating mix of literature and music, with many well-known international authors and artists arriving in town for spoken-word and musical performances.

Le Guess Who?
www.leguesswho.nl. **Date** Nov.
Originally focused on the Canadian independent scene, this festival in Utrecht now brings together the boldest and most unpretentious acts the world has to offer. A great way to discover not only the latest sounds, but also the various clubs of Utrecht. They also have a one-dayer in May.

ARTS & ENTERTAINMENT

Amsterdam Zuidoost

ArenA

*ArenA Boulevard 1 (311 1333, www.amsterdam
arena.nl). Metro/rail BijlmerArenA.* **Open** *varies.*
Admission *from €40.*

When the football season ends, Ajax's stadium is
reborn as a musical amphitheatre, hosting tours by
the likes of U2, the Rolling Stones, outdoor raves and
even a few Dutch stars. Bring your lighter, and don't
forget binoculars if you're stuck in those garishly
cheap seats.

Heineken Music Hall

*ArenA Boulevard 590 (0900 687 4242
premium rate, www.heineken-music-hall.nl).
Metro/rail BijlmerArenA.* **Open** *varies.*
Admission *from €30.*

A surprisingly cosy venue in the ArenA complex,
the Heineken Music Hall (capacity 5,500) regularly
plays host to pop, rock and dance acts that are too
big for the more central venues – from New Kids on
the Block to ZZ Top. The modern design may lack
character, but makes up for it in acoustics.

Ziggo Dome

*De Passage 100 (0900 235 3663 premium rate,
www.ziggodome.nl). Metro/rail BijlmerArenA.*
Open *varies.* **Admission** *from €40.*

With a staggering 17,000 seats, this behemoth towers over near neighbour Heineken Music Hall, so it's
not surprising it pulls in the biggest international
names: Lady Gaga, Madonna and George Michael,
for example. Bonuses: the acoustics are excellent,
and the logistical hiccups that often beset such large
venues non-existent.

JAZZ & BLUES

Classical music venues such as
Bethenienklooster (*see p203*) and
Splendour Amsterdam (*see p204*)
also feature regular jazz gigs.

Old Centre

Paleis van de Weemoed

*Oudezijds Voorburgwal 15-17 (625 6964,
www.paleis-van-de-weemoed.nl). Tram 4, 9, 14,
16, 24 or Metro Nieuwmarkt.* **Open** *varies.*
Admission *varies.* **Map** p312 K7.

This burlesque theatre and supperclub opens its red-
velvet curtains to a mixed bag of musicians, who
usually veer towards the jazzy side of things.
Though there's no official dress code, you may want
to consider a zoot suit and fedora as opposed to a
pair of tattered jeans.

Canals

★ Alto

*Korte Leidsedwarsstraat 115 (626 3249, www.jazz-
cafe-alto.nl). Tram 1, 2, 5, 7, 10.* **Open** *9pm-3am
Mon-Thur, Sun; 9pm-4am Fri, Sat.* **Admission**
free. **No credit cards. Map** p314 J12.

This intimate venue is one of the city's older and better jazz and blues venues. Famous Dutch saxophonist
Hans Dulfer has a long-running Wednesday evening
slot, but the quality is generally high on the other six
nights of the week. At time of writing, Alto was closed
for renovations – it should reopen later in 2014.

Bourbon Street

*Leidsekruisstraat 6-8 (623 3440, www.bourbon
street.nl). Tram 1, 2, 5, 7, 10.* **Open** *10pm-4am
Mon-Thur, Sun; 10pm-5am Fri, Sat.* **Admission**
before 11pm usually free; after 11pm €5-€10.
Map p314 J12.

In the heart of the tourist area, this blues club has a
spacious bar and a late licence. Musicians are welcome at the regular jam sessions, and international
acts drop by at least a couple of times a week. It's by
no means a glamorous venue, but if late-night music
played live is your thing, you won't be disappointed.

Jordaan & West

Maloe Melo

*Lijnbaansgracht 163 (420 4592, www.maloe
melo.com). Tram 7, 10, 13, 14, 17.* **Open** *9pm-
3am Mon-Thur, Sun; 9pm-4am Fri, Sat. Shows
from 10.30pm.* **Admission** *free-€10.* **No credit
cards. Map** p316 G11.

Bourbon Street.

ARTS & ENTERTAINMENT

'Well, I woke up this morning, feeling Maloe Melowed...' This small, fun juke joint on Lijnbaansgracht is Amsterdam's native house of the blues. Quality rockabilly and roots acts also play here on a regular basis, so shed your gloom and enjoy the boogie.

North Sea Jazz Club

Pazzanistraat 1, Westergasfabriek (722 0980, www.northseajazzclub.com). Tram 10. **Open** varies. **Admission** varies.
Associated with the annual festival North Sea Jazz (*see p199*), this club combines jazz and soul names, big and small, in an intimate setting – with both standing and dinner-club options. Next door, Pizza Pazzani is ideal for a quick meal, and hosts Kofferbak on the third Sunday of the month, with a savvy selection of spoken word, storytelling, comedy and music.

Zaal 100

De Wittenstraat 100, Westerpark (www.zaal 100.nl). Tram 3, 10 or bus 18, 21, 22. **Open** varies. **Admission** from €3. **No credit cards**. **Map** p311 D7.
Zaal 100 has its roots in the squatting scene, but is tastefully decorated, unlike some of its more grungy counterparts. The Thursday jazz workshops feature some of Amsterdam's best-known musicians; the venue also books a lot of singer-songwriters. Also a gallery space, it's frequently rented out by local artists. Vegetarian meals (three courses for €8 or less) are served on weekdays (except Tuesday) from 6pm.

Waterfront & Noord

Bimhuis

Piet Heinkade 3 (788 2188, www.bimhuis.nl). Tram 25, 26. **Open** varies. **Admission** from €16. **Map** p313 M5.
Jazz and improv musicians from far and wide queue for a chance to grace the stage at the Bimhuis. For decades a smoky jazz joint in the Old Centre, it moved some years back to the eye-catching new Muziekgebouw aan 't IJ complex – a bit of a shock for some fans, but it should ensure its healthy future. Since 2014 there have been sporadic pop nights too.

De Pijp

Badcuyp

1e Sweelinckstraat 10 (675 9669, www.badcuyp.nl). Tram 4, 16, 24. **Open** noon-1am Tue-Thur; noon-3am Fri; 1pm-3am Sat; 1pm-1am Sun. **Admission** free-€8. **Map** p315 N13.
The focus at this small, friendly venue is on world and jazz. An intriguing range of international talents plays the main hall, while the cute café has frequent open jams. The regular Brazilian jazz sessions are always worth a look.

North Sea Jazz Club.

ARTS & ENTERTAINMENT

Performing Arts

Welcome to a tiny city that likes to see itself as a huge hub in the cultural universe. Locals give standing ovations to Mahler symphonies and Russian pianist Alexander Melnikov, lap up the latest operas from Robert Wilson or Peter Sellars, and keenly support home-grown dance productions.

Amsterdam packs a real cultural punch with more than its fair share of world-class venues for every form of cultural endeavour. Add to this an active underground scene, and visitors are spoilt for choice. The breadth and quality of the Amsterdam arts experience was long due to enlightened funding from government and city council alike, resulting in a wealth of arts festivals, plus new buildings such as the Muziekgebouw. However, subsidy cutbacks have resulted in larger companies merging and smaller initiatives having to fight for their very existence (*see p134* **Culture Slash**). Much change is afoot...

TICKETS

Tickets for most performances can be bought at the venues themselves or via their websites (booking online is usually cheaper). Larger venues often include a free drink and even public transport in the ticket price. If you prefer to play it by ear, visit the **Last Minute Ticket Shop** (www.lastminuteticketshop.nl) on Leidseplein, where tickets for that night are sold at half price. You can also buy tickets from **Ticketmaster** (www.ticketmaster.nl).

Classical & Opera

One of the most heartwarming aspects of Amsterdam's classical scene is that the city promotes a classless adoration of beautiful music. Attending a concert is not a grand statement of one's arrival in society; it's simply about love of the music. Many of the greatest international orchestras perform in Amsterdam – typically for little more than the price of the biggest rock or pop concerts, and

frequently for considerably less. The city is also home to world-renowned orchestras and soloists, and renditions of the classics are not limited to the grand concert venues, but can be heard alongside canals, in parks, on the streets or in the halls of the new building of the **Conservatory of Amsterdam** – whose composers-in-training are being brought to the fore thanks to the likes of the new-music

IN THE KNOW
ORCHESTRAL MANOEUVRES

Amsterdam plays host to some of the most renowned orchestras and soloists in Europe. The superb **Royal Concertgebouw Orchestra** plays around 80 concerts a year in Amsterdam, while the highly respected **Nederlands Philharmonisch** (www.orkest.nl) and **Holland Symfonia** (www.hollandsymfonia. com) frequently stage wonderful opera and ballet productions.

specialist **Asko-Schönberg Ensemble**
(www.askoschoenberg.nl).

The **Royal Concertgebouw Orchestra**
(www.concertgebouworkest.nl), led by chief
conductor Mariss Jansons, is one of the world's
most famous orchestras. They play at home,
at the acoustically blessed **Concertgebouw**,
most weeks during the cultural season, which
kicks off in September – try to see them if
possible, even if just for a lunchtime concert.

Famed German conductor Marc Albrecht
is chief conductor of the **Dutch National
Opera** (formerly Netherlands Opera), the
Netherlands Philharmonic Orchestra
and the **Netherlands Chamber Orchestra**
(www.orkest.nl). Dutch composer Louis
Andriessen is still vying for immortality status;
his latest work for percussion and ensemble,
Tapdance, will have its premiere in Amsterdam
in 2014 as part of his 75th birthday celebrations.
And one of his students, Michel van der Aa, goes
from strength to strength as he incorporates
visual and theatrical elements into his often
site-specific work.

VENUES

Bethaniënklooster

*Barndesteeg 6b, Old Centre: Old Side (625
0078, www.bethanienklooster.nl). Tram 4,
9, 14, 16, 24 or Metro Nieuwmarkt.* **Open**
varies. **Tickets** varies. **No credit cards.**
Map p312 K8.
Hidden down a small alley off Nieuwmarkt, this former monastery is a wonderful stage for new classical
and jazz talent to cut its musical teeth. In between
enjoying free public performances by Amsterdam's
top music students, you'll have the chance to tune
into some reputable ensembles and quartets.

★ Concertgebouw

*Concertgebouwplein 2-6, Museum Quarter
(0900 671 8345 premium rate, www.concert
gebouw.nl). Tram 2, 3, 5, 12, 16, 24.* **Box
office** *By phone* 10am-5pm daily. *In person*
1-7pm Mon-Fri; 10am-7pm Sat, Sun. **Tickets**
from €15. **Map** p314 J15.
This beautiful neoclassical building, with crystal-
clear acoustics, is a favourite venue of many of
the world's top musicians. It's also home to the
renowned Royal Concertgebouw Orchestra. As you
would expect, the sound in the Grote Zaal (Great
Hall, capacity 1,974) is excellent. The Kleine Zaal
(Recital Hall, capacity 437) is perhaps less comfortable, but it's the perfect size for chamber groups and
soloists. For a taster, pop in for a free Wednesday
lunchtime concert: they often offer a trimmed-down
recital from one of the week's key performances. The
orchestra celebrated its 125th anniversary in 2013.
▶ *The Concertgebouw also holds regular concerts
for children; check the schedule for details.*

Conservatory of Amsterdam

*Oosterdokskade 151, Waterfront (527 7550,
www.ahk.nl/conservatorium). Tram 1, 2, 4, 5, 9,
13, 14, 16, 17, 24, 26.* **Open** varies. **Tickets**
varies. **Map** p313 M6.
Concerts and presentations take place almost daily,
and often for free, in the Amsterdam Conservatory's
new glass building just east of Centraal Station.
You'll find classical quartets to jazz big bands.

Engelse Kerk

*Begijnhof 48, Old Centre: New Side (624 9665,
www.ercadam.nl). Tram 1, 2, 4, 5, 9, 14, 16, 24.*
Open varies. **Tickets** varies. **No credit cards.**
Map p312 J10.
Nestled tightly within the idyllic courtyard of
Begijnhof, the English Reformed Church has been
hosting weekly concerts of baroque and classical
music since the early 1970s. Combined with a particular emphasis on the use of authentic period
instruments, the church's acoustics are genuinely
haunting. The busy evening schedule also raises
funds to help secure the building's future.

★ Muziekgebouw aan 't IJ

*Piet Heinkade 1, Waterfront (788 2000,
www.muziekgebouw.nl). Tram 26.* **Box office**
noon-6pm Mon-Sat. **Admission** €8-€30.
Map p313 M5.
Designed by the Danish architectural practice
3xNielsen, the Muziekgebouw is one of the most
innovative musical complexes anywhere in Europe,
befitting its previous incarnation as the IJsbreker,
whose long-lasting ethos was to promote modern

Concertgebouw.

variants of classical, jazz and world music. Never afraid to take risks, the centre's schedule bustles with delights, ranging from cutting-edge multimedia works to celebrations of composers from the last 150 years. It's also home to the Klankspeeltuin, where seven- to 12-year-olds can play with an inspired selection of musical machines, installations and computers.

▶ *The venue also hosts regular jazz concerts; see p201 Bimhuis.*

★ Nationale Opera & Ballet

Amstel 3, Old Centre: Old Side (625 5455, www.operaballet.nl). Tram 9, 14 or Metro Waterlooplein. **Box office** 10am-6pm Mon-Sat; 11.30am-2.30pm Sun; or until start of performance. **Tickets** from €15. **Map** p313 M9.

Until spring 2014, Amsterdam's showpiece venue for dance and opera, which is part of City Hall, was called the Muziektheater. But in the name of unified branding, the building – and its primary tenants, the Dutch National Ballet and Dutch National Opera – was reborn as the Nationale Opera & Ballet. The stage is also used for the latest Peter Sellars or Robert Wilson opera, and by leading dance companies on tour. Undoubtedly, it will maintain its reputation for high-quality performances at good prices. Tickets go on sale three months in advance and often sell out fast, so it's advisable to book early.

NedPhO-Koepel

Batjanstraat 3, Oost (521 7502, www.orkest.nl). Tram 7, 14. **Open** varies. **Tickets** varies.

In 2013, the Netherlands Philharmonic and the Netherlands Chamber Orchestra moved into a 1925-built church in Oost. The new rehearsal space also acts as a flexible performance space for 200 people to enjoy monthly open rehearsals (free), readings and educational programmes. Both orchestras, under conductor Marc Albrecht – a busy man as he's also conductor of De Nederlands Opera (now Nationale Opera) – perform regularly in the Concertgebouw.

Noorderkerk

Noordermarkt 48, Jordaan (620 4415, www. noorderkerkconcerten.nl). Tram 3, 10 or bus 18, 21, 22. **Concerts** 2-3pm Sat. **Tickets** €16-€19. **No credit cards. Map** p311 G7.

Sure, the wooden benches in this early 17th-century church are a bit on the hard side, but the Saturday concert programme is great, attracting accomplished musicians and a host of young talent.

▶ *Slip a little classical music into your grocery shop, by combining a Saturday classical concert here with a visit to Noordermarkt's delicious Boerenmarkt food market (see p121) outside.*

Orgelpark

Gerard Brandtstraat 26, Vondelpark (515 8111, www.orgelpark.nl). Tram 1. **Box office** *By phone* 2-5pm Tue-Fri. *In person* from 75mins before concert. **Tickets** €12.50-€20. **No credit cards. Map** p316 F15.

This church on the edge of Vondelpark provides space for ten organs, which are used for ambitious concerts – from Schubert to improv to electronica – in the hopes of bringing pipe-organ music kicking and wheezing into the 21st century.

★ Splendour Amsterdam

Nieuwe Uilenburgerstraat 116, Jodenbuurt (845 3345). Tram 4 or Metro Waterlooplein.

Muziekgebouw aan 't IJ. *See p203.*

PICK A FESTIVAL, ANY FESTIVAL

Modern dance? Experimental theatre? Circus? There's a festival to match.

Below are the major performing arts festivals, in chronological order. For more information on these, and other major annual events, *see pp34-43* **Diary**.

★ Holland Festival

Various venues (523 7787, www.hollandfestival.nl). **Date** June.
The month-long Holland Festival is the country's oldest and largest international arts festival, during which you can see a plethora of plays, operas, dance troupes, musical acts and exhibitions. Under artistic director Pierre Audi, recent guests have included Mikhail Baryshnikov, director Sam Mendes, musician Laurie Anderson, composer John Adams and Sonic Youth guitarist Lee Ranaldo.

Vondelpark Openluchttheater

Vondelpark, Zuid (www.openluchttheater.nl). Tram 1, 2, 3, 5, 12. **Date** early June-mid Aug.
Theatrical events have been held in Vondelpark (*see p128*) since 1865, and the tradition continues each summer with an assortment of free open-air shows, mostly on weekends. The programme includes dance, comedy and a variety of musical offerings.

Over het IJ

NDSM, Noord (www.overhetij.nl). Ferry from Centraal Station. **Date** early-mid July.
A summer feast of large-scale, site-specific performance and avant-garde mayhem, this 11-day festival is usually interesting and frequently compelling. Set in the appropriately apocalyptic setting of ex-shipyard NDSM *(see p158* **Northern Lights**), it brings together international troupes united by a love of absurdity and the latest in multimedia.

Julidans

Various venues (www.julidans.nl). **Date** July.
This two-week festival in July attracts many of the world's finest choreographers and dance companies, who showcase work around the city. Previous festivals have included premieres from Kathak master Akram Khan and an unexpected collaboration between Belgian dancer/choreographer Sidi Larbi Cherkaoui and flamenco star María Pagés.

★ Nederlands Theater Festival

Various venues (624 2311, www.tf.nl). **Date** end Aug/early Sept.
A jury-selected showcase of the best Dutch (and some Belgian) theatre that has been staged during the previous year. Running in tandem, the Amsterdam Fringe (www.amsterdamfringefestival.nl) is an uncurated mixture of experimental productions, in venues large and small, indoors and out.

De Parade

Martin Luther Kingpark, Zuid (033 465 4555, www.deparade.nl). Tram 12 or Metro Amstel. **Date** Aug.
This unique event has captured the essence of the old circus/sideshow atmosphere that's so conspicuously absent in today's commercial fairgrounds. Parade offers plenty of bizarre shows, many in beautiful circus tents; spread between them are cafés, bars and restaurants, as well as the odd roving performer. Theatre, music, art, magic, oddities and all kinds of attractions surround the audience, who are centre-stage instead of the other way around. The event also tours to Rotterdam, the Hague and Utrecht.

OUTSIDE AMSTERDAM
Holland Dance Festival

The Hague (070 361 6142, information 070 356 1176, www.holland-dance.com). **Date** late Jan-mid Feb.
The Holland Dance Festival takes place at three venues in the Hague, and is one of the biggest and most important festivals on the Dutch dance calendar. Its sterling reputation draws many of the world's leading companies, and the quality of the work is consistently high. Clips from previous festivals can be watched via the website's YouTube link.

★ Nederlandse Dansdagen

Maastricht (www.nederlandsedansdagen.nl). **Date** early Oct.
Held over the first weekend in October in Maastricht, Dutch Dance Days is a time when the season's best performances are repeated and the main Dutch dance prizes granted. It often coincides with National Dance Week (www.nationaledansweek.nl), when theatres across the country promote Dutch dance to a larger audience.

ARTS & ENTERTAINMENT

Discover the most powerful life on earth.
Right here in Amsterdam.

www.micropia.nl

Box office *By phone* from 4pm until start of performance. **Tickets** free-€16. **No credit cards**. **Map** p313 M8.
An inspiring local initiative for these cash-strapped times. A splendid old bathhouse has been renovated by a collective of musicians, composers and performing artists into rehearsals spaces, along with a bar and a performance hall where they give regular classical, jazz and pop concerts. Children's musical activities also occur frequently.

Stadsschouwburg
For listings, *see p212*.
This resplendent venue on Leidseplein is an impressive 19th-century building, originally constructed in a traditional horseshoe shape. It's known primarily for its theatre, dance and opera productions, but contemporary music performances occasionally manage to break into the schedule.

Westerkerk
Prinsengracht 281, Western Canal Belt (624 7766, www.westerkerk.nl). Tram 13, 14, 17.
Open 9am-5pm Mon-Fri. *Box office* 45mins before performance. **Tickets** varies. **No credit cards**. **Map** p312 G9.
This landmark church features a wide range of lunch and evening concerts, many free of charge. Cantatas are performed during services, a chance to hear the music in its proper setting. It's worth visiting to admire the stunning architecture alone.
▶ *From the top of Westerkerk's tower (see p93), you'll be treated to an incredible view of the surrounding area.*

Dance

Schizophrenic is probably the best way to describe Dutch dance. On the one hand, it has a boutique, experimental feel, with outlandish domestic creations that are hard on both eye and ear. On the other, its two headline companies, **Dutch National Ballet** (based in Amsterdam) and **Nederlands Dans Theater** (based in the Hague), are the envy of the international classical and contemporary dance worlds. Foreign choreographers such as Jiri Kylián, William Forsythe, Sidi Larbi Cherkaoui and Lightfoot León have seen their works flourish with regular premieres at the city's most important venues, the **Stadsschouwburg** (*see p212*) and **Nationale Opera & Ballet**. Commercial fare passes through the **Amsterdam RAI Theater** (*see p211*), care of the Kirov and Bolshoi Russian ballet companies, while the less classically minded should pay a visit to the city in July, when the Leidseplein theatres host **Julidans** (*see p205* **Pick a Festival, Any Festival**), a festival for the very latest international dance styles.

Het Veem Theater. *See p208.*

VENUES

Dance in all its forms is performed at a variety of venues in Amsterdam, the biggest of which are listed below. Other places that stage occasional events include **Theater Bellevue** (*see p212*), the **Frascati** (*see p211*), **De Brakke Grond** (*see p211*), **NDSM** (*see p158*) and **OT301** (*see p179*).

Dansmakers
Gedempt Hamerkanaal 203-205, Noord (689 1789, www.dansmakers.nl). Ferry from Centraal Station to IJplein. **Box office** varies. **Tickets** free-€15. **No credit cards**.
As well as staging work, Dansmakers is a production house that allows recent graduates to develop their choreographic talents. Established local names such as Ann van den Broek, Anouk van Dijk, Giulia Mureddu, Muhanad Rasheed and Sassan Saghar all began their careers here. It was formerly known as DansWerkplaats Amsterdam (DWA), and performances have been staged at least once a month, both here and elsewhere in the city or the Netherlands, since 1993. They also give workshops and lessons. Tickets for perfomances can be bought online or booked via reserveren@dansmakers.nl.

Toneelschuur.

Nationale Opera & Ballet

For listings, *see p204*.

Known as the Muziektheater until 2014, this plush, crescent-shaped building, which opened in 1986, is Amsterdam at its most ambitious. It has room for nearly 1,600 people and is home to both the Dutch National Ballet and Dutch National Opera (now known under the combined name of Nationale Opera & Ballet). Other major companies from home and abroad, such as Nederlands Dans Theater, also appear here. The lobby's panoramic glass walls offer impressive views over the River Amstel.

Podium Mozaïek

Bos en Lommerweg 191, Bos en Lommer (580 0381, www.podiummozaiek.nl). Tram 12. **Box office** 1-5pm and 1hr before performance; on performance days only. **Tickets** €5-€20.

In a district west of Westerpark, Bos en Lommer considers itself so up-and-coming that it's calling itself BoLo (to the general laughter of residents). But it does have this star venue in a former church, which specialises in presenting a multicultural range of dance, music and drama. The café is a real charmer as well.

Het Veem Theater

Van Diemenstraat 408-410, Western Docklands (626 9291, www.hetveemtheater.nl). Tram 3 or bus 18, 21, 22. **Box office** varies; shows usually 8.30pm. **Tickets** €7-€15; €5 reductions. **No credit cards**.

A homophone for 'fame', Het Veem Theater occupies the third floor of a renovated warehouse and hosts and co-produces modern dance and multimedia

productions from home and abroad. Café/restaurant Bak (737 2553, www.bakrestaurant.nl), in the same building, is a local foodie haven. *Photos p207.*

Outside Amsterdam

Lucent Danstheater

Spuiplein 150, Den Haag (070 880 0333, www.ldt.nl). NS rail Den Haag Centraal Station. **Box office** *By phone* 10am-6pm Mon-Fri; noon-6pm Sat. *In person* noon-6pm or until performance Mon-Sat. **Tickets** €15-€35.

Located right in the centre of the Hague, this is the fabulous home of the world-famous Nederlands Dans Theater, boasting a stage built especially for dance. As well as mounting high-quality Dutch dance and opera productions, it's also become one of the country's foremost venues in which to see international dance companies on tour.

Rotterdamse Schouwburg

Schouwburgplein 25, Rotterdam (010 411 8110, www.rotterdamseschouwburg.nl). NS rail Rotterdam Centraal Station. **Box office** 2-6pm or until performance Mon-Sat; 1hr before performance Sun. Closed July-mid Aug. **Tickets** €12-€42.50.

This large, square theatre opened in 1988 and soon became known by the waggish nickname Kist van Quist ('Quist's Coffin' – Wim Quist was the architect). It presents a generous variety of classical ballet and modern dance from both Dutch and international troupes in its two auditoria: one has 900 seats, the other a mere 150.

Toneelschuur

Lange Begijnestraat 9, Haarlem (023 517 3910, www.toneelschuur.nl). NS rail Haarlem Centraal Station. **Box office** 1.30-9.45pm daily. **Tickets** €10-€25. **No credit cards.**

Haarlem has every reason to be proud of its addition to the nation's cultural heritage, with two stages and two cinemas housed within its hypermodern home designed by cartoonist Joost Swarte. Its nationally renowned programme of theatre and modern dance has many culture vultures swooping in, especially from Amsterdam.

IN THE KNOW
ACROSS THE GREAT DIVIDE

Don't let the language issue put you off seeing a show. The Dutch have a distinctive, visual approach to theatre-making, and these days many companies, including **Toneelgroep Amsterdam**, employ English surtitles for their shows. All **Dutch National Opera** productions are surtitled in both Dutch and English.

COMPANIES

Amsterdam is home to countless choreographers and companies. As well as Dutch National Ballet (now part of Nationale Opera & Ballet), there are several smaller companies who've made a name on the world stage, including **Krisztina de Châtel** (www.kdechatel.com), **Het Internationaal Danstheater** (www.intdanstheater.net) and the more street-dance-flavoured **ISH** (www.thisisish.com), which often performs at the **MC Theater** (*see p197*) at Westergasfabriek. New arts centre **Tolhuistuin** (*see p198*), opening in summer 2014, is also home to several dance companies who will be holding regular performances there.

Don't Hit Mama
463 4449, donthitmama.nl.
Theatre-maker Nita Liem and writer/dramaturge Bart Deuss formed DHM in 2000. They reap inspiration from hip hop and urban dance traditions, while involving dancers and choreographers from the US, Africa and Asia.

Dutch National Ballet
www.operaballet.nl.
Amsterdam's foremost classical dance company recently fused with the Netherlands Opera under the name of Nationale Opera & Ballet (*see p208*). The company ranks alongside the Royal Ballet and New York City Ballet as one of the largest ensembles on either side of the Atlantic; it has the most comprehensive Balanchine repertoire of any European company. Under artistic director Ted Brandsen, the company attracts guest dancers and choreographers from around the world.

★ ICK Amsterdam
616 7240, www.ickamsterdam.com.
The Internationaal Choreografisch Kunstencentrum (ICK) Amsterdam was founded by Emio Greco and Pieter C Scholten – who in 2014 also became the artistic directors of Ballet National de Marseilles. The choreographer-director team produce high-quality contemporary dance with moody lighting and an unmatched sense of mise-en-scène. Works tour internationally, but can be seen locally at Frascati (*see p211*) and the Stadsschouwburg (*see p212*). ICK is also involved with hosting dance shows at the Felix Meritis debating centre (www.felix.meritis.nl), in an attempt to help the centre's financial problems.

Outside Amsterdam

★ Nederlands Dans Theater
www.ndt.nl.
Founded in 1959 and based at the Hague's Lucent Danstheater (*see p208*), NDT has transcended the Dutch dance scene and become an international force. Thanks to its former artistic director Jiří Kylián,

whose choreographies are desired by almost every high-profile company on the planet, NDT is met with open arms wherever it tours. In Amsterdam, performances usually take place at the Nationale Opera & Ballet (*see p208*), but NDTII – a second company of aspiring dancers – can be seen at the Stadsschouwburg (*see p212*) and elsewhere.

Scapino Ballet Rotterdam
010 414 2414, www.scapinoballet.nl.
The oldest dance company in the country (formed in 1945), Scapino used to be a little on the stuffy side. But in the 1990s, attention shifted from convention to innovation; once again, they're a force to be reckoned with, under the tutelage of Ed Wubbe.

TRAINING

Henny Jurriëns Foundation
Bellamystraat 49, Oud West (412 1510, www.hjs.nl). Tram 7, 17. **Classes** 9.30am (ballet), 11am (contemporary), 12.45pm (ballet) Mon-Fri; 11am (ballet) Sat. **Rates** €10 per class; €80 10 classes. **No credit cards. Map** p316 E13.
The Henny Jurriëns Foundation provides open training for professional dancers in both classical and modern dance techniques. The studio is at the top of the Olympia Building (an old cinema) and has the vibe of a New York loft. Instructors are a mix of locals and visiting teachers from abroad. The foundation also offers workshops, for which pre-registration is necessary. Full details on the website.

ICK Amsterdam.

ARTS & ENTERTAINMENT

ARTS & ENTERTAINMENT

ISLAND PLAYGROUND
An outdoor festival like no other.

Terschelling, one of the five Frisian islands that sit off the north coast of Holland, has a wonderful landscape of dunes, dykes and woodlands, shaped and shifted by the interaction of wind and man. A popular holiday destination for teenagers and twitchers (more than half the island is a bird sanctuary), it becomes a bohemian haven in mid June during the ten-day **Oerol** theatre festival (www.oerol.nl). The whole island is transformed into a stage for hundreds of acts to perform on; there might be international drama groups creating their own environments; world music gigs on the beaches; theatre expeditions through the woods; bicycle tours; or shows in boathouses or barns.

And as wacky as this all sounds, Oerol (founded in 1981) reflects a long legacy in Dutch theatre where all things absurd, over-the-top and technologically cutting-edge are embraced, and the dividing line between theatre, music, dance and circus is blurred. Think: sculpted dreamscape happenings rich in colour, technical wizardry, alien costuming and random exploding bits, all of which have evolved organically in response to the performance's site and context.

You can also witness similar versions of this particular school of performance at festivals in Amsterdam, such as **Parade** and **Over het IJ** (for both, *see p205*). But there's something very special about the epic natural setting of Oerol, which makes the performers, spectators and island residents all feel at home.

Parade.

Theatre

Even the flying visitor to Amsterdam will recognise it as a city of art and artists. Less evident, however, is its active and passionate theatre scene, which tends to thrive in secret in back-alley venues. As you might expect from this famously open-minded city, this is a place where performing artists are allowed – indeed encouraged – to experiment. Experimentation happens across all forms and genres, and the results are worth investigation, so be sure to hunt out smaller, alternative venues and off-centre cultural hubs. For the very bleeding edge of cutting-edge theatre, check out the absurdist multimedia works of **Pips:lab** (www.pipslab.org).

Public subsidy of the arts is under threat in the Netherlands, as elsewhere. As a sign of the times, witness the new **DeLaMar Theater**, which recently opened near Leidseplein, programming mostly Dutch-language theatre, cabaret and musicals. It was basically a €60 million gift from the VandenEnde Foundation, a cultural fund set up by insanely wealthy

international theatre producer Joop van den Ende to support cultural activities in the Netherlands (other beneficiaries include photography museum Foam and the Stedelijk Museum of Modern Art).

The language gap is often surprisingly well bridged by surtitles, audience interaction and strong visuals. If language is a barrier, then the multipurpose, multimedia **De Balie** is worth checking out. Alternatively, **NDSM** (*see p158* **Northern Lights**) mounts regular site-specific pieces that transcend linguistic limitations.

VENUES

Amsterdam Marionetten Theater
Nieuwe Jonkerstraat 8, Old Centre: Old Side (620 8027, www.marionettentheater.nl). Tram 4, 9. **Box office** *By phone* 10am-5pm Mon-Fri. *In person* from 2hrs before performance. **Tickets** €12-€15. **No credit cards. Map** p313 L7.
Opera as you've never seen it before. Imagine hand-crafted wooden marionettes wearing silk and velvet costumes, wielded by expert puppeteers in classic

works by Mozart and Offenbach, and you'll have an idea of what the AMT is all about. One of the last outposts of an old European tradition, the theatre also offers private lunches, dinners or high teas, to be taken while the puppets perform. Delightful.

Amsterdam RAI Theater
Europaplein 22, Zuid (549 1212, www.rai theater.nl). NS rail RAI Station. **Box office** from 1hr before performance until 30mins after. **Tickets** €20-€90.
A convention and exhibition centre by day, the RAI is a theatre by night and at weekends. Musicals, operas, comedy nights, ballets and spectacular shows can all be enjoyed in this sizeable hall.

De Balie
Kleine Gartmanplantsoen 10, Southern Canal Belt (553 5155, www.debalie.nl). Tram 1, 2, 5, 7, 10. **Box office** 5-9pm or until start of performance Mon-Fri; from 90mins before performance Sat, Sun. **Tickets** €7-€15. **No credit cards. Map** p314 J12.
This multipurpose venue presents all sorts of performances and events – theatre, films, photographic shows, literature – as well as numerous lectures and debates on topics of current interest, whether social, political or cultural. Add a visit to the café and you've got food for both mind and body. After all, what's culture without a little cake?

De Brakke Grond
Nes 45, Old Centre: Old Side (622 9014, www.brakkegrond.nl). Tram 4, 9, 14, 16, 24. **Open** varies. **Tickets** varies. **No credit cards. Map** p312 J9.

At the Flemish Arts Centre, you'll find visual art, literature, dance, theatre, music, performance, film and new media. If you're lucky, you might find an actor or two joining you at the bar of the adjacent café/restaurant. Tickets are also available from the box office at Frascati (*see p211*).

DeLaMar Theater
Marnixstraat 402, Western Canal Belt (0900 335 2627 premium rate, www.delamar.nl). Tram 1, 2, 5, 7, 10. **Box office** *By phone* 10am-10pm daily. *In person* noon-6pm daily; until 8.15pm on performance days. **Tickets** €11.50-€55. **Map** p314 H12.
The city's newest theatre and, at a cost of around €60 million, one of its most luxurious, the DeLaMar hosts major musicals, opera and drama. Its two auditoria can accommodate 600 and 900 people respectively. The management hope to make it the key destination in the Leidseplein theatre district.

★ Frascati
Nes 63, Old Centre: Old Side (626 6866, www.frascatitheater.nl). Tram 4, 9, 16, 24. **Box office** *By phone* 10am-7.30pm Mon-Fri. *In person* 5-7.30pm Tue-Sat. **Tickets** €8.50-€14. **No credit cards. Map** p312 K9.
Frascati has been a cornerstone of progressive Dutch theatre since the 1960s, and gives promising artists the chance to put their productions on one of its three stages. Their mission: to challenge the bounds of traditional theatre by teaming up professionally trained artists with those from the street, resulting in a variety of theatre and dance shows featuring MCs and DJs, as at the youthful Breakin' Walls festival. *Photo p212.*

DeLaMar Theater.

ARTS & ENTERTAINMENT

Frascati. *See p211.*

De Kleine Komedie
Amstel 56-58, Southern Canal Belt (624 0534, www.dekleinekomedie.nl). Tram 4, 9, 14, 16, 24. **Box office** 4-6pm or until start of performance Mon-Sat. **Tickets** €9-€20. **No credit cards.** **Map** p313 L10.
Built in 1786, De Kleine Komedie is Amsterdam's oldest theatre and still one of its most important. Extremely popular with locals, it's one of the city's most colourful venues as well as the nation's pre-eminent cabaret and music stage.

★ Koninklijk Theater Carré
Amstel 115-125, Southern Canal Belt (0900 252 5255 premium rate, www.carre.nl). Tram 4, 7, 10 or Metro Weesperplein. **Box office** *By phone* 9am-9pm Mon-Sat; 10am-8pm Sun. *In person* noon-6pm or until start of performance daily. **Tickets** €15-€55. **Map** p315 N11.
Many performers dream of appearing in this glamorous space, originally a 19th-century circus building and recently refurbished in a very grand style. The Carré hosts some of the best Dutch cabaret artists and touring operas, as well as the odd big music name. If mainstream musical theatre is your thing, this is the place to come for Dutch versions of popular blockbusters such as *Grease* and *Cats*. The annual Winter Circus brings in the world's classiest acts and clowns.

★ Stadsschouwburg
Leidseplein 26, Western Canal Belt (624 2311, www.ssba.nl). Tram 1, 2, 5, 7, 10. **Box office** noon-6pm or until start of performance Mon-Sat; from 2hrs before performance Sun. **Tickets** €10-€45. **Map** p314 H12.

The Municipal Theatre is a striking 19th-century building in the heart of the theatre, club and restaurant district. It's the chief subsidised venue for new drama, dance and music, featuring work by local companies and touring ensembles, and is the home of Toneelgroep Amsterdam (*see p213*). It has two stages: a traditional proscenium with a horseshoe-shaped auditorium (which means compromised sightlines if you sit too far to the left or right), and a gaping but flexible black box with raked seats. There's also a fine café, Stravinsky, and a stellar theatre and film bookshop.
▶ *Stadsschouwburg is also one of the main host venues for the Holland Festival; see p38.*

★ Theater Bellevue
Leidsekade 90, Southern Canal Belt (530 5301, www.theaterbellevue.nl). Tram 1, 2, 5, 7, 10. **Box office** 11am until start of performance daily. **Tickets** varies. **Map** p314 H12.
Dating from 1840, this is one of the city's most active venues, premiering lunchtime dramas by emerging Dutch playwrights as well as modern dance and cabaret in the evenings – the programme is extensive and its doors are rarely closed. The adjacent café, De Smoeshaan, is where local actors gather to gab. In February, look out for the Pop Arts Festival for international puppetry, a recently established Bellevue initiative.

Theater het Amsterdamse Bos
De Duizendmeterweg 7, Amstelveen (670 0250, www.bostheater.nl). Bus 66, 170, 172, 176, 199. **Tickets** €12.50. **No credit cards.**
Set in the wooded surrounds of Amsterdamse Bos, this is Amsterdam's answer to the Open-Air

ARTS & ENTERTAINMENT

Theatre in London's Regent's Park or New York's Delacorte Theater in Central Park. Dreamy midsummer nights can be spent with a picnic hamper and blanket watching an updated performance of, for example, Shakespeare. If, like many spectators, you're there for the champagne rather than the play, you won't mind listening to iambic pentameter in Dutch translation. The season runs from mid July to early September.

Westergasfabriek
Haarlemmerweg 8-10, West (586 0710, www. westergasfabriek.com). Tram 10 or bus 18, 22.

With a great variety of industrial buildings being reinvented as performance, event and exhibition spaces, the Westergasfabriek is quickly evolving into one of the city's premier cultural hubs – as it was through the 1990s, in fact, when it was a happening underground squatters' village. Two long-time dwellers, Cosmic Theater and Made in da Shade, fused to become the multicultural, street arts-savvy MC Theater (*see p197*).

▶ *With its marsh ponds, wildflower meadows and cypress trees, Westergasfabriek is lovely for a stroll, with plenty of little cafés to provide refreshment along the way.*

TONEELGROEP AMSTERDAM
The lowdown on the Netherlands' foremost theatre company.

Under the guidance of Flemish director Ivo van Hove, **Toneelgroep Amsterdam** (795 9900, www.tga.nl) has established itself as the biggest and boldest repertory company in the Netherlands. The 21-strong permanent ensemble has tackled the translated works of Shakespeare and Ibsen, Chekhov and Strindberg, among numerous others, and includes many actors who are nationally recognisable thanks to their appearances on Dutch television.

The company is based at the rear of the Stadsschouwburg (*see p212*) – which is also where it performs – in a state-of-the-art extension housing rehearsal studios and offices. As might be expected, productions are of a high quality and stand apart thanks to their sharp aesthetic choices and frequently avant-garde values. Past hits have included Tony Kushner's *Angels in America*, David Mamet's *Glengarry Glen Ross* and a trilingual staging (in Dutch, German and English) of Alfred Jarry's anarchic *Ubu Roi*. The last production resulted in the decision to employ English surtitles for main-stage productions, which has made the company more appealing to tourists and expats.

Toneelgroep also hosts lectures, symposiums and open rehearsals. The company tours Europe regularly and has longstanding relationships with theatres in Germany, including the Schauspiel Essen, with whom it collaborated on *Ubu*. 'Dutch theatre has learned to be open to new ideas, creative collaborations and different theatre languages,' says resident dramaturge Corien Baart. 'In a world where people are afraid of living together, where people feel overruled by unjust politics, it's important that theatre reaches out to its neighbours.'

Toneelgroep.

Stadsschouwburg.

ARTS & ENTERTAINMENT

Escapes & Excursions

Escapes & Excursions

Amsterdam is part of one of the world's most densely populated areas: no fewer than 40 per cent of the country's population inhabits the built-up sprawl known as the Randstad or 'Edge City' – which is named for its coastal location on the Netherlands' western edge. This region is made up of Delft, Haarlem, the Hague, Leiden and Utrecht, as well as bitter urban rivals Amsterdam and Rotterdam. The area's road, rail and waterway networks are impressive, making for a pleasant journey from the city to the countryside. All the destinations in this chapter can be visited on day trips, but they also stand up to more leisurely and sustained exploration.

Around Amsterdam
MUIDERSLOT & NAARDEN

Many important events in Dutch history took place in the legendary stronghold of **Muiderslot** in Muiden, about 12 kilometres (7.5 miles) south-east of Amsterdam. This moated castle, situated strategically at the mouth of the River Vecht, was built in 1280 for Count Floris V, who was murdered nearby in Muiderberg in 1296. Rebuilt in the 14th

---

IN THE KNOW
SURFERS' PARADISE

Wijk aan Zee (www.visitwijkaanzee.nl) rates as the country's only authentic surfing beach. And it's a surreal one: the North Sea on one side, transporter ships exiting and entering the North Sea Canal on another, and refinery chimneys jutting up above the dunes on yet another. You can be there in an hour from Amsterdam.

---

century, the fortress has been through many sieges and frequent renovations. The 17th-century furnishings originate from the period of another illustrious occupant, PC Hooft, who entertained in the castle's splendid halls.

A few kilometres away, the star-shaped stronghold of **Naarden** is not only moated, but has arrowhead-shaped bastions and a very well-preserved fortified town; it was in active service as recently as 1926. All is explained in the **Vestingmuseum**. The fortifications date from 1675, after the inhabitants were massacred by the Duke of Alva's son in 1572; the slaughter is depicted above the door of the Spaanse Huis (Spanish House). Today, however, Naarden is the perfect setting for a leisurely Sunday stroll.

Meandering down the River Vecht from Amsterdam towards Utrecht, boat passengers can glimpse some of the homes built in the 17th and 18th centuries by rich Amsterdam merchants. Local tour company **Schuttevaer** (030 272 0111, www.schuttevaer.com) runs boat trips (and can arrange English guides with advance notice). Two of the trips afford close-up views of castles, the first stopping on the way for a one-hour tour of **Slot Zuylen**, a 16th-century castle that was renovated in 1752. The collections of furniture, tapestries and objets d'art give an intriguing insight into the lives of the residents. Both Muiderslot and Naarden are part of the original defensive lines of Amsterdam called the **Stelling van Amsterdam**, now a UNESCO World Heritage Site. Visit www.stellingvanamsterdam.nl, if you're interested in exploring it further.

Muiderslot

Herengracht 1, Muiden (029 425 6262, www.muiderslot.nl). **Open** *Apr-Oct* 10am-5pm Mon-Fri; noon-5pm Sat, Sun. *Nov-Mar* noon-5pm Sat, Sun. **Admission** €13.50; €9 reductions; free under-4s, IAmsterdam, MK.

Vestingmuseum

Turfpoortbastion Westwalstraat 6, Naarden (035 694 5459, www.vestingmuseum.nl). **Open** 10.30am-5pm Tue-Fri; noon-5pm Sat, Sun. **Admission** €7; €5-€6 reductions; free under-4s, MK.

HAARLEM

Lying between Amsterdam and the beaches of Zandvoort and Bloemendaal, Haarlem – a gentler and older Amsterdam – is a mere stone's throw from the dunes and the sea, and attracts flocks of beach-going Amsterdammers and Germans every summer. And it's only 15 minutes by train from Centraal Station.

To catch up with Haarlem's history, head to **St Bavo's Church**, which dominates the main square. It was built around 1313 but suffered fire damage in 1328; rebuilding and expansion

lasted another 150 years. It's surprisingly bright inside: cavernous white transepts stand as high as the nave and are a stunning sight. The floor is made up of 1,350 graves, including a dedication to a local midget who died of injuries from a game he himself invented: dwarf-tossing. Then there's the famous Muller organ (1738): with an amazing 5,068 pipes, it's been played by Handel and the young Mozart.

Haarlem's cosy but spacious **Grote Markt** is one of the loveliest squares in the Netherlands. Just a few blocks away is the former old men's almshouse and orphanage, now home to the **Frans Halsmuseum**. Though it holds a magnificent collection of 16th- and 17th-century portraits, still lifes, various genre paintings and landscapes, the highlights are eight group portraits of militia companies and regents by Frans Hals (who is buried in St Bavo's). The museum also has collections of period furniture, Haarlem silver and ceramics, and an 18th-century apothecary with Delftware pottery. Nearby is art gallery **De Hallen**, whose two buildings, the Verweyhal and the Vleeshal, house an extensive range of modern art between them.

The **Teylers Museum** is also excellent. Founded in 1784, it's the country's oldest museum; fossils and minerals sit beside antique scientific instruments, and there's a superb collection of 10,000 16th- to 19th-century drawings by such eminent artists as Rembrandt, Michelangelo and Raphael.

However, Haarlem is more than just a city of nostalgia: it's one of vision, with a creative vibe that's felt all over town. Local illustrator/cartoonist Joost Swarte designed the theatre/

St Bavo's Church, Haarlem.

ESCAPES & EXCURSIONS

SAY CHEESE

In search of the yellow stuff.

Alkmaar Cheese Market.

Few things are held higher in national affections than cheese. When they're not munching on it or exporting more than 400,000 tonnes of it every year, the Dutch are making a tourist industry of it. So it shouldn't be a surprise that the Dutch have been known as 'cheeseheads' since medieval times, when they sported wooden cheese moulds on their heads in battle.

One ritual for both tourists and members of the cheese porters' guild is the **Alkmaar Cheese Market** (www.kaasmarkt.nl) – the oldest and biggest cheese market in the world – held in Alkmaar, a 40-minute train ride north of Amsterdam. It runs from 10am to noon every Friday between April and mid September. Pristine porters, wearing straw hats with coloured ribbons denoting their guild affiliation, weigh the cheeses and then carry them on wooden trays hung from their shoulders. Buyers test a core of cheese from each lot before the ceremony, which takes place at De Waag (Weigh House); you'll also find craft stalls, the tourist office and the cheese museum, **Het Hollands Kaas Museum** (072 515 5516, www.kaas museum.nl, closed Sun & Dec-Mar).

But Alkmaar has more than cheese on offer, and its medieval centre is worth a wander. Among the attractions at the **Biermuseum** (Houttil 1, 072 511 3801, www.biermuseum.nl, closed Sun) is a tasting cellar, while the **Stedelijk Museum** (Canadaplein 1, 072 548 9789, www.stedelijkmuseumalkmaar.nl, closed Mon) has impressive art and toy collections.

The Netherlands' famous red-skinned cheese is sold at **Edam**'s cheese market, every Wednesday in July and August from 10am until noon. Though the town, 20 kilometres (12.5 miles) north-east of Amsterdam and a prosperous port during the Golden Age, tells many stories through its exquisite façades and bridges, they can't compete with the cheese. In 1840, edams were used as cannon balls in Uruguay to repel seaborne attackers. In 1956, a canned edam (a relic from a 1912 expedition) was found at the South Pole and, when opened, proved to be merely a trifle 'sharp'. The town itself added to this lore in 2003 by building a colossal cheese cathedral from 10,000 of the unholy orbs to raise repair funds for the Grote Kerk.

Meanwhile, over in **Gouda** (less than an hour by train from Amsterdam), golden wheels of cheese go on sale at the market every Thursday from 10am in July and August. Near the town, there are also many *kaasboerderijen* (cheese farms). Look out for *kaas te koop* (cheese for sale) signs. The town does have other things going for it too: 20,000 candles light the main square during the Christmas tree ceremony.

Gouda.

cinema Toneelschuur in the town centre.
Patronaat (Zijlsingel 2, 023 517 5858,
www.patronaat.nl) books bands and DJs that
easily compete with anything in Amsterdam.
If you're more into wooden panelling, leather
wallpaper, chaotic conviviality and infinite beer
choices, then **In Den Uiver** (Riviervismarkt 13,
023 532 5399, www.indenuiver.nl) is definitely
worth investigating.

Frans Halsmuseum

*Groot Heiligland 62 (023 511 5775, www.frans
halsmuseum.nl).* **Open** 11am-5pm Tue- Sat; noon-
5pm Sun. **Admission** €12.50; €6-€9 reductions;
free under-18s, IAmsterdam, MK.

De Hallen

*Grote Markt 16 (023 511 5775, www.dehallen
haarlem.nl).* **Open** 11am-5pm Tue- Sat; noon-
5pm Sun. **Admission** €7.50; €4-€6 reductions;
free under-18s, MK.

Teylers Museum

*Spaarne 16 (023 516 0960, www.teylers
museum.nl).* **Open** 10am-5pm Tue-Sat; noon-
5pm Sun. **Admission** €11; €2-€8.50 reductions;
free under-5s, MK. **No credit cards.**

WATERLAND

Until the IJ Tunnel opened in 1956, the canal-
laced peat meadows of Waterland, lying north-
east of Amsterdam, were accessible mainly
by ferry and steam railway. This isolation
preserved much of the area's heritage; to see
a prime example, look around the old wooden
buildings at **Broek in Waterland**. This area
is best explored by bike before switching over
to a canoe or electric motor boat, both of which
can be rented from **Waterland Recreatie**
(020 403 3209, www.fluisterbootvaren.nl).

Marken, reached via a causeway, was
once full of fishermen (some of whom give
excellent boat tours), but is now awash with
tourists. Visit in the off-season, and you'll likely
find it quieter. To protect against flooding,
many houses are built on mounds or poles.
Marker Museum provides an overview of
the island's history. (For more on Marken,
see p222 **The Chain Gang**.)

The number of preserved historic buildings,
from Golden Age merchants' houses to the
famous herring-smokehouses, is what makes
Monnickendam special. The fine antique
carillon on the belltower of the old town hall
is also worth hunting down.

Such was **Volendam**'s success as a fishing
village that it's said the town flag was flown at
half-mast when the Zuider Zee was enclosed in
1932, cutting off access to the sea. The village's
enterprising spirit was soon applied to devising

a theme park from its fascinating historic
features but, sadly, the cheerily garbed locals
can barely be seen for the coachloads of tourists
dumped there every day – and invariably
pointed to the world's biggest collection of
cigar bands (11 million in total), all of them on
view to a seriously smoke-happy public at the
Volendams Museum (Zeestraat 41, 029 936
9258, www.volendamsmuseum.nl). These days,
Volendammers are better known nationally
for being heavy partygoers and, strangely,
producing an inordinate number of popular,
middle-of-the-road singers.

De Zaanse Schans is not your typical
museum village: people still live here. One
of the world's first industrial zones, Zaan
was once crowded with 800 windmills, which
powered the production of paint, flour and
lumber. Today, amid the gabled green and
white houses, attractions include an old-
fashioned Albert Heijn store. In nearby
Zaandam, you can visit **Czaar Peterhuisje**,
the tiny wooden house where Peter the Great
stayed in 1697 while he was honing his
shipbuilding skills and preparing for the
foundation of St Petersburg.

Czaar Peterhuisje

*Het Krimp 23, Zaandam (075 681 0000,
www.zaansmuseum.nl).* **Open** 10am-5pm Tue-
Sun. **Admission** €3; €2-€2.50 reductions;
free under-4s, MK.

Marker Museum

*Kerkbuurt 44, Marken (029 960 1904,
www.markermuseum.nl).* **Open** *Apr-Sept*
10am-5pm daily. *Oct-Mar* 11am-4pm Mon-
Sat; noon-4pm Sun. **Admission** €2.50;
€1.25 reductions; free MK.

De Zaanse Schans

*Pakhuis Vrede, Schansend 1 (075 681 0000,
www.dezaanseschans.nl).* **Open** *Museums,
shops & windmills* Apr-Nov 10am-5pm daily.
Dec-Mar varies. **Admission** varies.

WEST FRIESLAND

West Friesland faces Friesland across the
northern IJsselmeer. Despite being a part of
Noord-Holland for centuries, it has its own
customs and far fewer visitors than its near
neighbour. One way to get there is to take
a train to Enkhuizen (about an hour from
Amsterdam), then a boat to Medemblik.
From there, take the Museumstoomtram
(Museum Steam Train) to Hoorn.

The once-powerful fishing and whaling
port of **Enkhuizen** has many relics of its past,
but most people come here for the **Zuider
Zee Museum**. Wander around the indoor

Binnenmuseum, which has exhibits on seven centuries of seafaring life around the IJsselmeer, then explore the open-air Buitenmuseum, a reconstructed village (complete with 'villagers') of 130 late 19th- and early 20th-century buildings transplanted from nearby towns.

The Gothic **Bonifaciuskerk** and **Kasteel Radboud** dominate **Medemblik**, a port that dates from the early Middle Ages. The 13th-century castle is smaller than it was when it defended Floris V's realm but retains its knights' hall and towers. Glassblowers and leatherworkers show off their skills at the Saturday market during July and August. Close nearby is the 'long village' of **Twisk**, with its pyramid-roofed farm buildings, as well as the village of **Opperdoes**, built on top of a mound.

The pretty port of **Hoorn**, which dates from around 1310, grew rich on the Dutch East Indies trade; its success is reflected in its grand and historic architecture. Local costumes and crafts can be seen in July and August at the weekly Wednesday market. The local **Museum van de Twintigste Eeuw** (Museum of the 20th Century), while hardly living up to its name, does have plenty of interesting exhibits. The **Westfries Museum** focuses on the art, decor and history of the region.

Museumstoomtram Hoorn-Medemblik

Hoorn-Medemblik; tickets available behind the station at Van Dedemstraat 8, Hoorn (022 921 4862, www.museumstoomtram.nl). **Tickets** *Day trip (steam train & boat)* €21; €16 reductions.

Museum van de Twintigste Eeuw

Krententuin 24, Oostereiland, Hoorn (022 921 4001, www.museumhoorn.nl). **Open** 10am-5pm Mon-Fri; noon-5pm Sat, Sun. **Admission** €8; €3.50 reductions.

IN THE KNOW
WADDEN ISLANDS

The Frisian islands of Texel, Vlieland, Terschelling, Ameland and Schiermonnikoog (which are also known as the Waddeneilanden) are part of an archipelago that stretches from above North Holland and into Germany and Denmark. They're defined by sand dunes, beaches, ancient harbour towns and nature reserves. In short, the perfect getaways. You can be on a ferry to the largest one, Texel (www.texel.net), within an hour of leaving Amsterdam.

Westfries Museum

Rode Steen 1, Hoorn (022 928 0022, www.wfm.nl). **Open** 11am-5pm Tue-Fri; 1-5pm Sat, Sun. **Admission** €6.50; €5 reductions; free under-18s, MK.

Zuider Zee Museum

Wierdijk 12-22, Enkhuizen (022 835 1111, www.zuiderzeemuseum.nl). **Open** 10am-5pm daily (outdoor museum closed Nov-Apr). **Admission** €14.50; €7.25-€14 reductions; free under-4s, MK.

City Trips
DELFT

Imagine a miniaturised Amsterdam – canals reduced to dinky proportions, bridges narrowed down, merchants' houses shrunken – and you have the essence of Delft, a student town with plenty going on. It's an hour by train south-west from Amsterdam.

Delft was traditionally a centre for trade, producing and exporting butter, cloth and Delft beer – at one point, almost 200 breweries lined its canals – and, later, pottery. The subsequent loss in trade has been Rotterdam's gain, but the aesthetic benefits can be seen in the city's centuries-old gables, hump-backed bridges and shady canals. To appreciate how little has changed, walk to the end of **Oude Delft**, the oldest canal in Delft (it narrowly escaped being drained in the 1920s to become a sunken tramline), cross the busy road to the harbour, and compare the view to Vermeer's *View of Delft*, now on display in the Mauritshuis (*see p224*) in the Hague.

Delft is, of course, most famous for its blue and white tiles and pottery. There are still a few factories open to visitors – among them **De Delftse Pauw** and **De Porceleyne Fles**. The city has produced an enormous range of tiles, depicting everything from battling warships to randy rabbits, a dramatic contrast to today's mass-produced trinkets.

The town also has two spectacular churches. The **Nieuwe Kerk** (New Church) contains the tombs of philosopher Hugo de Groot and Prince William of Orange (alongside his dog, who faithfully followed him to death by refusing food and water). The church was completed in 1396. Across the market square is Hendrick de Keyser's 1620 **Stadhuis** (City Hall); De Keyser also designed Prince William's black and white marble mausoleum. Not to be outdone, the town's other splendid house of worship is the Gothic **Oude Kerk** (Old Church), dating from around 1200. It's known locally as 'Leaning Jan' because its tower stands two metres off-kilter.

Delft

Delft's museums have the calming air of quiet private residences. **Museum Het Prinsenhof**, located in the former convent of St Agatha, holds ancient and modern art exhibitions, along with displays about Prince William of Orange, who was assassinated here in 1584 by one of many keen to earn the price put on his head by Philip II of Spain during the Netherlands' 80-year fight for independence. The bullet holes are still clearly visible on the stairs.

It's enjoyable simply to stroll around town. The historic centre is home to more than 600 national monuments in and around the preserved merchants' houses, including the **Oostpoort** (East Gate, dating from 1394), the **Windmill de Roos** and the grim torture chamber in **Het Steen**, the City Hall's 13th-century tower.

There are several charming places to unwind over a drink or a meal. Don't miss **Stads-Koffyhuis** (Oude Delft 133, 015 212 4625, www.stads-koffyhuis.nl), which has a terrace barge in the summer and serves Knollaert beer, a local brew that's still made to a medieval recipe. **De Wijnhaven** (Wijnhaven 22, 015 214 1460, www.wijnhaven.nl) and **Vlaanderen** (Beestenmarkt 16, 015 213 3311, www.vlaanderen.nl) provide delicious meals and views at good prices.

FREE De Delftse Pauw

Delftweg 133 (015 212 4920, www.delftse pauw.nl). Open Apr-Oct 9am-4.30pm daily. Nov-Mar 9am-4.30pm Mon-Fri; 11am-1pm Sat, Sun. **Admission** free.

Museum Het Prinsenhof

Sint Agathaplein 1 (015 260 2358, www. prinsenhof-delft.nl). Open 11am-5pm Tue-Sun. **Admission** €8.50; €1-€5 reductions; free under-12s.

De Porceleyne Fles

Rotterdamseweg 196 (015 251 2030, www.royaldelft.com). Open Apr-Oct 9am-5pm daily. Nov-Mar 9am-5pm Mon-Sat; noon-5pm Sun. **Admission** €12; free under-12s.

GRONINGEN

A two-hour train ride from Amsterdam, the northern city of Groningen is pretty much the furthest one can get from the capital without leaving the country itself. Known as the 'Amsterdam of the North', it packs a similarly contemporary punch while still retaining plenty of old-world charm.

Groningen is a city that rocks – especially at night. But it's not just another student town. It's been around since BC became AD, when it was quick to evolve into a bustling walled city with

De Porceleyne Fles, Delft

THE CHAIN GANG

Cycle north beyond the city boundaries for a trip back in time.

Marken Lighthouse.

Start Amsterdam Centraal Station
Finish Marken (or further to Edam)
Distance About 40km/25 miles (round trip)
Duration A leisurely 8-10hrs

It's worth following in the tyre tracks of scores of Lycra-sheathed enthusiasts and heading out of Amsterdam by bike – thanks to the Netherlands' mercifully flat terrain, it's possible to cover surprising distances. The eastern Waterland region might be just 20 minutes away by bike from the city centre, but it's another world – at points, it feels as if you've cycled into a 17th-century Dutch landscape painting.

Starting at Centraal Station, catch the free ferry to Noord's Buiksloterweg (every five to ten minutes throughout the day), then follow the packs of competitive road cyclists (and the signposts when they become tiny luminous dots on the horizon) to **Durgerdam**. Riding into this tiny former fishing village, you'll find a tranquil scene: old painted wooden houses lining the cobbled street, pet rabbits grazing in their runs at the side of the road, and hundreds of bobbing masts on the IJmeer skyline.

Durgerdam consists of little more than this one perfect street, and halfway along is the village's only 'brown café', the **Oude Taveerne** (Durgerdammerdijk 73, 020 490 4259, www.deoudetaveerne.nl). It straddles the road: café to the left, wooden deck to the right. With its old-world charm and breathtaking stepped terrace projecting out into the tranquil water, it's the perfect place

to stop for a generous portion of *ontbijts* (breakfast). Make your way down the gangway-like wooden jetty to the furthest seats, where you can enjoy a gentle sea breeze and the sound of lapping water.

From here, set off to the north past the numerous former sea inlets, home to scores of bird colonies. Shortly after the village of **Uitdam**, turn west on to the causeway – the two-kilometre long and narrow Zeedijk – that has joined the former island of **Marken** to the mainland since 1957. It's generally peaceful, bar the occasional neon-clad cyclist zooming past. The village itself, with clusters of traditional green houses built on piles, is chocolate-box quaint. You can cycle lazily around the perimeter, taking in the sturdy lighthouse (nicknamed *de paard* – 'the horse' – for its shape) dating from 1700. You can also enjoy uninterrupted views across the IJmeer towards Almere and back towards the mainland to Volendam. Return to the village and linger around the harbour with its myriad cafés, bars and restaurants, just in time for a late lunch – perhaps a *broodje* (sandwich) at the **Oude Marken Lunchroom** (Buurtstraat 19) behind the harbour.

Legs aching, bike moaning, now's the time to consider your options. You could catch the ferry to the perfectly preserved 'theme park' village that is **Volendam**, or, if your legs are up to it, venture as far as the cheese paradise of Edam; less hardcore cyclists can head back to Amsterdam for a well-deserved rest.

a major grain market and high stakes in sugar and shipbuilding. Its history as a natural-gas reserve – which is a present reality, with an increasing number of earthquakes being caused by the extraction – is reflected in the **Aardgas Headquarters** (Concourslaan 17), a classic example of organic architecture.

In fact, you're greeted by several architectural classics as soon as you arrive. Centraal Station is across the street from the **Groninger Museum**, the funkiest art gallery on the planet – even Bilbao's Guggenheim looks prefabricated by comparison. Also nearby is an early work by superstar architect Rem Koolhaas: the **Urinoir**, featuring both stainless steel toilets and the homoerotic photography of Erwin Olaf. It's located on Kleine Der A in the scenic Westhaven district, also home to the **Nederlands Stripmuseum** (Comics Museum), which covers everything from Asterix to Zorro and beyond.

If you proceed up Folkingestraat, you'll soon find yourself at **Vismarkt** and **Grote Markt**. The latter's image-defining church and tower are the **Martinikerk** and **Martinitoren**. Historians claim they are named after St Martin rather than the cocktail, but suspicions rise, given that the surrounding square kilometre has the highest density of alcohol licences in the country. If all that isn't enough, the tower of nearby church **Jozefkerk** is nicknamed 'Drunken Man's Tower': each of its six faces has a clock and therefore at least two are always visible, creating a sense of double vision. Yep, it's a student town all right.

And if this thought is making you thirsty: there are two main strips. Peperstraat is middle-of-the-road, while Poelestraat is the trendier alternative.

Groningen also provides the perfect base to explore nature. There's much within cycling distance – for instance, the moated manors of **Menkemaborg** or **Fraeylemaborg** – but you can also take a bus to the nearby port towns, whence ferries go to the Wadden Islands of **Schiermonnikoog** and **Ameland**. Or, if you're returning to Amsterdam, you can stop halfway at the impossibly scenic village of **Giethoorn** with its higgledy-piggledy canal system.

Groninger Museum

Museumeiland 1 (050 366 6555, www. groningermuseum.nl). **Open** 10am-5pm Tue-Sun. **Admission** €13; €3-€10 reductions; free under-6s, MK.

Nederlands Stripmuseum

Westhaven 71 (050 317 8470, www.strip museum.nl). **Open** 10am-5pm Tue-Sun. **Admission** €9; €7.50 reductions; free under-3s, MK.

THE HAGUE

The Hague (Den Haag), adjacent to Delft and an hour's train ride from Amsterdam, is the nation's power hub and centre for international justice. It began life as the hunting ground of the Counts of Holland before being officially founded in 1248, when William II built a castle on the site of the present parliament buildings, the **Binnenhof**. It was here that the De Witt brothers were lynched after being accused of conspiring to kill William of Orange; they were brutalised nearby in **Gevangenpoort**, now a grimly evocative torture museum (no children under nine).

ESCAPES & EXCURSIONS

Groninger Museum.

Following in the tradition of his mother Queen Beatrix, King Willem-Alexander arrives at the Binnenhof in a golden coach every Prinsjesdag (third Tuesday in September) for the annual state opening of parliament. Guided tours are organised daily to the Knights' Hall, where the ceremony takes place. The freshly reopened **Mauritshuis**, a former royal home, has one of the most famous collections in the world: masterworks by Rubens, Rembrandt (including *The Anatomy Lesson of Dr Tulp*) and Vermeer (namely, *The Girl with a Pearl Earring*). Another work in the collection, *The Goldfinch*, by Carel Fabritius, became a global hit in 2013 as the title and inspiration for the latest novel of best-selling author Donna Tartt.

The Hague's city centre is lively, with a decent selection of shops lining the streets and squares around the palaces and along Denneweg. It's also one of the greenest cities in Europe and has a number of lovely parks: **Clingendael** has a Japanese garden; **Meijendael**, further out, is part of an ancient forest; and the **Scheveningse Bosje** is big enough to occupy an entire day.

Between the Bosje and the city is **Vredespaleis** (Peace Palace), a gift from American philanthropist Andrew Carnegie that is now the UN's Court of International Justice. On Churchillplein, the **International Criminal Tribunal** was the setting for former dictator Slobodan Milosevic's sulky theatrics – and, later, his death.

Beyond Scheveningse Bosje is **Scheveningen**, a former fishing village and now a resort. The highlight is the Steigenberger Kurhaus Hotel: built in 1887, it's a legacy of Scheveningen's halcyon days as a bathing place for European high society. Also here is the 'Sculptures by the Sea' exhibition,

a collection of statues at the **Museum Beelden aan Zee**.

The renovated **Panorama Mesdag** houses not only the single largest painting in the country – 120 metres (400 feet) in circumference – from which it takes its name, but also works from the Hague (most of them seascapes) and Barbizon (landscapes and pastoral scenes from peasant life) schools. None, though, is worth as much as *Victory Boogie Woogie*, Piet Mondrian's last work, which sold for a cool 80 million guilders (€36 million) in 1998. It's now on display at the **Gemeentemuseum**, which holds the world's largest collection of works by Mondrian, as well as many works of paradoxical art by MC Escher. The Gemeente's sister museum, **Escher in Het Paleis**, is filled with yet further examples of Escher's mind-melting art, supplemented with much interactive multimedia.

On the off-chance that your stopover in the country consists of one afternoon only, one way of seeing everything is by visiting **Madurodam**, an insanely detailed miniature city that dishes up every Dutch cliché in the book. Windmills turn, ships sail and trains speed around on the world's largest model railway. But if you happen to visit on a balmy summer's evening, when the models are lit from within by 50,000 miniature lamps, then Madurodam becomes a place of wonder.

If you need a beer, try **De Paas** (Dunne Bierkade 16a, 070 360 0019, www.depaas.nl). The living-room feel at **Murphy's Law** (Dr Kuyperstraat 7, 070 427 2507, www.murphys jazz.nl) attracts a friendly if unlikely mix of alternative folk and drunk diplomats. The Hague is also known to have some of the best Indonesian restaurants outside Indonesia.

Binnenhof, The Hague.

Binnenhof
Hofweg 1 (070 757 0200, www.prodemos.nl). **Open** 10am-5pm Mon-Sat. **Tours** from €5. **No credit cards.**

Escher in Het Paleis
Lange Voorhout 74 (070 427 7730, www.escherinhetpaleis.nl). **Open** 11am-5pm Tue-Sun. **Admission** €9; €6.50 reductions; free under-7s. **No credit cards.**

Gemeentemuseum
Stadhouderslaan 41 (070 338 1111, www.gemeentemuseum.nl). **Open** 11am-5pm Tue-Sun. **Admission** €14.50; free under-18s, MK.

Madurodam
George Maduroplein 1 (070 416 2400, www.madurodam.nl). **Open** *July, Aug* 9am-9pm daily. *Apr-June* 9am-8pm daily. *Sept, Oct* 9am-7pm daily. *Nov, Dec* 11am-5pm daily. *Jan-Mar* 9am-5pm daily. **Admission** €15.50; €13.50 reductions; free under-3s. **No credit cards.**

Mauritshuis
Korte Vijverberg 8 (070 302 3456, www.mauritshuis.nl). **Open** 11am-5pm Tue-Sun. **Admission** (incl audio tour) €14.50; free under-18s, MK.

Museum Beelden aan Zee
Harteveltstraat 1 (070 358 5857, www.beeldenaanzee.nl). **Open** 11am-5pm Tue-Sun. **Admission** €12; €5-€8.50 reductions; free under-13s.

Museum de Gevangenpoort
Buitenhof 33 (070 346 0861, www.gevangenpoort.nl). **Open** 10am-5pm Tue-Fri; noon-5pm Sat, Sun. **Tours** (hourly) from 10.45am Tue-Fri; from 12.45pm Sat, Sun. **Admission** €7.50; €5.50 reductions, MK. **No credit cards.**

Panorama Mesdag
Zeestraat 65 (070 364 4544, www.panorama-mesdag.nl). **Open** 10am-5pm Mon-Sat; noon-5pm Sun. **Admission** €10; €3-€5.50 reductions; free under-3s. **No credit cards.**

LEIDEN

Canal-laced Leiden derives a good deal of its charm from the Netherlands' oldest university, which was founded here in 1575 and includes such notable alumni as René Descartes, US president John Quincy Adams and many a Dutch royal. The old town teems with bikes and bars, and also contains the most historic monuments per square metre in the country, so it's a very rewarding place to visit. It's closer to Amsterdam then Delft or the Hague – about 35 minutes by train.

IN THE KNOW
DEER, BIKES AND ART

The country's biggest national park, the **Hoge Veluwe** (www.hogeveluwe.nl), has at its heart one of the Netherlands' best modern-art museums, plus an outdoor sculpture park, the **Kröller-Müller Museum** (www.kmm.nl). Rent a bike, feed the deer and gander at Van Goghs. It's about 75 minutes by car from Amsterdam.

In the Dutch Golden Age of the late 16th and 17th centuries, Leiden thrived on textiles. It also spawned three great painters of that era: Rembrandt van Rijn (born in a mill on the Rhine River), Jan van Goyen and Jan Steen. Although few works by these three Old Masters remain in the Leiden of today, the **Stedelijk Museum de Lakenhal** (Lakenhal Municipal Museum), where the Golden Age clothmakers met, does have a painting by Rembrandt, as well as works by other Old Masters and collections of pewter, tiles, silver and glass. Perhaps Leiden's most notable museum, though, is the **Rijksmuseum van Oudheden** (National Museum of Antiquities), which houses the largest archaeological collection in the Netherlands: in particular, the display of Egyptian mummies should not be missed. The excellent **Rijksmuseum voor Volkenkunde** (National Museum of Ethnology) showcases the cultures of Africa, Oceania, Asia, the Americas and the Arctic.

The ten million fossils, minerals and stuffed animals exhibited at **Naturalis Biodiversity Center** make it the country's largest museum collection, while the 6,000 species of flora at the **Hortus Botanicus**, one of the world's oldest botanical gardens, include descendants of the country's first tulips.

If Dutch clichés are the things you came here to see, head straight to the **Molenmuseum de Valk** (Falcon Windmill Museum), a windmill-turned-museum where you can see living quarters, machinery and a picturesque view out over Leiden. An even better panorama can be had from the top of the **Burcht**, a 12th-century fort on an artificial mound in the city centre.

To unwind after a long day of wandering, head to bar-restaurant **Annie's** (Hoogstraat 1a, 071 512 5737, www.annies.nu), which occupies eight candle-lit cellars underneath a bridge in the centre of town; its main selling point is the canal barge terrace. Another unique location is **Restaurant City Hall** (Stadhuisplein 3, 071 514 4055, www.restaurantcityhall.nl), a budget Italian restaurant-bistro in the city's ancient city hall.

ESCAPES & EXCURSIONS

Rotterdam's new station.

ESCAPES & EXCURSIONS

Hortus Botanicus Leiden

Rapenburg 73 (071 527 5144, www.hortus leiden.nl). **Open** *Apr-Oct* 10am-6pm daily. *Nov-Mar* 10am-4pm Tue-Sun. **Admission** €7; €2-€3 reductions; free under-4s, MK.

Molenmuseum de Valk

2e Binnenvestgracht 1 (071 516 5353, www. molendevalk.leiden.nl). **Open** 10am-5pm Tue-Sat; 1-5pm Sun. **Admission** €4; €2 reductions; free under-6s, MK. **No credit cards**.

Naturalis Biodiversity Center

Darwinweg 2 (071 568 7600, www.naturalis.nl). **Open** 10am-5pm daily. **Admission** €12; €4-€10 reductions; free under-4s, MK.

Rijksmuseum van Oudheden

Rapenburg 28 (071 516 6163, www.rmo.nl). **Open** 10am-5pm Tue-Sun. **Admission** €9.50; €3- €7.50 reductions; free under-5s, MK.

Rijksmuseum voor Volkenkunde

Steenstraat 1 (071 516 8800, www.rmv.nl). **Open** 10am-5pm Tue-Sun. **Admission** €11; €5-€8 reductions; free MK.

Stedelijk Museum de Lakenhal

Oude Singel 28-32 (071 516 5360, www.lakenhal.nl). **Open** 10am-5pm Tue-Fri; noon-5pm Sat, Sun. **Admission** €7.50; €4.50 reductions; free under-18s, MK. **No credit cards**.

ROTTERDAM

The antithesis of Amsterdam, both visually and in its vibe, the port city of Rotterdam (an hour's train journey south-west) brings an urban grit to the Dutch landscape. Almost completely flattened in World War II, it has blossomed as a concrete-and-glass jungle. From early 2014, you can be suitably welcomed via the new, gleaming, sci-fi-worthy **Centraal Station**.

The city has long been a haven for clubbers, artists, musicians, designers and cutting-edge architecture. Its citizens also love a good party – among its many festivals, the multicultural **Summer Carnival** (www.zomercarnaval.nl) draws some 900,000 spectators each July.

The city remains in a continual state of regeneration, including that of its futuristic skyline along the banks of the River Maas. The **Oude Haven** (Old Harbour) is a work of imaginative modernism, the pinnacle of which is Piet Blom's witty, bright-yellow cubic houses such as **Kijk-Kubus** (now also a hostel).

Across the splendid, white, asymmetrical **Erasmus Bridge** (nicknamed 'the swan'), don't miss activities in **Las Palmas** (Willeminakade 66), a remnant of the 1950s cruise ship era that's been restored as a cultural beacon, housing the **Nederlands Fotomuseum** (Dutch Photography Museum), among other institutions. This area, Kop van Zuid, received another architectural icon in late 2013 with the completion of **De Rotterdam** (Van der Vormplein 19, www.derotterdam.nl), the nation's largest building, by architectural wizard and local boy Rem Koolhaas. Conceived as a vertical city, it's set to house offices, apartments, shops, restaurants and a hotel. A nearby pedestrian bridge from historical (and now hip) **Hotel New York** (Koninginnenhoofd 1, 010 439 0500, www.hotelnewyork.nl) leads over to Katendrecht, once the go-to 'hood for randy sailors looking for company. Now it has Deliplein, a culinary square worth exploring. Another emerging district is the area just east of Centraal Station. Selling locally produced art, design, fashion and music, **Groos** (Schiekade 203, 010 414 5816, www.groosrotterdam.nl) is a ticket into the local creative scene. If it's good weather, settle down for a beer at nearby **Biergarten** (Schiestraat 18, 06 2470 8305 mobile, www.oktoberfestrotterdam.com) – it's outdoors, so isn't open all year.

If these initiatives have been forced to find other quarters due to the continued gentrification of the area, dart under the bridge to **Mini-Mall** (Raampoortstraat, www.mini-mall.nl), an abandoned railway station that now houses cafés, pop-up shops and modern-

jazz and world music venue **Bird**. Not far away towards the River Maas is breakfast and lunch spot **Picknick Rotterdam** (Mariniersweg 259, 010 280 7297, www.picknickrotterdam.nl), which is also known for wacky pop-ups, including a Tropicana Summer Terrace in a former indoor tropical water park. More urban hipness can be found further afield at **Uit je Eigen Stad** (Marconistraat 39, 010 820 8909, www.uitjeeigenstad.nl), an urban organic-farming project, market and restaurant. You can get there by following the new **Dakpark** ('roof park'; www.dakparkrotterdam.nl), a green strip covering a row of shops stretching from Hudsonplein in Delfshaven to Marconiplein.

FLOWER POWER

Tulips from Amsterdam, but also carnations, daffodils, gladioli...

Want a statistic that boggles the mind? Try this: the Netherlands produces a staggering 70 per cent of the world's commercial flower output, and still has enough left to fill up its own markets, botanical gardens, auctions and parades all year round.

The co-operative flower auction **FloraHolland** (www.floraholland.com) handles more than 12 billion cut flowers and over half a million plants a year, mostly for export, through a network of six national and international marketplaces (Aalsmeer, Naaldwijk, Rijnsburg, Venlo, Bleiswijk and Eelde). The most impressive auction is in **Aalsmeer**, in the world's biggest trading building (120 football fields' worth; Legmeerdijk 313, 029 739 7000). It's a 15-kilometre (ten-mile) drive south-west of Amsterdam; bus 172 runs there from Centraal Station.

Its unusual sales method gave rise to the phrase 'Dutch auction'. Dealers bid by pushing a button to stop a 'clock' that counts from 100 down to one; thus, the price is lowered – rather than raised – until a buyer is found. Bidders risk either overpaying for the goods or not getting them if time runs out. The auction is open to the public between 7am and 11am, Monday to Friday (Thursday until 9am). The earlier you get there, the better it is.

The 'countdown' bidding style was invented at **Broeker Veiling** (Museumweg 2,

Broek-op-Langerdijk, 022 631 3807, www.broekerveiling.nl, hours vary by season), the oldest flower and vegetable auction in the world. It's a bit of a tourist trap, but nonetheless includes a museum of old farming artefacts, plus a boat trip. The town of Broek-op-Langerdijk is 36 kilometres (22 miles) north of Amsterdam; if you're not driving, take a train from Centraal Station to Alkmaar, then catch bus 155.

Nowhere is the Dutch cult of the tulip celebrated in more glorious fashion than at the **Keukenhof** (025 246 5555, www.keukenhof.nl), located in South Holland's 'dune and bulb' region. Open for just eight weeks each year (from mid March to mid May), this former royal 'kitchen garden' has been a showcase since 1949 for local bulb growers, who still donate the staggering seven million bulbs planted by hand each year. There are other flowers, of course – crocuses, hyacinths and narcissi from late March; lilies and roses in early summer – but the tulip is the star, standing to attention in rows of glorious colour.

For more on the area's history, including the development of the bulb business, visit the **Museum de Zwarte Tulp** (Grachtweg 2a, 025 241 7900, www.museumdezwartetulp.nl, closed Mon) in Lisse. Keukenhof and Lisse are a 27-kilometre (17-mile) drive south-west of Amsterdam. Or take the train from Centraal to Leiden, then bus 54.

Keukenhof.

ESCAPES & EXCURSIONS

Rem Koolhaas also designed his city's cultural heart, the Museumpark, where you'll find outdoor sculptures and five museums. The top three are the **Het Nieuwe Instituut**, which gives an overview of the history and development of Dutch architecture, as well as covering design and new media; the **Museum Boijmans Van Beuningen**, which has a beautiful collection of traditional and contemporary art (including works by Bruegel, Van Eyck and Rembrandt); and the **Kunsthal**, which deals with art, design and photography.

Adjacent street Witte de Withstraat offers contemporary art hub **TENT** (Witte de Withstraat 50, 010 413 5498, www.tent rotterdam.nl), many smaller galleries and a variety of restaurants and bars. Fashionistas come here from afar to visit boutique **Margreet Holsthoorn** (Schilderstraat 5, www.margreetholsthoorn.nl). A bird's-eye view of the whole area can be had from the nearby **Euromast** (185 metres/607 feet).

If you're a backpacker, take advantage of **Use-it** (Vijjverhofstraat 47, 010 240 9158, www.use-it.nl). It offers great tips for what to do in the city, as well as free lockers.

Euromast

Parkhaven 20 (010 436 4811, www.euromast.nl). **Open** *Apr-Sept* 9.30am-10pm daily. *Oct-Mar* 10am-10pm daily. **Admission** €9.25; €6 reductions; free under-4s.

Het Nieuwe Instituut

Museumpark 25 (010 440 1358, www.het nieuweinstituut.nl). **Open** 10am-5pm Tue-Sat; 11am-5pm Sun. **Admission** €10; €6.50 reductions; free under-18s, MK.

Kijk-Kubus

Overblaak 70 (010 414 2285, www.kubuswoning.nl). **Open** 11am-5pm daily. **Admission** €2.50; €1.50-€2 reductions; free under-4s. **No credit cards**.

Kunsthal

Westzeedijk 341 (010 440 0301, www.kunsthal.nl). **Open** 10am-5pm Tue-Sat; 11am-5pm Sun. **Admission** €11; €2-€6 reductions; free under-6s, MK. **No credit cards**.

Museum Boijmans Van Beuningen

Museumpark 18-20 (010 441 9400, www.boijmans.nl). **Open** 11am-5pm Tue-Sun. **Admission** €12.50; €6.25-€10 reductions; free under-19s, MK.

Nederlands Fotomuseum

Wilhelminakade 332 (010 203 0405, www.nederlandsfotomuseum.nl). **Open** 10am-5pm Tue-Fri; 11am-5pm Sat, Sun. **Admission** €9; €4.50 reductions; free under-12s, MK.

UTRECHT

One of the oldest cities in the Netherlands, Utrecht (30 minutes by train from Amsterdam) was also, in the Middle Ages, the biggest. It was a religious and political centre for hundreds of years – at one point there were around 40 houses of worship in the city, all with towers and spires. The university is one of the largest in the Netherlands – still expanding and employing architects such as Rem Koolhaas (who designed the Educatorium) – and the centre bustles with trendy shops and cafés.

A starting place is the **Domtoren**, the cathedral tower. At over 112 metres (367 feet), it's the highest tower in the country, and it has more than 50 bells. The tower can be climbed, and the panorama is worth the 465 steps: vistas stretch to Amsterdam on a clear day. Buy tickets across the square at the **tourist office** (Domplein 9, www.bezoek-utrecht.nl), where you can also rent bikes and get details on the rest of the city and the castles on its outskirts.

The space between the tower and the **Domkerk** was originally occupied by the nave of the huge church, which was destroyed by a freak tornado in 1674. Another fascinating place to explore is the **Oudegracht**, the canal that runs through the centre of the city.

Of the city museums, the **Museum Catharijneconvent** (St Catharine Convent Museum) is situated in a beautiful late-medieval building. Mainly dedicated to Dutch religious history, it also has a great collection of paintings by Old Masters, including Rembrandt. The **Centraal Museum** has a varied collection, from paintings by Van Gogh to contemporary art and cutting-edge fashion. One wing is dedicated to illustrator Dick Bruna, who created that charming bunny, Nintje (known to some as Miffy). Another Utrecht-born celebrity in the collection is de Stijl architect and designer Gerrit Rietveld, known for his rectangular chairs and houses: the **Rietveld-Schröderhuis**, just outside the city centre, is part of the Centraal Museum and can be reached by a museum bus. The world's single biggest collection of automated musical instruments can be found at the fun **Nationaal Museum van Speelklok tot Pierement**. The **Universiteitsmuseum** (University Museum) focuses on science education and also has a centuries-old botanical garden.

A student town, Utrecht is, of course, rich with quality drinking holes. **De Winkel van Sinkel** (Oudegracht 158, 030 230 3030, www.dewinkelvansinkel.nl) is a grand setting, especially at night when its catacombs open for club nights and as a late-night restaurant. **ACU** (Voorstraat 71, 030 231 4590, www.acu.nl) has cheap eats and some of the city's edgier music

Utrecht.

events; **Kafe België** (Oudegracht 196, 030 231 2666, www.kafebelgie.nl) serves some 300 beers; **Ekko** (Bemuurde Weerd Westzijde 3, 030 231 7457, www.ekko.nl) focuses on indie and dance.

Centraal Museum
Nicolaaskerkhof 10 (030 236 2362, www.centraal museum.nl). **Open** 11am-5pm Tue-Sun. **Admission** €11; €5-€9 reductions; free under-13s, MK.

Museum Catharijneconvent
Lange Nieuwstraat 38 (030 231 3835, www.catharijneconvent.nl). **Open** 10am-5pm Tue-Fri; 11am-5pm Sat, Sun. **Admission** €12.50; €7 reductions; free under-5s, MK. **No credit cards**.

Nationaal Museum van Speelklok tot Pierement
Steenweg 6 (030 231 2789, www.museum speelklok.nl). **Open** 10am-5pm Tue- Sun. **Admission** €11; €6-€9 reductions; free under-4s, MK. **No credit cards**.

Universiteitsmuseum
Lange Nieuwstraat 106 (030 253 8008, www.universiteitsmuseum.nl). **Open** 11am-5pm daily. **Admission** €7; €3.50 reductions; free MK. **No credit cards**.

Around Utrecht

Utrecht is in an area rich with castles, forests and arboretums. **Slot Zuylen** (Zuylen Castle, Tournooiveld 1, Oud Zuilen, 030 244 0255, www.slotzuylen.nl) presides over exquisite waterfalls and gardens. Check the concerts and shows in **Kasteel Groeneveld**'s gorgeous gardens (Groeneveld Castle, Groeneveld 2, Baarn, 035 542 0446, www.kasteel groeneveld.nl), north-east of Utrecht. Stroll in the **Von Gimborn Arboretum** (Velperengh 13, 034 341 2144, www.gimbornarboretum.nl)

in Doorne, then head to **Kasteel Huis Doorn** (Langbroekerweg 10, 034 342 1020, www.huisdoorn.nl), where Kaiser Wilhelm II lived until his death in 1941.

Though **Kasteel De Haar** looks like the quintessential medieval castle, it's actually relatively recent. In 1892, the baron who inherited the ruins of De Haar (dating from 1391) re-created the original on a majestic scale, moving the entire village of Haarzuilens nearly a kilometre to make room for Versailles-styled gardens. The lavish interior is only visible on one of the informative guided tours.

Schoonhoven has been famous for its silversmiths since the 17th century, giving it its nickname of Zilverstad (Silver City). You can see antique pieces in the **Nederlands Goud-, Zilver- en Klokkenmuseum** and also at the former synagogue **Edelambachtshuis** (Museum of Antique Silverware). Olivier van Noort, the first Dutchman to sail around the world, and Claes Louwerenz Blom, who, locals believe, introduced the windmill to Spain in 1549, are buried in the 14th-century **Bartholomeuskerk**, whose tower leans 1.6 metres (five feet). Not buried here is Marrigje Ariens, the last woman to be burned as a witch in the country – but a circle of coloured stones by the city hall marks where she died in 1591.

Dating from the 11th century, **Oudewater** (north of Schoonhoven), once famed for its ropemaking, also has a rich witch-hunting past. Reaching its peak in the 1480s, the fashion didn't die out until the beginning of the 17th century. Oudewater achieved fame for its weighing of suspected witches and warlocks in the **Heksenwaag** (Witches' Weigh House).

Edelambachtshuys
Haven 13, Schoonhoven (0182 382614, www.rikkoert.nl). **Open** 10am-5.30pm Tue-Sat. **Admission** varies.

Heksenwaag
Leeuweringerstraat 2, Oudewater (034 856 3400, www.heksenwaag.nl). **Open** *Apr-Oct* 11am-5pm Tue-Sun. *Nov-Mar* 11am-5pm Fri-Sun. **Admission** €5; €2.50 reductions; free under-4s.

Kasteel De Haar
Kasteellaan 1, Haarzuilens (030 677 8515, www.kasteeldehaar.nl). **Open** *Castle* varies. *Grounds* 9am-5pm daily. **Admission** *Castle & grounds* €14; €9 reductions; free under-4s. *Grounds only* €4; €3 reductions; free under-5s.

Nederlands Goud-, Zilver- en Klokkenmuseum
Kazerneplein 4, Schoonhoven (0182 385612, www.zilvermuseum.com). **Open** noon-5pm Tue-Sun. **Admission** €7; €6 reductions; free under-13s.

ESCAPES & EXCURSIONS

In Focus

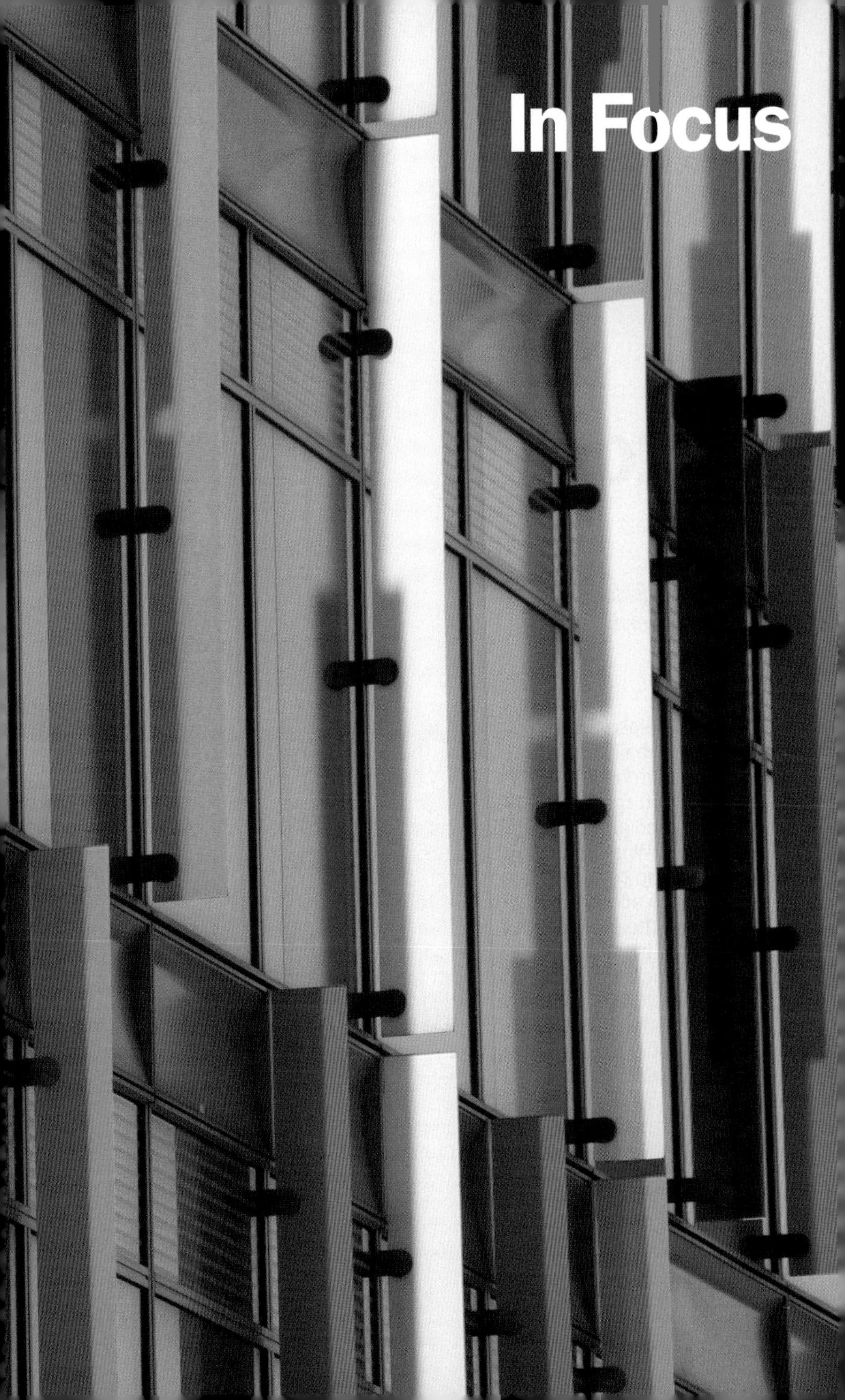

History

From Aemstelledamme,
a star city is born.

Technically speaking, Amsterdam is a city that shouldn't really have been a city. The boggy marshland surrounding a rising river wasn't ever a natural support for urban structures, so the locals built a dam and grouped their houses along the River Amstel. What sprang up as a result over the next eight or so centuries is a triumph of human engineering: a series of picturesque canal rings holding back the rising waters, and hundreds of thousands of buildings standing on pilings driven into sand. Pluck a cobblestone out of the streets today and you'll still find seashells right there.

Amsterdammers are proud that theirs is a city built on the sheer drive and ingenuity of its early inhabitants. In its Golden Age in the 17th century, Amsterdam was the centre of the western world. It was the birthplace of the first multinational corporation – the Dutch East India Company – and quickly became recognised as the cultural capital of northern Europe: Rembrandt, Frans Hals and Jan Steen gave way to Vincent van Gogh, Kees van Dongen, and later Karel Appel and Piet Mondrian. Not bad for a city built on such shaky foundations.

IN CONTEXT

BOGGY BEGINNINGS

According to legend, Amsterdam was founded by two lost fishermen who vowed to build a town wherever their boat came ashore. They reached terra firma, and their seasick dog promptly anointed the chosen patch with his vomit.

The reality is much more mundane. Although the Romans occupied the southern parts of Holland, they didn't reach the north. Soggy bog was not the stuff of empires, so the legions moved on. However, recent archaeological findings during the digging of the new Noord-Zuid metro line suggest there were some prehistoric settlements dating from 2500 BC. But Amsterdam's site spent most of its history at least partially underwater, and the River Amstel had no fixed course until enterprising farmers from around Utrecht built dykes during the 11th century. Once the peasants had done the work, the nobility took over. During the 13th century, the most important place in the newly reclaimed area was the tiny hamlet of Oudekerk aan de Amstel. In 1204, the Lord of Amstel built a castle nearby on what is now the outskirts of Amsterdam. After the Amstel was dammed in about 1270, a village grew up on the site of what is now Dam Square, acquiring the name Aemstelledamme.

BUILT ON BEER

In 1275, the Count of Holland, Floris V, gave Amsterdam a kickstart in becoming a vibrant trade port by exempting the area's traders from tolls. Then in 1323, his successor, Floris VI, made Amsterdam one of only two toll points in the province for the import of brews. This was no trivial matter at a time when most people drank beer; drinking the local water, in fact, was practically suicidal. Hamburg had the largest brewing capacity in northern Europe, and within 50 years a third of that city's production was flowing through Amsterdam. By virtue of its position between the Atlantic and Hanseatic ports, and by pouring its beer profits into other ventures, the city broadened its trading remit to take in various essentials.

Yet Amsterdam still remained small. As late as 1425, the 'city' consisted of a few blocks of houses with kitchen gardens and two churches along the final one-kilometre stretch of the River Amstel and enclosed by the canals now known as Geldersekade, Singel and Kloveniersburgwal. Virtually all the buildings were wooden (such as the Houtenhuis, still standing in the Begijnhof), and so fire was a perpetual threat; in the great fire of May 1452, three-quarters of the town was destroyed. One of the few examples of medieval architecture still standing is the Munttoren (Mint Tower) at Muntplein. Structures built after the fire were instead faced with stone and roofed with tile or slate. These new developments coincided with a rush of urban expansion, as – most notably – new foreign commerce led to improvements in shipbuilding.

RADICALISM AND REACTION

During the 16th century, Amsterdam's population increased from 10,000 (low even by medieval standards) to 50,000 by 1600. The city expanded, although people coming to the city found poverty, disease and squalor in the workers' quarters. Local merchants weren't complaining, however, as the city started to emerge as one of the world's major trading powers.

Amsterdam may have been almost entirely autonomous as a chartered city, but on paper it was still under the thumb of absentee rulers. Through the intricate marriage bureau and shallow genetic pool known as the European aristocracy, the Low Countries (the Netherlands and Belgium) had passed into the hands of the Catholic Austro-Spanish House of Habsburg. The Habsburgs were the mightiest monarchs in Europe, and Amsterdam was a comparative backwater among their European possessions; nonetheless, events soon brought the city to prominence among its near neighbours.

Amsterdam's new status as a trade centre attracted all kinds of radical religious ideas that were flourishing across northern Europe, encouraged by Martin Luther's condemnation of Catholicism in 1517. When Anabaptists first arrived from Germany in about 1530, the Catholic city fathers tolerated them. But when they started to run around naked and even seized the City Hall in 1534 during an attempt to establish a 'New Jerusalem' upon the River Amstel, the leaders were arrested, forced to dress, and then executed, signalling an unparalleled

Philip II (mounted on a cow), the Duke of Alençon, the Duke of Alba, William of Orange and Queen Elizabeth I.

period of religious repression: 'heretics' were burned at the stake on the Dam.

After the Anabaptists were culled, Calvinist preachers arrived from Geneva, where the movement had started, and via France. They soon gained followers and, in 1566, the religious discontent erupted into what became known as the Iconoclastic Fury. Churches and monasteries were sacked and stripped of ornamentation, and Philip II of Spain sent an army to suppress the heresy.

THE EMERGENCE OF ORANGE

The Eighty Years' War (1568-1648) between the Habsburgs and the Dutch is often seen as a struggle for religious freedom, but there was more to it than that. The Dutch were, after all, seeking political autonomy from an absentee king who represented a continual drain on their coffers. By the last quarter of the 16th century, Philip II of Spain was fighting wars against England and France, in the east against the Ottoman Turks, and in the New World for control of his colonies. The last thing he needed was a revolt in the Low Countries.

Amsterdam toed the Catholic line during the revolt, supporting Philip II until it became clear he was losing. Only in 1578 did the city patricians side with the Calvinist rebels, led by the first William of Orange. The city and William then combined to expel the Catholics

and dismantle their institutions in what came to be called the Alteration. A year later, the Protestant states of the Low Countries united in opposition to Philip when the first modern-day European republic was born at the Union of Utrecht. The Republic of Seven United Provinces was made up of Friesland, Gelderland, Groningen, Overijssel, Utrecht, Zeeland and Holland. Though initially lauded as a forerunner of the modern Netherlands, it wasn't the unitary state that William of Orange wanted, but rather a loose federation with an impotent States General assembly.

Each of the seven provinces appointed a Stadhouder (or viceroy), who commanded the Republic's armed forces and had the right to appoint some of the cities' regents or governors. Each Stadhouder sent delegates to the assembly, held at the Binnenhof in the Hague. While fitted with clauses set to hinder Catholicism from ever suppressing the Reformed religion again, the Union of Utrecht also enshrined freedom of conscience and religion (at least until the Republic's demise in 1795), thus providing the blueprint that made Amsterdam a safe haven for future political and religious refugees.

The obvious choice for Holland's Stadhouder after the union was William of Orange. After his popular tenure, it became a tradition to elect an Orange as Stadhouder. By 1641, the family had become sufficiently powerful for William II to marry a British princess, Mary Stuart; it was their son, William III, who set sail in 1688 to accept the throne of England in the so-called Glorious Revolution.

A SOCIAL CONSCIENCE WITH CLAWS

From its beginnings, Amsterdam had been governed by four Burgomasters (mayors) and a council representing citizens' interests. By 1500, though, city government had become an incestuous business: the city council's 36 members were appointed for life, 'electing' the mayors from their own ranks. Selective intermarriage meant that the city was, in effect, governed by a handful of families.

When Amsterdam joined the rebels in 1578, the only change in civic administration was that the Catholic elite were replaced by a Calvinist faction of equally wealthy families. The city, now with a population of 225,000, remained the third city of Europe, after London and Paris. Social welfare, though, was transformed under the Calvinists, and incorporated into government. The Regents, as the Calvinist elite became known, took over the convents and monasteries, starting charitable organisations such as orphanages. But they would not tolerate any kind of excess: drunkenness and immorality, like crime, were punishable offences.

In the two centuries before the Eighty Years' War, Amsterdam had developed its own powerful maritime force. Even so, it remained overshadowed by Antwerp until 1589, when that city fell to the Spaniards. In Belgium, the Habsburg Spanish had adopted siege tactics, leaving Amsterdam unaffected by the hostilities and free to benefit from the blockades suffered by rival ports. Thousands of refugees fled north, among them some of Antwerp's most prosperous merchants, who were mostly Protestant and Jewish (specifically Sephardic Jews who had earlier fled their original homes in Spain and Portugal to escape the Inquisition). The refugees brought the skills, the gold and, most famously, the diamond industry that would soon help make the city one of the greatest trading centres in the world.

THE GOLDEN AGE

European history seems to be littered with golden ages – but in Amsterdam's case, the first six decades of the 17th century genuinely deserve the label. It is truly remarkable that such a small and isolated city could come to dominate world trade and set up major colonies, resulting in a local population explosion and a frenzy of urban expansion. Its girdle of canals was one of the great engineering feats of the age. This all happened while the country was at war with Spain and presided over not by kings, but businessmen.

The Dutch East India Company, which was known locally as the VOC (Verenigde Oost Indische Compagnie), was the world's first transnational corporation. Created by the States General charter in 1602 to finance the wildly expensive and fearsomely dangerous voyages to the East, the power of the VOC was far-reaching: it had the capacity to found colonies, establish its own army, declare war and sign treaties. With 1,450 ships, the VOC made over 4,700 highly profitable journeys.

While the VOC concentrated on the spice trade, a new company received its charter from the Dutch Republic in 1621. The Dutch West India Company (West Indische Compagnie), while not as successful as its sister, dominated trade with Spanish and Portuguese territories in Africa and America, and in 1623 began to colonise Manhattan Island. Although the colony flourished at first, New Amsterdam didn't last long. After the Duke of York's invasion in 1664, the peace treaty between England and the Netherlands determined that New Amsterdam would change its name to New York and come under British control. The Dutch got Suriname in return.

Meanwhile, Amsterdam's port had become the major European centre for distribution and trade. Grain from Russia, Poland and Prussia, salt and wine from France, cloth from Leiden and tiles from Delft all passed through the port. Whales were hunted by Amsterdam's fleets, generating a thriving soap trade, and sugar and spices from Dutch colonies were distributed throughout Scandinavia and the north of Europe. All this activity was financed by the Bank of Amsterdam, which became the hub of the single most powerful money vault in all Europe, its notes exchangeable throughout the trading world.

PRESENT AND CORRECTED

From 1600 to 1650, the city's population ballooned four-fold, and it was obliged to expand once again. Construction on the most elegant of the major canals circling the city centre, Herengracht (Lords' Canal), began in 1613; this was where many of the ruling assembly had their homes. So that there would be no misunderstanding about status, Herengracht was followed further out by Keizersgracht (Emperors' Canal) and Prinsengracht (Princes' Canal). Immigrants were housed in the Jordaan.

For all its wealth, famine hit Amsterdam regularly in the 17th century. Guilds had benevolent funds for their members in times of need, but social welfare was primarily in the hands of the ruling merchant class. Amsterdam's elite was noted for its philanthropy, but only the 'deserving poor' were eligible for assistance. Those seen as undeserving were sent to houses of correction. The initial philosophy behind these had been idealistic: hard work would produce useful citizens. Soon, however, the institutions became little more than prisons for those condemned to work there.

Religious freedom wasn't what it might have been, either. As a result of the Alteration of 1578, open Catholic worship was banned in the city during the 17th century, and Catholics had to worship in secret. Some started attic churches, which are exactly what their name suggests; of those set up during the 1600s, only Our Lord in the Attic (*see p64*) survives in its entirety.

THE HARDER THEY FALL

Though Amsterdam remained one of the single wealthiest cities in Europe until the early 19th century, its dominant trading position was lost to England and France after 1660. The United Provinces then spent a couple of centuries bickering about trade and politics with Britain and the other main powers. Wars were frequent: major sea conflicts included battles against the Swedes and no fewer than four Anglo-Dutch wars, in which the Dutch came off worse. It wasn't that they didn't win any battles; more that they ran out of men and money. The naval officers who led the wars against Britain are Dutch heroes, and the Nieuwe Kerk has monuments to admirals Van

Kinsbergen (1735-1819), Bentinck (1745-1831) and, most celebrated of all, Michiel de Ruyter (1607-76).

In the 18th century, the Dutch Republic began to lag behind the major European powers. Amsterdam was nudged out of the shipbuilding market by England, and its lucrative textile industry was lost to other provinces. However, the city managed to exploit its position as the financial centre of the world until the final, devastating Anglo-Dutch War (1780-84). The British hammered the Dutch merchant and naval fleets with unremitting aggression, crippling profitable trade with their Far Eastern colonies.

THE NAPOLEONIC NETHERLANDS

During the 1780s, a republican movement known as the Patriots managed to shake off the influence of the Stadhouders in many smaller towns. In 1787, though, they were foiled in Amsterdam by the intervention of the Prince of Orange and his brother-in-law, Frederick William II, King of Prussia. Hundreds of Patriots then fled to exile in France, only to return in 1795, backed by a French army of 'advisers'. With massive support from Amsterdam, they thus celebrated the new Batavian Republic.

It sounded too good to be true, and it was. According to one contemporary, 'the French moved over the land like locusts.' Over 100 million guilders (about €50 million today) was extracted from the Dutch, and the French also sent an army, 25,000 of whom had to be fed, equipped and housed by their Dutch 'hosts'. Republican ideals seemed hollow when Napoleon installed his brother, Louis, as King of the Netherlands in 1806, and the symbol of Amsterdam's mercantile ascendancy and civic pride, the City Hall of the Dam, was requisitioned as the royal palace. However, after Louis had allowed Dutch smugglers to break Napoleon's blockade of Britain, he was forced to abdicate in 1810 and the Low Countries were absorbed into the French Empire.

French rule wasn't an unmitigated disaster for the Dutch. The foundations of the modern state were laid in the Napoleonic period, and a civil code introduced – not to mention a broadening of culinary possibilities. However, trade with Britain ceased, and the cost of Napoleon's wars prompted the Dutch to join

IN CONTEXT

IMMIGRATION MATTERS

The Netherlands is no longer as tolerant as it once was.

Historically, the Netherlands has been a haven for minorities and refugees fleeing persecution in their own countries, from Spanish and Portuguese Jews in the 16th century and the Huguenots in the 18th century to the Belgians during World War I and Hungarians after the 1956 revolution. Freedom of religion was accepted at an early stage in Dutch history, and laid down in the constitution of 1848, and there was never much tension between the Dutch and the communities of newcomers, which were always relatively small.

The situation changed, however, in the second half of the 20th century. After the Netherlands was forced to give up its colonies in the Dutch East Indies, 300,000 Indonesians came to the former motherland, followed, in the 1960s, by tens of thousands of labour migrants from Turkey and Morocco. The next wave of 300,000 foreigners came in the 1970s when another colony, Suriname, in South America, gained independence. Dutch passport-holders from the Netherlands Antilles and refugees from all over the world have also contributed to a serious shake-up of the demographic landscape, which had been pale white for centuries.

Initially, nothing much happened. The predominantly Christian Surinamese and Indonesians spoke Dutch, something the Muslim migrant workers from the Mediterranean countries did not. Not much attention was given to their language skills, because the idea was they would go home after a couple of years. But they didn't. They stayed, brought their families, and now, in 2014, this secularising nation of almost 17 million is faced with a million Muslims it finds rather difficult to deal with.

Until the 1990s, the Netherlands still had a great reputation for being a tolerant country. Meanwhile, an ever-growing number of non-Western immigrants and their offspring, badly educated and with low incomes, often on social welfare, were living in dilapidated apartment buildings in areas such as the Bijlmer (recently rebranded as Zuidoost), where crime rates were high and the future looked bleak.

Society chose to ignore the problem until Pim Fortuyn – a genuine populist politician, who made no secret of his anti-Islam feelings – made his voice heard. His assassination in 2002 shocked the nation. It wasn't a Muslim extremist who pulled the trigger, though, but a left-wing one. However, the next bullet did come from an Islamic extremist. In November 2004, Mohammed Bouyeri murdered provocative columnist and filmmaker Theo van Gogh, a big supporter of Fortuyn. For a while, everything seemed to change. Fortuyn's political allies even made it to the coalition government before the movement crumbled, through internal conflicts and empty-headedness.

The bleached blond and virulently anti-Islam Geert Wilders and his Freedom Party (PVV) stepped in to fill the void. In 2010, his party shot from nine to 24 seats, which gave him leverage to push through tougher immigration laws. Currently sidelined but still popular, Wilders has added EU bureaucracy to Islam as the two elements that are wrong with the Netherlands.

the revolt against France. After Napoleon's defeat, Amsterdam became the capital of a constitutional monarchy, including what is now Belgium; William VI of Orange was crowned King William I in 1815. But while the Oranges still reigned across the north, the United Kingdom of the Netherlands, as it then existed, lasted only until 1830.

A RETURN TO FORM

When the French were finally defeated and left Dutch soil in 1813, Amsterdam emerged as the capital of the new kingdom of the Netherlands but very little else. With its coffers depleted and colonies occupied by the British, it faced a hard fight for recovery.

The fight was made tougher by two huge obstacles. For a start, Dutch colonial assets had been reduced to present-day Indonesia, Suriname and the odd Caribbean island. Just as important, though, was the fact that the Dutch were slow to join the Industrial Revolution. The Netherlands had few natural resources to exploit, and business preferred sail power to steam. Add to this the fact that Amsterdam's opening to the sea, the Zuider Zee, was too shallow for new steamships, and it's easy to see why the Dutch struggled.

Still, by the late 19th century Amsterdam had begun to modernise production of the luxury goods for which it would become internationally famous: beer, chocolates, cigars and diamonds. The Noordzee Kanaal (North Sea Canal) was opened in 1876, while the city got a major rail link in 1889. Amsterdam consolidated its position at the forefront of Europe with the building of a number of landmarks, including Cuypers' Rijksmuseum (1885), the Stadsschouwburg (1894), the Stedelijk Museum (1895) and the Tropeninstituut (1926). The city's international standing soared – to the point where, in 1928, it hosted the Olympics.

MISERY OF THE MASSES

Amsterdam's population had stagnated at 250,000 for two centuries after the Golden Age, but between 1850 and 1900 it more than doubled. Extra labour was needed to fuel the revitalised economy, but the problem was how to house the new workers.

Today, the old inner-city quarters are desirable addresses, but they used to house Amsterdam's poor. The picturesque Jordaan, where regular riots broke out at the turn of the century, was occupied by the lowest-paid workers. Its canals were used as cesspits, and the mortality rate was high. Around the centre, new developments – De Pijp, Dapper and Staatslieden – were built: they weren't luxurious, but they enjoyed simple lavatory facilities, while the Amsterdam School of architects (see p251 **School of Rock**), inspired by socialist beliefs, designed now-classic housing for the poor. Wealthier citizens, meanwhile, lived in elegant homes near Vondelpark and further south.

The city didn't fare badly during the first two decades of the 20th century, but Dutch neutrality in World War I brought problems to parts of the population. While the elite lined their pockets selling arms, the poor faced crippling food shortages and unemployment, and riots broke out in 1917 and 1934. Many Dutch workers moved to Germany, where National Socialism was creating jobs. The city was just emerging from the Depression when the Nazis invaded in May 1940.

OCCUPATION

On 10 May 1940, German bombers mounted a surprise early-morning attack on Dutch airfields and barracks. The government and people had hoped that the Netherlands could remain neutral, as in World War I, so armed forces were unprepared. Queen Wilhelmina fled to London to form a government in exile, leaving Supreme Commander Winkelman in charge. After Rotterdam was destroyed by bombing and the Germans threatened other cities with the same treatment, Winkelman surrendered on 14 May.

During the war, Hitler appointed Austrian Nazi Arthur Seyss-Inquart as Rijkskommissaris (State Commissioner) of the Netherlands, and asked him to tie the Dutch economy to the German one and help to Nazify Dutch society. Though it gained less than five per cent of the votes in the 1939 elections, the National Socialist Movement (NSB) was the only Dutch party not prohibited during the occupation. Its doctrine resembled German Nazism, but the NSB wanted to maintain Dutch autonomy under the direction of Germany.

During the first years of the war, the Nazis let most people live relatively unmolested. Rationing, though, made the Dutch vulnerable

IN CONTEXT

IN CONTEXT

to the black market, while cinemas and theatres eventually closed because of curfews and censorship. Later, the Nazis adopted more aggressive measures: Dutch men were forced to work in German industry, and economic exploitation assumed appalling forms. In April 1943, all Dutch soldiers were ordered to give themselves up as prisoners of war. Within an atmosphere of deep shock and outrage, strikes broke out, but were violently suppressed.

As Nazi policies became more virulent, people were confronted with the difficult choice of whether to obey German measures or to resist. There were several patterns of collaboration: some people joined the NSB, while others intimidated Jews, got involved in economic collaboration or betrayed people in hiding. The most shocking institutional collaboration involved Dutch police, who dragged Jews out of their houses for deportation, and Dutch Railways, which was paid for transporting Jews to their deaths.

Others resisted. The Resistance was made up chiefly of Communists and, to a lesser extent, Calvinists. Anti-Nazi activities took various forms, including the production and distribution of illegal newspapers, which kept the population informed and urged them to resist the Nazi dictators. Some members of the Resistance spied for the Allies, while some fought an armed struggle against the Germans through assassination and sabotage. There were those who falsified identity cards and food vouchers, while others helped Jews into hiding. By 1945, more than 300,000 people had gone underground in the Netherlands.

THE HUNGER WINTER
In 1944, the Netherlands plunged into the Hongerwinter – the Hunger Winter. Supplies of coal vanished after the liberation of the south, and a railway strike, called by the Dutch government in exile in order to hasten German defeat, was disastrous for the supply of food. In retaliation, the Germans damaged Schiphol Airport and the harbours of Rotterdam and Amsterdam, foiling any attempts to bring in supplies, and grabbed everything they could. Walking became the only means of transport, domestic refuse was no longer collected, sewers overflowed and the population fell to disease.

To survive, people stole fuel: more than 20,000 trees were cut down and 4,600 buildings demolished. Floors, staircases, joists and rafters were plundered, causing the collapse of many houses, particularly those left by deported Jews. By the end of the winter, 20,000 people had died of starvation and disease, and much of the city was badly damaged. But hope was around the corner. The Allies liberated the south of the Netherlands on 5 September 1944, Dolle Dinsdag (Mad Tuesday), and complete liberation came on 5 May 1945, when it became apparent that the Netherlands was the worst-hit country in western Europe.

Amsterdam endured World War II without being flattened by bombs, but nonetheless its buildings, infrastructure, inhabitants and morale were reduced to a terrible state by the occupying Nazi forces. The Holocaust also left an indelible scar on a city whose population in 1940 was ten per cent Jewish. Only 5,000 Jews, out of a pre-war Jewish population of 80,000, remained. When the war was over, 450,000 people were arrested for collaboration, although most were quickly released; mitigating circumstances – NSB members who helped the Resistance, for example – made judgements complicated. Of 14,500 sentenced, only 39 were executed.

THE HOLOCAUST
'I see how the world is slowly becoming a desert, I hear more and more clearly the approaching thunder that will kill us,' wrote Anne Frank in her diary on 15 July 1944. Though her words obviously applied to the Jews, they were relevant to all those who were persecuted during the war. Granted, anti-Semitism in Holland had not been as virulent as in Germany, France or Austria. But even so, most – though not all – of the Dutch population ignored the persecution, and there's still a sense of national guilt.

The Holocaust happened in three stages. First came measures to enforce the isolation of the Jews: the ritual slaughter of animals was prohibited, Jewish government employees were dismissed, Jews were banned from public places and, eventually, all Jews were forced to wear a yellow Star of David. (Some non-Jews wore the badge as a mark of solidarity.) Concentration was the second stage. From early 1942, all Dutch

Jews were obliged to move to three areas in Amsterdam, isolated by signs, drawbridges and barbed wire. The final stage was deportation. Between July 1942 and September 1943, most of the 140,000 Dutch Jews were deported via the detention and transit camp of Kamp Westerbork. Public outrage at deportations was foreshadowed by the one and only protest, organised by dockworkers, against the anti-Semitic terror: the February Strike of 1941.

The Nazis wanted to eliminate Gypsies too: more than 200,000 European Gypsies, including many Dutch, were exterminated. Homosexuals were also threatened with extermination, but their persecution was less systematic: public morality acts prohibited homosexual behaviour, and gay pressure groups ceased their activities. Amsterdam has the world's first memorial to persecuted gays, the Homomonument (*see p180*), which incorporates pink triangles, turning the Nazi badge of persecution into a symbol of pride.

THE DUST SETTLES

Despite deep poverty and drastic shortages of food, fuel and building materials, the Dutch tackled the task of post-war recovery with a sense of optimism. Some Dutch flirted briefly with Communism after the war, but in 1948, a compromise was agreed between the Catholic KVP and newly created Labour party PvdA, and the two proceeded to govern in successive coalitions until 1958. Led by Prime Minister Willem Drees, the government resuscitated social programmes and laid the basis for a welfare state. The Dutch now reverted to the virtues of a conservative society: decency, hard work and thrift.

The country's first priority was economic recovery. The city council concentrated on reviving the two motors of its economy: Schiphol Airport and the Port of Amsterdam, the latter boosted by the opening of the Amsterdam-Rhine Canal in 1952. Joining Belgium and Luxembourg in the Benelux also brought the country trade benefits, and the Netherlands was the first European nation to repay its Marshall Plan loans. The authorities dusted off their pre-war development plans and embarked on rapid urban expansion. But as people moved into the new suburbs, businesses flowed into the centre, making congestion worse on the cramped roads.

After the war, the Dutch colonies of New Guinea and Indonesia were liberated from the Japanese and pushed for independence. Immigrants to the Netherlands included colonial natives, and Turkish and Moroccan 'guest workers'.

THE PROVOS

The 1960s proved to be one of the most colourful decades in Amsterdam's history. Popular movements very similar to those in other west European cities were formed, but because the Dutch have a habit of keeping things in proportion, popular demonstrations took a playful form.

Discontent gained focus in 1964, when a group of political pranksters called the Provos kickstarted a new radical subculture. Founded by anarchist philosophy student Roel van Duyn and 'anti-smoke magician' Robert Jasper Grootveld, the Provos – their name inspired by their game plan: to provoke – numbered only about two dozen, but were enormously influential. Their style influenced the major anti-Vietnam demos in the US and the Situationist antics in 1969 Paris, and set the tone for Amsterdam's love of liberal politics and absurdist theatre. Their finest hour came in March 1966, when protests about Princess Beatrix's controversial wedding to the German Claus van Amsberg

The Hunger Winter.

GOING WITH THE FLOW

Only by understanding water will you understand Amsterdam.

IN CONTEXT

Farmers, beer and water. An unlikely recipe for success, but they made Amsterdam what it is today. Not that the city's rise was universally greeted with delight. In 1652, during one of those periodic downturns in Anglo-Dutch relations, English poet Owen Felltham described the Low Countries as 'the buttock of the world, full of veins and blood but no bones.' But it's that boggy basis that is the foundation of Amsterdam's success and go-with-the-flow reputation.

Originating as a village that subsisted on a bit of fishing and some small-town frolicking, Amsterdam fostered some of the first cheerleaders of democracy: stubborn farmers, who set themselves to build dykes to keep the sea and the mighty Amstel river at bay. The teamwork needed for such a massive task formed the basis for today's famed but seemingly fading 'polder model', where all conflicts are resolved at endless meetings fuelled by coffee and the thirst for consensus. Of course, since flexibility and compromise also made good business sense, the approach turned out to be highly profitable (*see p238* **Immigration Matters**).

Amsterdam was only properly set up as a centre of pragmatic trade and lusty sin in the 14th century, when it was made exempt from the tax on beer. This opened the floodgates to a river of the stuff (flowing from Hamburg) and plenty of beer-drinking new settlers. After beer profits, other profits followed – from sea travels to both the East and the West – and before long Amsterdam was the richest and most powerful port on the planet. The resulting Golden Age saw the construction of the image-defining *grachtengordel* 'canal belt', which, together with the more ancient canals of the Old Centre, formed a full circulatory system – and, er, sewage system – in which goods, and people, from all over the world could flow in and out.

As well as demonstrating a flair for building canals, dykes, windmills and ships, the Dutch came up with a whole bevy of other water-worthy inventions during the

Golden Age. Inventor Cornelis Drebbel (1572-1634) designed the first prototype submarine (basically, a rowing boat fitted with rawhide and tubes), and local genius Jan van der Heyden (1637-1712) invented the first pump-action fire hose. More curious were the 'Tobacco-Smoke-Enema-Applicators', developed in an attempt to reanimate the drowning victims who were regularly pulled from the canals. This ancient technique – also applied with reversed 30-centimetre (12-inch) Gouda pipes – was standard practice and all part of the canalside scenery in Amsterdam until the 1850s, when the less dramatic but more effective mouth-to-mouth technique gained prominence. Talk about progress.

Development at the end of the 19th century allowed the building of the North Sea Channel, thus giving Amsterdam a more direct route to the open sea and triggering a second Golden Age of sorts. The 1990s can be seen in a similar light, when the Eastern Docklands began transforming into a showcase for modern architecture that sought to blend both private and public spaces with its watery surrounds. The artificial islands of IJburg further east continue this trend, as do ambitious plans to build vast windmill parks in the North Sea and create a floating runway for Schiphol Airport. While acceptance of this last idea is still far off, it's not as ridiculous as it sounds: Schiphol itself used to be five metres (16 feet) under water.

That water is of national importance in a country where two-thirds of the land is reclaimed was shown a few years ago. When King Willem-Alexander was still Crown Prince, he decided to slough off his image as a doltish young man and embrace water as a personal crusade. 'Water is beautiful. It's essential to life. It's about health, environment and transport. There's the fight against water and the fight against too little water. You can actually do everything with it, and it's primordially Dutch.' Anything you say, Crown Prince...

Amsterdam Port, 1928.

IN CONTEXT

Still, water does play a fundamental role in the recreational lives of many folk – and we're not just talking about boys peeing willy-nilly into the canals (*see p84* **Welcome to Uri-nation**). Admittedly, 'eel-pulling' – a folk game popular in the Jordaan, which the authorities tried to quash, resulting in the Eel Riot of 1886 and 26 fatalities – is no longer practised as a canal sport. But boating remains very popular (sadly, its winter counterpart, ice-skating, has suffered greatly from climate change). The opening of the city's first bona fide beach in IJburg was the news story of summer 2003, and inspired a slew of other urban beaches: Strand West (www.strand-west.nl), Strand Zuid (www.strand-zuid.nl) beside the RAI convention centre, and hipster paradise Roest (*see p156*).

And while the concept of making Prinsengracht swimmable remains a ploy by fringe political parties to get headline space, a more realistic plan – to redig canals that had been concreted over to cope with motor traffic, such as Elandsgracht and Lindengracht – was all set to go ahead until it was quashed by residents, who decided that since the city is already one-quarter water they didn't need any more of the stuff.

Regardless, Amsterdam remains aware that water is one of its strongest tourist magnets. Compared to the original Venice (aka the 'sewer of the south'), the waters of the 'Venice of the North' are essentially stench-free. And now that Amsterdam has its own gondola service (www.gondel.nl), there's really no competition. In fact, here you can meditate on the wiggly reflections in the canals from up close without fear of succumbing to fumes. Not merely trippy, they act as a constant reminder that Amsterdam is a happily twisted and distorted town – and also remarkably user-friendly; where you can throw your cares overboard and go with the flow. Just don't take that last part too literally.

turned nasty after the Provos let off a smoke bomb on the carriage route, and a riot ensued. Some Provos, such as Van Duyn, went on to fight the system from within: five won City seats under the surreal banner of the Kabouter (a mythical race of forest-dwelling dwarves) in 1970.

SQUATTERS

Perhaps the single most significant catalyst for discontent in the 1970s – which exploded into civil conflict by the '80s – was the issue of housing. Amsterdam's small size and historic centre had always been a nightmare for its urban planners. The city's population increased in the '60s, reaching its peak (nearly 870,000) by 1964. Swelling the numbers further were immigrants from the Netherlands' last major colony, Suriname, many of whom were dumped in Bijlmermeer. The district degenerated into a ghetto and, when a 747 crashed there in October 1992, the final number of fatalities was impossible to ascertain: many victims were unregistered. The metro link to Bijlmermeer is in itself a reminder of some of Amsterdam's most violent protests. Passionate opposition erupted against the proposed clearance in February 1975 of the Jewish quarter of Nieuwmarkt. Civil unrest culminated in 'Blue Monday' (24 March 1975) when police sparked clashes with residents and supporters. Police fired tear gas into the homes of those who refused to move out, and battered down doors.

Speculators who left property empty caused acute resentment, which soon turned into direct action: vacant buildings were occupied illegally by squatters. In March 1980, police turned against them for the first time and used tanks to evict squatters from a former office building in Vondelstraat. Riots ensued, but the squatters were victorious. In 1982, as the squatting movement reached its peak, clashes with police escalated: a state of emergency was called after one eviction battle. Soon, though, the city – led by new mayor Ed van Thijn – had gained the upper hand over the movement, and one of the last of the big squats, Wyers, fell amid tear gas in February 1984 to make way for a Holiday Inn. Squatters were no longer a force to be reckoned with, though their ideas of small-scale regeneration have since been absorbed into official planning.

THE SHAPE OF THINGS TO COME

Born and bred in Amsterdam, Ed van Thijn embodied a new strand in Dutch politics. Though a socialist, he took tough action against 'unsavoury elements' – petty criminals, squatters, dealers in hard drugs – and upgraded facilities to attract new businesses and tourists. A new national political era also emerged: the welfare system and government subsidies were trimmed to ease the country's large budget deficit, and more businesslike policies were introduced to try and revitalise the economy.

The price of Amsterdam's new affluence has been a swing towards commercialism. Flashy cafés, galleries and restaurants replaced the alternative scene, and a mood of calm settled on the city. Still, a classic example of Dutch compromise is the development of 'breeding grounds of the arts', which are basically unused buildings that are handed over to artists and other creative types to do with what they will – for a couple of years at a time.

During the recent economic downturn, the main advantages of nurturing Amsterdam's reputation as a hotbed for edgy creativity became more apparent – proving it isn't ready to relinquish its rebel status just yet.

Protestors demonstrate about squatting rights in 1980.

KEY EVENTS
All the Dutch dates that matter.

EARLY HISTORY

1204 Gijsbrecht van Amstel builds a castle in the area that will eventually become the city of Amsterdam.

1270 Amstel dammed at Dam Square.

1300 Amsterdam is granted city rights by the Bishop of Utrecht.

1306 Work begins on the Oude Kerk.

1313 The Bishop of Utrecht grants Aemstelledamme full municipal rights and leaves it to William III of Holland.

1421 The St Elizabeth's Day Flood; Amsterdam's first great fire.

WAR AND REFORMATION

1534 Anabaptists try to seize City Hall but fail. A sustained and brutal period of anti-Protestant repression begins.

1565 William the Silent organises a Protestant revolt against Spanish rule.

1566 Iconoclastic Fury unleashed. Protestant worship is made legal.

1568 Eighty Years' War with Spain begins.

1577 Prince of Orange annexes city.

1578 Catholic Burgomasters replaced by Protestants in the Alteration.

1579 The Union of Utrecht is signed, allowing freedom of religious belief.

THE GOLDEN AGE

1602 The Dutch East India Company (VOC) is founded.

1606 Rembrandt van Rijn is born.

1611 The Zuiderkerk is completed.

1613 Work starts on the Canal Belt.

1623 The Dutch West India Company colonises Manhattan Island.

1625 Peter Stuyvesant founds New Amsterdam.

1642 Rembrandt finishes *The Night Watch*.

1648 The Treaty of Munster is signed, ending Eighty Years' War with Spain.

1654 England begins a bloody, drawn-out war against the United Provinces.

1667 England and the Netherlands sign the Peace of Breda.

DECLINE AND FALL

1672 England and the Netherlands go to war; Louis XIV of France invades.

1675 Portuguese Synagogue is built.

1685 French Protestants take refuge after revocation of the Edict of Nantes.

1689 William of Orange becomes King William III of England.

1787 Frederick William II, King of Prussia, occupies Amsterdam.

1795 French revolutionaries set up the Batavian Republic.

1813 Unification of the Netherlands.

1815 Amsterdam becomes the capital.

BETWEEN THE OCCUPATIONS

1848 City's ramparts are pulled down.

1876 Noordzee Kanaal links Amsterdam with the North Sea.

1885 The Rijksmuseum is completed.

1889 Centraal Station opens.

1922 Women are granted the vote.

1928 Olympic Games are held in Amsterdam.

WORLD WAR II

1940 German troops invade.

1941 The February Strike, in protest against the deportation of Jews.

1944-45 20,000 people die in the Hunger Winter.

1945 Canadian soldiers liberate Amsterdam.

1947 Anne Frank's diary is published.

THE POST-WAR ERA

1966 The wedding of Princess Beatrix and Prince Claus ends in riots.

1968 The IJ Tunnel opens.

1976 Cannabis is decriminalised.

1977 First Metro line is opened.

1980 Queen Beatrix's coronation.

1997 The Euro approved as European currency in the Treaty of Amsterdam.

1999 Prostitution is made legal after years of decriminalisation.

2002 Dutch politician Pim Fortuyn is murdered.

2004 Filmmaker Theo van Gogh is murdered by an Islamic fundamentalist.

2007 'Project 1012' clean-up begins.

2009 Bystanders killed in assassination attempt on the Dutch royal family.

2013 Reopening of Rijksmuseum.

IN CONTEXT

Architecture

A 17th-century skyline in transition.

TEXT: STEVE KORVER

For the last several years, Amsterdam might have done well by its visitors to post signs reading, 'Please pardon our appearance while we are undergoing renovations.' But slowly, all the construction is rounding off, with the completion of the Stedelijk Museum (2012) and Rijksmuseum (2013). Only Centraal Station and the central transit thoroughfares down Damrak and into De Pijp where the new Metro line is currently being installed are still causing disruption. It's a pity that the municipal powers-that-be didn't put their heads together to co-ordinate this chaos rather better...

In spite of what might appear to be a lot of change, the 17th-century skyline in the centre of Amsterdam isn't likely to alter any time soon. In 2010, the city's famous canal district, or *grachtengordel*, was named a UNESCO World Heritage Site, and as such is protected against development. The once-ignored Amsterdam Noord, meanwhile, is quickly reinventing itself with the new EYE Film Institute as its compelling centrepiece, luring visitors via the free ferry from behind Centraal Station.

THE VIEW FROM AFAR

'The colours are strong and sad, the forms symmetric, the façades kept new,' wrote Eugène Fromentin, the noted 19th-century art critic, of Amsterdam. 'We feel that it belongs to a people eager to take possession of the conquered mud.'

The treacherous, blubbery soil on which the merchants' town of Amsterdam is built meant that most attempts at monumental display were destined soon to return to their original element. It's this unforgiving land, combined with the Protestant restraint that characterised the city's early developments and the fact that there were no royals out to project monstrous egos, that have ensured Amsterdam's architectural highlights are often practical places like warehouses, homes, the stock exchange and former city hall, rather than overblown palaces and castles.

Amsterdam's architectural epochs have followed the pulse of the city's prosperity. The highly decorative façades of wealthy 17th- and 18th-century merchant houses still line canals. A splurge of public spending in the affluent 1880s gave the city two of its most notable landmarks – **Centraal Station** and the **Rijksmuseum**. Rather conversely, social housing projects in the early 20th century stimulated the innovative work of the Amsterdam School, while Amsterdam's late 1980s resurgence as a financial centre and transport hub led to an economic upturn and thickets of ambitious modern architecture on the outskirts of town and along the Eastern Docklands.

Prime viewing time for Amsterdam's architecture is late on a summer's afternoon, when the sun gently picks out the varying colours and the patterns of the brickwork. Then, as twilight falls, the canal houses – most of them more window than wall – light up like strings of lanterns, and you get a glimpse of the beautifully preserved, frequently opulent interiors that lie hidden behind the façades.

UNDERNEATH THE PAVING STONES

Amsterdam is built on reclaimed marshland, with a thick, soft layer of clay and peat beneath the topsoil. About 12 metres (39 feet) down is a hard band of sand, deposited 10,000 years ago during the

Houtenhuis, Begijnhof.

Little Ice Age, and below that, after about five metres of fine sand, is another firm layer, this one left by melting ice after the Great Ice Age. A further 25 metres (82 feet) down, through shell-filled clay and past the bones of mammoths, is a third hard layer, deposited by glaciers over 180,000 years ago.

The first Amsterdammers built their homes on muddy mounds, making the foundations from tightly packed peat. Later on, they dug trenches, filled them with fascines (thin, upright alder trunks) and built on those. And yet still the fruits of their labours sank slowly into the swamp. By the 17th century, builders were using longer underground posts and were rewarded with more stable structures, but it wasn't until around 1700 that piles were driven deep enough to hit the first hard sand layer.

The method of constructing foundations that subsequently developed has remained more or less the same ever since, though nowadays most piles reach the second sand level and some make the full 50-metre (164-foot) journey to the third hard layer. To begin, a double row of piles is sunk along the line of a proposed wall (since World War II, concrete has been used instead of wood).

Then, a crossbeam is laid across each pair of posts, planks are fastened longitudinally on to the beams, and the wall is built on top. Occasionally, piles break or rot, which is why Amsterdam is full of old buildings that teeter precariously over the street, tilt lopsidedly or prop each other up in higgledy-piggledy rows.

TRIALS BY FIRE

Early constructions in Amsterdam were timber-framed, built mainly from oak with roofs of rushes or straw. Wooden houses were relatively light and therefore less likely to sink into the mire, but after two devastating fires (in 1421 and 1452), the authorities began stipulating that outer walls be built of brick, though wooden front gables were still permitted. In a bid to blend in, the first brick gables were shaped in imitation of their spout-shaped wooden predecessors.

But regulations were hardly necessary, for Amsterdammers took to their brick with relish. Granted, some grander 17th-century buildings were built of sandstone, while plastered façades were first seen a century later and reinforced concrete made its inevitable inroads in the 20th century. But Amsterdam is still essentially a city of brick: red brick from Leiden, yellow from Utrecht and grey from Gouda, all laid in curious formations and arranged in complicated patterns. Local architects' attachment to – and flair with – brick reached a zenith in the highly fantastical, billowing façades designed by the Amsterdam School early in the 20th century.

FORCE AND REINFORCEMENT

Only two wooden buildings remain in central Amsterdam: one (built in 1460) in the quiet courtyard of the **Begijnhof** (no.34, known as the Houtenhuis; *see p75*), and the other on Zeedijk. The latter, **In't Aepjen** (Zeedijk 1; *see p60*), was built in the 16th century as a lodging house, getting its name from the monkeys that impecunious sailors used to leave behind as payment. Though the ground floor dates from the 19th century, the upper floors provide a clear example of how, in medieval times, each wooden storey protruded a little beyond the one below it, allowing rainwater to drip on to the street rather than run back into the body of the building. Early brick gables had to be built

'Amsterdam is still essentially a city of brick: red brick from Leiden, yellow from Utrecht and grey from Gouda.'

at an angle over the street for the same reason, though it also allowed objects to be winched to the top floors without crashing against the windows of the lower ones.

Amsterdam's oldest building, however, is the **Oude Kerk** (Old Church, Oude Kerksplein 23; *see p64*). It was begun in 1300, though only the base of the tower dates from then: over the ensuing 300 years, the church, once having the simplest of forms, developed a barnacle crust of additional buildings, mostly in a Renaissance style with a few Gothic additions. The finest Gothic building in town is the **Nieuwe Kerk** (at Dam and Nieuwezijds Voorburgwal; *see p79*), still called the 'New Church' even though work on it began at the end of the 14th century.

When gunpowder first arrived in Europe in the 15th century, Amsterdammers realised that the wooden palisade that surrounded their settlement would offer scant defence, and so set about building a new, stone wall. Watchtowers and gates left over from this wall make up a significant proportion of the city's surviving pre-17th-century architecture, though most have been altered over the years. The **Schreierstoren** (Prins Hendrikkade 94-95; *see p60*) of 1480, however, has kept its original shape, with the addition of doors, windows and a pixie-hat roof. The base of the **Munttoren** (Muntplein; *see p76*) originally formed part of the Regulierspoort, a city gate built in 1490. Another city gate from the previous decade, the St Antoniespoort (Nieuwmarkt 4;), was converted into a public weighhouse, **De Waag** (*photo p250*), in 1617, then further refashioned to become a guild house and finally a café-restaurant. It remains one of Amsterdam's most menacing monuments – *see p77* **Nieuwmarkt**.

IN CONTEXT

De Waag. *See p249.*

CALL OF THE CLASSICAL

A favourite 16th-century amendment to these somewhat stolid defence towers was the later addition of a sprightly steeple. Hendrick de Keyser (1565-1621) delighted in designing such spires, and it is largely his work that gives Amsterdam's present skyline a faintly oriental appearance. He added a lantern-shaped tower with an openwork orb to the Munttoren, and a spire that resembled the Oude Kerk steeple to the **Montelbaanstoren** (Oudeschans 2), a sea-defence tower that had been built outside the city wall. His **Zuiderkerk** (Zuiderkerkhof 72; *see p142*), built in 1603, sports a spire said to have been much admired by Christopher Wren.

De Keyser's appointment as city mason and sculptor in 1595 gave him free rein, and his buildings represent the pinnacle of the Dutch Renaissance style (also known as Dutch Mannerist) – perhaps the greatest being the **Westerkerk** (Prinsengracht 279; *see p93*), completed in 1631 as the single biggest Protestant church in the world. Since the very beginning of the 17th century, Dutch architects had been gleaning inspiration from translations of Italian pattern books, adding lavish ornament to the classical system of proportion they found there. Brick façades were decorated with stone strapwork (scrolls and curls derived from picture frames and leatherwork). Walls were built with

'Before house numbers appeared in the 18th century, ornate gables and wall plaques were a means of identifying addresses.'

alternating layers of red brick and white sandstone, a style that came to be called 'bacon coursing'. The old spout-shaped gables were also replaced with cascading step-gables, often embellished with vases, escutcheons and masks. There was also a practical use for these adornments: before house numbers were introduced in Amsterdam in the 18th century, ornate gables and wall plaques were a means of identifying addresses.

The façade of the **Vergulde Dolphijn** (Singel 140-142), designed by De Keyser in 1600 for Captain Banning Cocq (the commander of Rembrandt's *The Night Watch*), is a lively mix of red brick and sandstone, while the **Gecroonde Raep** (Oudezijds Voorburgwal 57) has a neat

IN CONTEXT

SCHOOL OF ROCK

The influential Amsterdam School movement.

Characterised by its (often rounded) brick constructions and intricate detailing, the Amsterdam School style was used for working-class housing, institutions and schools during the early 20th century. Hendrik Berlage formed the nexus of the movement. Not only did his work reject all the 'neo-'styles that defined most 19th-century Dutch architecture, he also provided the opportunity to experiment with new forms by coming up with the urban development scheme, Plan Zuid.

Although the Amsterdam School was short-lived – it was forced to simplify within a decade when money ran out, and its greatest proponent, Michel de Klerk, died – examples of its work are visible in Spaarndammerbuurt, Rivierenbuurt, Concertgebouwbuurt and the area around Mercantorplein.

Located along the waterfront, the epic **Scheepvaarthuis** (now the Grand Hotel Amrâth Amsterdam, Prins Hendrikkade 108-114; *see p277*) is generally considered to be the school's first work. Completed in 1916, it was created by JM van der Mey, Piet Kramer and De Klerk. Among the hallmarks on show are obsessively complex brickwork, allegorical decorations (reflecting its use as shipping companies' offices), sculptures and seamlessly fused wrought-iron railings.

The Spaarndammerbuurt sports the school's most frolicsome work and remains a huge draw for more dedicated architectural tourists. **Het Schip** (The Ship), as locals call it, takes up the whole block between Zaanstraat, Hembrugstraat and Oostzaanstraat. Completed in 1919, it was commissioned by the Eigen Haard housing association and includes 102 homes and a school. The grand archway at Oostzaan 1-21 leads to the Ship's courtyard and central meeting hall. **Museum Het Schip** (*see p114*), once a post office, is now an exhibition space devoted to the school; it also runs Amsterdam School tours.

Located at the border of De Pijp and Rivierenbuurt is **Plan Zuid**. It is here that socialist housing association De Dageraad (the Dawn) allowed De Klerk and Kramer (together with their favourite sculptor, Hildo Krop) to do their hallucinatory best. Josef Israelkade, Burg Tellegenstraat and the courtyard of Cooperatiehof are its highlights.

Elsewhere in the city (on Waalstraat and Vrijheidslaan, for example), you'll find later, more restrained examples of the school's work. A window seat at **Café Wildschut** (Roelof Hartplein 1-3, 676 8220, cafewildschut.nl) offers spectacular views of a whole range of architectural goodies, including **Huize Lydia** (across the street at no.2), which first served as a home to Catholic girls. Finished in 1927, it stands as one of the very last buildings in which wacky window shapes and odd forms were allowed.

Plan Zuid.

IN CONTEXT

step-gable, with riotous decoration featuring busts, escutcheons, shells, scrolls and volutes. De Keyser's magnificent **Huis Bartolotti** (Herengracht 170-172), a 1617 construction that hugged the canal, is the finest example of the style.

This decorative step-gabled style was to last well into the 17th century. But gradually a stricter use of classical elements came into play; the façade of the Bartolotti house features rows of Ionic pilasters, and it wasn't long before others followed where De Keyser had led. The Italian pattern books that had inspired the Dutch Renaissance were full of the less-ornamented designs of Greek and Roman antiquity. These appealed to many young architects who followed De Keyser, and who were to develop a more restrained, classical style. Many, such as Jacob van Campen (1595-1657), went on study tours of Italy, and returned fired with enthusiasm for the symmetric designs, simple proportions and austerity of Roman architecture. The buildings they constructed during the Golden Age are among the finest Amsterdam has to offer.

THE GOLDEN AGE

The 1600s were a boom time for builders as well as for businessmen. There was no way it could have been otherwise, as Amsterdam's population more than quadrupled during the first half of the century. Grand new canals were constructed, and wealthy merchants lined them with mansions and warehouses. Van Campen, along with fellow architects Philips Vingboons (1607-78) and his younger brother Justus (1620-98), were given the freedom to try out their ideas on a flood of new commissions. Stately façades constructed of sandstone began to appear around the city, but brick remained the most popular material. Philips Vingboons's **Witte Huis** (Herengracht 168) has a white sandstone façade with virtually no decoration: the regular rhythm of the windows is the governing principle of the design. The house he built in 1648 at **Oude Turfmarkt 145** has a brick façade adorned with three tiers of classical pilasters – Tuscan, Ionic and Doric – and festoons that were characteristic of the style. However, the crowning achievement of the period was Amsterdam's boast to the world

of its mercantile supremacy and civic might: namely, the Stadhuis (City Hall) on the Dam, designed by Van Campen in 1648 and now known as the **Koninklijk Paleis** (*see p78*).

There was, however, one fundamental point of conflict between classical architecture and the requirements of northern Europe. For more practical reasons, wet northern climes required steep roofs, yet low Roman pediments and flat cornices looked odd with a steep, pointed roof behind them. The architects solved the problem by adapting the Renaissance gable, with its multiple steps, into a tall, central gable with just two steps. Later, neck-gables were built with just a tall central oblong and no steps. The right angles formed at the base of neck-gables were often filled in with decorative sandstone carvings called claw-pieces.

On very wide houses, it was possible to build a roof parallel to the street rather than end-on, making an attractive backdrop for a classical straight cornice. The giant **Trippenhuis** (Kloveniersburgwal 29, De Wallen), built by Justus Vingboons in 1662, has such a design, with a classical pediment, a frieze of cherubs and arabesques, and eight enormous Corinthian pilasters. It wasn't until the 19th century, when zinc cladding became cheaper, that flat and really low-pitched roofs became feasible.

RESTRAINT VS REFURBISHMENT

Working towards the end of the 17th century, Adriaan Dortsman (1625-82) had been a strong proponent of the straight cornice. His stark designs – such as for the **Van Loon house** at Keizersgracht 672-674 – ushered in a style that came to be known as Restrained Dutch Classicism (or the 'Tight Style', as it would translate directly from the Dutch description: Strakke Stijl). It was a timely entrance. Ornament was costly and, by the beginning of the 18th century, the economic boom was over.

The merchant families were prosperous, but little new building went on. Instead, the families gave their old mansions a facelift or revamped the interiors. A number of 17th-century houses got new sandstone façades (or plastered brick ones, which were cheaper), and French taste – said to have been introduced by Daniel Marot, a French architect based in Amsterdam – became hip.

Oude Turfmarkt.

As the century wore on, ornamentation regained popularity. Gables were festooned with scrolls and acanthus leaves (Louis XIV), embellished with asymmetrical rococo fripperies (Louis XV) or strung with disciplined lines of garlands (Louis XVI). The baroque grandeur of **Keizersgracht 444-446**, for example, is hardly Dutch at all. Straight cornices appeared even on narrow buildings, and became extraordinarily ornate: a distinct advantage, this, as it hid the steep roof that lay behind, with decorative balustrades adding to the deception. The lavish cornice at **Oudezijds Voorburgwal 215-217** stands as a prime example of such construction.

REMIXING MASONRY

Fortunes slumped after 1800, and during the first part of the 19th century more buildings were demolished than constructed. When things picked up after 1860, architects raided past eras for inspiration. Neoclassical, neo-Gothic and neo-Renaissance features were sometimes lumped together in a mix-and-match style. The **Krijtberg Church** (Singel 446) from 1881 has a soaring neo-Gothic façade and a high, vaulted basilica, while the interior of AL van Gendt's **Hollandsche Manege** (Vondelstraat 140; *see p130*), also 1881, combines the classicism of the Spanish Riding School in Vienna with a state-of-the-art iron and glass roof.

In stark contrast, the **Concertgebouw** (Van Baerlestraat 98; *see p203*), a Van

Gendt construction from 1888, borrows from the late Renaissance, while the **City Archive** (Amsteldijk 67), from 1892, is De Keyser revisited. But the period's most adventurous building is the **Adventskerk** (Keizersgracht 676), which has a classical base, Romanesque arches, Lombardian moulding and fake 17th-century lanterns.

The star architect of the period was PJH Cuypers (1827-1921), who landed commissions for both the **Rijksmuseum** (Stadhouderskade 41; *see p130*) of 1877-85 and what would become its near mirror twin on the other side of town, **Centraal Station** (Stationsplein; *see p74*), built 1882-89. Both are in traditional red brick, adorned with Renaissance-style decoration in sandstone and gold leaf. Responding to those who thought his tastes too catholic, Cuypers – while still slipping in some of his excesses later during the construction – decided to organise each building according to a single coherent principle. This became the basis for modern Dutch architecture.

A NEW AGE DAWNS

Brick and wood – good, honest, indigenous materials – appealed to Hendrik Petrus Berlage (1856-1934), as did the possibilities offered by industrial developments in the use of steel and glass. A rationalist, he took Cuypers' ideas a step further in his belief that a building should openly express its basic structure, with a modest amount of ornament in a supportive role. Notable also was the way he collaborated with sculptors, painters and even poets throughout construction. His **Beurs van Berlage** (Beursplein; *see p62*), built between 1898 and 1903 – a mix of clean lines and functional shapes, with the mildest patterning in the brickwork – was startling at the time, and earned him the reputation of being the father of modern Dutch architecture.

Apart from the odd shopfront and some well-designed café interiors, the art nouveau and art deco movements had little direct impact on Amsterdam, though they did draw a few wild flourishes: HL de Jong's **Tuschinski Cinema** (Reguliersbreestraat 26; *see p176*) of 1918-21, for example, is a delightful and seductive piece of high-camp fantasy. Instead, Amsterdam architects developed a style of their own, an mix of art nouveau and Old Dutch using their favourite materials: wood and brick.

A LOCAL MOVEMENT

This movement, known as the **Amsterdam School** (*see p251* **School of Rock**), reacted against Berlage's sobriety by producing its uniquely whimsical buildings with waving, almost sculptural brickwork. Built over a reinforced concrete frame, the brick outer walls go through a complex series of pleats, bulges, folds and curls that earned them the nickname *Schortjesarchitectuur* ('Apron Architecture'). Windows can be trapezoid or parabolic; doors are carved in strong, angular shapes; brickwork is highly decorative and often polychromatic; and sculptures are abundant.

The driving force behind the school came from two young architects, Michel de Klerk (1884-1923) and Piet Kramer (1881-1961). Two commissions for social housing projects – one for **Dageraad** (constructed around PL Takstraat, 1921-23), one for **Eigen Haard** (located in the Spaarndammerbuurt, 1913-20) – allowed them to treat entire blocks as single units. Just as importantly, the pair's adventurous clients gave them freedom to express their ideas. The school also produced more rural variants suggestive of village life, such as the rather charming BT Boeyinga-designed 'garden village' **Tuindorp Nieuwendam** (Purmerplein, Purmerweg).

ARCHITECTURAL REBELLION

In the early 1920s, a new movement emerged that was the very antithesis of the Amsterdam School – although certain crossover aspects can be observed in JF Staal's 1930-completed **Wolkenkrabber** (Victorieplein), the first ever residential high-rise in the country, whose name appropriately translates as 'cloudscraper'. Developing rather than reacting wildly against Berlage's ideas, the Functionalists believed that new building materials such as concrete and steel should not be concealed, but that the basic structure of a building should be visible. Function was supreme, ornament anathema. Their hard-edged concrete and glass boxes have much in common with the work of Frank Lloyd Wright in the USA, Le Corbusier in France and the Bauhaus in Germany.

Perhaps unsurprisingly, such radical views were not shared by everyone, and the period was a turbulent one in Amsterdam's architectural history. Early Functionalist work, such as the 1930s **Openluchtschool** (Open-air School, Cliostraat 40), 1934's striking **Cineac Cinema** (Reguliersbreestraat 31) and the **Blauwe Theehuis** (in Vondelpark; *see p134*), has a clean-cut elegance, and the Functionalist garden suburb of **Betondorp** (literally, 'Concrete Village'),

Tuschinski Cinema.

built between 1921 and 1926, is much more attractive than the name might suggest. But after World War II, Functionalist ideology became an excuse for more dreary, derivative, prefabricated eyesores. The urgent need for housing, coupled with town-planning theories that favoured residential satellite suburbs, led to the appearance of soulless, high-rise horrors on the edge of town.

A change of heart during the 1970s refocused attention on making the city centre a pleasant jumble of residences, shops and offices. At the same time, a quirkier, more imaginative trend began to show itself in building design. The **ING Bank** (Bijlmerplein 888), inspired by Rudolf Steiner's philosophy of anthroposophy and built in 1987 of brick, has hardly a right angle in sight. A use of bright colour, and a return to a human-sized scale, is splendidly evident in Aldo van Eyck's **Hubertushuis** (Plantage Middenlaan 33-35) from 1979, which seems to personify the architect's famed quotation: 'my favourite colour is the rainbow.' New façades – daringly modern, yet built to scale – began to appear between the old houses along the canals. The 1980s also saw, amid much controversy, the construction of what soon became known as the 'Stopera', a combined **City Hall** (Stadhuis) and opera house on Waterlooplein; the eye-catching brick and marble of the **Muziektheater** (see p204, Nationale Opera & Ballet) is more successful than the dull oblongs that make up City Hall.

Housing projects of the 1980s and 1990s have provided Amsterdam with some imaginative modern architecture – especially on the islands of the once-derelict Eastern Docklands (see p256 **Along the Watefront**). You can get a good view from the roof of Renzo Piano's recognisable **NEMO** building (see p154). While the area did not achieve the dream of becoming a harbourfront on par with that of Sydney, Australia, it did help put local architecture on the global map.

EYES FORWARD

At the municipal information centre for planning and housing in **Zuiderkerk** (see p142), visitors can admire scale models of current and future developments set to transform the city within the near future. Those interested should pay a visit to

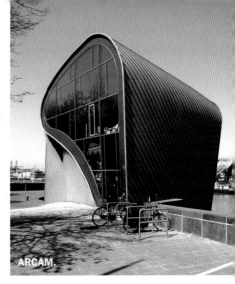
ARCAM.

NEMO's neighbour, mighty **ARCAM** – the **Architectuurcentrum Amsterdam** (see p154) – or pick up a copy of its excellent publication 25 Buildings You Should Have Seen, Amsterdam. Bureau Monumenten & Archeologie Amsterdam (BMA), meanwhile, provides an overview of the city's architecture from its origins to 1940 at www.bma.amsterdam.nl (Dutch only).

Architectural travesties of the past have politicised the populace and referendums are held prior to many developments. Although 130,000 local votes against the construction of IJburg – a residential community built on a series of man-made islands in the IJmeer, just east of Amsterdam – was not enough to arrest development around this ecologically sensitive area, they did inspire the promise that ƒ15 million (now around €7 million) would be invested in 'nature development'. Parts of the area have also become a showcase for the recently hyped Dutch concept of wilde wonen – 'wild living' – where residents get to design and build their own houses, a radical concept in this space-constrained country.

Similarly, the referendum result against the new **Noord-Zuidlijn** on the Metro network didn't halt the project, but it did establish that the city government needed to be considerably more diligent in its thinking. When planning the line, the powers-that-be apparently overlooked such significant

ALONG THE WATERFRONT

Experimental and enthralling: is this the future of modern housing?

Amsterdam's Eastern Docklands area is one of the city's premier eating and entertainment hotspots. But it's also a fantastic showcase for the Netherlands' daring experiments in residential living. If you want to explore the future of Amsterdam, hop on a bike.

Head north-west of Centraal Station, past the startling modern architecture of the new Palace of Justice and IJDock development (www.ijdock.nl) along Westerdok, to the **Westelijke Eilanden** (Western Islands) near the Jordaan, for a taste of life during the Golden Age, when Amsterdam was the richest port in the world. These artificial islands were originally created in the 17th century to sustain maritime activity. Although there are trendy warehouse flats and a yacht basin on Realeneiland, Prinseneiland and Bickerseiland – where one-time shipyards, tar distillers and salters and smokers of fish were based – the area still remains the city's best setting for a scenic stroll (helped by the sizeable community of local artists) evoking seafaring times.

Since 1876, the route to the open sea has been the North Sea Canal. Because the working docks also lie to the west, there's little activity on the IJ behind Centraal Station, aside from a handful of passenger ships and free ferries sailing across the water to Amsterdam Noord – one of which will take you to the vibrant cultural breeding ground that is the former shipping yard **NDSM** (*see p158* **Northern Lights**).

Back on the south side, follow the water eastwards from Centraal Station before joining up with and following Oostelijke Handelskade and its parallel boardwalk. You pass the **Nationale Opera & Ballet** (*see p204*), an epicentre of new music,

Palace of Justice

which includes exhibition galleries and a grand café and restaurant (complete with a terrace overlooking the scenic waters of the IJ). Its close neighbour is the spectacular, wave-shaped, glass passenger terminal for luxury cruise ships (www.ptamsterdam.nl).

Before proceeding to clubs **Café Pakhuis Wilhelmina** (*see p198*) and **Panama** (*see p195*), and the **Lloyd Hotel** (*see p289*), take a walk down the airy Jan Schaeferbrug to the left – starting off by going through the **Pakhuis de Zwijger** (*see p156*), an old cocoa storage warehouse reinvented as a new-media centre. It has a charming café.

The bridge will take you to the tip of Java-eiland, which, at first glance, may look like a dense, designer confinement, but it's not hard to be charmed by the island's dividing pedestrian street, which will have you crossing canals on funky bridges and walking past a startling variety of architecture.

At Azartplein, the island suddenly changes its name to KNSM-eiland, in honour of the Royal Dutch Steam Company (KNSM), once based here. Here, you can visit the excellent local bookshop **Van Pampus** (KNSM-laan 303, 419 3023,

NDSM

www.boekhandelvanpampus.nl) or **De Kompaszaal** (KNSM-laan 311, 419 9596, www.kompaszaal.nl), a café and restaurant in the former KNSM arrivals and departures hall, which has the feel of a 1950s cruise ship, complete with watery views from the terrace. Otherwise, veer north and follow Surinamekade, with houseboats on one side and artist studios on the other. Pass the 'Black Widow' tower and loop around the island's tip and back along KNSM-laan, turning left into Barcelonaplein, and then right when you pass through the abstract sculpted steel archway. Linger and look at the imposing residential **Piraeus** building by German architect Hans Kollhoff, if only for its eye-twisting inner court.

The two peninsulas to the south are Borneo and Sporenburg, the work of urban-planning and landscape architecture firm West 8. The plots are all differently sized, to encourage the many architects involved – a veritable who's who of international stars – to come up with creative low-rise living. Cross over to Sporenburg via the Verbindingsdam to the mighty silver **Whale** residential complex, designed by architect Frits van Dongen, over on Baron GA Tindalplein. In folky contrast, a floating Styrofoam park produced by erstwhile Provo Robert Jasper Grootveld has been set in front of it on Panamakade.

From here, cross over to Borneo on the swooping red bridge. Turn left up Stuurmankade – past a still more violently

undulating pedestrian bridge – and pause to enjoy the view at the end. Then return west along Scheepstimmermanstraat, easily Amsterdam's most eccentric architectural street, where every single façade on show – from twisting steel to haphazard plywood – manages to be more bizarre than the next.

Where Panamalaan meets Piet Heinkade, you can take the IJtram from CS to IJburg (the stop is right by the huge public artwork *Folly for the Bees*), or return to Oostelijk Handelskade and to the Lloyd Hotel and its neighbouring café **De Kantine** (Rietlandpark 375, 419 4433). Or head up Czar Peterstraat, a once dangerous street, but now pleasant area with quirky shops and cafés, and hit urban beach **Roest** (*see p156*) or go for a home-brewed beer at **Brouwerij 't IJ** (*see p151*).

More energetic types might prefer to take a 20-minute bike ride to IJburg, heading south via C van Eesterenlaan and Veelaan, then left down Zeeburgerdijk. This in turn connects up with Zuiderzeeweg, which then merges into a bridge that ends at a set of traffic lights. Here, follow the cycle path to the right, to IJburg.

Originally intended to be completed in 2012, seven artificial islands were to be home to 45,000 people inhabiting more than 18,000 units, many floating on the water. Economic problems mean that, currently, there are only three islands and 16,000 residents – a subdued version of what was hyped as a showcase for Dutch landscape and residential architecture. There's still plenty to look at, but funky beach **Blijburg** (*see p157*) is a highlight.

On the way back to town, you can stop at equally funky café-restaurant **Magetico** (*see p40*) or at the chip stand, **Eiburgh Snacks** (Zuiderzeeweg, beside no.2). The snack store serves some of the best fries in town, along with a hearty pea soup.

For more detailed information on architectural tours of all these areas and more, contact ARCAM (www.arcam.nl).

IN CONTEXT

Lloyds Hotel.

'Since 2009, 40 per cent of the country's architects have lost their jobs.'

details as financing, loss of revenue for shopkeepers, and the potential for all this digging to bring about the speedier sinking of historical buildings, none of which endeared them to voters.

SUPERDUTCH

Modern Dutch architecture – thanks in part to notable exponents such as Rem Koolhaas (his ugly 1991 work, **Byzantium**, is viewable at the north entrance to Vondelpark on Stadhouderskade) – remains very much in vogue. Brad Pitt's own favourite architecture firm, MVRDV, which renovated the **Lloyd Hotel** (*see p289*), shot to prominence at Hanover World Expo 2000 with its 'Dutch Big Mac', featuring such delicious ingredients as watermills and windmills for electricity on the roof, a theatre on the fourth floor, an oak forest on the third floor, flowers on the second floor, and cafés,

shops and a few dunes on the first floor. Yes, dunes.

International periodicals continue to see the 'Dutch Model' – where boundaries between building, city and landscape planning have blurred beyond recognition – as both pragmatic and futuristic. After all, ecological degradation is now a worldwide phenomenon, and the space-constrained Netherlands has long seen nature as a construct that needs to be nurtured. Expect this principle to define some of the Dutch architecture of the future.

High-budget architectural statements are still arising. For example, construction in Zuidoost around the Amsterdam Bijlmer ArenA train station has pumped much-needed life into what was once essentially an architectural prison. Another hotspot that roped in a veritable who's who of architects is **Zuidas** (www.zuidas.nl) in the south. Zuidas is grouped around the World Trade Center, close to the wacky **ING House** (Amstelveenseweg 500); spot this clog-shaped glass edifice on the ride in from Schiphol Airport. And then there's the compelling **EYE Film Institute** (*see p176*) in Amsterdam Noord, which looks as if it might actually take flight.

BACK TO BASICS?

With the global economic meltdown, the golden years are over. Since 2009, 40 per cent of the country's architects have lost their jobs. With dwindling budgets, architects are now looking for less pretentious solutions. They're becoming more inspired by such projects as the hundreds of old steel containers turned into living spaces for students in 2004 at both **NDSM** (*see p158*) in the north and **Houthavens** in the west.

Others are seeking to rejuvenate the millions of square metres of empty office space by turning them into residences, hotels, care facilities and indoor farms. In 2013, more than 80,000 square metres of offices were given a new function – with a hope to double that amount in 2014. In another project, DUS architects are looking both to the past and the future in Amsterdam Noord by 3-D printing over the next couple of years an updated 17th-century canal house. In short: the future looks bright, sustainable and more than just a little bit wacky.

Zuidas.

Art

Ah, the Golden Age. The living was sweet during those first six decades of the 17th century, starting with the founding of the East India Company (VOC) and ending when the British changed New Amsterdam to New York. Not only did the economic benefits of being the world's leading trading power result in the building of Amsterdam's image-defining ring of canals, but it also led to a flourishing of the arts that continues to this day. That's why it's easy to get lost in the sheer number of viewable works in Amsterdam. Sometimes, it's just better to focus on a few prime works – to stop and smell the tulips, as it were.

MEDIEVAL ROOTS

The groundwork for the blooming of art in Amsterdam's Golden Age was laid by the city's rich medieval artistic tradition under the sponsorship of the Church. Later artists, not content to labour solely *ad majorem dei gloriam*, found more 'individual' masters in the Flemings Bosch and Brueghel. Foremost among these early artists was **Jacob Cornelisz van Oostsanen** (c1470-1533). Also known as Jacob van Amsterdam, he represents the beginning of the city's artistic tradition, and his sharpness of observation became a trademark for all Dutch art that was to follow. The one painting of his that survived the Iconoclastic Fury, *Saul and the Witch of Endor* (on display at the **Rijksmuseum**; *see p130*), tells the whole biblical story in one panoramic, almost comic-book-like, swoop: beginning on the left where Saul seeks advice from a witch about his impending battle with the Philistines and ending in the far distance, behind the central witches' sabbath, with his 'poetic justice' of a suicide in the face of defeat.

The Baker of Eeklo is another example that seemingly comes from a very much pre-modern time. It hangs in the **Muiderslot** (*see p216*), the castle outside Amsterdam

built for Count Floris V. Painted in the second half of the 16th century by two rather obscure painters, **Cornelis van Dalem** and **Jan van Wechelen**, the depicted tableau – of a busy bakery, where people whose heads have been replaced by cabbages await patiently the rebaking of their actual heads – can probably only make sense to a populace weaned on medieval stories of magic windmills that could grind old people up and them churn them out young again. In this related story, bakers are slicing the heads off clients to rebake them to specification; a cabbage – a symbol for the empty and idle head – was used to keep the spewing of blood to a minimum, although sometimes people's heads came out 'half-baked' or 'misfired'.

OLD MASTERS

Painters had no problems with marketing once the Golden Age proper arrived and the aspirant middle classes became hungry for art. **Rembrandt van Rijn** (1606-69) is, of course, the best known of all those who made art while the money shone. However, *The Company of Captain Frans Banning Cocq and Lieutenant Willem van Ruytenburch* (1642) didn't prove the snappiest title

GALLERY HOPPING

Take a tour of the city's most interesting art spaces.

Galleries, mini museums, ateliers and non-traditional art spaces abound in Amsterdam, in just about every area of the city. The Jordaan is still the congregation point for the more established and internationally minded contemporary-art galleries, while the Spiegelkwartier (literally, 'mirror quarter') in the Southern Canal Belt is where you'll find anything pre-dating 1945, including Old Master paintings, CoBrA art, antiques and genuine Delftware. In recent years, urban art pioneers have headed to Noord, where the massive shipyard turned studio complex **NDSM** (*see p158* **Northern Lights**) is a breeding ground of creative production; while others have migrated to De Pijp, West and Oost (*see p149* **Eastern Promise**) for cheaper or funkier art digs.

Amsterdam's art spaces can be divided into two categories: commercial art galleries devoted to selling work by more established artists; and non-profit project spaces, where emerging and non-traditional artists have more opportunities to 'play'. Among the first group, **Annet Gelink**

Mediamatic.

Gallery, **Torch Gallery**, **Galerie Gabriel Rolt** and **Galerie Fons Welters** are always good bets (for all, *see p124* **Art Throb**). For project spaces, **Mediamatic Factory** (*see p154*) in the Waterfront is not to be missed; for younger, fresher, edgier work, head to **W139** (*see p67*) in the Old Centre or **Studio/K** (*see p179*) in Oost. Meanwhile, Amsterdam continues its rich tradition of nourishing a street-art culture (in spite of the police's efforts to curb graffiti), so you'll also find plenty of eye candy pretty much everywhere around town (*see p120* **Painting the Town**).

For the most up-to-date list of current shows and spaces, buy the monthly *Art Alert* (www.artalert.nl – available at **Athenaeum Nieuwscentrum**; *see p82*); it's in Dutch, but the galleries are sorted by area and marked on maps. You can also download a bimonthly calendar from AKKA (www.akka.nl). English-language city marketing magazine *A-Mag*, available at most newsstands and tobacconists, has extensive arts listings too.

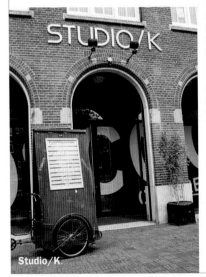

Studio/K.

for a painting. *The Night Watch*, though, is rather more memorable, and it's by this name that the most famous work by Rembrandt is now known (it's on display at the Rijksmuseum). Amsterdam's Civic Guard commissioned this group portrait to decorate their new building, but rather than conjure up a neat, unexciting portrait, Rembrandt went for spontaneity, capturing a moment of lively chaos: the captain issuing an order as his men jostle to his rear. It's now the city's most popular work in the city's most popular museum.

Rembrandt couldn't decorate Amsterdam on his own, however, and the likes of Jan Vermeer, Frans Hals, Ferdinand Bol, Jan Steen and Jacob van Ruisdael thrived creatively and economically during this time. Delft-born painter **Jan Vermeer** (1632-75) painted pictures, such as *The Milkmaid* (also on display at the Rijksmuseum), that radiate an extraordinary serenity. In his essential essay, 'Vermeer in Bosnia', Lawrence Weschler suggests that the artist's works are not depictions of actual peace but rather hopeful invocations of a peace yet to come. For Vermeer was painting at a time when exhausted, war-weary Europe was slowly emerging from the ravages of the Thirty Years War (1618-48); at the time, peace still remained a fervent hope rather than a definite expectation.

> *'Van Gogh set out to reinvent the very relevance of painting in a post-photography world.'*

Leiden's **Jan Steen** (c1625-79) dealt with the chaos of the times in another way – a way that got him a bad rep as a rowdy. While he did run a tavern in his own home, his patchy reputation is more likely based on the drunken folk that inhabit his paintings of everyday life. In fact, if one looks carefully at, for example, *The Merry Family* (at the Rijksmuseum), Steen comes across as highly moralistic. With the inscription over the mantelpiece ('As the Old Sing, So Pipe the Young') putting literally what the painting reflects figuratively – through a plethora of symbols that represent the emptiness of a life spent smoking, drinking and talking about nothing – the picture offers a lesson as valid today as when it was painted. Steen himself has a cameo as the puffy-cheeked bagpiper.

After the Golden Age began to tarnish, art continued to develop. The Jordaan-born

Jan Steen's *The Merry Family*.

Jacob de Wit (1695-1754), long before the invention of sticky glow-in-the-dark stars, brightened up many a local ceiling with cloud-dappled skies, gods and flocks of cherubs. Initially influenced by Rubens's altar work in Antwerp, De Wit developed a much more delicate and sympathetic touch, which he used to great rococo effect in a number of Amsterdam buildings. Among these are the attic church at **Ons' Lieve Heer op Solder** (*see p64*), the Rijksmuseum, the **Pintohuis** (now a community-run library and reading room; Sint Antoniesbreestraat 69, Jodenbuurt, 624 3184) and **Huis Marseille** (*see p93*). However, his mastery of trompe l'oeil, later named *witjes* after him, is probably best seen at the **Bijbels Museum** (*see p92*). One ceiling was painted for local merchant Jacob Cromhout, while the other, entitled *Apollo and the Four Seasons*, was salvaged in the 1950s from a nearby property on Herengracht. Both paintings have recently been stylishly restored.

THE ARRIVAL OF VINCENT

The 18th century produced Monet's inspiration, **Johan Jongkind**, while the 19th century offered **George Breitner** and Van Gogh – two artists out to reinvent the very relevence of painting in a post-photography world. The career of everyone's favourite earless genius, **Vincent van Gogh** (1853-90), is on full display in Amsterdam, most notably at the **Van Gogh Museum** (*see p133*). Here, you can marvel at the fact that the creator of the dark shadows of *Skull with Smoking Cigarette* went on to paint, a mere two years later, in 1888, the almost kinetic *Bedroom*. By then, Van Gogh had settled in France's clearer light and abandoned the Vermeer-inspired subdued colouring of his earlier work to embrace the Expressionist style that would make him famous. While the self-portrait clearly reflects his restless nature, *Bedroom* depicts the very bed he would, perhaps, have been better off sleeping in. Just two months later, he had the first of the nervous breakdowns that led finally to his suicide.

Like Van Gogh, **Isaac Israëls** (1865-1934) sought to reinvent the relevance of painting in a post-photographic age. But unlike his buddy George Breitner, who chose to embrace this new technology by using photographs as the basis for his paintings, Israëls chose a more athletic path and achieved the 'snapshot'

FAKING IT

When is a Vermeer not a Vermeer?

The Dutch are as famed for their business acumen as their dykes, but this has sometimes led the less scrupulous to a somewhat free and easy attitude towards a work's provenance. An estimated 30 per cent of the world art market consists of forgeries, and even the most famous institutions can be caught out. In 1938, the Rijksmuseum (*see p130*) lost a bidding war for a Vermeer to Rotterdam's Museum Boijmans Van Beuningen (*see p228*), which bought the painting for the then-astronomical price of 550,000 guilders. Proof, if it were needed, that desire blinds, for how else could Hans van Meegeren's heavy-handed *De Emmaüsgangers* be mistaken for a Vermeer? It was only in 1945, when the forger was facing a traitor's death penalty for selling the Nazis another 'Vermeer', that Van Meegeren admitted both works were forgeries, painted to avenge himself on a critic's poor reviews. That self-same critic had fallen for the forgeries, although it's unlikely that the sweet taste of revenge was sufficient compensation for Van Meegeren's subsequent imprisonment: he died in jail a couple of years later.

Isaac Israëls' *Two Girls by a Canal.*

GIVING A SQUAT

The squat ethic lives on in the city's creative scene.

OT301.

Amsterdam has a lot of nostalgists weeping for those 1980s and '90s salad days when cultural squats such as Silo and Vrieshuis Amerika were the coolest, edgiest and most frolicsome things around. But while no one likes a whiner, when the powers-that-be closed these cultural beehives in order to make Amsterdam the 'business gateway to Europe', it was soon seen as a monumental blunder in a city defined by its artistic traditions. So the city bureaucrats, in an effort to claw back lost prestige and emigrating artists, did what all such functionaries do and threw money at the problem, creating non-squat squats called *broedplaatsen* ('breeding grounds').

Don't worry if it gets confusing: the world of Amstersquats is nothing if not divided into umpteen different categories – and it only got more confusing in 2010 when squatting was made illegal. Consequently, many squats were emptied, but others were ignored since there were no owners pushing for redevelopment. Some of the evicted squatters were given permission to take over other underused spaces (such as **Vondelbunker**; *see p198*) – let's call these 'post-squats'. There are also 'bought squats' (old squats that were sold cheaply by the city to their inhabitants), such as **Vrankrijk** (www.vrankrijk.org), which remains a hotbed of cheap beer and radical politics.

Meanwhile, *broedplaatsen* are coming of age, and working to bring cultural activities to the outer reaches of the city by embedding artists and creatives straight into the community. They've already pumped plenty of life into Noord, Oost and even the Red Light District. Also, *broedplaatsen* aren't always put into economically challenged neighbourhoods such as Zuidoost and Nieuw West; for example, a former school in the rather dull but flush financial district Zuid-As is now engaging the area's stockbrokers through art and a highly rated restaurant, **Old School** (www.oldschoolamsterdam.com). Magazine and website **Nieuw Amsterdam** (www.nieuwamsterdam.nu) does a great job of following all the developments – albeit in Dutch.

But it's still the places that began as bona fide squats that are making the crossover most efficiently. One-time film academy **OT301** (*see p198*) is totally happening, as is former shipyard turned arts complex **NDSM** (*see p158* **Northern Lights**). And while not actually itself a *broedplaats*, **Westergasfabriek** (*see p116*) oozes reclaimed industrial cred.

IN CONTEXT

the easiest solution but may be costly. For on-street parking, look for the blue boxes marked with a white P to pre-pay with a credit card. You'll have to enter your registration – parking officials from Cition (the local traffic authority) then just scan the plate to see if you've paid. Depending on the area, you'll pay €3-€5/hr.

When leaving your car anywhere in the city, be sure to empty it of valuables and leave your glovebox open: cars with foreign plates are vulnerable to break-ins.

Car parks

Car parks are indicated by a white 'P' on a blue square sign. Also worth considering are the very economical Park and Rides (see www.bereikbaaramsterdam.nl for locations), which cost between €1 and €8 per day. For more information and a list of locations in English, see www.iamsterdam.com/park-and-ride.

P1 Parking Amsterdam Centraal

Prins Hendrikkade 20, Old Centre: New Side (638 5330, www.p1.nl). **Open** 24hrs. **Rates** €5/hr; €55/24hrs. **Map** p312 J6.
Many nearby hotels offer a 10% discount on parking here. You can also save by booking ahead online.

Q-Park Europarking

Marnixstraat 250, Oud West (0900 446 6880 premium rate, www.q-park.nl). **Open** 24hrs. **Rates** €2/26mins; €40/24hrs. **Map** p316 F11.

Q-Park De Kolk

Nieuwezijds Kolk 18, Old Centre: New Side (0900 446 6880 premium rate, www.q-park.nl). **Open** 24hrs. **Rates** €2/21mins; €52/24hrs. **Map** p312 J7.

Parking fines

Fines are €55.50, plus the price of one hour's parking in that section of town, and can only be paid via your bank. For more details, visit www.cition.nl and click on 'parking'; include your registration and ticket number when transferring funds. If you suspect your car has been towed, call 14 020 (8am-6pm Mon-Fri) or 251 3322 (24hrs). If this is the case, you'll have to pay €419 plus €30/day. Payment is only possible with a credit card.

Car pound

Daniël Goedkoopstraat 9, Oost (251 2121, www.stadstoezicht.

amsterdam.nl). **Open** 7am-11pm daily.

Petrol

There are 24-hour petrol stations (*tankstations*) at Gooiseweg 10, Sarphatistraat 225, Marnixstraat 250 and Spaarndammerdijk 218.

WATER TRANSPORT

Amsterdam is best seen from the water. There are plenty of canal cruises, but they don't offer the freedom to do your own exploring. For ways to get around on the water, *see pp50-53* **Tour Amsterdam** and *p88* **Canal Cruising**. When renting a boat, don't ignore the basic rules of the water (put simply: stick to the right and beware of canal cruisers).

CYCLING

Cycling is the most convenient means of getting from A to B: there are bike lanes on most roads, marked by white lines and bike symbols. When cycling, unless indicated otherwise by signs, traffic from the right has priority, and watch out for pedestrians stepping into your path. Bike lights are compulsory in the dark; police set up periodic checkpoints and will fine you on the spot if you don't have any. Avoid catching your tyre in the tram rails (always cross them at an angle) and never leave a bike unlocked – Amsterdam has one of the highest bicycle theft rates in the world. If someone on the street offers you a bike for sale (*fiets te koop*), don't be tempted: it's almost certainly stolen, and there are plenty of good, cheap bike hire companies around, of which we list a selection below and in **Tour Amsterdam** (*see pp50-53*). Apart from these, check www.goudengids.nl under the section 'Fietsen en Bromfietsen Verhuur'.

Note that almost every bicycle in Amsterdam now uses the reverse pedal braking system rather than a pair of manual brakes attached to the handlebars. Those who are used to the latter will find it takes some time to adjust, so be sure to allow time to practise before setting out on the streets. *See also pp272-273.*

Bike rental

There are many places to rent a bike, for about €10 a day. A passport and/or credit card is required.

Bike City

Bloemgracht 68-70, Jordaan (626 3721, www.bikecity.nl). Tram 10, 13, 14, 17. **Open** 9am-5.30pm daily. **Rates** from €13.50/day. *Deposit €50.* **Map** p311 F9.

Frederic Rentabike

Brouwersgracht 78, Jordaan (www.frederic.nl, 624 5509). **Open** 9am-5.30pm daily. **Rates** from €10/24hrs. **Map** p312 G7.
These bikes are not as aggressively branded as elsewhere in the city. Frederic also rents out houseboats, apartments and rooms (*see p286*).

Mac Bike

For listings, *see pp50-53* **Tour Amsterdam**.

Mike's Bike Tours

Kerkstraat 134, Southern Canal Belt (622 7970, www.mikesbike toursamsterdam.com). Tram 1, 2, 5. **Open** *Apr-Sept* 9am-6pm daily. *Oct-Mar* 10am-6pm daily. **Rates** from €10/day. **Map** p314 K12.
Guided tours available.

Rent-A-Bike

Damstraat 20-22, Old Centre: Old Side (625 5029, www.renta bike.nl). Tram 4, 9, 14, 16, 24. **Open** 9am-6pm daily. **Rates** €9.50/24hrs; €25 deposit and passport/ID card or credit card photocopy. **Map** p312 J9.

StarBikes Rental

De Ruyterkade 127, Waterfront (www.starbikesrental.com, 620 3215). **Open** 8am-7pm Mon-Fri; 9am-7pm Sat, Sun. **Rates** from €9/24hrs. **Map** p313 L6.
Complete with 'bike gallery' and tour options, StarBikes also has a nice café overlooking the waters of the IJ, and very friendly staff. You may be tempted to just forget the bikes and hang out.

WALKING

Amsterdam is a compact city and everything is easy to reach on foot. The canals, cobbled streets, stunning architecture and sheer number of cafés make a stroll through the city a very pleasant experience. Just be aware that cyclists are ruthless – they stop for nothing and no one, so don't get in their way. For details on walking tours, *see pp50-53* **Tour Amsterdam**.

ESSENTIAL INFORMATION

LIVING BY DESIGN

Good design is part of everyday life in the Netherlands.

The Dutch love of design comes into view as you descend towards Schiphol Airport and glide over a Mondrian-like grid-pattern landscape. A dedication to arrangement is apparent in the ballet-like elegance of Dutch football players, who open space to score and close lines to defend. And an eye for detail underpins a multitude of creative spheres, from art to architecture, whether on paper, canvas or computer.

The history of Dutch design has been influenced by the orderliness of Calvinism and the modernist movement De Stijl, founded in Amsterdam in 1917. Drawing upon that part of the Dutch psyche that craves order, abstract artists such as Theo van Doesburg, Piet Mondrian and Gerrit Rietveld sought rules of equilibrium, which can be applied to everyday design as much as art. Just surf the web or leaf through *Wallpaper** magazine to see the legacy of the style today. And yet a counterpoint has always existed in the Dutch people's strong desire for personal expression (perhaps an echo of the stubbornness required to battle the sea).

Worldwide acclaim has greeted this eclectic mix of functionality and wit – just consider the playful, Lego-like residential building Silodam by MVRDV Architects or the sharp angles exhibited on the new Palace of Justice, both in the Western Docklands. Furthermore, there's an active sense of 'city design' at work: urban planners carefully quote from the work of American sociologist Richard Florida, who argues that the 'creative class' can play a beneficial role in urban development (*see p263* **Giving a Squat**). Creative types are working in deprived neighbourhoods, ranging from the Red Light District to the Baarsjes and Bos en Lommer

districts west of the Jordaan, and the former shipyard NDSM.

To witness how design has infiltrated every level of Dutch life, cross the Damrak from the Red Light District to visit a major outlet of department store **HEMA** (Nieuwendijk 174-176, www.hema.nl). A quarter of the Dutch population wakes to the ring of a HEMA alarm clock; one in three men wear HEMA underwear; and one in four women a HEMA bra. Every year, the store sells 506,000 kilograms of liquorice and 14 million units of *tompouce* (a pink-glazed custard cake), as well as one smoked sausage every second. Currently, there's even an improbably successful *HEMA the Musical* touring the country. It may be an economical place to shop for basics, but the store has also made a name for itself as a source of affordable design objects – even their sales flyers are graphics classics. It has featured products by leading designers such as Piet Hein Eek, Gijs Bakker and Hella Jongerius, and over the past 20 years has shifted 250,000 units of its Le Lapin whistling kettle. You might also want to check out supermarket **Marqt** (*see p136*), which has taken branding to the next level.

For a stroll deep into the heart of local design, head to **Frozen Fountain** (*see p98*) in the Western Canal Ring or **Hotel Droog** (*see p72*) in the Old Centre. You can also visit that most higgledy-piggledy area, the Jordaan. A former school here is now the studio of design star Marcel Wanders, where you'll find his homewares store **Moooi** (*see p122*). Another disciple of Richard Florida, Wanders is now 'designing' other creative hubs elsewhere in the city, as well as newly opened hotel **Andaz Amsterdam** (*see p283* **Designer Dreams**).

Frozen Fountain.

'Mondrian moved through Realism, Impressionism and Cubism, before embracing the purely abstract.'

feel of his paintings by running around like a ninny and painting very fast. *Two Girls by a Canal* (on show at the **Amsterdam Museum**; *see p76*) does successfully reflect a quintessentially Impressionist view of dynamic Amsterdam.

DE STIJL AND COBRA

There's a fair case to be made that the 20th century belonged to **Piet Mondrian** (1872-1944), whose career can also be used as a one-man weathervane of modern art. He moved through Realism, Impressionism and Cubism, before embracing the purely abstract and becoming one of the founders of **De Stijl** ('The Style'). His use of only lines and primary colour blocks inspired accusations of sterility, but actually represented a very personal and subjective quest for essence and harmony. He was also something of a wit, tilting his late and ultra-minimal canvas, *Composition with Two Lines* (on display at the **Stedelijk Museum**; *see p130*) by 45 degrees.

Karel Appel (1920-2001) once said, 'I just mess around' – and many agree when met with his childish forms, bright colours and heavy strokes. But art that chose instinct over intellect was just what the world needed after World War II, when **CoBrA** (*see p138* **The Serpent's Tale**) exploded on to the scene. Appel's rate of production was so huge that Amsterdam ex-forger Geert Jan Jansen claims Appel verified several of Jansen's works as his own. You can admire an Appel mural by the entrance of restaurant **Bridges** (*see p67*), part of the Grand Amsterdam hotel.

ONWARD TO THE FUTURE?

As we move deeper into the 21st century, the focus has shifted away from painting and towards design (*see p264* **Living by Design**). **Marcel Wanders**' 1997-produced Knotted Chair could not be more different from that other iconic Dutch chair of the 20th century: the highly geometric Red-Blue Chair (1918-23) by De Stijl co-founder Gerrit Rietveld. But Knotted Chair – which reinvents the frumpy hippie art of macramé with the aid of high-tech epoxy – came to represent the work of a new vanguard of local designers who seek to achieve a fusion of wit, hipness and function – also to be witnessed in **Piet Hein Eek**'s Waste Table, made of recycled timber.

It has often been said that Amsterdam, with its soggy climate and bleak winters, was designed to look as good in black and white as it does in colour, making it especially appealing to amateur photographers. And, as home to **Ed van der Elsken** (1925-1990), **Anton Corbijn** and **Rineke Dijkstra**, the city is a strong supporter of the photographic arts, with photography museum **Foam** (*see p104*) providing solid institutional backing. The studio of **Erwin Olaf** functions as a graduate school of sorts for young photographers.

Although painters such as **Marlene Dumas** keep the medium fresh, the local art scene now seems more interested in embracing the blur between street art, design, photography, new media and so on. Since the 1980s, there's been a backlash against conceptual art's anti-functional rhetoric – which would have pleased adherents of De Stijl, who hoped the future would bring a frenzy of cross-disciplinary activity. Photographers, cartoonists and architects are considered to be 'artists', and it's not surprising that the

IN CONTEXT

Marcel Wanders' Knotted Chair.

city's creative atmosphere has lured many an expat (one such is UK artist and filmmaker Steve McQueen) to set up canalside studios.

EMBRACING THE NEW

Amsterdam has embraced new media like few other cities. The pioneering **Waag Society** (www.waag.org) and the happily subversive **Mediamatic** (www.mediamatic.net) both arose from the 'tactical media' scene. Mediamatic received particular acclaim for its 2007 'El HEMA' project, which remixed iconic Dutch department store HEMA into an outlet for Muslim-inspired design.

Pakhuis de Zwijger (*see p156*) acts as a hub for numerous cutting-edge outfits, complete with a programme of events, conferences and exhibitions – and a great café. Artist/entrepreneur/designer **Daan Roosegaarde** (www.studioroosegaarde.net) is quickly becoming a household name as his studio pumps out interactive wheat fields, LED lights that respond to touch, and dresses that get more transparent based on the wearer's heartbeats.

What makes Amsterdam such a hotbed for creative types? One simple answer might be: money. Historically, the Dutch government has been incredibly generous with subsidies for artists (for a while, every art-school grad got financial assistance for five years after leaving college). The government is less keen to splash the cash in times of austerity, of course, and the right-wing coalition in the

Hague cut cultural subsidies by 25 per cent in 2011 (*see p134* **Culture Slash**). Still, as the home of prestigious art residency the **Rijksakademie** (www.rijksakademie.nl) and acclaimed art/design university **Gerrit Rietveld Academie** (www.gerritrietveld academie.nl), Amsterdam is teeming with young, up-and-coming artists from all over the world, who are producing work, in all media, like crazy. This international influence helps explain why the city's galleries are more adventurous and welcoming to young artists and curators than elsewhere.

In some respects, the city is one huge gallery. All new construction projects have long had to dedicate a percentage of their costs to public art, so one can hardly walk a metre without bumping into some kind of creative endeavour. Not all attempts are successful, but there's no doubt that the urban landscape is a much richer place thanks to **Hans van Houwelingen**'s bronze iguanas frolicking in the grass of Kleine Gartmanplantsoen; **Atelier Van Lieshout**'s breast-appended houseboat floating in the Langer Vonder in Amsterdam Noord; the stained-glass of cartoonist **Joost Swarte** in buildings on the east side of Marnixstraat's northern end; and **Rombout & Droste**'s demented walking bridges on Java-eiland.

To miss out on Amsterdam's art offerings would be a sin comparable with anything you might contemplate in the Red Light District. So open your eyes and start looking.

Daan Roosegaarde installations.

Sex & Drugs

It's pragmatism at its finest: what better way to stamp out crime than by legalising it? Granted, the story of Amsterdam's liberal attitudes isn't quite so straightforward, but here's a fact known the world over: this city does sex and drugs with fewer hang-ups than anywhere else on the planet. It's little wonder that visitors are drawn like iron filings to a magnet. Some elements of the local authorities would like to clean up Amsterdam and attract a higher-minded breed of tourist. However, if you ask most non-residents the first words that come to mind when they hear 'Amsterdam', their answers will be 'Red Light District' or 'coffeeshops'. And since the city has long been at the forefront of forward-thinking policies on sex and drugs, who can really blame them?

Of course, we wouldn't want you to forget the other 95 per cent of the guide to this most multi-faceted city – but we'd be shirking our duty if we didn't tell you the history behind the naked ladies in their neon-framed windows, and the availability of joints the size of Oklahoma. The fun starts here.

SEX

The recorded history of prostitution in Amsterdam dates from the city's 13th-century roots. Amsterdam has always resisted all efforts to banish sex as an industry, and eventually the Dutch came to accept the advantages of a more pragmatic approach. Although working as a prostitute has been completely legal here since 1911, it wasn't until 2000 that the ban on brothels was lifted, thus formally permitting window and brothel sex work. But with the legalisation of brothels came bureaucratisation: now, all sex workers must be in possession of an EU passport; and a 200-page rule book was introduced to govern the whole business of selling sexual services, covering everything from fire escapes to the appropriate length of a prostitute's fingernails.

By the 15th century, Amsterdam was a bustling port attracting plenty of money, merchants and sailors – or, more specifically, merchants and sailors with money – which in turn increased the amount of sex for sale. However, it wasn't only randy men who influenced the industry's growth, but also the fact that many local women, separated from their seafaring husbands for months on end, were left with little or no means to sustain themselves or their children. Prostitution was one of the few money-making options available.

In the Middle Ages, prostitutes had been permitted to work in one of the brothels located on what is now Damstraat. Keeping a whorehouse was the exclusive privilege of the city's sheriff, and women found working elsewhere in the city were marched to said sheriff to the 'sound of drums and flutes'. But in the 15th century, prostitutes began working the area around Zeedijk; and by the 17th century, some were walking through the Old Side with red lanterns to advertise their profession. Soon after, enterprising women turned to advertising themselves in the windows of their own homes or from front-facing rooms rented from other homeowners; it's from this practice that today's rather more garish window trade is descended.

More 'traditional' methods of conducting business still apply, but it's the red-lit windows that have earned Amsterdam's notoriety as a major sex capital. And no matter how prepared you think you are, you'll be taken aback the first time you see street after street of huge picture windows, each decorated with red velvet-effect soft furnishings, each sparingly lit, and each dominated by a nearly-naked woman. The women are in your face, obliging you to notice them. They come in all shapes, sizes, skin tones and ages (but in recent years there's been a move to uniformity

COFFEESHOP PROTOCOL

The where, the when, the how.

IN CONTEXT

In terms of ambience, every coffeeshop is different. Some offer amazing food, others great couches. Some have a terrible atmosphere but the best hash in town. Others have it all. And they are all bound by strict regulations. Coffeeshops can only sell you five grams. They are banned from advertising; so if they have a website at all, they are 'fan sites'. Since 2007, alcohol has been prohibited in coffeeshops (which motivated a few to set up sister bars next door or across the street). Since 2008, it has been illegal to smoke tobacco in a working environment – including, perversely, coffeeshops. You can still smoke 'pure' weed, and many shops have sealed smoking rooms for tobacco, or offer bongs or herbal mixes as alternatives. Some rent out vapourisers: a gizmo that vapourises THC (the active ingredient) at a low temperature so that the leaves stay uncombusted, resulting in a smokeless toke. Another way to save your lungs is a spacecake – but be very careful with dosage as they take a while to kick in.

When you first walk in, ask to see a menu: it will list the available drugs and their prices, and staff can explain the effects of each and give you a look and a smell. Prices vary: expect to pay around €8 for a gram of decent bud or hash, and more for better quality. Hash is

typically named after its country of origin (Moroccan, Afghan, Lebanese), whereas cannabis usually bears invented names loosely referring to an element of the strain (White Widow, Super Skunk, Silver Haze). These are mostly genetic hybrids developed over the years for supreme effect. Previously, the big rage was for extremely potent weed grown hydroponically under indoor lights. This is still available, but avoid it if you prefer remaining conscious while getting high. Various coffeeshops carry a good bio (organic) selection; some sell nothing but.

All shops provide free rolling papers and tips – which is handy if you still need practice on how to roll a proper one. If you're in a rush, pre-rolled joints are always available, but usually contain low-grade ingredients (though a few shops pride themselves on excellent pre-rolls).

as 75 per cent are now likely to be from Romania or Bulgaria). Not all of them look terribly excited to be there, but neither would you if your job involved standing up for hours and answering a string of stupid questions. Many of the women pass the time between clients by gossiping with colleagues, dancing and cavorting or teasing passers-by. If you see someone who takes your fancy, talk to her politely and you'll be behind the curtain before you can say, 'I love Amsterdam.'

Amsterdam's best-known red-light district spreads out around the Oudezijds Voorburgwal and Oudezijds Achterburgwal canals, and the famous windows alternate with the butcher, the baker and the candlestick-maker. Two smaller, less-heralded red-light areas sit on the New Side (between Kattengat and Lijnbaanssteeg) and in the Pijp (Ruysdaelkade, from Albert Cuypstraat to 1e Jan Steenstraat).

What you see is not all you get: there are loads of other options to choose from. A quick scan of the internet will lead you to escort services, professional S&M services, sex clubs, striptease clubs, swingers' clubs, brothels, live sex shows, sex services for gay men, peep shows, sex cinemas and more. Only a few things are not permitted, such as street prostitution and sex workers under the age of 21.

In the game of commercial sex, the big losers are female customers whose options are limited. There are a few escort services that will supply male or female prostitutes for you, and you may find a window prostitute who is happy to get busy with a woman – though this is more likely to happen if you visit with your male partner. Another option for the adventurous is to visit a swingers' club; they generally have an overabundance of single men looking for a free frolic. You could also make a point of visiting the most female-friendly sex shop in Amsterdam, **Female & Partners** (see p82) to pick up a little consolation gift for yourself (though remember, batteries are rarely included).

The most unusual quality about the Red Light District is its integration into the Old Centre neighbourhood (for more, see p56). Police patrol the area with just enough visibility to dissuade most troublemakers. CCTV cameras keep a close eye on street activity and every window is equipped with an emergency alarm system that the woman behind it can activate if necessary. While the majority of clients, almost half of whom are locals, have no interest at all in harming a prostitute, these safeguards give workers a feeling of reassurance. One misdemeanour that's guaranteed to cause trouble is taking a photo of a window prostitute. If you get the urge, try to imagine yourself in their place and remember that they're not zoo animals. If you really need a picture of an Amsterdam window gal, pop into a tourist shop that sells suitable postcards.

The subject of prostitution always raises concerns about STDs. Sex workers take their healthcare seriously and will insist on using a condom – and clients should do likewise. There are no laws requiring prostitutes to have medical check-ups but there's an STD clinic in the Old Side's Red Light District where sex workers can go anonymously for free check-ups. The prostitute-rights organisation, De Rode Draad, went bankrupt in 2012, but there's still a sex workers' union, Vakwerk. You can find out about both at the **Prostitution Information Centre** (PIC, Enge Kerk Steeg 3, 420 7328, www.pic-amsterdam.com). Recently, a couple of other 'educational centers' have opened up. **Red Light Secrets – Prostitution Museum** (Oudezijds Achterburgwal 60h, www.redlightsecrets.com) allows you to touch, feel and empathise with the job of the sex worker (and take a nice snap of yourself in an S&M room). **Yab Yum** (Singel 295, 624 9503, www.yabyum.com) is a notorious brothel turned overpriced museum (ideal if you happen to be passionate about excessive 1980s kitsch).

Despite the increased openness, the situation does remain imperfect. The legal reforms in 2000 were aimed in part at reducing the number of illegal immigrants working in prostitution; but in actual fact, only a minority of prostitutes have no legal status. There are still exploitative situations involving coercion, parasitic and controlling 'boyfriends', and problems related to substance abuse. And while Project 1012 (see p57 **Red Light Blues**) was rationalised by the city as a way to battle human trafficking, critics believe that the cutting back of windows has only pushed the industry underground where it can't be regulated – thereby making conditions for sex workers even worse. Perhaps the most positive effect of all the legal changes has been to legitimise prostitution as a profession, which means that sex workers have access to social services and can legitimately band together to improve their working conditions. However, the stigma remains. Even in the most ideal circumstances, it's still difficult for prostitutes to balance their work and private lives. Further, prostitutes have problems when trying to get bank accounts, mortgages and insurance, despite being liable for taxes and generating an estimated half a billion euros a year.

Certainly, the locals' liberal, grown-up attitudes merit applause, and the methods they've employed to deal with the inevitability of a sex industry have arguably resulted in a better deal for both customer and sex worker. Visit with an open mind, but just don't be too surprised if Amsterdam's fabled Red Light District falls short of at least some of the hype.

DRUGS

You strut in through the front door of the coffeeshop, engage in a simple transaction and then smoke the sweet smoke. You strut out through the front door, wiggly, wasted and – most importantly, for you have done no wrong – free of any paranoia. Welcome to the Netherlands.

A large part of the country's image has been defined by its apparently lax attitude towards drugs. But this is misleading: soft drugs are still only semi-legal. Simply put, the famously pragmatic Dutch began to put drug laws into perspective back in the early 1970s. Swamped with heroin and repeatedly reminded by the ex-Provos and hippies then entering mainstream politics of the relatively benign nature of pot, the fight against wimpy drugs came to be seen as a ludicrous waste of time and money.

And so, in 1976, a vaguely worded law was passed to make a distinction between hard and soft drugs, effectively separating their markets from each other's influence and allowing the use and sale of small amounts of soft drugs – under 30 grams (one ounce). The 'front door' of the then embryonic 'coffeeshop' was now legal,

although the 'back door', where produce arrived by the kilo, looked out on an illegal distribution system. While the coffeeshop owner deals on the condoned side of this economy and can redirect his profits into other legal ventures (as many do, investing in hotels and nightclubs), and while suppliers experience the profitability of being illegal, the couriers who provide the link and run the risks without high returns remain in a legal limbo where such clichés as 'Kafkaesque' or 'catch-22' seem all too real.

And yet the wobbly system has worked. Time has passed without the increase in soft drug use that doomsayers predicted. The coffeeshop has become a part of the Amsterdam streetscape. And the concerted efforts against hard-drug use – less through law enforcement and more via education, methadone programmes, needle exchanges, drop-in shoot-up centres and counselling – have resulted in one of the lowest junkie populations in the world.

Moves towards complete legalisation of soft drugs have always been thwarted by a variety of factors: pressure from fellow EU members (France – which, funnily enough, is Holland's pipeline for heroin – and more recently Germany); tension between the government and coffeeshop owners (who have come to enjoy testing the boundaries of the vague laws); and the lack of a local supply. This last factor, though, was weakened by the 'green wave' of the early '90s, when the US-designed skunk blew over and was found to grow very nicely under artificial light; its descendants are the basis for the near-infinite variety of Nederweeds. Technology has even produced viable hash from the local harvest: foreign suppliers need no longer be involved.

In the name of keeping the peace with the EU, some politicians recently suggested making coffeeshops into private clubs, solely for local use – essentially sending tourists on to the street to score. But as things stand, that won't be happening any time soon. But the power of the anti-coffeeshop movement and new regulations have resulted in a halving of the number of coffeeshops in the Netherlands: from 1,200 in 1997 to 600 in 2013 (25 per cent of which are in Amsterdam). Meanwhile, local weed entrepreneurs are instead investing in countries such as Spain and Portugal that have come closer to the Netherlands' policies towards soft drugs.

Many other countries are also waking up to the advantages of the once-derided policies of the Dutch. Uruguay completely legalised weed in 2013. A similar trend is occurring state by state in the USA – once the staunchest of soldiers in the war against drugs. So the time might be on hand that those estimated 40,000 growing operations in the Netherlands may finally become legal, regulated and taxed. But yes, that might take a while.

There's an obvious difference between the locals' blasé attitude and how visitors behave. The majority of Amsterdammers treat soft drugs as just something else to do. Dope tourists, though, hit the coffeeshops with wide-eyed, giggling greed, then face a painful comedown when they belatedly realise that Dutch drugs are far stronger than those they're used to at home. (In hindisght, perhaps that third spacecake might have been two too many...)

Then there's the issue of organised crime. Every country has it in some form, of course, but the gangs in the Netherlands are able to go about their drug-running businesses with more ease than the government would like. Worse still, many Dutch gangs are believed to be freely trafficking drugs both hard and soft all over Europe, a fact that hasn't endeared the Netherlands to its neighbours.

And yet, and yet... the policy works. And before the world has caught up, the Dutch have moved on: since 1998, the pleasure-seeking public has become less hedonistic, smoking fewer joints (from 28 per cent to 19 per cent), dropping less ecstasy (from 27 per cent to eight per cent) and snorting less coke (ten per cent to three per cent). So you might want to put a bit of that in your pipe and smoke it.

ROLL UP

How to craft the perfect joint.

REGULAR EUROPEAN

STEP 1 Fold 50 per cent of your roach into a concertina and then smoothly roll the remaining cardboard around it.
STEP 2 Spread an even layer of tobacco down the middle of a king-sized paper, with slightly more at one end than the other. Spread your weed down the middle of the tobacco (this will make the spliff burn evenly). Position the roach.
STEP 3 Roll the tobacco back and forth between the paper until it's firm, which will help with rolling the final spliff.

SPLIFF DESIGN CLASS

CAMBERWELL CARROT

STEP 1 Stick two papers together at an angle slightly greater than 90 degrees, with the gummed edges at a right angle. Add additional papers as required. Create a fold in the angled papers in line with the first.
STEP 2 Add your tobacco, weed and roach as for the Regular European.
STEP 3 Roll carefully and expect spillage – don't worry; you can put it back into the top afterwards. Secure the first papers, then the angled ones, keeping the rolling tight.

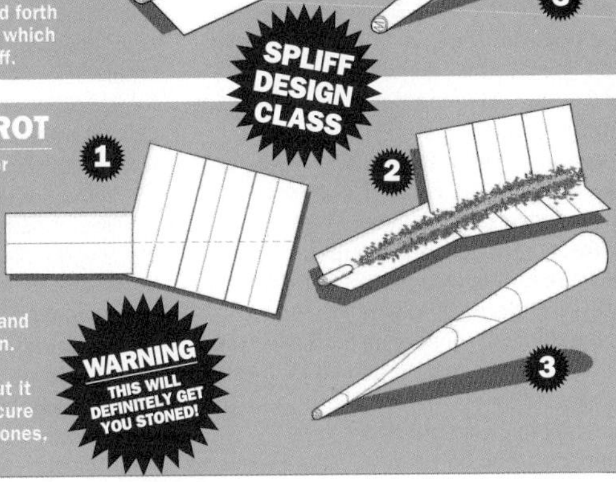

WARNING THIS WILL DEFINITELY GET YOU STONED!

IN CONTEXT

Cycling

Bicycles may be largely taken for granted these days, but as 'iron horses that need no feeding', they are still majestic beasts whose invention transformed life as much as the car and commercial flight. The *fiets* – as the Dutch call it – democratised movement by being both functionally and financially accessible. As an efficient agent of mobility, freeing up time for more noble pursuits, bikes also participated in the emancipation of women and found one of their biggest local cheerleaders in pioneering feminist Alleta Jacobs, the Netherlands' first female doctor and inventor of the family-planning 'Dutch cap'. And thanks to a bicycle's mechanical nudity – the artist Saul Steinberg called it an 'X-ray of itself' – bikes are easy to maintain as well. And did we mention their eco-friendly nature?

IN CONTEXT

TWO-WHEELED NATION

Don't mention it to the Dutch (more on this later), but it was a German, Karl van Drais (1785-1851), who envisioned two in-line wheels being steered by handlebars at the front. But this was only a 'walking bike', and it was not until 1861 that Ernest Michaux, a son of a Parisian wagon-maker, put pedals on the front wheel and created the *vélocipède*. Then, in 1871, Englishman James Starley made the discovery that a huge front wheel made things more efficient – only to be outdone in 1885 by his own nephew John Kemp Starley, who made his 'Rover' with two equal-sized wheels being back-propelled with a chain.

While later appended with rubber tyres to cure riders of headaches, this design had already achieved near-perfection. And it's this standard old 'bone-shaker', called an *oma fiets* ('granny bike'), that you still see most around town. This horizontal land – where only the wind offers any real challenges – has no need for light frames.

Bicycles, in their simplest incarnations, are intrinsic to Dutch identity: sensible, sober and befitting of the Calvinist doctrine of 'no pain, no gain'. Politicians and royals always take to the saddle for a photo shoot.

The Dutch also show their respect by buying 1.5 million bikes annually and then, in Amsterdam alone, stealing 150,000 of them. (Professional thieves steal 40 per cent, junkies 30 per cent, and 'occasion stealers' – read: broke students – account for the other 30 per cent.) It has been calculated that if the city's 881,000 bikes were all put together, they would fill Vondelpark thrice over.

Bike terms have entered the language in many ways. 'Bicycle bread' refers to raisin bread that is so skimpy on the raisins that a bike could ride between them. And if you see someone with gapped teeth, feel free to point, laugh and call them 'bike rack'. But the most widely used cycling phrase is 'Okay, first return the bike', which means 'first things first'. This commemorates the requisition by retreating Germans of the nation's bikes at the end of World War II, and provides part of the reason why spiteful locals still occasionally direct German tourists to the Anne Frankhuis when asked about the location of the nearest coffeeshop.

Bicycles played a particularly heady role for the Provos in the 1960s. This left-wing group combined anti-capitalist politics with a sense of the absurd, and their 'happenings' – which were to become blueprints for both the Yippies in America and the Situationists in France – were actually orchestrated mind games meant to provoke the authorities into embarrassing actions such as drug busts of haystacks. Their 1965 'White Bicycle Plan' donated a white painted bicycle to the citizens of Amsterdam for their free use in the hope that the city would follow through with thousands more. But it only provoked the police to impound it.

While there were many other 'White Plans' – such as the 'White Constable Plan' that envisioned white-clad cops equipped with lighters for joint-smokers, chickens for the hungry and oranges for the thirsty – only the 'White Bicycle Plan' managed to enter the realm of the nearly-real. The idea was formulated by Luud Schimmelpenninck who, as a newly elected councillor in 1967, tried to push the plan through over the next 30 years. He managed to deal with the logistics of finding sponsorship, weaving through the required bureaucracy, inventing an 'asshole-proof' bicycle and developing a computerised distribution system that would minimise theft. But after several trials and millions of guilders of investment, the plan proved unworkable in Amsterdam. But versions of the plan are currently very successful in Paris, Antwerp and Copenhagen.

The city is full of other cycling visionaries. Local squatters invented 'tall bike jousting', a recreation using bikes made of spare parts and welded together to reach dizzying heights. Perhaps you can convince **Recycled Bicycles** (Spuistraat 84a, www.recycled bicycles.org) to even build you one. And the **Fietsfabriek** (Sarphatistraat 141, www.fietsfabriek.nl) continues its quest to bring cargo bikes to the world. For a trendier tone, check out the minimal street bikes of **Vanmoof** (www.vanmoof.com) or the bamboo bikes of **Blackstar** (www.blackstarbikes.nl).

'Politicians and royals always take to the saddle for a photo shoot.'

A visionary touch is also required to deal with the mountains of parked bikes. VMX Architect built a shed for 2,500 bicycles that was pile-driven in a canal by Centraal Station, but it wasn't nearly enough to deal with the chaos. The city hopes to build 40,000 more spots by 2020, a third of them in manned parking lots underground. But will the stubborn Amsterdam cyclist be lured into them? Biking remains an emotional issue, as witnessed by the brouhaha surrounding the bike path under the Rijksmuseum (*see p131* **The 'Museum of the Netherlands'**).

To learn how rich the history of cycling is in Amsterdam, get a copy of Pete Jordan's obsessively researched and excellently written *In the City of Bikes: The Story of the Amsterdam Cyclist*. It tells the story of the author's own love affair with bikes – and using them to explore the city's streets – while weaving in the history of cycles since the locals went crazy for them in the 1890s.

ON YOUR BIKE
For those who want to ride, here are some tips. Firstly, only cycle if you know how. Ignore traffic lights (unless the police are around of course). Amsterdam cyclists hate to queue behind people waiting for a red light, and in general regard traffic lights as charmingly inconsequential pop-art town decorations. If you do get into an accident, it's usually the car drivers who lose in court and hence are the ones who will pay for your shiny new wheelchair. Also, remember to stick to your right and watch out for the tram tracks and tourists reading maps on the bike path. It may also help to read a few books on chaos theory before setting out. Oh, and avoid travelling in packs; yes, we're talking to you British rugby players and Italians.

Amsterdam cyclists are rightfully proud, or perhaps even a little smug, about their rights to the road. So they should be, since bikes play a key role in achieving the long-term sustainability of our planet. Happy pedalling!

IN CONTEXT

Essential Information

Hotels

With accommodation options in the city running the gamut from B&Bs and privately owned small hotels to enormous, and enormously posh, establishments, Amsterdam does its best to find a bed for everybody. Nonetheless, there is still a shortage of places to stay: the question is, where to put new hotels in this densely packed environment. Thankfully, people are coming up with some wonderfully inspired solutions, whether it's updating a youth prison or building designer suites in a crane. Limited space in the city centre means that hotel rooms there tend to be on the small side, and you don't get that much bang for your buck. Still, many make up for their somewhat modest dimensions with that most prized commodity: a canal view.

STAYING IN AMSTERDAM

Despite the economic downturn, new luxury hotels have continued to pop up around town. With 93 rooms and suites spread across six canal houses, the **Waldorf Astoria Amsterdam** (Herengracht 542-556, 710 6090, www.3.hilton.com) is one of the most hotly anticipated hotel openings of 2014. Other relative newcomers include the **Conservatorium**, located in a former 19th-century music conservatory, and the **Sir Albert Hotel**, in a former diamond

IN THE KNOW
APARTMENT RENTALS

Longer-term accommodation options do exist, though the range isn't enormous. A few hotels have apartments, or you can try **Apartment Services** (www. apartment services.nl) or **StayAmsterdam** (www.stayamsterdam.com). **City Mundo** (http://amsterdam.citymundo.com) matches visitors to assorted kinds of accommodation – anything from a room in a flat to a houseboat or a traditional Dutch windmill.

factory. Both exhibit a local pattern whereby existing buildings are revamped in favour of construction from scratch.

These two may well have been inspired by the earlier successes of former shipping office **Grand Hotel Amrâth Amsterdam** and onetime youth prison **Lloyd Hotel**. The latter has also opened **Hotel The Exchange**, in a prime central location, with each room decked out by a different fashion designer.

The budget end of the market has been just as creative. Plus, they've had to face some fierce competition from the likes of Airbnb and Couchsurfing, which have proved popular in a city where the residents are both relaxed and hospitable. **CitizenM** – local folks with global ambitions – came up with their own unique solution: stacking up some shipping containers and renting them out as 'budget luxury' accommodation. Meanwhile, in neighbouring Sloterdijk to the west, hostel **Meineger Hotel** (Orlyplein 1, 808 0502, www.meininger-hotels.com) has been built in an abandoned office building. Nearby, the new **Student Hotel Amsterdam** (Jan van Galenstraat 335, Bos en Lommer, 422 8669, www.thestudenthotel.com) combines a campus vibe with extended-stay deals. The best way to experience the local version of Dutch hospitality is to stay in a B&B. These are often stylish affairs, with prices to match (*see p287* **Small and Suite**).

Hotels cluster around particular districts of Amsterdam: the Museum Quarter and the Canals district have plenty, whereas De Pijp and Jordaan, alas, contain only a few. A general rule of thumb is to avoid those near Centraal Station or the Red Light District.

If you want to rent a houseboat for your stay, check out www.houseboats.nl. For campsites, *see p288* **Canvas Nights**.

MONEY MATTERS

Hotels are graded according to an official star-rating system designed to sort the deluxe from the dumps – but we haven't followed it in this guide, as the ratings merely reflect room size and amenities such as lifts or bars, rather than other important factors such as decor, staff or atmosphere. Instead, we've divided the hotels by area, then listed them in five categories, according to the standard prices (not including seasonal offers or discounts) for one night in a double room with en suite shower/bath. For **Deluxe** hotels, you can expect to pay more than €350; for properties in the **Expensive** bracket, €225-€350; for **Moderate** properties, allow €100-€225; while **Budget** rooms go for less than €100. For **Hostels**, you'll pay €50-€75 for a double, around €20 for a dorm bed. For gay hotels, *see p182*.

Note that credit cards aren't always accepted in this quaint old city, particularly in smaller places. The room rate may, or may not, include the city tax of five per cent; it could be added to your final bill. Most hotels have Wi-Fi, but you may be charged extra for it. Before booking, it's always worth checking for special deals on the hotel's own website or on more commercial websites – www.tripadvisor.com and www.booking.nl (also in English) are good places to start.

THE OLD CENTRE

Deluxe

Grand Hotel Amrâth Amsterdam

Prins Hendrikkade 108-114 (552 0000, www. amrathamsterdam.com). Tram 1, 2, 4, 5, 9, 13, 14, 16, 17, 24, 26. **Map** p313 L7.

The Grand Hotel Amrâth nods handsomely to both Dutch sea-faring supremacy and the birth of an architectural movement. Considered to be the first example of the Amsterdam School, this century-old shipping office, known as the Scheepvaarthuis (Maritime House), bursts with creative brickwork and sculpture. The hotel's feeling of timelessness remains, although you can expect the usual range of deluxe frills and fripperies, plus (a rarity here) a pool. Some rooms have supplements for specific views. There's also the prestigious three-storey suite in the front tower.
▶ *For more on this monumental building, see p251 School of Rock.*

Grand Hotel Krasnapolsky

Dam 9 (795 6088, www.nh-hotels.nl). Tram 4, 9, 14, 16, 24. **Map** p312 J8.

Slap-bang in the middle of the action, the Grand Hotel Krasnapolsky is Amsterdam's best-known

ESSENTIAL INFORMATION

Art'otel Amsterdam. *See p278.*

hotel. It's directly opposite the Koninklijk Paleis (Royal Palace; *see p78*), and it can certainly compete when it comes to looks, grace and glamour. Accommodation ranges from the full-on indulgence of the Tower Suite to cheaper, more compact rooms at the rear, which is where you'll end up if you book one of the bargain deals. The spectacular glass Winter Garden (a listed monument) is open to non-guests for weekend brunch.

★ Hotel de l'Europe
Nieuwe Doelenstraat 2-14 (531 1777, www.leurope.nl). Tram 4, 9, 14, 16, 24. **Map** p312 K10.
A luxury landmark with fabulous views across the Amstel, this is the place to head for an indulgent splurge or a honeymoon hideaway. As should be expected at these prices, every detail is taken care of. The Provocateur suite has a round bed and an in-room jacuzzi big enough for two. The hotel is one of the few in Amsterdam to boast a pool, and its Bord'Eau restaurant, with two Michelin stars, is highly rated. Freddy's Bar – named after beer king Heineken – is a woody and evocative place in which to sip a cocktail or suck back a cigar.

★ Sofitel Legend The Grand Amsterdam
Oudezijds Voorburgwal 197 (555 3111, www.sofitel-legend-thegrand.com). Tram 1, 2, 4, 5, 9, 13, 14, 16, 17, 24. **Map** p312 K9.
Steeped in centuries of history, the Grand is located near the centre of the Red Light District. But the moment guests step into the luxurious courtyard, they feel as if they've been whisked a million miles away from the risqué surroundings. Rooms are spacious and airy, and the art deco-style bathrooms come supplied with Hermès and L'Occitane smellies. There's also a stellar restaurant, Bridges (*see p67*).

Expensive

Art'otel Amsterdam
Prins Hendrikkade 33 (719 7222, www.artotel amsterdam.com). Tram 1, 2, 4, 5, 9, 13, 14, 16, 17, 24. **Map** p312 J7.
See p283 **Designer Dreams**. *Photo p277.*

Hotel The Exchange
Damrak 50 (523 0080, www.hoteltheexchange. com). Tram 1, 2, 4, 5, 9, 13, 14, 16, 17, 24. **Map** p312 J8.

HOME FROM HOME
Consider a B&B.

While B&Bs are often seen as a cheap and cheerful option, Amsterdam's versions tend to be chic affairs, kitted out to their stylish owners' exacting specifications. You'll need to book ahead – restrictions limit the number of guests allowed to stay in a house at any one time to four.

Between Art & Kitsch
Ruysdaelkade 75-2, De Pijp (679 0485, www.between-art-and-kitsch.com). **No credit cards.** **Map** p315 L14.
Technically speaking, this B&B is located between the museums and De Pijp. Set on a delightful canal, it's great for culture vultures keen to get out and explore. There are just two guest rooms: one is decorated in mock art deco with authentic period knick-knacks; the other works a faux baroque look. Both live up to the name's promise, making it the quirky choice.

Kamer01
Singel 416, Southern Canal Belt (06 5477 6151 mobile, www.kamer01.nl). Tram 1, 2, 5. **Map** p315 J10.
A very stylish, gay-friendly place designed by Atelier Hertogh. The Red Room is sensually scarlet and comes with a shower big enough for an entire football team; the Blue Room has a sexy circular bed. Both share a private roof terrace. Then there's the grand Green Suite. Rooms are equipped with iMacs, flatscreen TVs and DVD players. The downstairs kitchen offers a help-yourself 'maxi bar' and titbits from nearby bakery Holtkamp. Minimum stay is two nights.

Kamer01.

Swissotel Amsterdam.

A simple hallway leads back to a red gift-box of a reception, offering just a peek of the statement seating in the mezzanine above. Each of the 61 rooms in this hotel (graded from one to five stars) has been exquisitely designed by Amsterdam fashion graduates – and it shows.

NH Barbizon Palace
Prins Hendrikkade 59-72 (556 4564, www. nh-hotels.nl). Tram 1, 2, 4, 5, 9, 13, 14, 16, 17, 24. **Map** p312 K7.
A flash branch of the reliable NH chain, the Barbizon is opposite Centraal Station. Public areas are decked out in sleek monochrome, which makes the rooms themselves a bit disappointing. The on-site facilities, however, couldn't be accused of being run-of-the-mill. They include a meeting room in the 15th-century St Olof Chapel and Michelin-starred restaurant Vermeer.

Renaissance Amsterdam
Kattengat 1 (621 2223, www.renaissance amsterdam.nl). Tram 1, 2, 5, 13, 17. **Map** p312 H7.
This 400-room hotel is a smart option for exploring the bohemian charms of the Haarlemmerstraat and Jordaan areas. It compensates for its flowery decor with top-end hotel luxuries such as in-house films, interactive videos and a fitness centre, making it a good bet for flush families with recalcitrant kids. There's also a babysitting service. High-tech conference facilities bring in business travellers.

Swissotel Amsterdam
Damrak 96 (522 3000, www.swissotel.com/hotels/ amsterdam). Tram 4, 9, 16, 24. **Map** p312 J8.
Geared firmly towards the business market, the handsome Swissotel is also a good choice for holidaymakers. All rooms are soundproofed against the hullabaloo outside and come with big beds, and on-demand film and music. Fork out for a pricier room and you'll get an espresso machine and some swish design. The suites overlook Dam Square.
▶ *For some serious retail therapy, pop across to department store De Bijenkorf; see p71.*

★ Victoria Amsterdam
Damrak 1-5 (623 4255, www.parkplaza.com/ victoriaamsterdam). Tram 1, 2, 4, 5, 9, 16, 24, 26. **Map** p312 J7.
A reliable option, the 300-room Victoria is located opposite Centraal Station. The public areas, decked out in browns, creams and reds, are very dapper indeed. Bedrooms are of a good size and come with all the expected trappings. A big plus is the excellent health club and pool, open to non-guests for a fee.

Moderate

Hotel V Nesplein
Nes 49 (662 3233, www.hotelv.nl). Tram 4, 10. **Map** p312 K9.

Located on a charming theatre street, this boutique B&B-style hotel is ideal for business travellers sick of corporate sterility. All rooms have new-age, sleek decor, and the lounge-cum-restaurant, known as the Lobby, looks lovely with its open fireplace and opulent finishings.
Other location Hotel V Frederiksplein, Weteringschans 136, Southern Canal Belt (662 3233).

Nova
Nieuwezijds Voorburgwal 276 (623 0066, www.novahotel.nl). Tram 1, 2, 5, 13, 14, 17. **Map** p312 J9.
Arranged across five townhouses, the rooms here are plainly furnished yet good-looking in an Ikea kind of way, and comfortable. Bathrooms, though, can be a tight squeeze. Nova is handily located for the Nieuwezijds nightlife, as well as all the cultural sights. For longer stays, it rents apartments at Nicolaas Maesstraat 72, near Museumplein.

★ Residence le Coin
Nieuwe Doelenstraat 5 (524 6800, www.lecoin.nl). Tram 4, 9, 14, 16, 24. **Map** p312 K10.
On a quiet, café-lined street between the Old Centre and the main shopping district, this medium-sized hotel arranged across seven buildings has spacious, stylish rooms in muted colours with minimal fussy extras. Big windows mean they're drenched in light. Furniture is a classy mix of old and new; the attic rooms are particularly full of character. Many of the rooms have kitchenettes.

RHO Hotel
Nes 5-23 (620 7371, www.rhohotel.com). Tram 1, 2, 4, 5, 9, 13, 14, 16, 17, 24. **Map** p312 J9.

Make the most of the city with Time Out

timeout.com/london

If your budget doesn't stretch quite as far as the swankier hotels on and around Dam Square, this is a match for them in terms of location – it's set on an interesting backstreet bustling with lovely bars, restaurants and theatres. The lobby is pure 1930s glam (reflecting the building's past as a gold merchant's offices), though bedrooms are merely plain and tidy. The single rooms, it has to be said, are really rather minuscule.

Budget

★ Greenhouse Effect

*Warmoesstraat 53-55 (624 4974, www.
greenhouse-effect.nl). Tram 1, 2, 4, 5, 9,
14, 16, 24.* **Map** p312 K7.

Planning on immersing yourself in cannabis culture? Then this might be just the place to rest your addled head. Some rooms have shared facilities; several are kitted out in suitably trippy style, while others are just plain, old-fashioned sweet, overlooking one of the canals. To take the edge off any sore heads, breakfast is served until noon. The bar has an all-day happy hour and arranges drum 'n' bass, reggae and rare groove nights.

▶ *You can toke on some high-quality ganja in the coffeeshop downstairs; see p70.*

Winston Hotel

*Warmoesstraat 129 (428 4934, www.winston.nl).
Tram 1, 2, 4, 5, 9, 14, 16, 24.* **Map** p312 K8.

The legendary Winston, now part of St Christopher's Inns, is renowned for its youthful, party-loving atmosphere, and arty rooms decorated in eccentric, eclectic style by local businesses and artists. The dorms (of four, six or eight beds) are much cheaper – but much less fun. There's a late-opening bar on site, and a good club, Winston Kingdom (*see p191*).

Hostels

★ Flying Pig Downtown

*Nieuwendijk 100 (420 6822, www.flying
pig.nl). Tram 1, 2, 3, 5, 13, 16, 17, 24, 26.*
Map p312 J7.

Not so much a hostel, more a way of life. Young backpackers flock here from around the world, as much for the social life as the accommodation; the hostel organises walking tours and in-line skating for free, and there are regular parties and cheap beer. A pool table, chill-out room, DJ nights, 'munchies' for sale: Flying Pig hostels are for visitors who giggle when they say the word 'Amsterdam'. They don't accept guests aged under 16 or over 40 – and our guess is that anyone over 30 will feel like a senior citizen. With locations near Leidseplein and at the beach in Noordwijk (and free shuttle buses between them), you're sure to find multiple ways to get your party on and make plenty of friends.

Other locations Flying Pig Uptown, Vossiusstraat 46-47, Vondelpark (400 4187).

Shelter City Christian Hostels

*Barndesteeg 21 (625 3230, www.shelter.nl).
Metro Nieuwmarkt.* **Map** p312 K8.

Virtuous visitors who don't want to participate in the vices Amsterdam has to offer can enjoy the peace and quiet of the alcohol-, drug- and smoke-free Shelter City Christian Hostels. With single-sex dorm rooms, activities such as cookie-baking and daily Bible discussion, guests might even be able to counteract the sins they've inadvertently witnessed. Dorm beds are charitably cheap at both locations, and you don't even have to be Christian to stay here.

Other locations Bloemstraat 179, Jordaan (624 4717).

WESTERN CANAL BELT

Deluxe

★ Dylan

*Keizersgracht 384 (530 2010, www.dylan
amsterdam.com). Tram 1, 2, 5.* **Map** p314 H11.

Outrageous elegance is the selling point here. Guests are made to feel like superstars and lodge in colour-coded chromotherapy rooms – such as zingy raspberry, zen-like black or toasty turmeric – designed to enhance your mood. Every detail, from Michelin-starred chef Dennis Kuipers' contemporary French-inspired menu in the Vinkeles restaurant, to the careful alignment of the cushions in the public areas, is well thought out by the owners.

Eden Amsterdam American Hotel

*Leidsekade 97 (556 3000, www.edenamsterdam
americanhotel.com). Tram 1, 2, 5, 7, 10.*
Map p314 H12.

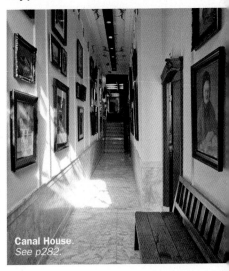

Canal House.
See p282.

The public areas of this dazzling art nouveau monument are all eye-pleasers – especially the magnificently buttressed Café Americain. The rooms, though (excepting the suites), are pretty cramped and decorated in smart-but-bland standard hotel fittings. They do have good views, either on to the canal or the bustling square below, and some have their own balcony. Meeting facilities are available.

★ Hotel Pulitzer
Prinsengracht 315-331 (523 5235, www.hotelpulitzeramsterdam.nl). Tram 13, 14, 17. **Map** *p312 G10.*
Sprawling across 25 canal houses, the Pulitzer is an ideal destination for indulgent getaways. Guests can arrive by boat, there are antiques galore, rooms are big and stylish, and the facilities are top-notch. A lovely garden nestles at the back. In August, the Grachtenfestival (*see p41*) of classical music takes place in and around the hotel grounds, making it an excellent choice for music fans.

Expensive

★ Ambassade Hotel
Herengracht 341 (555 0222, www.ambassade-hotel.nl). Tram 1, 2, 5. **Map** *p312 H10.*
Known as the 'literary' hotel, where many famous authors check in when visiting the city, the Ambassade has a library full of books signed by its more illustrious guests, which you're free to peruse. It also has a magnificent collection of art by famous CoBrA artists. Taking up ten canal houses on the Herengracht, it's also a stone's throw from the Spui, where there are plenty of new and second-hand

bookshops for furthering your reading, and browsing, pleasure.

Andaz Amsterdam
Prinsengracht 587 (523 1234, www.amsterdam.prinsengracht.andaz.hyatt.com). Tram 1, 2, 5. **Map** *p314 H11.*
See p283 **Designer Dreams**.

★ Canal House
Keizersgracht 148 (622 5182, www.canalhouse.nl). Tram 13, 17. **Map** *p312 G8.*
After recent renovations, these three 17th-century canal houses are certainly fresh in the way they combine old (ornate chimneys, heavy ceiling beams and a tasteful array of knick-knacks) and new (plush modern furnishings, and obsessive but not intrusive service). After reopening in 2012, it was quickly acclaimed as one of Europe's great hotels by such heavy-hitters as *Condé Nast Traveler* and the *New York Times*. *Photo p281.*

Maison Rika
Oude Spiegelstraat 12 (330 1112, www.rika int.com). Tram 2, 13, 14. **Map** *p312 H10.*
A chic two-bedroom canal house across the way from Ulrika 'Rika' Lundgren's Nine Streets fashion emporium, where the Swedish fashion maven provides a carefully curated to-do list so guests can experience Amsterdam like a local – albeit a very well-heeled one.

Toren
Keizersgracht 164 (622 6352, www.thetoren.nl). Tram 1, 13, 17. **Map** *p312 G8.*
This building has been a Golden Age mansion, a prime minister's home, a university and even a hiding place for persecuted Jews during World War II. Now, it's a family-run, 37-room hotel with all the usual trappings: opulent fabrics, grand public rooms and attentive staff. The standard rooms are a bit cramped, but deluxe rooms have jacuzzis, and the bridal suites come with double whirlpool baths.

Moderate

Estherea
Singel 303-309 (624 5146, www.estherea.nl). Tram 1, 2, 5. **Map** *p312 J10.*
Spread over several charming canal houses at the heart of this elegant district, this private hotel has been run by the same family for decades. The emphasis is on understated, simple luxury. Rooms come equipped with DVDs and marble bathrooms, ensuring that once you're in, you won't want to stray from your front door. The Estherea also has a library.

't Hotel
Leliegracht 18 (422 2741, www.thotel.nl). Tram 1, 2, 5, 13, 14, 17. **Map** *p312 G8.*

Maison Rika.

DESIGNER DREAMS

From snot vases to penis lamps, a new breed of art hotels has arrived.

Andaz Amsterdam.

The love child of Dutch design maestro Marcel Wanders and hospitality super-group Hyatt, the **Andaz Amsterdam** (*see p282*) is stuffed with playful references to Amsterdam and 'Dutchness'. Then again, its lush worldliness makes it positively un-Dutch. With images of giant tulips and Wanders' 'airborne snotty vases' also on display, the 122-room hotel can seem plain surreal.

Wanders, who is renowned for his Knotted Chair and design hub **Moooi** (*see p122*), has transformed a notoriously ugly public library into something entirely worthy of Hyatt's 'luxury boutique division'. The location is ace: beside the Prinsengracht canal, in the middle of the quirky Nine Streets shopping district.

The public spaces are bold and dramatic. Huge bell-shaped chandeliers hang above carpets that feature cartographic patterns reminiscent of the Golden Age of exploration. The wallpaper is covered in graphic motifs (in Delft blue) that reference Amsterdam's long relationship with literature and the arts; and monitors beam the very latest in video art.

The rooms themselves are bright and modern, with a pair of 'screaming' clogs mounted on the wall and Delftware-style washbasins. To reflect the building's bibliophile past, each room comes with

an excellent selection of books about design and Amsterdam; the five luxury rooftop suites get their own mini libraries.

Meanwhile, **Art'otel Amsterdam** (*see p278*) has penis lamps in its library and huge airborne sperm flying high in the atrium – yet it's all very tasteful. Opened in 2013 just across from Centraal Station, the hotel's restaurant/lounge **5&33** (*see p80*) is already one of the city's hippest hangouts.

Part of an art-meets-life hotel chain, Art'otel uses specific artists to decorate their hotels. Globally acclaimed Rotterdam artist Joep van Lieshout was asked to be the artist-in-residence for the Amsterdam outpost. Specialising in sculptures and installations that blur the boundaries between art, design, architecture, the rational and the irrational, he's given the world fully-realised slave camps, rectum bars and even his own take on handbags.

The hotel is dotted with Van Lieshout's works, all themed around the cycle of life. As if to compensate, the 107 rooms are more about efficient elegance and are equally suitable for work and lounging, with large-screen LED TVs, multimedia panels for your electronics, and Illy espresso machines – with, you guessed it, Van Lieshout cups. Take a sip and live the life...

A stylish bolt-hole near some lovely restaurants and bars, and ideally placed for scenic strolls. This prosaically named place is fitted throughout in 1920s-inspired style: Bauhaus prints adorn the walls, the colour scheme is muted, and the armchairs are design classics. The spacious rooms have great views, whether to the canal in front or the garden behind. The characterful split-level room in the eaves sleeps up to five.

Truelove Guesthouse

Prinsenstraat 4 (320 2500, 06 2480 5672 mobile after 6pm, www.truelove.be). Tram 1, 2, 5. **Map** p312 G8.
Set above an old antiques shop (which now serves as the hotel reception), this dinky place is decorated with the odd quirky piece from the selection downstairs. The attic room is the best, but all come with fridge, TV and kettle. There's also an apartment located on Langestraat.

Budget

★ Hotel Brouwer

Singel 83 (624 6358, www.hotelbrouwer.nl). Tram 1, 2, 4, 5, 9, 13, 16, 17, 24, 26. **No credit cards. Map** p312 H8.
The eight neat, en suite rooms are named after Dutch painters, and all look on to the Singel canal. Don't expect rafts of extra touches, just honest, reasonably priced accommodation in a long-standing family-run hotel. A traditional Dutch breakfast is included in the price. Unusually for budget class, there's a lift, plus TVs in the double rooms.

Singel Hotel

Singel 13-17 (626 3108, www.singelhotel.nl). Tram 1, 2, 4, 5, 9, 13, 16, 17, 24, 26. **Map** p312 H7.
Ideally located for canal and Jordaan strolls, and for arrival and departure by train, the Singel is a five-minute walk from the station, and right next door to the beautiful, domed Koepel church. Inside its 17th-century walls, rooms are plain and furnished in a modern, basic style; they're generally clean and tidy, and all are ensuite. Front-facing rooms can be noisy due to their proximity to the nightlife.

SOUTHERN CANAL BELT

Deluxe

★ Hotel 717

Prinsengracht 717 (427 0717, www.717hotel.nl). Tram 1, 2, 5. **Map** p314 J12.
A rather well-kept secret, this small, flower-filled boutique hotel only offers suites and is the epitome of understated glamour. The emphasis is on searching the globe for the best accoutrements – linens from the USA, bespoke blankets from Wales, boxspring mattresses from London. Afternoon tea

is served every day, and there's a patio for summer breakfasts or general lounging. Guests are the type that like to shed their euros on antiques in the Spiegelkwartier. The room rate includes breakfast, house wines, TV, wireless internet and a DVD collection. A lovely choice.

★ InterContinental Amstel Amsterdam

Professor Tulpplein 1 (622 6060, www.amsterdam. intercontinental.com). Tram 4, 7, 10 or Metro Weesperplein. **Map** p315 O11
They don't come much posher than this. Standing imperiously over the Amstel river, this is where movie stars or royalty lay their heads when they come to town, on a supersoft pillow in one of the huge, soundproofed rooms. Everything here is superlative: arrival by the hotel's own boat is possible; staff are both liveried and top-hatted; the galleried lobby is breathtaking; regional French restaurant La Rive (*see p106*) has a Michelin star; even the swimming pool looks out on to the river. If money is no object or you're after that once-in-a-lifetime splurge, this is the place to go.

Expensive

Banks Mansion

Herengracht 519-525 (420 0055, www.banks mansion.nl). Tram 16, 24. **Map** p314 K11.
Once you've checked in to this grand hotel in a former bank building, everything is yours: drinks and snacks in the lounge, films and minibar in your room – they're all free, because the owners want to create a homely feel. This all-inclusive hotel also provides a pillow menu, rain showerheads, plasma TVs and DVD players in every room.

Dikker & Thijs Fenice Hotel

Prinsengracht 444 (620 1212, www.dtfh.nl). Tram 1, 2, 5, 7, 10. **Map** p314 J12.
A long-established name on Amsterdam's hotel scene, this upmarket place in an 18th-century warehouse building near Leidseplein often has authors dropping in to stay. Rooms are plain but smart, while the glamorous penthouse has a wall made of glass for unsurpassed views over the city rooftops. At breakfast time, guests are bathed in jewel-coloured light from the stained-glass windows.

★ Mercure Hotel Arthur Frommer

Noorderstraat 46 (721 9175, www.mercure.com). Tram 4, 16, 24. **Map** p315 L12.
Occupying a series of attractive townhouses arranged around a courtyard, this Mercure hotel is a real oasis of relaxation. Set on a charming residential street within walking distance of the sights and the nightlife, and a couple of minutes' stroll from the Amstelkerk, it's also in one of the finest locations in town. Rooms are both spacious and smart, and there's a cosy bar and stylish public areas.

Moderate

Amsterdam Wiechmann

Prinsengracht 328-332 (626 3321, www.
hotelwiechmann.nl). Tram 1, 2, 5, 7, 17.
Map p314 G11.

From a suit of armour in the reception to 1950s teapots and toasters in the breakfast room, retro touches from every era adorn this rather eccentric, long-established hotel. Room decoration tends towards the chintzy, but things are brought up to date with free Wi-Fi. Check the website for plenty of special deals.

Bridge Hotel

Amstel 107-111 (623 7068, www.thebridge
hotel.nl). Tram 4, 7, 9, 10 or Metro Weesperplein.
Map p315 N11.

Feeling gloriously isolated on the eastern banks of the River Amstel, this private hotel in a former stonemason's workshop is just a few minutes' stroll from the bright lights of Rembrandtplein and the rest of the city centre. It's also well situated for exploring the Plantage and Jodenbuurt. Rooms are simple and bright; ones that command a river view cost more, of course. For longer stays, there are self-catering apartments and a studio.

Hotel de Munck

Achtergracht 1-3 (623 6283, www.hoteldemunck.
com). Tram 4, 7, 10. **Map** p315 N11.

This higgledy-piggledy place in an old Dutch East India Company captain's house is perched on a secluded little canal near the river. Rooms are plain and basic (and some are looking rather tired), though they are clean and neat. The breakfast room is a delight, though, with a 1950s jukebox and walls plastered with old album covers.

Nicolaas Witsen

Nicolaas Witsenstraat 4 (626 6546, www.hotel
nicolaaswitsen.nl). Tram 4, 7, 10 or Metro
Weesperplein. **Map** p315 M12.

One of the few hotels to fill the gap between the museums and De Pijp, this place, though plain, functional and a tad overpriced, is well placed for culture- and fun-seekers. The excellent delicatessen on the corner of the street encourages in-room midnight feasting.

★ Seven Bridges

Reguliersgracht 31 (623 1329, www.sevenbridges
hotel.nl). Tram 4, 16, 24. **Map** p315 L11.

Ideal for those who want a luxury hidey-hole far from the madding crowd that's also conveniently located for the museums and city centre. There are no public spaces here, apart from the lobby and garden, just ten lovely rooms stuffed mainly with antiques. This lack of shared space means all guests must suffer the privation of compulsory breakfast in bed. It's one of Amsterdam's best-kept secrets, although we have a strong feeling that it won't remain one for much longer.

Budget

★ Hotel Prinsenhof

Prinsengracht 810 (623 1772, www.hotel
prinsenhof.com). Tram 4, 7, 10, 16, 24.
Map p312 M11.

College Hotel. *See p286.*

A good option for budget travellers, this diminutive, ten-room hotel with helpful and friendly staff is right near the city's nightlife, and foodie Utrechtsestraat. The stairs are positively vertiginous – luggage is hauled up on a pulley. Rooms are simple, clean and tidy; some have shared facilities. Best of all, rooms with canal views don't attract a premium.

JORDAAN & WEST
Moderate

Frederic Rentabike
Brouwersgracht 78 (624 5509, www.frederic.nl). *Bus 18, 21, 22.* **No credit cards. Map** p312 G7.
This bike shop has a nice little sideline in renting out rooms, apartments and six houseboats (mostly in the Jordaan), ranging from the sleek to the downright homely. Houseboat no.5 on the Prinsengracht is big, stylish and comes with free internet access.

MUSEUMS, VONDELPARK & ZUID
Deluxe

Conservatorium
Van Baerlestraat 27 (570 0000, www. conservatoriumhotel.com). Tram 1, 2, 3, 5, 12, 16, 24. **Map** p314 J14.
With a prestigious location on the Museumplein, this grand 19th-century neo-Gothic building, latterly the Sweelinck music conservatory, has been transformed into a wonderfully stylish place to stay. Italian architect Piero Lissoni has embraced the building's rich historical heritage while introducing

contemporary clean lines and a muted colour scheme to the 129-room hotel. As well as ultra-luxe suites and upmarket spa and gym facilities, there's some excellent drinking and dining to be had. The brasserie/lounge is a striking space, set in a brick courtyard with soaring windows and a glass ceiling.

Expensive

College Hotel
Roelof Hartstraat 1 (571 1511, www.thecollegehotel. com). Tram 3, 5, 12. **Map** p315 L16.
All the staff at this outpost of Amsterdam's college for the hotel and catering trades are students, who are training in situ. The boutique styling and glamorous touches (bathrooms are a strong point) ensure that prices are far from pocket money, though the downside is that service is unpredictable. Some rooms are small, though you get oodles of space if you're prepared to pay top dollar. There's a bar and ambitious modern Dutch restaurant. *Photos p285.*

Moderate

★ Bilderberg Jan Luyken
Jan Luykenstraat 58 (573 0730, www. bilderberg.nl). Tram 2, 5, 7, 10. **Map** p314 J14.
One of the city's most stylish secrets, this place is just a kitten-heeled skip away from the designer shops of PC Hooftstraat. Rooms – slickly done out, with designer touches – are something of a bargain for a place with such looks and facilities. Check the website for special deals.

CitizenM
Prinses Irenestraat 30 (811 7090, www.citizenm. com). Tram 5, 16.
Welcome to the future of hotels: the shipping container. Due to the housing shortage in Amsterdam, local students have long been living in these humble units, but CitizenM is now using them as the basis for a 'budget luxury' designer-hotel chain. Created and assembled off-site, the 14sq m (150sq ft) rooms have a wall-to-wall window, a king-size bed with luxury linens, a shower pod, a toilet pod, and a flatscreen TV. Refreshments are available 24/7 from the 'canteen'.
Other locations Jan Plezierweg 2, Schiphol Airport (811 7080).

Conscious Hotel Museum Square
De Lairessestraat 7 (671 9596, www.conscious hotels.com). Tram 2, 3, 5, 12. **Map** p314 J16.
This relatively new, fairly priced and sustainable Dutch chain fashions an 'eco design' vibe while being careful not to come across as 'hippy'. Expect desks made from recycled plastics, upside-down plants over the bed, and the use of enviromentally friendly cleaning products.
Other locations Conscious Hotel Vondelpark, Overtoom 519-521, Vondelpark (820 3333).

CitizenM.

ESSENTIAL INFORMATION

SMALL AND SUITE
Want an alternative to a conventional hotel?

The city's hunger for new places to stay has resulted in some imaginative and unusual accommodation solutions – the only drawback is that most are only big enough for a couple.

'Boutique hostel' **Cocomama** (Westeinde 18, Southern Canal Belt, 627 2454, www.cocomama.nl) is located in a former brothel. In the past, it cost €200 for an hour of fun at 'gentlemen's club' Princess; now it costs from €26 for a whole night. The rooms have been rebuilt to sleep groups of two to six; one room still suggests the house's rosy origins, while the others have been decorated with more traditional Dutch themes. Every Tuesday, the friendly lady proprietors cook a meal – plus there's a garden for further interaction.

Faralda NDSM Crane Hotel Amsterdam (NDSM-Plein 78, Noord, 06 5580 0659 mobile, www.faralda.nl) is a much posher and less down-to-earth (literally) affair. Three luxury double suites – 'Mystic', 'Free Spirit' and 'Secret' – have been built into the old crane that was once used to position ships in dry dock at former shipyard NDSM (*see p158* **Northern Lights**). For €435 a night, you can enjoy all mod cons and amazing views of the city.

In another industrial monument, over in the Westergasfabriek, the **Leidinghuis** (Klönneplein 1, 586 0711, www.westergasfabriek.nl) consists of two interconnected semi-circular buildings attached to the massive Gashouder, which once held gas and now holds events. Acclaimed Dutch designer – and king of recycled wood – Piet Hein Eek designed the interior. There's a brilliant orange table downstairs, a kitchenette and library on the mezzanine, and a bathroom and bedroom nestled in the rafters. By day, it's used for workshops or parties, but it can also act as the ultimate suite for two. Rental costs €200 for part of the day – double that if you want to stay the night.

If it's more legendary Dutch design you're after, you can stay at **Hotel Droog** (*see p72*). The Droog team originally planned to expand their shop to include a proper hotel, but were stymied by permit issues, so they ended up with just one suite. A large and lovely one, of course, that's filled with Droog design prototypes and can be rented

Cocomama.

for around €200 per night. The suite is located in a pair of 17th-century buildings (formerly the city's STD clinic) that are divided into shop sections meant to amplify the idea of what a hotel actually is. For example, the 'dining room' is a relaxing public café, a 'washroom' sells cosmetics and a 'wardrobe' features fashion.

Finally, dozens of Amsterdam's empty *brugwachtershuisjes* ('bridgemaster houses') could be reinvented as hotel suites. These tiny elevated houses, located on drawbridges across city canals, provided shelter to bridge operators. But they're becoming obsolete due to automatisation. Local business people, architects and hoteliers have joined forces, under the name **Sweets Amsterdam**, to renovate them for public use. The first ones are set to be available by early 2015.

ESSENTIAL INFORMATION

★ Hotel Vondel

Vondelstraat 28-30 (612 0120, www.vondel hotels.nl). Tram 1, 2, 3, 5, 7, 10. **Map** *p314 H13.*
Another hidden gem near museums and upmarket shopping opportunities, this thoroughly chic place is festooned with art and has a lovely decked garden. Rooms, ranging from small to huge, are designer-driven, with chandeliers and swanky bathrooms. Unusually for such a trendy hotel, families are positively encouraged. They run three other places to stay, and a fourth (Hotel de Hallen) opens in 2014.
Other locations Hotel JL No.76, Jan Luijkenstraat 74-76, Museum Quarter (348 5555); Hotel Roemer, Roemer Visscherstraat 10, Vondelpark (589 0800); b&nb Herengracht, Herengracht 176, Western Canal Belt (515 0453).

JODENBUURT, PLANTAGE & OOST

Moderate

Arena

's Gravesandestraat 51 (850 2400, www.hotel arena.nl). Tram 3, 7, 9, 10, 14. **Map** *p317 Q10.*
A holy trinity of hotel, restaurant and nightclub in a former Catholic orphanage, Arena is ideal for lazy young scenesters looking for a one-stop shop. The standard and large rooms are a bit boring from an aesthetic point of view; the extra-large ones and suites, kitted out by leading local designers, look great but come with matching price tags. The location is a bit out of the way, but trams can whizz you into the centre in ten minutes.

Eden Lancaster

Plantage Middelaan 48 (535 6888, www.eden lancasterhotel.com). Tram 9, 14. **Map** *p317 P9.*

Even though it's rather far from some sights, this hotel is a short tram ride (or a 20-minute walk) from Centraal Station, and there are several decent cafés nearby. It's quite basic (and bathrooms are cramped), but rooms are good for business travellers, equipped as they are with Wi-Fi and desks. The hotel's triple and quad rooms are very much aimed at families.
▶ *Artis Royal Zoo (see p147), one of the oldest zoos in the world, is across the road.*

Budget

Hotel Adolesce

Nieuwe Keizersgracht 26 (626 3959, www. adolesce.nl). Trams 9, 14 or Metro Waterlooplein. **Map** *p313 N10.*
You won't get any breakfast at this unfussy place near the Skinny Bridge, but guests can help themselves to a buffet in the lounge with sandwiches, drinks, fruit and chocolate. Rooms are pretty plain – the attic room is nicest – but it's close to both the Hermitage Amsterdam museum (*see p143*) and Waterlooplein flea market (*see p146*).

Hostels

★ Stayokay Amsterdam Zeeburg

Timorplein 2 (551 3190, www.stayokay.com). Tram 10, 14.
Located in a grand old school building that also houses fab cinema and club Studio/K (*see p179*), this branch of the reliable hostel chain is part of Stayokay's designer concept from Edward van Vliet. It's done out in warm reds, with mosaic floors, sleek but simple furniture and huge photos on the walls. Perfect for families and the more discerning hosteller – HI members get a discount – it offers several special packages; check the website for details.

CANVAS NIGHTS

Camping is a great choice for a budget, family-friendly stay.

Camping is a national pastime for the Dutch, so you can expect well-maintained sites with good facilities, including laundries and supermarkets. Although none of these campsites is close to the city centre, all have good transport links. **Zeeburg** is a young people's site, **Gaasper** and **Amsterdamse Bos** are aimed at families, while everyone mixes happily together at **Vliegenbos**.

Gaasper Camping Amsterdam

Loosdrechtdreef 7, Amsterdam Zuidoost (696 7326, www.gaaspercamping.nl). Metro *Gaasperplas or nightbus 355, 357.* **Open** mid Mar-early Nov; sometimes at New Year.

★ Het Amsterdamse Bos

Kleine Noorddijk 1, Amstelveen (641 6868, www.campingamsterdamsebos.nl). Bus 171, 199. **Open** Apr-mid Oct (mid Oct-Mar call for details).

Vliegenbos

Meeuwenlaan 138, Amsterdam Noord (636 8855, www.vliegenbos.com). Bus 32, 33 or nightbus 361. **Open** Apr-Sept.

Zeeburg

Zuider IJdijk 20, Zeeburg (694 4430, www.campingzeeburg.nl). Tram 14 or bus 22, 37. **Open** all year.

Other locations Kloveniersburgwal 97, Old Centre: Old Side (624 6832); Zandpad 5, Vondelpark (589 8996).

WATERFRONT & NOORD
Expensive

Doubletree by Hilton
Oosterdoksstraat 4 (530 0800, http://doubletree3.hilton.com). Tram 1, 2, 4, 5, 9, 13, 14, 16, 17, 24. **Map** p313 L6.
Just east of Centraal Station near the new public library, this is one of the largest hotels in the country. Rooms feature floor-to-ceiling windows, and are equipped with an iMac and free Wi-Fi, while the rooftop SkyLounge bar-restaurant offers a spectacular view across the city and harbour. Corporate clients are particularly well served, thanks to the business centre and convention facilities.

Mövenpick Hotel Amsterdam City Centre
Piet Heinkade 11 (519 1200, www.moevenpick. com). Tram 26. **Map** p313 N5.
Large, tall and glamorous, this striped, stone-coloured hotel is a great base for exploring the Waterfront and Noord on the banks opposite. Rooms are decorated in soothing greys and woods; pricier ones grant access to an executive lounge and have great views over the cruise liners ploughing through the waters, or over the city's rooftops.

Moderate

Amstel Botel
NDSM-Pier 3 (626 4247, www.amstelbotel.nl). Ferry from Centraal Station to NDSM.
A 15-minute cruise from Centraal Station across the river IJ to NDSM in Noord, this hotel-on-a-boat is a safe bet if you're looking for good, clean accommodation. Unless you're fooled by the 'luxury' rooms boast and come expecting the *QE2*, you'll be perfectly happy. The bar has long opening hours, games such as pinball and pool, and a jukebox. The last ferry leaves Centraal Station at 11.45pm (12.45am Fri, Sat), but a free shuttle bus runs during the night.

★ Lloyd Hotel
Oostelijke Handelskade 34 (561 3604, www.lloyd hotel.com). Tram 10, 26. **Map** p313 N5.
This one-time youth prison has been reinvented as a stylish hotel offering one- to five-star accommodation, complete with a new 'cultural embassy'. Lloyd features the work of hotshot Dutch designers Atelier van Lieshout and Marcel Wanders. Expect the unexpected – in the best possible way, of course. The restaurant, with its sunny terrace and modishly simple menu, is a bonus. Sibling is the fashion-conscious Hotel The Exchange (*see p278*).

Lloyd Hotel.

DE PIJP
Deluxe

★ Hotel Okura Amsterdam
Ferdinand Bolstraat 333 (678 7111, www.okura.nl). Tram 12.
This smart stopover has everything captains of industry need. There's a pool and health club (open to non-guests); state-of-the-art conference facilities; top-notch sushi bars; and a high-end French restaurant, Le Ciel Bleu, and smart cocktail bar on the 23rd floor. Rooms offer no surprises in terms of facilities – they've got the lot – or looks. They range from small standard to the huge suite on the 21st floor.

Sir Albert Hotel
Albert Cuypstraat 2-6 (305 3020, www.siralbert hotel.com). Tram 16, 24. **Map** p315 M14.
Once a diamond factory, Sir Albert is a new four-star 'luxury boutique' hotel featuring the interior stylings of BK Architects. High-ceilinged rooms are inspired by the great design movements of the past, while old-school service is balanced by the latest mod cons. Japanese pub-style restaurant Izakaya has already been embraced by local foodies.

Budget

★ Bicycle Hotel
Van Ostadestraat 123 (679 3452, www.bicycle hotel.com). Tram 3, 12, 16, 24. **Map** p315 N15.
This beloved, cheap 'n' cheerful staging post for pedal-pushers was one of the first (and is still one of the few) places to stay in De Pijp. It has good bike access to popular out-of-town routes, and the friendly staff can provide advice and rent out bikes; if you bring your own, you can park it securely for free. Rooms are comfy, the breakfast room is cute and there are loads of excellent places nearby to refuel for the energetic day ahead.

Getting Around

ARRIVING & LEAVING

By air

Amsterdam's **Schiphol Airport** (0900 0141 premium rate, www. schiphol.nl) lies 18 kilometres (11 miles) south-west of the city. There's only one terminal building, but within that there are four departure and arrival halls.

Taxis

A fixed fare from the airport to the south and west of the city costs around €40, and to the city centre about €50. Bear in mind that there are always plenty of licensed taxis beside the main exit. You can book taxis on the Schiphol website.

Connexxion Airport Hotel Shuttle

Connexxion desk, Schiphol Plaza, near Arrivals Hall 4, Schiphol Airport (038 339 4741, www.schipholhotelshuttle.nl). Departures from Platform A7. This bus from Schiphol to Amsterdam runs at least every 30 minutes between 6am and 9.30pm. Anyone can buy a ticket (€17 single, €27 return), not just hotel guests. Drop-off points are the 100-odd allied hotels; see the website for schedules.

Trains

Trains leave every ten minutes or so between 5am and midnight (after which they depart hourly). The journey to Centraal Station takes about 20 minutes. Buy tickets (€4 single) before you board or you're likely to incur a €35 fine. There's a €0.50 surcharge if you buy tickets over the counter; use the machines (with English instructions) instead.

Airlines

Aer Lingus
0900 265 8207 premium rate, www.aerlingus.com.

British Airways
346 9559, www.britishairways.com.

EasyJet
0900 040 1048 premium rate, www.easyjet.com.

KLM
474 7747, www.klm.com.

By car

Options for crossing the Channel with a car include: Harwich to Hook of Holland with **Stena Line** (www.stenaline.nl); Newcastle to Amsterdam (IJmuiden) with **DFDS Seaways** (www.dfdsseaways. co.uk); Hull to Rotterdam or Zeebrugge with **P&O Ferries** (www.poferries.com); and Dover to Calais with P&O Ferries or **MyFerryLink** (www.myferry link.com). **Irish Ferries** from Ireland go from Rosslare to either Roscoff or Cherbourg in France (www.irishferries.com). Another option is the **Eurotunnel** to France (www.eurotunnel.com).

By coach

International coach services arrive at Amstel Station, with easy connection to Centraal Station. To book a ticket, visit the **Eurolines** website (www.eurolines.nl), which is in English. Fares start from around €51.50 for a single from London Victoria to Amsterdam.

By rail

The fastest route from London is to catch a **Eurostar** train (www. eurostar.com) from St Pancras International to Brussels, then change to an InterCity or Thalys high-speed train to Amsterdam.

The 'Dutch Flyer' train and ferry service involves a train from Liverpool Street Station to Harwich, Stena Line's superferry crossing to Hook of Holland, and then a train to Amsterdam Centraal (with a change in Rotterdam).

If you live in the North of England or Scotland, take the ferry from Hull or Newcastle (*see above*). Transfer buses shuttle from the port to either Rotterdam Centraal or Amsterdam Centraal train stations.

PUBLIC TRANSPORT

Getting around Amsterdam is very easy: there are efficient, cheap and integrated trams, metros and buses, and in the centre most places can be reached on foot. Locals tend to get around by bike, and there are also boats and water taxis. Be warned that public transport provision for those with disabilities is dire.

For information, tickets, maps and an English-language guide to all types of public transport tickets, visit the website of **GVB**, Amsterdam's municipal transport authority (www.gvb.nl).

The **9292ov** website (www.9292.nl) combines national bus, train, taxi, tram and ferry information, and its 'door-to-door' journey planner is invaluable.

Trams are the best way to travel around the city by public transport, with a network of routes through the centre (buses and the metro are more useful for outlying suburbs). For a basic map of the tram network, *see p306*.

Fares & tickets

An **OV-chipkaart** ('chip card') system operates across the tram, bus and metro network. The card, which is valid for five years, incurs a one-off €7.50 fee and can be purchased at station ticket machines, tobacconists and many supermarkets, as well as GVB Tickets & Info offices (www.gvb.nl). You can load the card in the ticket vending machine, paying with cash or card, and use it immediately. You can also load the card in yellow Add Value Machines at tobacconists and various other shops.

An unlimited 24-hour OV-chipkaart costs €7.50. You can also buy unlimited 48-, 72-, 96-, 120-, 144- and 168-hour cards (ranging from €12 to €32). With any type of OV-chipkaart, you have to check in and out when boarding or disembarking a tram, bus or metro, using the card readers in the trams and buses, at the entryway to metro stations or on the metro platform. Hold your card in front of the reader and wait for a beep and green light to flash.

An alternative to the OV-chipkaart is the **IAmsterdam City Card**, which includes unlimited public transport and free entrance to 38 museums and attractions. It can be purchased at shops and newsagents across Amsterdam, or at one of the IAmsterdam tourist offices (*see p297*). The card costs €47 (24 hours), €57 (48 hours) or €67 (72 hours). Don't even think about travelling without a ticket: inspectors make regular checks, and passengers without tickets are hit with €35 on-the-spot fines.

Trams & buses

Trams run from 6am (6.30am Sat, 7.30am Sun). Night buses (nos.348-369) take over at other times. All night buses go to Centraal Station, except 369 (Station Sloterdijk to Schiphol Airport).

Night-bus stops are indicated by a black square with the bus number printed on it. During off-peak hours and at quiet stops, stick out your arm to let the driver know you want to get on. Signs at tram and bus stops show the name of the stop and line number, and boards indicate the full route.

Tram rules

Other road users need to be aware that a tram will only stop if absolutely necessary. Cyclists should listen for tram warning bells and cross tramlines at an angle that avoids the front wheel getting stuck. Motorists should avoid blocking tramlines: cars are allowed to venture on to them only if turning right.

Metro

The metro uses the same ticket system as trams and buses (see p290) and serves suburbs to the south and east. Three separate lines – 51, 53 and 54 – terminate at Centraal Station (sometimes abbreviated to CS), while line 50 connects west with south-east. Metro trains run from 6am (6.30am Sat, 7.30am Sun) to around 12.15am.

TAXIS

Since Taxi Centraal Amsterdam was decentralised, there are more and more independent taxi companies on the market, which unfortunately means there are some opportunist drivers out there, while others have no idea where they're going. Your best bet is to opt for a cab that has the red and black 'TCA/7x7' rooflight on it whenever you can, or you can phone 777 7777.

Sometimes it's hard to hail a taxi in the street, but ranks are dotted around the city. The best central ones are outside Centraal Station; alongside the bus station (at Kinkerstraat and Marnixstraat); Rembrandtplein; and Leidseplein. Always ask your driver how much

your journey will cost before you set off – they should be able to give you an approximate figure; that way you'll know if you've been ripped off. (You can also try to ask for a flat rate.) Make sure the meter starts at the minimum charge (€2.80); you're then charged €2.03/km. If you feel you've been ripped off, ask for a receipt before handing over cash. If the fare seems too high, phone the central taxi office (650 6506, 24hrs) or contact the police. Wheelchairs will only fit in taxis if they're folded. If you're a wheelchair user, you can call the special car transport service (633 3943, 7am-5pm daily). You'll need to book one or two days in advance and the service costs around €2.20/km.

Alternatively, hail a **bicycle cab** – basically a high-tech rickshaw – or order one (06 1859 5153 mobile, www.wielertaxi.nl), €1/3mins per person, free under-2s). There's a €2.50 surcharge for phone orders. You could also look into hiring a water taxi.

DRIVING

If you're coming by car to the Netherlands, it's wise to join a national motoring organisation before you leave. To drive in the Netherlands, you'll need a valid national driving licence; **ANWB** (see right) and many car-hire firms favour photocard licences (Brits need the paper version as well for this to be legal). You'll need proof that your vehicle has passed a road safety test in its country of origin, an international identification disc, vehicle registration papers and insurance documents.

The Dutch drive on the right. Motorways are labelled 'A'; major roads 'N'; and European routes 'E'. Seatbelts are compulsory for drivers and all passengers. Speed limits are usually 50km/h (31mph) within cities, 80km/h (50mph) outside, and 100km/h (62mph) on motorways. Speeding and other traffic offences are subject to heavy on-the-spot fines.

If you're driving in Amsterdam, look out for cyclists. Always check carefully before you make a turn and when you open your door. Many streets in Amsterdam are one-way – for cars, that is, not bikes, so don't be surprised to see people cycling against the traffic flow.

Strict drink driving laws only allow 0.5 milligrams of alcohol per millilitre of blood.

Royal Dutch Automobile Club (ANWB)

Buikslotermeerplein 307-311, Noord (088 269 3080, customer services 088 269 2222, 24hr emergency line 088 269 2888, www.anwb.nl). Bus 31, 38, 46, 230, 245. **Open** *Customer services* noon-5.30pm Mon; 9.30am-5.30pm Tue-Fri; 8.30am-5pm Sat.

An annual membership fee (from €55) covers the cost of breakdown assistance. Members of foreign motoring organisations may be entitled to free help. Crews may not accept credit cards at the scene.

Car hire

Dutch car hire (*autoverhuur*) firms generally expect at least one year's driving experience and will want to see a valid national driving licence (with photo) and passport before they hire a vehicle. All will require a deposit by credit card, and you generally need to be over 21. Prices given below are for one day's hire of the cheapest car available excluding insurance and VAT.

Adam's Rent-a-Car

Nassaukade 344-346, Oud West (685 0111, www.adams rentacar.nl). Tram 7, 10, 17. **Open** 8am-6pm Mon-Fri; 8am-8pm Sat. **Map** p316 G12.

One-day hire costs from €32; the first 100km (62 miles) are free, and after that the charge is €0.14/km. There's a branch at Middenweg 51.

Dik's Autoverhuur

Van Ostadestraat 278-280, De Pijp (662 3366, www.diks.net). Tram 3, 4. **Open** 8am-7.30pm Mon-Sat; 9am-12.30pm, 8-10.30pm Sun. **Map** p315 O14.

Cars from €28 per day. The first 100km are free, then it's €0.16/km.

Hertz

Overtoom 333, Oud West (612 2441, www.hertz.nl). Tram 1. **Open** 8am-6pm Mon-Fri; 8am-2pm Sat; 9am-2pm Sun. **Map** p316 F15.

Cars from €50 per day. The first 300km are free, then it's €0.15/km.

Parking

All of central Amsterdam is metered from 9am until at least 7pm – and in many places to midnight – and spaces are difficult to find. Most spaces are only for official resident permit-holders – especially within the Canal Ring. Official parking garages are often

Resources A-Z

ADDRESSES

Addresses take the form of street name and then house number, such as Damrak 1.

AGE RESTRICTIONS

In the Netherlands, only those over the age of 18 can purchase alcohol, buy cigarettes, smoke dope or drive.

ATTITUDE & ETIQUETTE

Amsterdam's reputation as a relaxed city is well founded, as anyone will find out after a wander around the Red Light District. But not everything goes. Smoking dope is not OK everywhere: spliffing up in restaurants is usually frowned upon, and many nightclubs ban sportswear and trainers.

BUSINESS

Banking

ABN-Amro *0900 0024 (24hrs daily), www.abnamro.nl.* Locations all over Amsterdam.
ING Group *228 8800 (24hrs daily), www.ing.com.* Locations all over Amsterdam.
Rabobank *0900 0905 (8am-10pm Mon-Fri; 9am-5pm Sat), www.rabobank.nl.* 30 locations around town.
For information on currency exchange, *see p296*.

Couriers & shippers

FedEx *0800 0222 333, www.fedex.com/nl_english.* **Open** *Customer services* 8am-7pm Mon-Fri.
PostNL *088 868 6868, www.postnl.nl.* **Open** 24hrs daily.

Office services

Many tobacconists and copy shops have fax facilities.

Euro Business Center
Keizersgracht 62, Western Canal Belt (520 7500, www.ebc amsterdam.nl). Tram 1, 2, 5, 13, 14, 17. **Open** 8.30am-5pm Mon-Fri. **Map** p312 G7.
Office leases, virtual offices, meeting rooms and secretarial services.
World Trade Center
Strawinskylaan 1, Zuid (575 9111, www.wtcamsterdam.com). Tram 5 or NS rail Amsterdam Zuid-WTC Station. **Open** *Office & enquiries* 8.30am-5.30pm Mon-Fri.
Long or short term lets and business services available.

Translators & interpreters

AVB Vertalingen
Ouderkerkerlaan 50, Amstelveen (645 6610, www.avb-vertalingen.nl). Bus 142, 149, 165, 166, 170, 171, 172, 175, 186, 187, 199, 215, 216, 300. **Open** 9am-5pm Mon-Fri. **No credit cards.**
Mac Bay *PC Hooftstraat 15, Museum Quarter (24hr line 662 0501, www.macbay.nl). Tram 2, 5.* **Open** 9am-7pm Mon-Fri. Specialists in financial and legal document services.

Useful organisations

For details of embassies and consulates, *see p294*.

Expat Center *Startbaan 8, Amstelveen (0900 9811, www.expatcenter.nl). Metro Marne.* **Open** 9am-5pm Mon-Fri; 1-6pm Sat, Sun (weekends & after office hours by appt only).

This initiative, which recently opened a service centre, makes it much easier to negotiate all the relevant Dutch bureaucracy if you decide to move and/or set up a business here.
Kamer van Koophandel (Chamber of Commerce)
De Ruyterkade 5, Waterfront (531 4000, www.kvk.nl). Tram 1, 2, 4, 5, 9, 13, 16, 17, 24. **Open** 8.30am-5pm Mon-Fri. **Map** p312 H6.
Offers lists of import/export agencies, trade representatives and companies by sector.
Ministerie van Buitenlandse Zaken *Bezuidenhoutseweg 67, The Hague (070 348 6486, www.rijks overheid.nl/bz).* **Open** 7am-8pm Mon-Fri for the legalisation of documents. The Ministry of Foreign Affairs. Detailed enquiries may be referred to the Netherlands Enterprise Agency (*see below*).
Ministerie van Economische Zaken *Bezuidenhoutseweg 73, The Hague (070 379 8911, www.rijksoverheid.nl/ez).* **Open** 9am-5.30pm Mon-Fri.
The Ministry of Economic Affairs helps with general queries about the Dutch economy. Detailed enquiries may be referred to the Netherlands Enterprise Agency (*see below*).
Netherlands-British Chamber of Commerce *Oxford House, Nieuwezijds Voorburgwal 328-L, Old Centre: New Side (421 7040, www.nbcc.co.uk). Tram 1, 2, 5, 13, 14, 17.* **Open** 9am-5pm Mon-Fri. **Map** p312 J10.
Netherlands Enterprise Agency
Prinses Beatrixlaan 2, The Hague (088 602 8060, www.hollandtrade.com). **Open** 8.30am-5.30pm Mon-Fri (by appt).
This government agency is a handy source for all kinds of business information – they share an address

ESSENTIAL INFORMATION

with the Netherlands Foreign Investment Agency (*see below*).

Netherlands Foreign Investment Agency *Prinses Beatrixlaan 2, The Hague (088 602 1142, www.nfia.nl).* **Open** by appt.
The Foreign Investment Agency is a first port of call for businesses relocating to the Netherlands.

CONSUMER

If you have a complaint about the service you've received from Dutch businesses that you're unable to resolve, contact the **National Consumentenbond** (070 445 4545, www.consumentenbond.nl, open 8am-8pm Mon-Thur, 8am-5.30pm Fri, Dutch only) for advice.

CUSTOMS

If you're entering the Netherlands from another EU country, you may import limitless goods that are for your own personal use. If you enter the country from a non-EU country, the following limits apply:

● 1 litre of spirits or 2 litres of sparkling wine or 2 litres of fortified wine, such as sherry or port (or a proportional assortment of these products) and 4 litres of non-sparkling wine and 16 litres of beer.
● 200 cigarettes or 250 grams of smoking tobacco or 100 cigarillos or 50 cigars (or a proportional assortment of these products).
● Other goods to the value of €430.

The import of meat or meat products, fruit, plants, flowers and protected animals to the Netherlands is illegal.
  For more information, go to the English website of the tax authorities: www.belastingdienst.nl.

DISABLED

Winding cobbled streets, poorly maintained pavements and steep canal house steps can present real difficulties to the physically less able, but the pragmatic Dutch can generally solve problems quickly. Most large museums, cinemas and theatres have decent disabled facilities. The metro is accessible to wheelchair users with normal arm function, but most trams are inaccessible to wheelchair users due to their high steps. The website www.toegankelijkamsterdam.nl has a list of hotels, restaurants and attractions that cater well for the physically less able. **StarBikes** (*see p292*) also rents a special bicycle for the disabled.

DRUGS

Locals have a relaxed attitude to soft drugs, but smoking isn't acceptable everywhere. Use discretion. Outside Amsterdam, public consumption of cannabis is largely unacceptable. Foreigners found with hard drugs should expect to face prosecution. Organisations offering advice can do little to help foreigners with drug-related problems, although the **Jellinek Drugs Prevention Centre** is happy to provide help in several languages, including English. Its helpline (590 1515, open 3-5pm Mon-Thur) offers advice and information. There's also a 24-hour crisis/detox emergency number: 590 5000. *Also see pp267-271* **Sex & Drugs**.

ELECTRICITY

Electricity in the Netherlands runs on 220V. Visitors with British 240V appliances can change the plug or use an adaptor. For US 110V appliances, you'll need to use a transformer.

EMBASSIES & CONSULATES

American Consulate General
Museumplein 19, Museum Quarter (575 5309 8am-4.30pm daily, 070 310 2209 outside business hours, http://amsterdam.usconsulate.gov). Tram 3, 5, 12, 16. **Open** *US citizens services* 8.30-11.30am Mon-Fri. *Immigrant visas* by appt.
Map p314 K15.

Australian Embassy
Carnegielaan 4, The Hague (070 310 8200, Australian citizen emergency phone 0800 0224 794, www.netherlands.embassy.gov.au). **Open** 8.30am-5pm Mon-Fri. *Passport & notarial services* 9am-1pm Mon-Fri.
This embassy cannot issue visas or accept visa applications. The nearest Department of Immigration and Multicultural Affairs is at the embassy in Berlin. Note that only general visa information is available from the Visa Information Officer.

British Consulate *Koningslaan 44, Vondelpark (676 4343, www.gov.uk).* Tram 2. **Open** *British citizens* 9am-12.30pm Mon, Tue, Thur, Fri. *Phone enquiries* 9am-1pm, 2-4.30pm Mon-Fri. *Visa enquiries* by appt 3-4.30pm Mon-Fri.

British Embassy *Lange Voorhout 10, The Hague (070 427 0427, www.gov.uk).* **Open** 9am-5.30pm Mon-Fri.

For visa and tourist information, contact the British consulate (*see left*).

Canadian Embassy *Sophialaan 7, The Hague (070 311 1600, www.canadainternational.gc.ca).* **Open** 9am-1pm, 2-5.30pm Mon-Fri. *Consular & passport section* 9.30am-12.30pm Mon-Fri (afternoons by appt only).

Irish Embassy *Scheveningseweg 112, The Hague (070 363 0993, www.embassyofireland.nl).* **Open** 10am-12.30pm, 2.30-5pm Mon-Fri. *Visa enquiries* 10am-12.30pm Mon-Fri.

New Zealand Embassy *Eisenhowerlaan 77N, The Hague (070 346 9324, www.nzembassy. com/netherlands).* **Open** 9am-12.30pm, 1.30-5.30pm Mon-Fri.

EMERGENCIES

In an emergency, call **112** (free from any phone) and specify police, fire service or ambulance. For helplines and hospitals, *see p295*; for police stations, *see p296*.

GAY & LESBIAN

See pp180-189 **Gay & Lesbian**.

HEALTH

Nationals of non-EU countries should take out insurance before leaving home. UK residents travelling in Europe require a European National Health Insurance Card (EHIC). This allows them to benefit from free or reduced-cost medical care when travelling in a country belonging to the European Economic Area (EEA) or Switzerland. The EHIC is free of charge. For further information, refer to www.dh.gov.uk/travellers.

Apotheek Leidsestraat
Leidsestraat 74-76, Western Canal Belt (422 0210, www.leidsestraat apotheek.nl). Tram 1, 2, 5. **Open** 8.30am-11pm daily.
The central night chemist for filling prescriptions.

Sint Lucas Andreas Apotheek *Jan Tooropstraat 164, West (510 8826, www.sintlucasandreasziekenhuis.nl/afdeling/apotheek).* Tram 13, bus 64. **Open** 24hrs daily.
A 24/7 chemist for prescriptions.

Centraal Doktorsdienst/Atacom *592 3333, www.atacom.nl.*
A 24-hour English-speaking line for advice about symptoms.

Accident & emergency

Go to the **eerste spoedhulp** (A&E) of any hospital (*ziekenhuis*). The Dutch emergency number is 112; *see also p294* **Emergencies**.

In the case of minor accidents, call 088 003 0600 (open 24/7) and the service will connect you with an emergency GP in your area. There's also **Tourist Medical Service Amsterdam** (592 3355, http://touristdoctor.nl), which you can call 24 hours a day for free advice.

You can also just turn up at the outpatient departments of the following city hospitals (*ziekenhuis*). All are open 24 hours a day, seven days a week.

Hospitals

Academisch Medisch Centrum *Meibergdreef 9, Zuid (566 9111, first aid 566 2222). Metro Holendrecht.*
Boven IJ Ziekenhuis *Statenjachtstraat 1, Noord (634 6346, first aid 634 6200). Bus 34, 36, 37, 125, 245, 363, 392.*
Onze Lieve Vrouwe Gasthuis *'s Gravesandeplein 16, Oost (599 9111, first aid 599 3016). Tram 3, 7 or bus 37, or Metro Weesperplein or Wibautstraat.*
St Lucas Andreas Ziekenhuis *Jan Tooropstraat 164, West (510 8911, first aid 510 8911). Tram 13 or bus 64 or Metro Jan van Galenstraat.*
VU Ziekenhuis *De Boelelaan 1117, Zuid (444 4444, first aid 444 3636). Tram 16, 24 or bus 62, 142, 170, 171, 172, 176, 310 or Metro Amstelveenseweg.*

Contraception & abortion

The morning-after pill is available over the counter from pharmacies (*see right*).

CASA Amsterdam *Sarphatistraat 618-628, Oost (088 888 4444, www.casaklinieken.nl). Tram 9, 10, 14.* **Open** 8.30am-5pm Mon-Fri. Phone for information or an appointment (8am-8pm Mon-Fri, 9am-1pm Sat). CASA Amsterdam performs surgical and medical abortions, and offers advice about youth sexuality, the pill, IUD insertion and Implanon.

Dentists

Tandartsenpraktijk AOC *Wilhelmina Gasthuisplein 167, Oud West (616 1234, www.tandarts*
enpraktijk-aoc.nl). Tram 1, 2, 3, 5, 12. **Open** 9am-5pm Mon-Fri. AOC offers emergency dental treatment and a recorded service: call 686 1109 for information on where a walk-in clinic in your area will be open at a specific time.
TBB *0900 821 2230 premium rate, 506 3841, www.tandarts bemiddelingsbureau.nl.* Operators can put you in touch with your nearest dentist, and telephone lines are open 24 hours for those with dental emergencies.

Opticians

Check under 'Opticiens' at www.goudengids.nl.

Pharmacies

Chemists (*drogists*) are usually open from 9.30am to 5.30pm Monday to Saturday. For prescription drugs, go to a pharmacy (*apotheek*), usually open from 9.30am to 5.30pm Monday to Friday. Outside these hours, *see left*.

STDs, HIV & AIDS

The **AIDS Information Line** (689 2577) run by HIV Vereniging offers advice and can put you in contact with every department you need. **SOA AIDS Nederland** has a more general information line (0900 204 2040 premium rate) for questions about safe sex and sexually-transmitted diseases.

The city's health department, the GGD, runs free STD clinics that are anonymous and open to all. You can also arrange testing through a GP. An AIDS test can also be done at thrift shop chain **Out of the Closet** (www.outofthecloset.org).

There are many active AIDS/HIV-related organisations in Amsterdam, including **Stichting AIDS Fonds** (www.aidsfonds.nl), **Stop AIDS Now!** (www.stop aidsnow.nl) and **Dance4Life** (www.dance4life.nl).

GGD *Weesperplein 1 (555 5822, www.ggd.amsterdam.nl). Tram 7, 10 or Metro Weesperplein.* **Open** 8.30-10.30am, 1.30-3.30pm Mon-Fri. **Map** p313 O10. Examinations and treatment of STDs, including free and anonymous HIV tests.
HIV Vereniging *1e Helmersstraat 17 B3, Oud West (689 3915, www.hivnet.org). Tram 1, 2, 5.* **Map** p316 F14.
The Netherlands HIV Association supports those who are HIV
positive, including offering legal help. You can get HIV test results in an hour. Call 689 2577 (2-6pm Mon, Tue, Thur) to chat, ask questions or make an appointment for a visit or workshop.
SOA AIDS Nederland Info Line *0900 204 2040 premium rate, www.soaaids.nl.* **Open** 10am-6pm Mon-Tue, 2-6pm Wed-Fri.
If you need any information or advice on safe sex, AIDS or any other sexually-transmitted infections and diseases, call this friendly phone line (€0.10/min).

HELPLINES

Alcoholics Anonymous *085 104 5390 (24hrs daily), www.aa-netherlands.org.*
English and Dutch information on the times and dates of meetings, and contact numbers for counsellors. The website has an English section, and you can locate meetings by day or by town.
Narcotics Anonymous *06 2234 1050, www.na-holland.nl.*
Offers a 24-hour answerphone service in English and Dutch, with counsellors' phone numbers.

ID

Everyone has to carry some sort of identification all the time. If you're moving to Amsterdam, you have to register with the local council, in the same building as the Aliens' Police (*see p297* **Visas & immigration**).

INTERNET

All global ISPs have a presence here (check websites for numbers). Most hotels are well equipped, with dataports in the rooms, terminals in the lobby or Wi-Fi throughout. Many cafés and restaurants have Wi-Fi – just ask for the access code.

Internet Café *Martelaarsgracht 11, Old Centre: New Side (no phone, www.internetcafe.nl). Tram 4, 9, 16, 24.* **Open** 9am-1am Mon-Thur, Sun; 9am-3am Fri, Sat. **Rates** from €1/30mins plus compulsory beverage. **No credit cards**.

LEFT LUGGAGE

There's a staffed left-luggage counter at **Schiphol Airport** (795 2843, www.schiphol.nl), where you can store luggage for up to one month, open daily from 6am to 10pm (€7/24hrs). There are also automatic left-luggage lockers, accessible 24 hours a day (from €6/24hrs, for up to 168 hours). There are also plenty of lockers at **Centraal Station**, with 24-hour access (from €3.85/24hrs).

LEGAL HELP

Access – The Hague International Centre *City Hall, Spui 70, The Hague (0900 222 2377 premium rate, www.access-nl.org)*. **Open** 9am-5pm Mon-Fri. This volunteer-run organisation for the international community runs a helpline for all matters (10am-4pm Mon-Fri). If you happen to be in the Hague, you can visit in person. **Juridisch Loket** *Vijzelgracht 21-25, Southern Canal Ring (0900 8020 premium rate, www.juridischloket.nl). Tram 1, 2, 5*. **Open** 9am-5pm Mon-Fri. **Map** p315 L12. Qualified lawyers offering free or low-cost legal advice.

LOST PROPERTY

Report lost property to the police (*see right*). Inform your embassy or consulate, too, if you lose your passport. For things lost at the Hoek van Holland ferry terminal or Schiphol Airport, contact the company you're travelling with. For lost credit cards, *see right*.

Centraal Station *Stationsplein 15, Old Centre: Old Side (0900 202 1163 premium rate, www.ns.nl). Tram 1, 2, 4, 5, 9, 13, 16, 17, 24, 26*. **Open** 24hrs daily. Items found on trains are kept for four days at the office on the east side of the station (0900 321 2100 premium rate), after which they're forwarded to the Centraal Bureau Gevonden Voorwerpen (Central Lost Property Office) in Utrecht (www.nshispeed.nl, 8am-5pm Mon-Fri), where they're stored for three months. Fill in the 'tracing' form on the website and have items posted (collecting them personally isn't possible) from €15.

GVB Lost Property *Arlandaweg 100 (0900 8011 premium rate, 2pm-6.30pm Mon-Fri). Tram 12 or Sloterdijk rail*. **Open** 9am-6.30pm Mon-Fri. Wait at least a day or two before you call and describe what you've lost on the bus, metro or tram. If your property has been found, you can pick it up at GVB head office at Arlandaweg. If you've lost your keys, you don't have to call ahead. **Municipality Lost Property** *Korte Leidsedwarsstraat 52 (251 0222). Tram 1, 2, 5, 7, 10*. **Open**

In person 9am-4pm Mon-Fri. *By phone* noon-4pm Mon-Fri. If you've lost your passport or ID card, ask at the local police station.

MONEY

Since January 2002 the Dutch currency has been the Euro.

ATMs

Cash machines are found at banks, supermarkets and larger shops such as HEMA. If your card carries the Maestro or Cirrus symbol, you should be able to withdraw cash from ATMs, although it's worth checking with your bank before you go, and also what the charges are.

Banks

Amsterdam has more than its fair share of vast banks. Most are open 9am to 5pm, Monday to Friday, with Postbank opening on Saturday mornings as well. For a full list of banks, check www.goudengids.nl under 'Banken'. There's little difference between exchange rates offered by banks and bureaux de change. Dutch banks buy and sell foreign currency and exchange travellers' cheques, but few give cash advances against credit cards.

Bureaux de change

GWK Travelex *Centraal Station, Old Centre: Old Side (627 2731, www.gwktravelex.nl). Tram 1, 2, 4, 5, 9, 13, 16, 17, 24, 26*. **Open** 8am-8pm Mon-Sat; 10am-5pm Sun. **Map** p312 J6. Other locations include Leidseplein 31 (10.15am-5.30pm daily); Schiphol Airport (6am-10pm daily); Damrak 86 (9am-8pm Mon-Sat, 11am-6pm Sun); and Dam 1-5 (9am-7pm Mon-Sat, 11am-6pm Sun).

Credit cards

Credit cards are widely used. Most restaurants will take at least one type of card; they're less popular in bars and shops, and most supermarkets don't accept them at all, so always check first and carry some cash. The most popular cards are Visa, MasterCard, American Express and Diners Club. If you lose your card, call the relevant 24-hour number immediately:

American Express 504 8000
Diners Club 654 5500 (office hours)
MasterCard 660 0611
Visa 0800 022 3110

Tax

Sales tax (BTW) – 19 per cent on most items, six per cent on goods such as books and food, more on alcohol, tobacco and petrol – will be included in prices quoted in shops.

OPENING HOURS

As a general rule, shops are open from 1pm to 6pm on Monday (if they're open at all); 10am to 6pm Tuesday to Friday, with some open until 9pm on Thursdays; and 10am to 5pm on Saturdays. Smaller shops are more erratic; if in doubt, phone. Many central shops are open on Sunday. The city's bars tend to open at various times during the day and close at around 1am throughout the week, except for Fridays and Saturdays, when they stay open until 2am or 3am. Restaurants generally open in the evening from 5pm until 11pm (though some close as early as 9pm); many are closed on Sunday and Monday.

POLICE

For emergencies, call 112. There's also a 24-hour police service line (0900 8844) for the Amsterdam area. To report a crime anonymously, call 0800 7000.

Dutch police (www.politie.nl) are under no obligation to grant a phone call to those they detain – they can hold people for up to six hours for questioning for minor crimes, 24 hours for major matters – but they'll phone the relevant consulate on behalf of a foreign detainee.

Hoofdbureau van Politie (Police Headquarters) *Lijnbaansgracht 219, Jordaan (0900 8844 premium rate). Tram 1, 2, 5, 7, 10*. **Open** 24hrs daily. **Map** p314 H12.

POSTAL SERVICES

Following a reorganisation of the postal services, all but one of the post offices in Amsterdam have closed. Instead, many tobacconists, supermarkets and book shops offer postal services. Look for the orange illuminated sign with the PostNL logo. The postal information line is available on 0900 0990 (premium rate).

Post office *Singel 250, Old Centre: New Side (www.postnl.nl)*. **Open** 7.30am-6.30pm Mon-Fri; 7.30am-5pm Sat.

THE LOCAL CLIMATE

Average temperatures and monthly rainfall in Amsterdam.

	°C/°F	Rainfall (mm/in)	Sun (hrs/day)
Jan	4/39	68/2.7	1.8
Feb	6/43	48/1.9	2.8
Mar	9/48	66/2.6	3.7
Apr	13/55	53/2.1	5.5
May	17/63	61/2.4	7.2
June	20/68	71/2.8	6.6
July	22/72	76/3.0	6.9
Aug	22/72	71/2.8	6.7
Sept	19/66	66/2.6	4.4
Oct	14/57	73/2.9	3.3
Nov	9/48	81/3.2	1.9
Dec	6/43	84/3.3	1.5

SAFETY & SECURITY

Amsterdam is a relatively safe city, but do take care. The Red Light District is rife with undesirable characters who, though not violent, are expert pickpockets; be vigilant, especially on bridges; and don't ever make eye contact with anyone who looks as though they're up to no good.

Be careful to watch out for thieves on the Schiphol train. If you cycle, lock your bike up well (two locks are advisable). Keep valuables in your hotel safe, don't leave bags unattended, and ensure your cash and cards are well tucked away, preferably zipped up in your bag.

SMOKING

In 2008, the Netherlands imposed a smoking ban in all public indoor spaces. As for cannabis, locals have a relaxed attitude, but smoking it isn't acceptable everywhere in the city: use your discretion, and if in doubt, ask before you spark up. For more on Amsterdam's dope laws, *see p294*.

TELEPHONES

We list Amsterdam numbers without the city code, which is 020. To call within the city, just dial the seven-digit number. To phone Amsterdam from elsewhere in the Netherlands add 020 at the start of the listed number. Numbers in the Netherlands outside Amsterdam are listed with their code. There are other types of numbers that appear in this book. 06 numbers are for mobile phones; 0800 numbers are freephone numbers; and 0900 numbers are charged at premium rates. The latter two can't be reached from abroad.

Dialling & codes

Listen for the dialling tone (a hum), insert the phonecard, dial the code (none for calls within Amsterdam), then the number. On public phones, a digital display indicates credit left. International calls can be made from all phone boxes. For details on rates, phone international directory enquiries (*see below*).

From the Netherlands

Dial the following code, then the number you're calling.
Australia 00 61
Irish Republic 00 353
UK 00 44 (then drop the first '0' from the area code)
USA & Canada 00 1

To the Netherlands

If dialling from outside the Netherlands, use the country code 31, followed by the number. Drop the first '0' of the area code. The first 0 on mobiles is also dropped.
From Australia 00 11 31
From UK & Irish Republic 00 31
From USA 011 31

Operator services

Within the Netherlands

National directory enquiries 1888 (€0.90/min)
International directory enquiries 1889 (€0.90/min)
Local operator 0800 0101
International operator 0800 0410

Mobile phones

Check with your service provider before leaving about service while you're in the Netherlands. US mobile phone users should make sure they call their phone provider before departure to check their mobile's compatibility with GSM bands.

Public phones

Phonecards are available from stations, the Amsterdam Tourist Board, post offices and tobacconists. You can also use credit cards in many public phones.

TIME

The Netherlands is an hour ahead of Greenwich Mean Time (GMT). The Dutch use the 24-hour clock.

TIPPING

Service charges are included in hotel, taxi, bar, café and restaurant bills. It's polite to round up to the nearest euro for small bills or the nearest five for larger sums, although tipping 10% is becoming more common. In taxis, most people tip 10%.

TOURIST INFORMATION

IAmsterdam Visitor Information Centre *Stationsplein 10, Old Centre: Old Side (702 6000, www. iamsterdam.com). Tram 1, 2, 4, 5, 9, 13, 16, 17, 24, 26.* **Open** *Mar-Oct* 9am-5pm Mon-Sat; 10am-4pm Sun. *Nov-Feb* 10am-2pm Mon; 10am-5pm Tue, Wed, Sun; 9am-5pm Thur-Sat. The main tourist office is outside Centraal Station.
Other location Schiphol Airport, Arrivals Hall 2 (7am-10pm daily).

VISAS & IMMIGRATION

Citizens from the EU, USA, Canada, Australia and New Zealand just need a valid passport for stays of less than three months. Citizens of other countries must have a tourist visa. For stays longer than three months, apply for a residents' permit at the Immigration and Naturalisation Service (Stadhouderskade 85, 088 043 0430, www.ind.nl).

WHEN TO GO

See above **The Local Climate**.

Public holidays

Public holidays are listed on p36.

WOMEN

Central Amsterdam is fairly safe for women: use your common sense when travelling alone. Call emergency number 112 if you're in danger. The helpline 611 6022 is available for support if you've been a victim of rape, assault, sexual harassment or threats.

Further Reference

BOOKS

Fiction

Baantjer *De Cock series* Crime novels by a local ex-cop. Also a TV series.
Albert Camus *The Fall Man* Recalls his Parisian past in Amsterdam's 'circles of hell'.
Tracy Chevalier *Girl with a Pearl Earring* Inspired by Vermeer's painting; set in 17th-century Delft.
Arnon Grunberg *Blue Mondays* Philip Roth's *Goodbye Columbus* goes Dutch in this 1994 bestseller.
David Liss *The Coffee Trader* Thriller focused on a 17th-century Portuguese Jewish financier, tempted into the emerging coffee trade.
Harry Mulisch *The Assault* A boy's perspective on World War II. Also a classic film.
Multatuli Max *Havelaar, or the Coffee Auctions of the Dutch Trading Company* A colonial officer and his clash with the corrupt government.
Janwillem van der Wetering *The Japanese Corpse* An off-the-wall police procedural set in Amsterdam.
Manfred Wolf (ed) *Amsterdam: A Traveller's Literary Companion* The country's best writers on the city.

Non-fiction

Timothy Brook *Vermeer's Hat: The 17th Century and the Dawn of the Global World* An exploration of the Golden Age via various works of art.
Ian Buruma *Murder in Amsterdam: The Death of Theo van Gogh and the Limits of Tolerance* An analysis of tensions over immigration and tolerance in the Netherlands.
Christian Ernsten (ed) *Mokum: A Guide to Amsterdam* Offers quirky approaches to discovering the city's liberties.
Fred Feddes *A Millennium of Amsterdam* An illustrated history of Amsterdam's changing landscapes.
Anne Frank *The Diary of Anne Frank* Still-shocking wartime diary.
RH Fuchs *Dutch Painting* A comprehensive guide.
Marielle Hageman and Gerlinde Schuller *Amsterdam in Documents 2010-1275* An illustrated history of the city's most important documents and artworks.

Etty Hillesum *An Interrupted Life: The Diaries and Letters 1941-1943* The moving wartime experiences of a young Amsterdam Jewish woman who died in Auschwitz.
Lisa Jardine *Going Dutch: How England Plundered Holland's Glory* Cultural interaction between British and the Dutch in the Golden Age.
Pete Jordan *In the City of Bikes: The Story of the Amsterdam Cyclist* A personal history of the city's fave mode of transportation.
Geert Mak *Amsterdam: A Brief Life of the City* The city's history told through the stories of its people.
Benjamin B Roberts *Sex and Drugs before Rock 'n' Roll: Youth Culture and Masculinity during Holland's Golden Age* Young, male and horny in the 17th century.
Simon Schama *The Embarrassment of Riches* A lively social and cultural history of the Netherlands.
Russell Shorto *Amsterdam: A History of the World's Most Liberal City* Title nails it. A compelling read.
Russell Shorto *The Island at the Center of the World: The Epic Story of Dutch Manhattan* The Dutch as seen through their influence in the New World.
David Winners *Brilliant Orange: The Neurotic Genius of Dutch Football* More than just a football book: a look into the Dutch psyche.
Wim de Wit *Amsterdam School: Dutch Expressionist Architecture*

MUSIC

Arling & Cameron *Music for Imaginary Films (2000)* Eclectic duo reinvent the history of the soundtrack.
Chet Baker *Live at Nick's (1978)* In front of his favourite rhythm section, Chet simply soars.
Beach Boys *Holland (1973)* Californians hole up in Holland and start recording.
Herman Brood & His Wild Romance *Shpritsz (1978)* The classic album from the nation's iconic rocker and cuddle junkie.
The Ex + Getatchew Mekuria *Moa Anbessa (2006)* Anarcho squat punks/improv jazzsters team up with Ethiopian sax legend.
De Jeugd van Tegenwoordig *Ja, Natúurlijk! (2013)* Amsterdam hip hop legends, often incoherent and therefore universal.

FILMS

Amsterdam Global Village *dir Johan van der Keuken (1996)* A meditative meander through the city's streets (and people).
Amsterdamned *dir Dick Maas (1987)* Psychotic frogman, lots of canal chase scenes and continuity problems that lead to characters turning an Amsterdam corner and ending up in Utrecht.
Black Book *dir Paul Verhoeven (2006)* A Jewish singer goes undercover for the Dutch Resistance.
The Fourth Man *dir Paul Verhoeven (1983)* Melodrama seething with homoerotic desire.
Hufters en Hofdames (Bastards and Bridesmaids) *dir Eddy Terstall (1997)* Amsterdam as a backdrop to twentysomething relationship pains.
Karacter (Character) *dir Mike van Diem (1997)* An impeccable father-son drama.
De Noorderlingen (The Northerners) *dir Alex van Warmerdam (1992)* Absurdity and angst in a lonely Dutch subdivision by the director of *Borgman* (2013)
Turks Fruit (Turkish Delight) *dir Paul Verhoeven (1973)* Sculptor Rutger Hauer's rich young wife is killed by a brain tumour.
Yes Nurse! No Nurse! *dir Pieter Kramer (2002)* Musical cult classic for connoisseurs of camp.
Zusje (Little Sister) *dir Robert Jan Westdijk (1995)* A family affair with voyeuristic overtones.

WEBSITES

www.9292.nl GVB's excellent door-to-door route-planner.
www.amsterdam360.com Over 300 360-degree shots of Amsterdam.
www.archined.nl News and reviews of Dutch architecture.
www.dutchnews.nl Dutch news summarised in English.
www.englishbreakfast.nl Early morning radio show.
www.gayamsterdamlinks.com
www.holland.com National tourism board website.
www.iamsterdam.nl Official Amsterdam Tourist Board website.
www.iens.nl Diner reviews.
www.specialbite.com Reviews of the best new restaurants.
www.subbacultcha.nl All things counterculturally musical.

Index

INDEX

INDEX

INDEX

INDEX

Maps

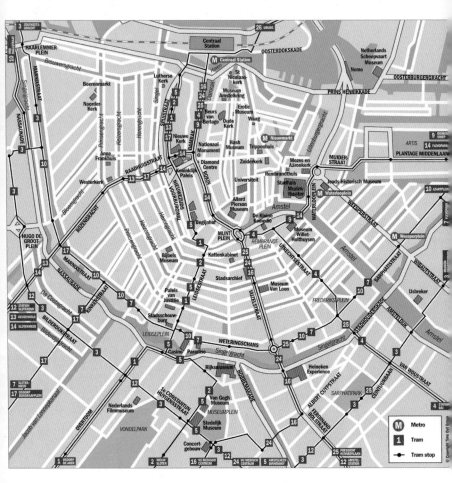

MAPS

MAPS

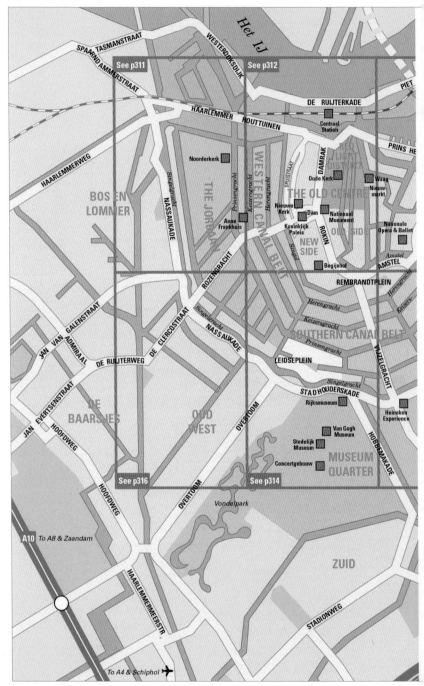

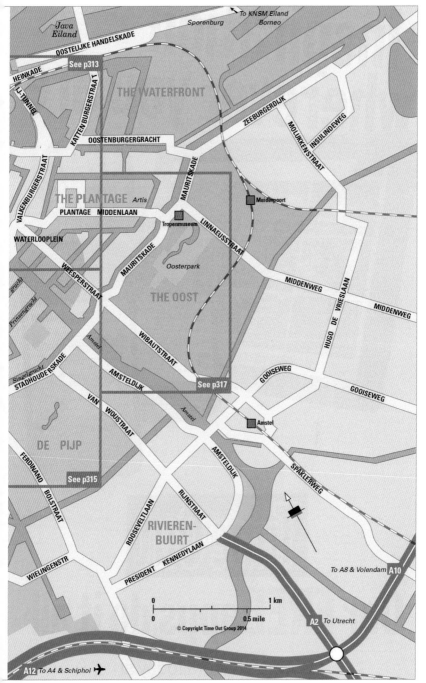

Java Eiland

To KNSM Eiland
Sporenburg   Borneo

OOSTELIJKE HANDELSKADE

HEINKADE

See p313

IJ TUNNEL

KATTENBURGERSTRAAT

THE WATERFRONT

ZEEBURGERDIJK

MOLUKKENSTRAAT

INSULINDEWEG

OOSTENBURGERGRACHT

VALKENBURGERSTRAAT

MAURITSKADE

THE PLANTAGE   Artis

PLANTAGE   MIDDENLAAN

Muiderpoort

WATERLOOPLEIN

Tropenmuseum

LINNAEUSSTRAAT

gracht

WEESPERSTRAAT

MAURITSKADE

Oosterpark

THE OOST

MIDDENWEG

HUGO DE VRIESLAAN

MIDDENWEG

Prinsengracht

Amstel

WIBAUTSTRAAT

Singelgracht

STADHOUDERSKADE

AMSTELDIJK

GOOISEWEG

VAN

Amstel

GOOISEWEG

See p317

MAPS

WOUSTRAAT

Amstel

DE PIJP

FERDINAND BOLSTRAAT

AMSTELDIJK

Amstel

SPAKLERWEG

See p315

ROOSEVELTLAAN

RIJNSTRAAT

RIVIEREN-
BUURT

WIELINGENSTR

PRESIDENT   KENNEDYLAAN

To A8 & Volendam   A10

0   1 km
0   0.5 mile
© Copyright Time Out Group 2014

A2   To Utrecht

A12   To A4 & Schiphol

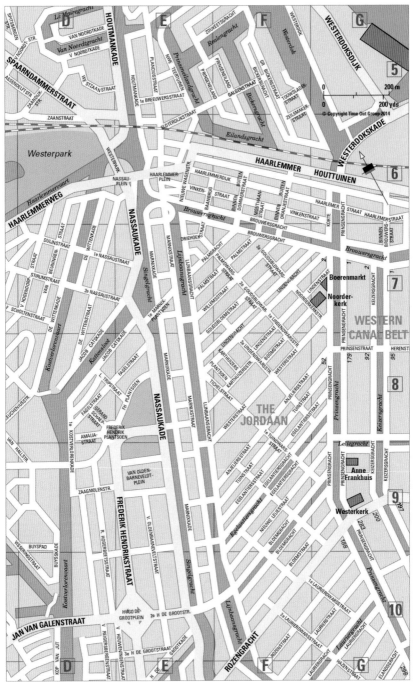

MAPS

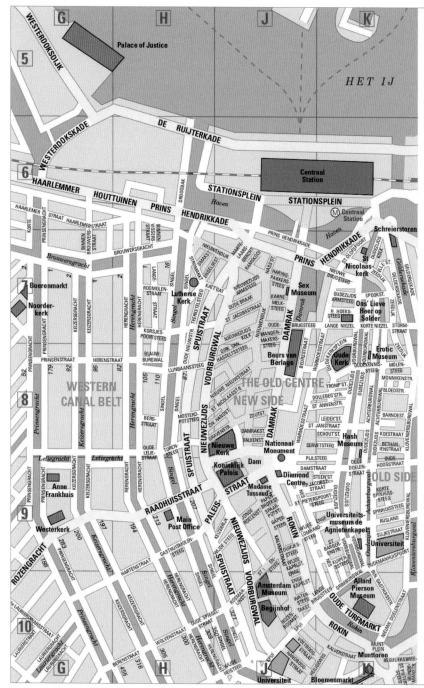

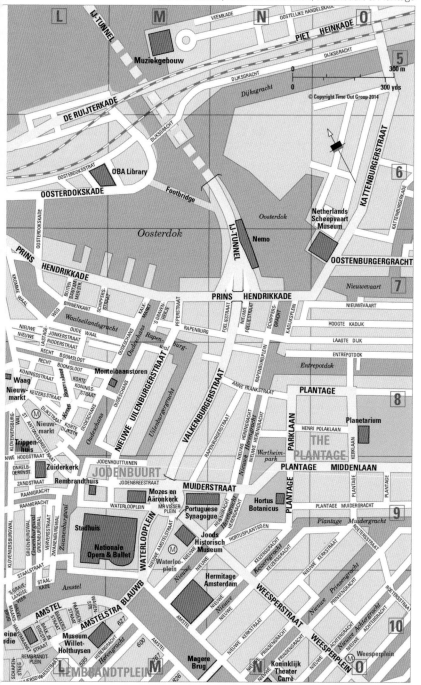

MAPS

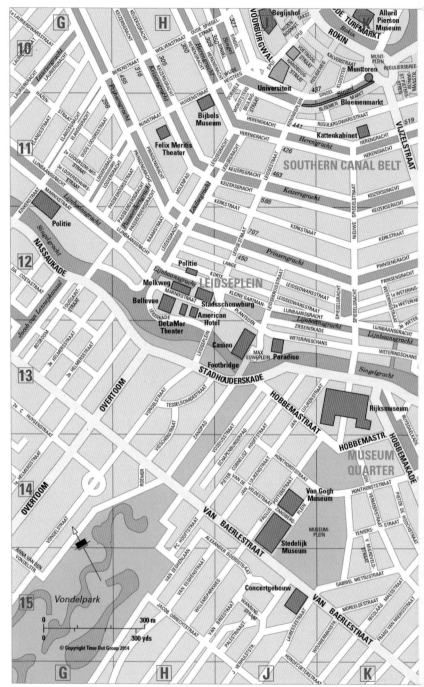

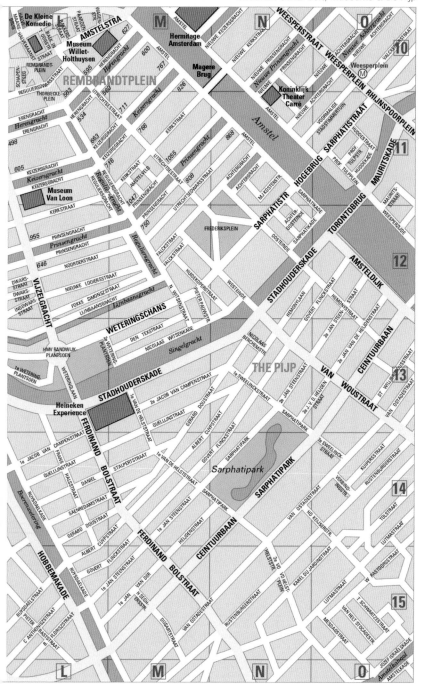

MAPS

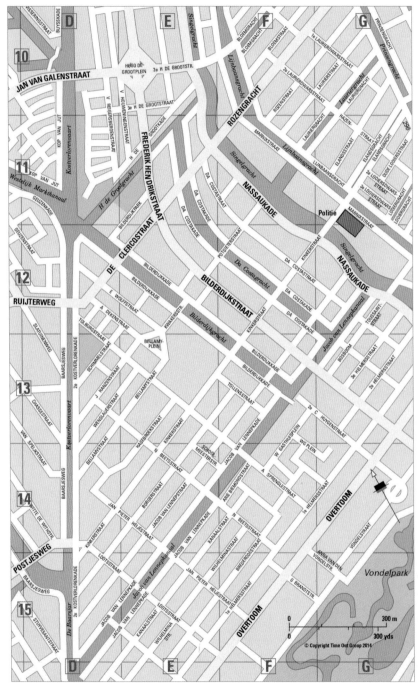

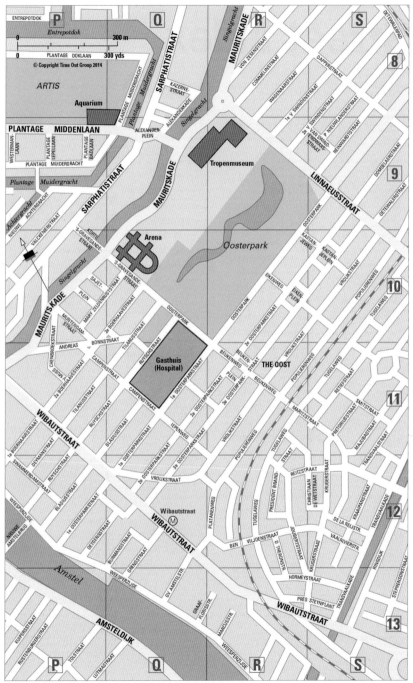

Street Index